# THE BAKU COMMUNE
## 1917–1918

STUDIES OF THE RUSSIAN INSTITUTE

COLUMBIA UNIVERSITY

# THE
# BAKU
# COMMUNE
## 1917-1918

CLASS AND NATIONALITY IN THE
RUSSIAN REVOLUTION

*Ronald Grigor Suny*

1972
*Princeton, New Jersey*
PRINCETON UNIVERSITY PRESS

The Russian Institute of Columbia University sponsors the
*Studies of the Russian Institute* in the belief that their publication contributes to scholarly research and public understanding.
In this way the Institute, while not necessarily endorsing their
conclusions, is pleased to make available the results of some of
the research conducted under its auspices. A list of the *Studies
of the Russian Institute* appears at the back of the book.

This book has been composed in 9 on 12 pt. Primer type.
Printed in the United States of America
by Princeton University Press

233701

TO MY MOTHER AND FATHER

# Preface

The historiography of the Russian Revolution in Western countries, for all its peculiar advantages of objective distance from the events, has produced a distorted view of the vast canvas of 1917–1918 by its almost exclusive concentration on the central cities, Petrograd and Moscow. Despite some interesting studies on the national regions during the revolution, important industrial centers have been overlooked, centers in which the revolution ran a course distinctly different from the pattern evident in Petrograd. This study endeavors to redress the balance somewhat by presenting a close look at the first year and a half of the revolution in the Caspian seaport and oil capital of the Russian empire, Baku. The very uniqueness of Baku, where class and national struggles were intertwined, offers a useful corrective to generalizations based on the better-known case of central Russia.

The revolution of 1917 was the culmination of a long process of social development and disintegration, the origin of which lay deep in Russia's past and in the peculiar characteristics of her society. A predominantly peasant country with an insignificantly small working class, Russia underwent the first so-called "socialist" revolution. This paradoxical occurrence, apparently inconsistent with orthodox Marxist prediction, was, in fact, explained by some of the Russian Marxists. From his earliest writings the "Father of Russian Marxism," Georgii Valentinovich Plekhanov, had maintained that the Marxist timetable would apply to Russia in a somewhat unusual form. Marx had argued that, in the transition from feudal society through capitalism to socialism, two great revolutions had to be endured: a bourgeois-democratic revolution which would abolish feudal relationships and permit the mature development of capitalist society; and a proletarian-socialist revolution which would liquidate capitalist exploitation and begin the transition to the classless society. Plekhanov carefully distinguished between these two revolutions, but contended that in backward, peasant Russia the miniscule urban proletariat would have to help the pusillanimous bourgeoisie carry out the bourgeois-democratic revolution. During this first revolution the working class would be allied with the bourgeoisie and had to refrain from taking power. Only after a long interim period under a parliamentary republic, with the establishment of civil liberties and the slow development of an organized labor movement, could the second revolution be accomplished. This discipline and restraint of the working class were to characterize the Menshevik approach from the break with the Leninists in 1903 right through the revolution.

Lenin also maintained a distinction between the two revolutions; but in 1905 and again in 1917 he began to flirt with the notion of "continuous" or "permanent" revolution, a theory first expounded by the Social Democrats Helphand-Parvus and Leon Trotsky.[1] According to Lenin the period between the two revolutions was of indeterminate length and could very probably be shortened, i.e., the proletariat might be able to take power in the course even

[1] "Permanent revolution," according to Trotsky, was inevitable in Russia, given the fact that the bourgeoisie could not make its own revolution without the proletariat. Once the revolution was undertaken, workers' representatives would enter the government and be compelled by their constituents to introduce socialist legislation. Trotsky wrote: *"Political supremacy of the proletariat is incompatible with its economic slavery.* Whatever may be the banner under which the proletariat will find itself in possession of power, it will be compelled to enter the road of Socialism." (L. Trotsky, *Results and Prospects* [1906], trans. as *Our Revolution* by M. J. Olgin [New York, 1918], and republished in Robert V. Daniels [ed.], *A Documentary History of Communism* [New York, 1960], I, p. 46.)

of a revolution which in its first stages was a bourgeois-democratic revolution. This would be accomplished, not with the aid of the liberal bourgeoisie, but in alliance with the poor and middle peasantry. Such a revolution in Russia he conceived as the opening shot in the international proletarian revolution. Believing that by herself Russia could not achieve socialism, Lenin argued that the aid of the advanced industrial states of Western Europe was essential for the final transition to socialism. Lenin was more radical in his approach to the workers than Plekhanov, more receptive to the potential of the peasantry, and more impatient in his anticipation of the international revolution.

All Marxists agreed in 1917 that the February Revolution was "bourgeois-democratic," despite the fact that the revolution in Petrograd had been made by workers and soldiers. Two contenders for power sprang up to fill the vacuum: the Provisional Government, made up of bourgeois, professionals, and liberal intellectuals, and the Soviet of Workers' Deputies. Evident from the beginning was the fact that real power rested with the soviet, which alone could order people into the streets and command the local soldiers. But the soviet leadership, largely Menshevik and Socialist Revolutionary, reluctant to take formal state power into its own hands, recognized the Provisional Government. The workers had made the revolution, but their leadership considered it a "bourgeois" revolution and gave its conditional support to the "bourgeois" government. Thus, the "dual power" or *dvoevlastie* was created, in part as a result of fears that a workers' government could not unify Russia in its crisis and in part because of the notion that in a bourgeois-democratic revolution state power should remain in the hands of the bourgeoisie.[2]

The implicit conflict between the Menshevik view and the Leninist approach did not come out into the open until

[2] I. G. Tseretelli, *Vospominaniia o fevral'skoi revoliutsii*, I (Paris and The Hague, 1963), pp. 22–23.

Lenin's return to Russia in April. The Bolshevik leader's attention was turned first to his own party in an attempt to win it over to his more radical position, appealing to the Bolsheviks to break decisively with the Provisional Government and adopt the slogan "All Power to the Soviets." The implications of this slogan were clear: immediate transition to the socialist revolution. Not only did Lenin's *April Theses* shock the Bolshevik moderates, it traumatized the conciliatory leadership of the soviet. Within a surprisingly short time, however, Lenin had won over his own party as well as a significant number of the city's workers. By May the conference of factory committees was passing Bolshevik resolutions.

The weakness of the Provisional Government and its absolute dependence on the support of the soviet was made abundantly clear in the "April Crisis," during which soviet discontent with Miliukov's annexationist foreign policy led to the foreign minister's resignation. In the aftermath of the crisis the government itself began to break up. Early in May a coalition government, made up of members of the old governing group and a number of socialist ministers from the soviet, was formed. The coalition was a stopgap government, designed to lead the country through the war until a Constituent Assembly could be convened and a constitution adopted. But, unlike the *dvoevlastie*, the coalition tried to link the leadership of the workers with the representatives of the upper classes, and the divergence of interests of these groups led to a complete impasse in the government. The failure of the coalition government to respond to the deepening social crisis in the country and its inability to bring the war to an end worked to the advantage of the one party which promised immediate social reforms and an end to the war—the Bolsheviks.

Shortages of food combined with the failure of the "Kerensky Offensive" to increase the volatility of the workers and soldiers. Outside the cities the peasants undertook their own kind of land reform by seizing the land themselves, killing the landlords, and burning their manor houses. By September the Bolsheviks had majorities in both the Moscow and the Petrograd soviets. The coalition government had thus been *de facto* repudiated by the soviet electorate. The October Revolution, while in form a conspiratorial *coup d'état*, came about after a steady draining away of Kerensky's support. Just as in February 1917 no troops could be found to defend the tsarist order, so in October few but the famous Women's Battalion of Death were prepared to stand up for the coalition government.

The Bolsheviks came to power in Petrograd, Moscow, and a number of other cities in October and November 1917, but by overthrowing the Provisional Government they in effect declared war on the rest of Russia, which was unwilling to recognize a soviet monopoly of power. On the eve of the Civil War a deceptive calm lay over Russia, while elections to the Constituent Assembly were held. Those elections reflected the widespread opposition to the Bolsheviks and the peasants' support for the Socialist Revolutionaries. When two months later the soviet government dispersed the Assembly after a one-day session, the lines were finally drawn for the fratricidal struggle. On one side were those who accepted the October Revolution and soviet power; on the other was a diverse group unified by their rejection of October but only in part committed to February.

A thousand miles to the south, in Transcaucasia, the revolution resembled the pattern in Petrograd, at least for the first year. A "dual power" was created in both Tiflis and Baku, but in both cities real power was held by the soviet. There too the moderate socialists dominated the local soviets and refused to seize power in their own name. Only after a long and gradual radicalization of the workers were the Bolsheviks in Baku in a position to make a bid for power. In Tiflis the Georgian Mensheviks, considerably more radical than their Russian brethren, formed an independent Georgian government.

Similarities disappeared, however, soon after October. In Baku the local Bolsheviks decided not to seize power by force but to work toward a "peaceful transition" to soviet power. Thus Baku's "October" was delayed. Not until March 1918 did the soviet win the political monopoly in the city which it had sought since the fall of 1917. The consequences of this delay are discussed in this study.

The moderate Bolshevism of Baku had deep roots in the history of the local labor movement and Social Democracy in the city. Faced with a politically unconscious working class that was divided by nationality, skills, and wage-levels, the Baku Bolsheviks adapted their appeals to the particular interests of the oil workers. Thus Bolshevism in Baku, especially after 1905, developed a sensitivity toward workers' economic desires. Bolsheviks dominated trade unions, workers' clubs, and the legal labor movement. The underground party continued to exist, but often played a subordinate role to the legal institutions. The Bolshevik leaders did not simply respond to any spontaneously generated impulse of the workers but rather worked to shape those impulses and provide the economic struggle of workers with organization, appropriate rhetoric, and some political overtones.

A local history study such as this one can in some detail describe the growth of Bolshevik receptivity to workers' demands in both the pre-1917 and the revolutionary periods. This work attempts to demonstrate the dialectical relationship between the workers and the Bolsheviks in which the party taught and from which the party learned. The chapters that follow describe the origins, evolution, and eventual disintegration of the Bolshevik hegemony over the workers of Baku.

Any researcher dealing with the revolution in Baku must address himself to the perplexities which punctuate the events themselves. Questions arise how the Bolsheviks achieved paramountcy in the Baku soviet without a majority. Why did *dvoevlastie* continue after October 1917? What were the reasons for the revolution's "delay" in Baku? Particularly fascinating are the problems of the nationalist struggle within the city and its relationship to the class struggle. Was the insurrection in March 1918 the result of class or national antagonism? On this very point Soviet and non-Soviet historians are divided. Finally, why did the Baku Commune fail? Were the Bolsheviks at fault or were the objective circumstances beyond the capacity of any party to control?

Historical writing on the revolution in Baku has always been abundant but has never enjoyed freedom from partisanship (or, in Soviet terminology, *partiinost'*). Whether the writer wanted to prove his party comrades innocent of the tragic murder of the Twenty-six Commissars,[3] to demonstrate the correctness of Shaumian's general line,[4] or to defend Great Britain from the accusations of the Soviet government,[5] those who have taken up their pens to describe the confusion of those years in Baku have usually served a mistress less worthy than Clio. Needless to say, the cause of objectivity has not been served by the political shifts within the Soviet Union which have resulted in artificial reevaluations of various aspects of revolutionary history. As with most Soviet historiography, so with the material on Baku, the most productive period was between the Civil War and the consolidation of Stalin's dictatorship in the early 1930s. During that period the study of history

[3] V. A. Chaikin, *K istorii rossiiskoi revoliutsii*, vypusk 1; Kazn' 26 bakinskikh komissarov (Moscow, 1922); an account of the execution by a Right S.R.

[4] Artashes Karinian, *Shaumian i natsionalisticheskie techeniia na Kavkaze* (Baku, 1928); by the Bolshevik commissar of justice in the Baku Commune.

[5] C. H. Ellis, *The British "Intervention" in Transcaspia, 1918–1919* (Berkeley, 1963); by a member of the British force in Transcaspia at the time of the execution of the Baku Commissars.

was "Bolshevized," but not yet "Stalinized." The former process implied merely that the point of view of the Bolshevik party during the revolution was identified as the only correct position and that those of the rival parties were seen as ranging from "mistaken" to "anti-Soviet" and "counterrevolutionary." The works on Baku written in the twenties read as if they had been dictated by the participants in the events themselves, as if the old Bolsheviks were rationalizing their own actions in the recent past.[6] Facts are not distorted, but they are interpreted in agreement with an *a priori* understanding of the "laws" of history.

Particularly important in the 1920s was the work of the *kolletiv* of scholars who eventually formed the Shaumian Institute of Party History in Baku. Collections of documents, memoirs, and secondary accounts by the leading Marxist historians in Transcaucasia were published by the Institute. Such writers as A. Dubner, Ia. A. Ratgauzer, S. A. Sef, and A. Raevskii provided Soviet readers with the first thoroughly analytical accounts of the revolution in one of the major cities of their country.[7] Because the archive of the Baku soviet had been destroyed during the

[6] For a general survey on Soviet historiography of the 1920s on the revolution in Baku, see N. M. Kuliev, "Sovetskaia istoriografiia sotsialisticheskoi revoliutsii v Azerbaidzhane," *Istoriia SSSR*, no. 3 (1967), pp. 38–50.

[7] A. Dubner, *Bakinskii proletariat v gody revoliutsii (1917–1920 gg.)* (Baku, 1931).

Ia. A. Ratgauzer, *Bor'ba bakinskogo proletariata za kollektivnyi dogovor 1917 g.* (Baku, 1927).

———, *Revoliutsiia i grazhdanskaia voina v Baku, I: 1917–1918 gg.* (Baku, 1927).

S. E. Sef, *Revoliutsiia 1917 g. v Zakavkaz'e (dokumenty, materialy)* (Tiflis, 1927).

———, *Kak bol'sheviki prishli k vlasti v 1917–1918 gg. v bakinskom raione* (Baku, 1927).

A. M. Raevskii, *Partiia "Musavat" i ee kontrrevoliutsionnaia rabota* (Baku, 1928).

Turkish occupation of the city, these researchers relied primarily on the stenographic reports of soviet sessions given in the local press. The completeness and apparent accuracy of these accounts make Baku newspapers the single most valuable primary source for investigations of the revolutionary events. Scholarly works of the 1920s are admittedly "Bolshevik" in tone, but they are invaluable to scholars as sources of information. Based on solid research and candid in dealing with controversial issues, their failure usually lies in the authors' readiness to impute the most diabolical motives to leaders of other political parties and to identify Bolshevik policies, as a rule, with an objectively correct course. These writers consistently argue the primacy of the class struggle within Baku over the nationalist conflict, often objecting strenuously to certain mistakes committed by the Bolshevik leadership. Debates raged in the 1920s, and the historiographical conflicts have been preserved in published symposia.[8] They appear all the more lively when compared with the dearth of controversy which followed the establishment of the "Cult of Personality."

Stalinized history on the revolution in Baku grew out of the famous speech of Lavrenti Beria given in Tiflis on July 21–22, 1935.[9] Stalin's lieutenant in Transcaucasia attempted to demonstrate to his audience, indeed to a generation of readers, that both the prerevolutionary and postrevolutionary history of Georgia and its neighbors had been dominated by the single figure of Iosif Dzhugashvili. Events which had occurred in Stalin's absence were attributed to him. Articles by other revolutionaries were said to have been written by him. He had been omniscient and ubiquitous. During his frequent stays in prison he managed,

[8] S. E. Sef, *Kak bol'sheviki prishli k vlasti.* . . .
[9] Lavrenti Beria, *On the History of the Bolshevik Organizations in Transcaucasia* (Moscow, 1949).

in Beria's account, to carry on the business of the party from his cell. Stalin had, in fact, spent part of his revolutionary youth in Baku, and the party chief of Azerbaijan, M. D. Bagirov, in a speech which rivaled Beria's in imagination, celebrated Stalin's sixtieth birthday (1939) with a lengthy account of the General Secretary's years in that city.[10] These two works determined the nature of all writing on party history in Transcaucasia until the death of Stalin (1953) and the Twentieth Party Congress (1956). The other major studies of this period, by Burdzhalov, Tokarzhevskii, and Ibragimov, share this fawning dedication to Stalin and a rigid uncompromising view of the "enemies" of the Bolsheviks.[11] Those scholars who found it impossible to elevate Stalin to the position of prime mover in Transcaucasian politics either remained silent or spent years in the aimless pursuit of nonexistent material.

Since the Twentieth Party Congress Soviet historiography on Baku has returned to the position of the 1920s, i.e., to a Bolshevik approach without Stalinist distortions. But the best-known works of the recent past have not yet rid themselves of the formulistic and oppressively dull style developed in the Stalin years. The role of the opposition parties has not yet been adequately investigated, and certain unrehabilitated figures have been neglected in the retelling of the revolution. In 1957, on the fortieth anniversary of the revolution, collections of documents were issued, but the processes of selection require that they be

[10] M. D. Bagirov, *Iz istorii bol'shevistskoi organizatsii Baku i Azerbaidzhana* (Moscow, 1946).

[11] E. Burdzhalov, *Dvadtsat' shest' bakinskikh komissarov* (Moscow, 1938).

E. A. Tokarzhevskii, *Bakinskie bol'sheviki—organizatory bor'by protiv turetsko-germanskikh i angliiskikh interventov v Azerbaidzhane v 1918 godu* (Baku, 1949).

The work of Z. I. Ibragimov is largely in the Azeri language; for a complete list see the bibliography in I. A. Guseinov *et al.* (eds.), *Istoriia Azerbaidzhana*, III, pp. 504–505.

used with utmost care:[12] many interesting documents were left out or abridged—and only a close reading of the Baku press provides a true picture. The most interesting work in recent years has appeared in articles in *Istoriia SSSR* and other journals, rather than in book-length studies. First-hand experience in the USSR indicates that historical thinking is somewhat ahead of publications and that Soviet historians impatiently await the total eradication of the unscientific habits of an older generation.

[12] Z. I. Ibragimov and M. S. Iskenderov (eds.), *Bol'sheviki v bor'be za pobedu sotsialisticheskoi revoliutsii v Azerbaidzhane. Dokumenty i materialy, 1917–1918 gg.* Hereafter this work will be cited as *"Dok."*

# Acknowledgments

The completion of this work would not have been possible without "a little help from my friends," relatives, and teachers both in the United States and in the Soviet Union. I began the investigation of Social Democracy in Transcaucasia under the guidance of Professor Henry Roberts, then of the Russian Institute, in a seminar in Soviet history. Professor Roberts is personally responsible for making possible my year-long sojourn in the USSR, as well as for penetrating and friendly criticism of my work in New York. I must thank Dr. Nina Garsoian, likewise of Columbia University, who introduced me to the intricacies of the Armenian language and taught me invaluable lessons about historical methodology. The most important of all my mentors at Columbia was Professor Leopold Haimson, whose unrivaled knowledge of Russian Social Democracy and the social history of the late imperial period has shaped this study decisively. Also at Columbia I would like to acknowledge Professors Alexander Erlich, Loren Graham, and George Fischer, and Mr. Peter Linebaugh, who read and criticized this work when it was in dissertation form. Special thanks as well are due to Richard Green for permission to use materials he collected.

The bulk of the research was done in the Soviet Union, where I participated in the Cultural Exchange of Young Professors and Graduate Students in 1965–1966. At that time I was privileged to work in the Lenin Library, the Central State Archive of the October Revolution and Socialist Construction (TsGAOR), the State Archive of the Armenian Soviet Socialist Republic, and the Institute of

Party History in Erevan. It is impossible to repay all the men and women in these institutions who helped me in my research. I can here only acknowledge that help, as well as the assistance received from people connected with Moscow State University, Erevan State University, and the Academy of Sciences of the Armenian SSR. Especially I extend my gratitude to: Miss Knarik Hovhannessian, Mkitch Vahanovich Arzumanian, Lev Stepanovich Shaumian, Vahak Mesropian, Nina Mirzoeva, Academician Artashes Karinian, and Iurii Stepanovich Kukushkin.

RONALD GRIGOR SUNY

*Oberlin, Ohio*

# Glossary of Terms and Abbreviations

*"Biulleten'"*—*Biulleten' komiteta revoliutsionnoi oborony,* the newspaper of the committee of revolutionary defense.

*"Biulleten' diktatury"*—*Biulleten' diktatury Tsentrokaspiia i prezidiuma vremennogo ispolnitel'nogo komiteta soveta.*

Cheka (*Chrezvychainaia Komissiia*)—the Extraordinary Commission set up by the Soviet Government in December 1917 to combat counterrevolutionary forces: the predecessor to the Soviet secret police agencies, e.g., the OGPU, NKVD, KGB.

Dashnak—member of the Dashnaktsutiun (Armenian Revolutionary Federation), the most influential Armenian political party in Transcaucasia.

desiatina—a measure of land equal to 2.7 acres.

*"Dok."*—Z. I. Ibragimov and M. S. Iskenderov (eds.), *Bol'sheviki v bor'be za pobedu sotsialisticheskoi revoliutsii v Azerbaidzhane. Dokumenty i materialy, 1917–1918 gg.* (Baku, 1960).

*dvoevlastie*—"dual power": refers to the period when the Provisional Government and the Petrograd soviet both held power in the capital.

Glavkoneft (*Glavnyi Neftianoi Komitet*)—the Central Oil Committee, established on May 19, 1918, in Moscow to supervise the oil industry throughout Russia.

Hnchak—member of the Hnchak Party, an Armenian Marxist party.

Hummet—the Azerbaijani Social Democratic Party, affiliated with the RSDRP.

IKOO (*Ispolnitel'nyi Komitet Obshchestvennykh Organizatsii*)—the Executive Committee of Public Organizations: the official governing agent of the Provisional
Government in Baku, established in the first days of
the revolution (March 1917) and disbanded by the Soviet in November 1917.

IKS (*Ispolnitel'nyi Komitet Soveta*)—the executive committee of the Baku Soviet.

Kadet—member of the Party of People's Freedom, the principal liberal party in Russia.

Musavat—the Azerbaijani nationalist party.

"*Ocherki*"—M. S. Iskenderov *et al., Ocherki istorii kommunisticheskoi partii Azerbaidzhana* (Baku, 1963).

Ozakom (*Osobyi Zakavkazskii Komitet*)—the Special
Transcaucasian Committee established by the Provisional Government as the highest governing authority in
Transcaucasia. It exercised little actual power during its
existence from March to November 1917.

"*Pis'ma*"—S. G. Shaumian, *Pis'ma, 1896–1918* (Erevan,
1959).

pood—a measurement of weight equal to 36.11 pounds.

RSDRP (*Rossiiskaia Sotsial-Demokraticheskaia Robochaia
Partiia*)—the Russian Social Democratic Workers' Party.

RSDRP(b)—the Bolshevik Party.

S.D.—Social Democrat: a member of the RSDRP.

S.R.—Socialist Revolutionary: a member of the principal
peasant socialist party.

"Shaumian, I"—S. G. Shaumian, *Izbrannye proizvedeniia*,
I: 1902–1916 *gg.* (Moscow, 1957).

"Shaumian, II"—S. G. Shaumian, *Izbrannye proizvedeniia*,
II: 1917–1918 *gg.* (Moscow, 1958).

Sovnarkhoz (*Sovet Narodnogo Khoziastva*)—Supreme
Council of People's Economy, both in Petrograd–Moscow and in Baku.

Sovnarkom (*Sovet Narodnykh Komissarov*)—Council of People's Commissars, both in Petrograd–Moscow and in Baku.

Tsentrodom—an agency set up in Baku to organize municipal services, such as sanitation, when order broke down in 1917.

Tsentrokaspii—the Union of Caspian Sailors, a Socialist-Revolutionary stronghold.

*tsentsovoe obshchestvo*—the former ruling classes in tsarist Russia.

TsK (*Tsentral'nyi Komitet*)—the Central Committee of the RSDRP.

uezd—an administrative sub-division of a province.

verst—a measurement of distance equal to 1.06 kilometers.

Zafatem—the Union of Plant, Factory and Technical Workshop Owners, an association of oil industrialists.

Zavkom (*Zakavkazskii Komisariat*)—the Transcaucasian Commissariat formed on November 15, 1917, as the successor to the Ozakom in Tiflis.

# A Note on Transliteration and Dating

Transliteration from Russian is based on the Library of Congress system, although common English usage has been adopted for certain names and terms. Transliteration from Armenian is based on the eastern Armenian dialect which is spoken in the Armenian SSR. Azeri words and names have been transliterated according to the Russian system except in cases where accepted practice has established other spellings.

The dates are given according to the Julian calendar, then in use in Russia, which was thirteen days behind the Gregorian calendar used in the West. Where the latter calendar is used indications are made in the text.

# Contents

THE BAKU COMMUNE

1917–1918

# 1

## Nationality and Class in Baku

A POPULAR ETYMOLOGICAL EXPLANATION of the name "Baku" is that it comes from two Persian words (*bad* and *kube*) which roughly translate as "buffeted by winds." Baku is indeed subject to winds, blowing in from the Caspian and bringing the little relief from the heat that its inhabitants enjoy. The city is today the fourth largest in the Soviet Union, the elegant capital of the Azerbaijani Soviet Socialist Republic, and the home of more than a million people. The oil industry which spawned it is remote from the downtown boulevards, yet its influence is felt everywhere. Baku's history, both before and after the revolution of 1917, is intimately connected with its principal resource, oil. As early as the tenth century an Arab traveler wrote that Baku's wells provided both white and black oil, useful for lighting, heating, and lubrication, as well as medicine. In the ensuing centuries a modest but profitable trade in oil made the city an important link with Iran and Russia. In 1723 Tsar Peter I sent an expedition to Baku and ordered his victorious general to bring several poods of the renowned white oil back to Russia. The city remained in Russian hands until 1735 when a weakened empire returned it to Iran in exchange for trading privileges.

Russia's mercantile interest in Baku never slackened, however, and many Russian and Armenian merchants settled in the city. At the beginning of the nineteenth century Baku had about five hundred buildings and three thousand inhabitants, and was the center of a small Persian khanate. Three powers—Iran, Russia, and Turkey—

coveted the town, and a series of campaigns finally culminated in its annexation by the Romanovs.

Travelers to Baku marveled at the ancient temple of the fire-worshipers, where a flame fed by the petroleum underground burned constantly. With the coming of the Russians in 1806 enterprising men began systematically to exploit the natural riches of the Caspian shore. In the district of Surakhany, near the fire-temple, the production of kerosene was begun in 1859, the same year that Edwin Drake drilled the first oil-well in Titusville. A successful attempt to drill a well near Baku was made by a local entrepreneur in 1869; and in the following decades the industry, based on this more efficient method of obtaining petroleum, surrounded the sleepy port of Baku with a forest of derricks. The first gusher came in 1873 amid cries of "We have our own Pennsylvania now!"[1] Within a few years oil had turned Baku from an oriental curiosity into a modern cosmopolitan city.

With the development of the oil industry in the last decades of the nineteenth century a new class of entrepreneurs appeared in Baku side by side with the older commercial bourgeoisie. The *neftepromyshlenniki* ("oil industrialists") soon dominated the economy and politics of the Apsheron Peninsula, displacing the older-established elites. At first Armenian capitalists were favored by the tsarist government. During the period (1821–1872) when the government held a state monopoly on the oil-fields and leased them for four-year terms to selected entrepreneurs, the Armenians were given special treatment. From 1850 to 1872 a monopoly on the pumping of oil was granted first to the Armenian capitalist Ter-Gukasov, and later to his countryman Mirzoev.[2] Local Azerbaijani capitalists, cut off from the pumping of oil, managed in this period to gain control of more than half the refineries in the area.[3]

[1] I. A. Guseinov *et al.* (eds.), *Istoriia Azerbaidzhana* (Baku, 1959–1963), II, pp. 201–202.

[2] *Ibid.*, p. 200.   [3] *Ibid.*, p. 255.

When the government abolished the state monopoly and began selling the fields to the highest bidders, the dominance of the Armenians was challenged but only slightly shaken. Paradoxically, with the influx of Russian, Georgian, Jewish, and foreign capital, the relative position of the Azerbaijanis deteriorated sharply.[4] Azerbaijanis owned none of the larger companies (those producing over ten million poods of oil a year), being primarily involved in smaller enterprises. It was the Russian and Armenian owners who shared control of the middle and large companies with the foreign investors.[5]

While local Baku entrepreneurs lived in splendor by the Caspian, the real control of the oil industry steadily drifted from the city to foreign investors with their headquarters either in Saint Petersburg or abroad. More than half the capital in Russia's oil industry came from abroad. British capital alone accounted for 60 percent of the total capital investment in Baku's oil industry.[6] The largest company at the time of the revolution was owned by foreigners, the Nobel brothers, Robert and Ludwig. During the First World War their company, the Société Anonyme d'Exploitation du Naphte Nobel Frères, acquired the majority of stock in the giant Russian General Oil Company, thus becoming the single largest oil producer in the empire.[7]

The trend toward monopoly, so often cited by Marxist historians, was clearly evident in Baku, particularly after

[4] By the beginning of the twentieth century, of the 167 oil companies around Baku, only 49 (29.3%) were owned by Azerbaijanis, while 55 (32.9%) were owned by Armenians, 21 (12.8%) by Russians, 17 (10.2%) by Jews, 6 (3.6%) by Georgians, and 19 (11.3%) by foreigners (ibid.).

[5] Ibid., p. 256; this national breakdown was not characteristic of all industries. For example, Azerbaijanis dominated Caspian shipping, owning 80% of all vessels. Armenians, however, ran the fishing industry. The only large textile mill in Transcaucasia belonged to the Azerbaijani millionaire, Z. A. Tagiev.

[6] Heinrich Hassmann, *Oil in the Soviet Union* (Princeton, 1953), p. 28.

[7] Ibid., pp. 26–27.

the turn of the century. Baku had assumed world-wide significance as a source of oil and had played a leading role in the industrial expansion of Russia in the 1890s. From 1898 to 1901 the oil fields of Baku produced more oil than all the fields in the United States.[8] Then, suddenly, a general economic crisis hit Russia with immediate and disastrous effect on Baku. Primitive technology and heavy taxes made competition with the Americans difficult, and after 1901 Baku suffered a net decline in the amount of oil drilled and refined.[9] The industry never fully recovered. Demand for oil declined, prices fell, and panic gripped the Baku stock-exchange. Drilling was halved between 1900 and 1902. Output dropped 11 percent from 1901 to 1903.[10] The smaller firms were the greatest losers; many went bankrupt. Because of their resources for flexible operation, the larger firms survived the crisis, often showing a profit.[11] As a result consolidation of companies took place, giving the larger companies even greater influence and power in the industry. In 1900 the six largest companies—Nobel, Mantashev, the Caspian–Black Sea Corporation, the Baku Oil Society, the Caspian Company, and the Society for Drilling Russian Oil and Liquid Fuel— produced 50 percent of the oil drilled in Baku.[12] In 1912 Russian banks and industrialists combined the Mantashev Company with G. M. Lianosov, and the Neft Company to form Russian General Oil. That same year the Royal Dutch–Shell group bought the Rothschilds' Caspian–Black Sea Company to add to their other holdings.[13] Consolidation, however, did not affect the net decline in production which continued irregularly until the second decade of the century. Thus, just as the labor movement began to have an effect in Baku, the industry as a whole faced a crisis of shrinking output.

---

[8] A. M. Raevskii, *Bol'sheviki i Men'sheviki v Baku v 1904–05 godakh* (Baku, 1930), p. 26.

[9] I. A. Guseinov *et al.*, II, p. 433.

[10] *Ibid.*, p. 434.   [11] *Ibid.*, p. 436.

[12] *Ibid.*, p. 437.   [13] Hassmann, p. 27.

The development of the oil industry had made Baku in a few short decades a capitalist city in a feudal land, a proletarian oasis surrounded by a peasant population. With the industry the city itself grew rapidly in the last decades of the nineteenth century. In the mid-1870s Baku housed only about 15,000 people; according to the census of 1913 it had grown to be the largest city in Transcaucasia, with a population of 214,600 in the city proper and 119,300 in the industrial districts.[14] Baku was structured in three distinct concentric circles of population. In the center were the city districts (Maritime, Bailov, Railroad Station, City, and Armenikend) where most of the educated elite, the skilled workers, and the propertied classes had their homes. Surrounding the city were the industrial districts (*promyslo-zavodskoi raion*), divided between factory districts (*zavodskoi raion*) (Black City, White City, and the villages of Zlykh, Akhmedly, and Kishly) and the more distant oil-field districts (*promyslovoi raion*) which contained the villages of Sabunchi, Balakhany, Ramany, Zabrat, Bibi-Eibat, Surakhany, Binagady, Amirazhany, Biul'-Biuli, Shikhovo, and Baladzhary. At the limits of Baku *uezd* and interspersed among the oil-fields lived the simple Azerbaijani peasants, the vast majority of the population of eastern Transcaucasia. These peasants, poor and completely uneducated, were cut off from the city and remained politically passive until well after the revolution.[15] The government of Baku was largely in the hands of

[14] G. A. Arutiunov, *Rabochee dvizhenie v Zakavkaz'e v period novogo revoliutsionnogo pod"ema* (*1910–1914 gg.*) (Moscow-Baku, 1963), pp. 34, 43.

[15] The districts were ethnically mixed, though there were districts largely populated by one nationality. For example, the Armenians were heavily concentrated in Armenikend. Russians had a majority in White City (75%), Black City (61%), and large minorities in Sabunchi, Balakhany, and Bibi-Eibat. The Azerbaijanis had majorities in the villages of Zabrat, Surakhany, and Balakhany. Generally the Azerbaijanis were losing ground in the Baku area, as the non-Azerbaijani populations increased more rapidly than they. (V. V. Pokshishevskii, *Polozhenie bakinskogo proletariata nakanune revoliutsii* [*1914–1917 gg.*] [Baku, 1927], pp. 7–8.)

officials appointed by the tsarist government. Local self-government came late to Baku (not until 1878) and never developed independently of the tsarist appointees. In many respects Baku was treated as a semicolonial area. The government's main concern was keeping order and exploiting the oil reserves. Consideration of public welfare was left to the local authorities or to the charity of private persons It is not surprising, therefore, that both workers and the propertied classes agitated for political reforms.

In 1878, after considerable delay, the Municipal Statute of 1870 was extended to Baku, thus ending police and military rule in the city. The provincial governor, appointed by the tsar, was given limited powers over the urban self-government. A city duma was created, which in turn elected a city board (*gorodskaia uprava*), and a mayor (*gorodskoi golova*) who chaired both the duma and the city board. These new institutions were to concern themselves with the social, educational, and health needs of the municipality, and to assist in keeping order. Government was paternalist in nature, though men of property could participate in the duma elections. A law stipulated that not more than half the members of the duma could be non-Christians.[16] In this way both the lower classes and the Moslems were effectively kept from the seat of power.

Even these small concessions to urban self-government by the Tsar-Liberator, Alexander II (1855–1881), were rescinded by his more conservative son, Alexander III (1881–1894). In 1892 he issued a municipal "counter-reform," in which the franchise was further limited, the powers of the governor were increased, and non-Christian

---

[16] A. Sh. Mil'man, *Politicheskii stroi Azerbaidzhana v XIX–nachale XX vekov* (*administrativnyi apparat i sud, formy i metody kolonial'nogo upravleniia*) (Baku, 1966), p. 211. The electorate, based on tax assessments, was divided into three groups. The top dozen or so taxpayers by themselves chose one-third of the duma members.

representation was reduced to one-third of the duma membership. In Baku at the turn of the century only 1,631 people, or less than 1.5 percent of the population, had the right to vote in elections to the duma.[17] Although the duma did intensify its activities in the fields of sanitation and education in the 1890s (fourteen elementary schools were opened in that period), the general public was apathetic about the duma, and only about one-quarter of the electorate participated in elections.[18] Every third duma session had to be canceled because of the lack of a quorum. The Baku city duma was thus a body elected, attended, but only occasionally supported by the *grande bourgeoisie.*

In the first decades of the twentieth century, labor agitation, national animosities, and revolution led to a repressive response by the tsarist government. The powers of the police, the military, and the tsarist bureaucracy were increased, while former concessions of self-government and political rights were withdrawn. In January 1902 a "state of emergency" was declared in Baku. This permitted the police to circumvent the established judicial system in dealing with labor disorders and political agitation. In February 1905 Baku was placed under martial law (*na voennom polozhenii*), and a temporary governor-general was appointed.[19] That summer Baku was declared to be "in a state of siege" (*na osadnom polozhenii*). Not until October 1906 was the government of the city normalized. At that point a new official, the *gradonachal'nik*, was appointed by the tsar on the recommendation of the viceroy of the Caucasus. The *gradonachal'nik* was given the powers of a governor in administrative and police matters in the city and represented the city in the councils of the governor of Baku Province. As if to underline the fact that this latest administrative reform had increased the military nature of the municipal government, every six months the tsar decreed that Baku remained in a state of

[17] *Ibid.,* p. 217.    [18] *Ibid.,* p. 213.    [19] *Ibid.,* p. 247.

(9)

emergency (*chrezvychainaia okhrana*).[20] With the coming of the First World War Baku returned to martial law. Unpredictably vacillating between military rule, police repression, and "days of freedom," the government of Baku never won the confidence of the city's population. A tradition of local self-government did not develop either among the men of property or among the lower classes who remained completely estranged from urban politics.

Characteristic of Baku's working class was its lack of deep roots in the city. Sixty-four percent were Russians from the central provinces, Moslems from the Volga region, Armenians who had come down from the mountains of Karabagh, or immigrants from Northern Persia.[21] Of the population of the oil-fields 72.6 percent had not been born there. About the same percentage owned land in their place of birth, and every year some of the workers returned to their farms while others took their place at the drilling-site. Those who had not come from great distances maintained direct ties with their families in the villages. Most lived alone—especially the Moslem workers. For every thousand men there were only 394 women.[22] The oil-field workers lived in a compact workers' ghetto without the comfort of wives or families. They were actually half peasants, half workers, a phenomenon well known to other parts of Russia, especially in the early years of industrialization. The Moslems experienced most notably this semiproletarian existence; they were the most transient, the most closely tied to the village, the least proletarianized. Of the various nationalities the Russians were the most settled, judging by the higher proportion of women among them.[23]

Identification with the city was slight among workers,

20 *Ibid.*, p. 269.
21 Arutiunov, p. 58.
22 S. S. Aliiarov, "Izmeneniia v sostave rabochikh Baku v gody pervoi mirovoi voiny," *Istoriia SSSR*, no. 2 (1969), p. 56.
23 Pokshishevskii, p. 8.

especially among the unskilled who lived outside the city in the districts where the only government known was that provided by the owners of the oil industry. Negotiations for improvements in housing, schools, welfare, sanitation, etc. had to be carried out with the Unions of the Oil In-dustrialists, not with the municipal government in Baku. The tendency of the workers up to and through 1917 was to agitate for piecemeal and immediate alleviation of spe-cific hardships, rather than for basic reforms.

The economic orientation of the Baku workers cannot, however, be explained solely by their transience and iso-lation from the political order. The wage system and the attitude of the employers also contributed. Workers, as is true everywhere, could be distinguished as skilled and un-skilled, but there was the difference in Baku that the two groups tended to live separately, were usually of different nationalities, and had different cultural and political affi-liations. The social distance between skilled and unskilled workers was accentuated by the system by which the em-ployers paid their employees. Separate agreements were reached by the individual firms with the various categories of workers, so that workers doing the same work for differ-ent firms received different wages while the wage-rates within each factory showed considerable differentials.

The system of separate agreements was combined with a program of bonuses and subsidies rather than simple increases in wages. These bonuses could be rescinded without changing the basic wage-rates, and made the workers dependent on the good will of their employers. This *beshkesh* policy, as it was called, was a contributing factor in the tendency of the Baku workers to be con-cerned primarily with economic improvement rather than with political change. The discontent of the workers was easily alleviated by small grants of subsidies and bonuses. Moreover, the Baku industrialists were flexible in their dealings with their workers, making concessions unknown in the rest of Russia. The willingness of the industrialists to grant the workers the substance of their demands often distracted the labor movement from considering long-range political programs.[24]

In Baku wages were high in comparison with the rest of Russia, but living and working conditions were abominable by any standard. In her memoirs Eva Broido, a Menshevik who worked in Baku in 1905, describes the physical conditions she found on her arrival in a workers' settlement in Balakhany:

> I was immediately plunged into the very midst of toil and soot—the road to hell, I thought, would be very similar to the one we were driving on. It was narrow and indescribably dirty; and on both sides of it towered the dark and gloomy derricks from which minute droplets of oil escaped in clouds and slowly settled on everything. On the skin of my face, neck and hands it felt like prickly dust; my clothes were sticky with it. We were surrounded by derricks on all sides. As far as the eye could reach there was nothing but derricks and an

[24] The "liberalism" of the Baku industrialists stands out in sharp contrast with the behavior of the bourgeoisie in the rest of Russia. The attitude of the oil industrialists toward their workers may have its origin in the paternalism of the owners toward their employees. Many firms were owned by men who employed only members of their nationality and who provided schooling, housing, and welfare for their workers. A unique personal link thus developed between employer and employee in the oil-fields and refineries. Another explanation for the liberalism of Baku oil capitalists has been provided by a Social Democrat active in Baku after the 1905 revolution. Iurii Larin (Lur'e) writes:

> The oil industry's possession of a firm base in the form of a guaranteed and growing domestic market put it on its own feet, made it self-sufficient. This explains to a significant degree the independent tone and well-known liberalism of the Baku industrialists in comparison with their colleagues in the rest of Russia. . . . A large role in this was played by the pressure of the intensive workers' movement, of course, with which they thought to deal at first with "gentle measures." (Iurii Larin, *Rabochie neftianogo dela* [*iz byta i dvizheniia 1903–1908 gg.*] [Moscow, 1909], p. 10.)

occasional factory chimney. Along both sides of the road, and completely dwarfed by the derricks, stood rows of squat, one-storied dwelling-houses with windows darkened by soot and sometimes covered with wire netting. Crawling around the derricks were some tall black figures in long, greasy Persian coats and high ginger-colored sheepskin hats. It was a picture of unremitting and hopeless gloom.[25]

The hierarchy of workers by skills and wages was closely related to the national differences within the Baku working class. By 1917 the total number of workers in and around Baku numbered about 108–110 thousand.[26] Of these, Azerbaijanis made up 36.9 percent, Russians 23 percent, Armenians 21.4 percent, Daghestanis 11.3 percent, and Volga Tatars 3.6 percent.[27] Most of the skilled workers, office employees, and administrators were Armenians and Russians, while the Azerbaijanis and Daghestanis formed the bulk of the drillers and field workers.[28] Nationality tended to accentuate differences of status within the work-

[25] Eva Broido, *Memoirs of a Revolutionary*, trans. and ed., Vera Broido (New York and Toronto, 1967), pp. 68–69.

[26] This estimate is made in S. S. Aliiarov, "Chislennost', professional'nyi i natsional'nyi sostav bakinskogo proletariata v period pervoi mirovoi voiny," *Uchenye zapiski azerbaidzhanskogo gosudarstvennogo universiteta imeni S. M. Kirova, Seriia istorii i filosofskikh nauk*, no. 1 (1967), p. 73.

[27] *Ibid.*, p. 78.

[28] *Ibid.* Among office workers the national breakdown was as follows:

| | |
|---|---|
| Azerbaijanis | 11.1% |
| Russians | 33.0% |
| Armenians | 29.8% |
| Daghestanis | 3.4% |
| Volga Tatars | 1.0% |

Among highly skilled workers the national breakdown was:

| | |
|---|---|
| Azerbaijanis | 16.1% |
| Russians | 46.8% |
| Armenians | 24.9% |
| Daghestanis | 4.7% |
| Volga Tatars | 2.1% |

ing class. National animosities were thus coupled with social and economic antagonisms which led to tension and disunity in the working class rather than the cohesion which the Social Democrats tried to promote. At times class interests prevailed over national antagonisms, as in the great strikes of 1903, 1904, 1913, and 1914; at other times, notably in 1905 and in the "March Days" of 1918, proletarian solidarity disappeared in a frenzied interethnic bloodletting.

Nationality reinforced class, but at the same time national loyalties cut across class lines. A poor unskilled Moslem worker had little in common with a skilled Armenian worker apart from their memories of the massacres of 1905, whereas he had the bonds of religion and custom tying him to a Moslem peasant and, indeed, to a Moslem capitalist. Moslem workers occupied the bottom of the labor hierarchy while at the same time Moslem industrialists experienced condescension from Armenian, Russian, and foreign capitalists. The Azerbaijani community did not participate as fully in the economic and political life of Baku as did their neighbors, though they

---

Yet among unskilled workers the Moslems predominated:

| | |
|---|---|
| Azerbaijanis | 54.0% |
| Russians | 10.7% |
| Armenians | 13.9% |
| Daghestanis | 17.0% |
| Volga Tatars | 3.1% |

Altogether 71% of all workers in and around Baku were Moslems—northern Azerbaijanis, southern Azerbaijani immigrants from Persia, Volga Tatars from the region of Kazan, or north Caucasian Moslems who were usually from Daghestan and sometimes called "Lezgins." The largest single contingent within the Moslem working class was the Azerbaijani, about 46%. Most of these men were from eastern Transcaucasia and were Russian subjects. During the First World War they replaced their brothers from Persia who returned home when the ruble exchange proved disadvantageous to them. (*Ibid.*, no. 2, p. 35.)

(14)

made up an absolute majority in Baku *uezd* and considered eastern Transcaucasia as their historic homeland.

In describing the Azerbaijani peasantry of Transcaucasia, the urban intelligentsia always resorted to words like "dark," "unconscious," or "reactionary." Most vexing to liberals and radicals in Baku was the peasants' loyalty to the landlords, the noble beks and khans, and their obedience to the Moslem clergy, the mullahs and imams. Although they were the poorest peasants in Transcaucasia, the Moslems were also the least revolutionary. Perhaps the answer to this paradox lies in the unique village society in which they lived. The Azerbaijani village did not suffer from absentee landlordism and consequently the peasants did not share a common antagonism to an invisible exploiter. Instead the nobles lived in the villages, only slightly distinguishable from their peasant neighbors. Their landholdings were small. Altogether Moslem nobles owned only 18.9 percent of the arable land.[29]

Within the village there was little influence of the urban culture or the secular nationalism which developed among Baku Moslems in the decade from 1905 to 1917. Village needs were satisfied by a natural, nonmonetary economy, which effectively isolated one village from another. The periodic crisis suffered by Georgian and Armenian peasants because of market fluctuations did not affect the Azerbaijani peasants.[30] Surplus labor on the land was

[29] N. Pchelin, *Krest'ianskii vopros pri musavate* (1918–1920). *Ocherki* (Baku, 1931), pp. 2–5: 32.4% was state land; 48.7% was owned by the peasants. Seventy-two percent of the landlord class owned less than twenty-five desiatins (on the average, 6.31 desiatins). Sixteen percent of the beks owned from twenty-five to one hundred desiatins, the average holding in this group being 45.64 desiatins. A small group of rich beks, 8% of the nobility, owned the great estates (averaging about 155 desiatins), while a still wealthier group, 4% of the nobility, owned estates which averaged 1,580 desiatins.

[30] Grigorii Uratadze, *Vospominaniia gruzinskogo sotsial-demokrata* (Stanford, Calif., 1968), pp. 26–27.

siphoned off by Baku, thus preventing the development of a rural proletariat.

Called Tatars or Turks until the 1930s, the Azerbaijanis developed a national consciousness only in the recent past. Though they had lived in the Baku area for centuries, Azerbaijanis never thought of themselves as a distinct national group until late in the nineteenth century. Even after the Russian conquest, Persia maintained a cultural and religious dominion over the Transcaucasian Azerbaijanis, just as she maintained a political hold on the southern Azerbaijanis. This cultural domination was reinforced by the Iranized clergy of the Shiite wing of Islam. Sixty percent of Azerbaijanis considered themselves Shiite, and only a minority Sunni.[31] Linguistically the Azerbaijanis were closer to the Ottoman Turks, though the Ottomans were Sunni. To combat this Persian influence, young intellectuals fashioned a national literary movement to renew interest in the Turkish language, a linguistic challenge specifically directed against the conservative nobility and the clergy who insisted on the use of Persian.[32]

The first newspaper in the Azeri vernacular, considered at the time a "peasant dialect," was published in 1875 but lasted only two years. *Ekinchi* ("Laborer") was designed to reach the Azerbaijani peasant, and contained much material on agricultural techniques. Politically *Ekinchi* was representative of the newly emerging Azerbaijani intelligentsia; it was anti-Iranian, anti-Shiite, and secular in its outlook.[33] In this initial period the pro-Turkish posture of Baku's Moslem intellectuals was shaped by the Pan-Turkism of the Tatar thinker Ismail Bey Gasprinskii, and closer to home by the Azerbaijani playwright Mirza Feth-'Ali

[31] A. Bennigsen and C. Lemercier-Quelquejay, *La presse et le mouvement national chez les musulmans de Russie avant 1920* (Paris and The Hague, 1964), p. 28.

[32] Serge A. Zenkovsky, *Pan-Turkism and Islam in Russia* (Cambridge, Mass., 1960), pp. 92–94.

[33] Bennigsen and Lemercier-Quelquejay, p. 28.

Akhundzade (1812–1878), known to his admirers as the "Molière of the Orient." Generally in Baku the differences between Shiite and Sunni were muted, as Pan-Turkism became the dominant ideological tendency in the Azeri press. To Azerbaijanis these internal squabbles were irrelevant in the face of the political strength of the Russians and Armenians in Baku.

Baku and Kazan, the Tatar city on the Volga, were the two centers of the Moslem literary and political renaissance of the early twentieth century. From 1875 to February 1917, Moslems in Russia published 172 periodicals, of which nearly a half appeared in these two cities: 60 in Baku, 23 in Kazan.[34] Yet the two cities were significantly different. In Kazan the commercial bourgeoisie was the chief promoter of the national movement, while in Baku the industrial bourgeoisie shared the direction of the movement with the landed nobility.[35] The active labor movement in Baku tinted all politics with a deeper shade of red than in Kazan. The more politicized press of the Azerbaijanis did not include a single religious or conservative periodical, while Kazan had several.

After a lull from 1891 to 1903, during which time no periodicals in Azeri were published, Azerbaijani political life intensified. Liberal Turkophiles contributed to the influential Russian-language newspaper *Kaspii*, owned by the Moslem millionaire Zein ul-'Abdin Tagiev. Most of the Azeri press was unknown outside Transcaucasia, but *Kaspii* had an international reputation. It shared this renown with the famous satirical journal *Molla Nasreddin* (1906–1914), which cleverly disseminated a mixture of democratic, semisocialist, anticlerical, and anticolonialist ideas. Apart from these two journals Baku's influence among Russian Moslems did not extend across the Caucasus; the rest of Russia was under the sway of the Pan-Turks of Kazan.

---

[34] *Ibid.*, p. 48.   [35] *Ibid.*, p. 104.

The political and literary monopoly among Azerbaijanis held by the liberal intelligentsia was broken by 1904. In that year a socialist group called "Hummet" ("Endeavor") was formed in the wake of the first series of labor strikes. Attached to the Baku Committee of the Russian Social Democratic Workers' Party and dominated by the Bolsheviks, Hummet was the single exception to the party's rule that no national Social Democratic organization was to be permitted within it. Its spokesmen argued well for making an exception in order to concentrate all efforts to agitate among Azerbaijani workers in a single organization.[36] Hummet's distinct appeal to one national group within the proletariat made it a most effective weapon in the Bolshevik arsenal. It counterbalanced the appeal of the nationalist Armenian parties among the Armenian workers and was responsible for the high degree of Bolshevik support among Moslem workers.

With the collapse of the labor movement in 1908, many of the former leaders of Hummet drifted away from Social Democracy. Typical of these defectors was Mehmet Emin Bey Resul Zade, who left Russia that year to participate in the revolution in Persia.[37] A few years later he and some

[36] A. Bennigsen and C. Lemercier-Quelquejay, *Islam in the Soviet Union* (London, 1967), p. 244. Its earliest leaders included men from all classes of Azerbaijani society: noblemen like Nariman Bey Narimanov, Meshedi Aziz Bey Azizbekov, and Mehmet Emin Bey Resul Zade; bourgeois like Sultan Mejid Efendiev, Asadullah Akhundov, and Dadash Bunyatzade; and workers like Zeinal Zeinalov and Ali Husein Resul Zade.

[37] Mehmet Emin Bey Resul Zade (1884–1954) was a socialist until 1910 when he left Persia for Turkey and Pan-Turkism. On his return to Russia in 1913 he resumed his political activity in the Musavat Party, founded in 1911. In 1917 he was elected chairman of the party, leading its faction in the Baku soviet. His political position was somewhere between the Moslem liberals and Hummet. With the fall of the independent republic of Azerbaijan he was taken to Moscow and in 1922 was permitted to emigrate to Germany. Later he moved to Poland, Rumania, and finally to Turkey, remaining throughout an influential person in the emigration.

of his former associates formed a new political party called "Musavat" ("Equality"), which called for the "unification of all Moslem peoples without discrimination by nation or religious practices."[38] Musavat's call for unity was a far cry from the specifically labor-oriented appeals of the Social Democrats from whose ranks the Musavat leaders had emerged. The only trace of the Bolshevik past were the rules for entering the party—only by acceptance of the program and active participation in a party group could one be considered a party member—and the "democratic centralist" organization of the party, according to which lower party organs were subordinate to the higher ones. Interestingly enough, there is no mention of Azerbaijan, either autonomous or independent, in the program, nor is there reference specifically to the Turks. Moslem unity, Pan-Islamism, dominated this first program of the Musavat Party.

The affinity of the Azerbaijanis to the Ottoman Turks seemed to lose political significance with the outbreak of the war between Turkey and Russia in 1914. Both *Kaspii* and *Achiz-soz*, the newspaper founded by Resul Zade in October 1915, supported Russia in the war. The Russian government did not overly concern itself about the possible defection of Moslems to the Turks, and expressed its confidence in its Turkic subjects by the appointment of an Azerbaijani commander of the elite Guard Cavalry Corps.[39] Prominent Azerbaijanis worked actively for the war effort. Tagiev financed the creation of Azerbaijani volunteer units to fight the Germans and supported a large military hospital in Baku.[40] Pan-Turkism seemingly had been laid to rest in the first flush of patriotism. The ideal of Moslem

[38] The Musavat program has been published in M. D. Guseinov, *Tiurkskaia demokraticheskaia partiia federalistov "Musavat" v proshlom i v nastoiashchem*, 1: programma i taktika (Tiflis, 1927), pp. 71–78.
[39] Zenkovsky, p. 122.     [40] *Ibid.*, p. 124.

unity had been replaced by limited cultural demands, such as those made by *Achiz-soz* for schools in the national language, the establishment of state-supported Moslem seminaries, and the return of the Moslem clergy's funds and real estate confiscated by the government.[41] The Moslem revolt in central Asia in 1916 found no resonance in the Caucasus. *Kaspii* referred to the protest against mobilization of the Moslems of Turkestan as a "dark spot" which weakened the common effort against the external enemy.[42] The Azerbaijanis by 1917 were a nationality in the process of self-definition, with a nationalist resurgence still ahead of it. The liberal Azerbaijani intelligentsia saw in the February Revolution the opportunity to redress the wrongs they felt had been done their people, to lift the Moslems to the level of their Christian neighbors, and to gain for them a proportionate share of the political power in Baku.

The sixty-three thousand Armenians held the political balance between the Moslem community (95,000) and the Russians in the city (90,000), playing a role in the government of the city and the management of the oil industry far out of proportion to their actual numbers.[43] Their weight in the city was much greater than that of the Moslems, and in the surrounding districts the Armenians preferred to live among their own, employ their countrymen, and in general to cultivate a nationally exclusive mode of life. The great factories of the Armenian capitalists, Mantashev, Lianozov, and Mirzoev, hired almost exclusively Armenian labor and housed their workers in settlements around their plants. The ancient Armenian language was spoken; Russian was often unknown. Wom-

---

[41] M. D. Guseinov, pp. 36–37.

[42] *Kaspii*, no. 7, January 10, 1917.

[43] These figures are from the 1916 census as reported in *Baku*, no. 191, August 31, 1917.

en were kept in a subordinate position and not permitted to participate in political life or even to acquire education.[44] While among the Moslem Azerbaijanis the first loyalty was to religion, for the Armenian it was to nationality, not class. Until the international labor movement developed in Baku, the masses of Armenians did not join with their alien neighbors in political and social organizations. The only political party which could claim massive support among the Armenians had to combine its political program with an explicitly national appeal.

The Armenian Revolutionary Federation, known as the "Dashnaktsutiun," had been founded in 1890 in Tiflis with the aim of fostering democratic liberties and equality for the peoples of the six eastern provinces of Anatolia. The party directed its initial efforts solely toward improving the lot of Turkish Armenians, and until 1903 its committees in Transcaucasia, Persia, and Europe operated only as sources of men and money for the emancipation movement within Turkey.[45] By 1894 a Dashnak organization had already been set up in Balakhany outside of Baku, and when Kristafor Mikaelian, a founder of the party, visited the local Dashnaks in that year, he spoke not only of the party's responsibility in revolutionizing the Armenian people but also of the necessity of carrying on propaganda among the Kurds and Persians. There was no revolutionary message for those Armenians living within Russia.[46]

Together with a program of emancipation leftist Dashnaks adopted a socialist line. In 1896 the Dashnaks informed the Second International that although there was no capitalist development in Turkish Armenia the Dashnaks wished to work toward the socialist destiny of hu-

---

[44] Broido, p. 83.
[45] *Rapport présenté au Bureau Socialiste International par le parti socialiste et révolutionnaire arménien Daschnaktzoutioun* (Stuttgart, 1907), p. 9.
[46] *Arev*, no. 48, March 19, 1918.

manity.[47] Their tactic at that time was based on individual acts of terrorism which would instigate intervention by the European powers on behalf of the Armenians.[48] Not until 1907 did the Dashnaktsutiun adopt an explicitly socialist program.

The Dashnaks turned their attention toward Transcaucasia in 1902–1903 and began a campaign of anti-tsarist activity when in 1903 the Russian government seized the lands of the Armenian Church. By 1905 the Dashnaks had penetrated the labor movement, particularly in Baku where they formed ten trade unions with a total of about two thousand members.[49] Two years later the Dashnaks could claim 265 circles in Baku and its outlying districts.[50] Besides their economic and political roles, the Dashnaks planned an important military role as the self-styled defenders of the local Armenian population. When in 1905 a series of armed fights broke out between Armenians and Azerbaijanis, the Dashnaks alone of the political parties took to the streets. They assassinated the governor of Baku, Prince Nakasheidze, after declaring him responsible for the February 1905 pogrom in Baku, and terrified Prince Golitsyn, the viceroy of the Caucasus. With all Armenians facing a common Moslem threat, the Dashnaks were able to cement an alliance with the Armenian middle class. Vorontsov-Dashkov, Golitsyn's successor and the initiator of a policy of tolerance toward the Armenians, wrote to the prime minister, Stolypin, about the change in orientation and tactics of the Dashnaks which had resulted from the 1905 pogroms:

> In this period the organization "Dashnaktsutiun" obtained a special dominant influence in the city of Baku after the Armeno-Tatar disorders and the troubled period of 1905–1906. This is explained by the fact that

[47] *Au congrès international socialiste de Londres. La Fédération révolutionnaire arménienne* (Geneva, 1896), p. 4.
[48] *Ibid.*, p. 5.      [49] *Ibid.*, p. 20.      [50] *Ibid.*, p. 22.

at that time the most influential and richest part of the Armenian population saw in the organization its armed protection against the Moslems and the anarchistic organizations created by the revolution, and supported widely the Dashnaks with material means, and that's why the latter are so well armed; besides the purpose of protecting their persons, the richer Armenians used the Dashnaks for the protection of their property and property interests; thus it happened that in the oil-fields the Dashnaks stopped strikes by means of a threat, and, on the other hand, when they wanted to take revenge on someone or other of the industrialists who had not wanted to satisfy their demands for money, they forced the workers on his field to strike.[51]

By the end of 1906 the menace from the Moslems had disappeared, and Armenian capitalists were no longer willing to submit to the extortion by the Dashnaks.[52] The alliance between the Dashnaks and the middle-class Armenians broke down. Even as this occurred the party was shifting dramatically to the left.

In 1907 the Dashnaks not only adopted a socialist program but also drafted a program for Transcaucasia that envisioned a democratic republic independent in internal affairs though tied in foreign affairs to the Federal Russian Republic. Transcaucasia was to be divided into cantons that would approximate the national divisions of the region. The Dashnaks favored "nonterritorial cultural autonomy," a principle which guaranteed each citizen national cultural rights no matter where he lived.[53] The adoption of this policy and of a socialist program drove a number of

[51] P. A. Stolypin and I. I. Vorontsov-Dashkov, "Bor'ba s revoliutsionnym dvizheniem na Kavkaze v epokhu stolypinshchiny (Iz perepiski P. A. Stolypina s gr. I. I. Vorontsovym-Dashkovym)," *Krasnyi arkhiv*, no. 3 (34) (1929), p. 206.

[52] *Ibid.*, pp. 206–207, 211.

[53] *Programma armianskoi revoliutsionnoi i sotsialisticheskoi partii Dashnaktsutiun* (Geneva, 1908), *passim*.

militant nationalists, such as Antranik and Mihran, from the party.[54]

Inevitably, the schism in the party, coupled with an intensified campaign by the tsarist government against the Dashnaks, led to a decline in the party's fortunes in the years from 1907 to 1914. Scores of Dashnaks were rounded up by the police and held until mass trials were organized in 1912. The young lawyer Alexander Kerensky lent his oratorical talents to the defense of the "terrorists."[55] To escape harassment many Dashnaks left Russia to work in the revolutionary movements in Persia and Turkey. Programmatically and tactically akin to the Russian Socialist Revolutionaries, the Dashnaktsutiun made its appeal to all classes within the Armenian nation, with the aim of leading a common front against the states which suppressed Armenian national expression. In this basic strategic conception the Dashnaks opposed the internationalist Social Democrats, whose appeal, especially after 1905, was limited to one class, the workers.

To the left of the Dashnaktsutiun were a number of Armenian socialist organizations—the Hnchak Party, a Marxist party founded in 1887; the Union of Armenian Social Democrats, which lasted only a few months; and the Armenian Social Democratic Workers' Organization.[56]

[54] K. S. Papazian, *Patriotism Perverted: A discussion of the deeds and misdeeds of the Armenian Revolutionary Federation, the so-called Dashnagtzoutune* (Boston, 1934), pp. 28–29.

[55] Alexander Kerensky, *Russia and History's Turning Point* (New York, 1963), pp. 80–81.

[56] For a brief account of the early years of the Hnchak Party, see Louise Nalbandian, *The Armenian Revolutionary Movement: The Development of Armenian Political Parties through the Nineteenth Century* (Berkeley and Los Angeles, 1963), pp. 104–131.

The Armenian Social Democratic Workers' Organization was founded in 1904 in order to form circles and unions exclusively of Armenian workers; in this respect it was similar in form to the Jewish Bund. More active than the Dashnaktsutiun in the labor movement, it led thirty strikes, all of them successful, between

After a schism in the Hnchak Party in 1896, a left wing, which became vocally socialist and less committed than the body of the party to independence for Turkish Armenia, gained supporters in Transcaucasia. These Left Hnchaks vacillated in the prerevolutionary years between occasional ententes with the Dashnaks and, more often, temporary alliances with Russian Social Democrats. In 1902 a few influential Hnchaks, such as Sergo Khanoian and Ashot Khumarian, joined with a Left Dashnak, Arshak Zurabian, and some novices in the revolutionary movement, Bogdan Knuniants and Stepan Shaumian, to form the Union of Armenian Social Democrats.[57] This small

---

1906 and 1917. At that time they claimed two thousand workers organized in their unions. (Martov *et al.*, III, pp. 315–316.)

In 1917 this small party supported the Provisional Government, opposed any slackening in the war effort, and, in contrast to the Dashnaktsutiun, disapproved of a federalist solution to the nationality problem. The Armenian Social Democrats called for "broad local government and national-cultural autonomy." Midway through 1917 the party merged with the Mensheviks and the Jewish Bund to form a united Social Democratic opposition to the Baku Bolsheviks. Their influence, however, remained negligible. (*Banvor*, no. 14, July 16, 1917; S. M. Dimanshtein [ed.], *Revoliutsiia i natsional'nyi vopros*, III [Moscow, 1930], pp. 402–403.)

[57] All of these men later became important figures in Transcaucasian Social Democracy. Zurabian became a Menshevik and was elected to the Second State Duma. Bogdan Knuniants (1878–1911) was a Bolshevik until 1908 when he turned toward liquidationism; he had been prominent as a Bolshevik member of the Petersburg soviet in 1905.

Stepan Georgievich Shaumian (1878–1918) was a Social Democrat from 1900 and a Bolshevik from 1903, a personal friend of Lenin's, and a delegate to the Fourth and Fifth Congresses of the Russian Social Democratic Workers' Party. From 1907 until his death he worked in Baku. In 1917 Shaumian was elected to the Central Committee of the Bolshevik Party, and on December 16, 1917, he was appointed Provisional Extraordinary Commissar for Caucasian Affairs, i.e., the highest representative of the Soviet government in the Caucasus. He was chairman of the Baku Sovnarkom in 1918 and a specialist on the nationality question. On September 20, 1918, he was killed as one of the Twenty-six Commissars.

(25)

circle, known primarily through Lenin's attack on its federalist program, merged within a year with the Tiflis Committee.[58] Out of this group emerged the future leader of the Baku Commune, Stepan Shaumian.

Armenians in both Turkey and Transcaucasia lived in fear of their neighbors. Periodically the Turks had organized massacres of the Christian minorities, and in 1896 and again in 1909 they turned against the Armenians. The First World War threatened the Armenians with the ultimate disaster—genocide. The Young Turk government of Enver, Djemal, and Talaat Pasha decided in 1915 to deport or liquidate the Armenians in Anatolia, whom they considered a potential internal threat to the war effort against the Russians. The Transcaucasian Armenians formed self-defense regiments to operate with the Russian Army on the Caucasian Front. Turkish Armenians cooperated with the Russian Army and retreated with it when it withdrew. By the end of 1915 almost two hundred thousand refugees had crossed the Arax River into Transcaucasia.[59] Thousands reached Baku, bringing with them tales of atrocities at the hands of the Moslems. Realizing that only a Russian victory could prevent the extermination of their people, the Armenians of Baku and their Dashnak leadership adopted a "Russian orientation," strongly supporting the war and resisting all "defeatist" propaganda.[60]

[58] S. T. Arkomed (G. Karjian), *Rabochee dvizhenie i sotsialdemo-kratiia na Kavkaze* ( *s 80-kh gg. po 1903 g.* ) (Moscow-Petrograd, 1923), p. 83. Lenin's article, "O manifeste 'Soiuz armianskikh sotsial-demokratov,' " appeared in *Iskra*, no. 33, February 1, 1903, and has been reprinted in V. I. Lenin, *Polnoe sobranie sochineniia* (5th ed.), VII, pp. 102–106.

[59] *The Treatment of Armenians in the Ottoman Empire: Documents Presented to Viscount Grey of Fallodon* (London, 1916), p. 206.

[60] In May 1917 an Armenian Kadet, Khristofor Vermishev, editor of the liberal newspaper *Baku*, told the Eighth Congress of the Kadet Party:

The attacks on what is called Russian imperialism are

The war increased the national and class tensions in Baku. The city seemed prepared for a repetition of the 1905 Armeno-Azerbaijani massacres. Rumors circulated within the city that one or the other side was arming for a showdown. Not only the threat but the actuality of violence gripped the city. It was a "frontier" town, with poorer men armed and richer men accompanied by bodyguards. Killings were frequent. No one thought it strange that political parties filled their coffers by "shaking down" local merchants and industrialists. The greatest fear of party leaders was that the incipient violence would erupt into an uncontrollable interethnic bloodletting. When the revolution finally came, however, it was not a national conflict which erupted in Baku, but rather a classical class struggle between workers and their employers. The roots of that conflict lay in the short history of the labor movement and its Social Democratic leadership in Baku.

---

completely beyond understanding. In the Caucasus this imperialism created a legal order and a secure life which Armenians had not known before. Russian imperialism had its dark sides, but in general it was a positive force. And when I see that Russians are afraid of this word and that everyone rejects it, then as an Armenian I feel sad for the past of Russia. Between Russian imperialism and German there is an impassable difference. You bear freedom to peoples, you bear security for life to those who groaned under the Moslem yoke, and your rejection of imperialism, as you understand it at this moment, would be in relation to the East a fatal mistake. Armenia has waited for long years for Russian imperialism to say its mighty word in Turkish Armenia and lead the Armenians from under the Turkish yoke. And the denial of imperialism would be met in the Turkish Armenian slums by great despair. Do not deny these slums, because thus you will denigrate your history. (*Rech'* no. 109, May 11, 1917; Dimanshtein, p. 401.)

# 2

# Social Democracy
# and the Labor Movement in Baku
# 1898-1917

SOCIAL DEMOCRACY, with its offspring, the mass labor movement, began its history in Baku later than in other industrial centers of the Russian empire. Originating as a small socialist study circle in 1898, it did not reach the dimensions of a mass movement until the general strike of 1903. Nevertheless, as a center for party activity Baku rivaled Saint Petersburg and Moscow in importance, and the gains made by Baku workers—which included the first labor–management contract in Russia's history—inspired their comrades in the capitals and elsewhere to emulate the efforts of the oil workers.

Social Democracy found its first response in Transcaucasia among Russian and Georgian railroad workers in Tiflis.[1] In 1898 a turner named Popov arrived in Baku from Moscow and established at the Nobel Plant the first Social-Democratic circle in Baku, largely of Russian workers.[2] The next year Avel Enukidze came from Tiflis to Baku and organized a small circle of railroad workers

[1] S. T. Arkomed (G. Karjian), *Rabochee dvizhenie i sotsial-demokratiia na Kavkaze (s 80-kh gg. po 1903 g.)* (Moscow-Petrograd, 1923), p. 59.

[2] The members of this first circle were I. O. Vatsek, Ivan Ulianov, Ivan Konkushkin, the Mazilkin brothers, and the Blinov brothers. (*Deiateli revoliutsionnogo dvizheniia v Rossii: Biograficheskii-bibliograficheskii slovar'*, v: Sotsial-Demokraty 1880–1904, comp. E. A. Korol'chuk and Sh. M. Levin, ed. V. I. Nevskii [Moscow, 1931–1933], p. 715.)

from the local depot. Twenty men met every two weeks to discuss economic and, sometimes, political problems.[3] At the end of that year "Lado" Ketskhoveli, another Georgian socialist and the "teacher" of Stalin, arrived in Baku. The history of the Russian Social Democratic Workers' Party (RSDRP) in Baku can be dated from 1900, when a four-man center for the Social Democrats was informally organized as the antecedent to the Baku Committee of the Party.[4] That year May Day was celebrated for the first time in Baku by twelve men.[5] Although the demonstration could not be compared with the Kharkov march of over five thousand workers, it marked a beginning for Baku. The next year two hundred were on the streets.[6]

The initial support for the socialists came primarily from workers in the factories and refineries. Only in late 1904, when a unique trade-unionist movement came into being, were the workers in the outlying oil-fields, the least skilled and worst paid, attracted to the movement.[7] The Social Democrats achieved their greatest success among Russian workers.[8] At first the Armenian workers were not interested in Social Democracy, remaining loyal to the national parties, the Dashnaktsutiun and the Hnchak Party. But in 1903 Armenians joined in the series of strikes, and soon afterwards the Armenian parties ended their active interference with socialist propaganda.[9] The Azerbaijani workers also began joining socialist circles in 1903, but were even less enthusiastic about the movement than the Armenians. Local Social Democrats were heartened by the

[3] *Dvadtsati piat' let bakinskoi organizatsii bol'shevikov (Osnovnye momenty razvitiia bakinskoi organizatsii)* (Baku, 1924), p. 9.

[4] *Ibid.*, p. 11.

[5] *Ibid.*, p. 12.

[6] *Ibid.*

[7] *Ibid.*, p. 7; *Vtoroi s"ezd RSDRP, Iiul'–Avgust 1903 goda: Protokoly* (Moscow, 1959), p. 515.

[8] *Iskra*, no. 53, November 25, 1903.

[9] *Vtoroi s"ezd . . .* , p. 515.

fact that sixty Azerbaijanis had joined the circles by the Second Party Congress. The next year the Social Democrats formed the exclusively Azerbaijani group, Hummet, which cooperated with the Baku Committee. Most reluctant to participate in the labor ferment were the immigrants from Persia who spent only a few years in the oilfields with the intention of returning to their native land. Their passivity was, in part, responsible for the slowness of recruitment in the fields.[10] Another reason for the failure of socialist propaganda to spread to the lower strata of field workers was the unwillingness of the small number of socialist intellectuals to disperse their meager resources too far from the center of the city, the homeground of the more skilled workers, the worker elite. The lack of cadres who knew the languages of the Moslem workers, and the complete absence of socialist literature in those languages, further contributed to the neglect by the socialists of the poorest of their constituents.

By 1902–1903 Baku had acquired a reputation as a city continually disrupted by strikes and demonstrations. The underlying reason for the ferment in Baku was undoubtedly the miserable physical conditions in which the workers existed, conditions in which it seemed as if nature itself had conspired to deprive men of simple pleasures such as trees or fresh air. But credit must be given to the Social Democrats for furnishing the stimulus for the strikes and demonstrations, by printing in the fall and winter of 1901 a series of leaflets and of newspapers spelling out for the first time the inequities the workers knew from experience.[11] The rapidity of the growth of the labor movement can be gauged from the fact that the 1902

[10] *Ibid.*, p. 517. Not surprisingly, the least transient nationalities—the Russians and Armenians—were the first attracted to the labor movement. The Moslems—native Azerbaijanis, Volga Tatars, and immigrants from Persia—were the least active workers in the movement and, coincidently, the most transient.

[11] Arkomed, p. 102.

May Day celebration brought five thousand people into the streets.[12] And a year later the number of demonstrators had doubled.[13]

The early Social Democrats in Baku not only made the workers conscious of the terrible conditions in which they lived and worked but also awoke the workers to the possibility of a better life beyond their day-to-day physical exertions. Men who had never known anything but physical labor were made aware of the world of the mind, and, through the mind, of the possibility of improving their situation. As one agitator remembers: "A worker who joined our organization was conscious of partaking in higher culture, his horizons became wider, his understanding deeper and his moral standards higher. And this was reflected even in his outward appearance."[14] In the oil districts—where soot rained down constantly on everything, where the danger of assault kept men armed and women indoors—life was brutish and short, but the Social Democrats brought light into the physical darkness of the workers' world by teaching reading, lecturing on the latest leaflet, and instilling new values that replaced vodka as the solace of the underdog.

The series of minor economic strikes and political demonstrations climaxed in the general strike of July 1903. The strike began spontaneously on July 2 in a few workshops in Bibi-Eibat and Black City. The following day, as shops and plants throughout the city joined the strikers, the Baku Committee issued leaflets supporting the ill-defined demands of the workers.[15] The strike quickly reached proportions far beyond the expectations of the

---

[12] *Ibid.*, p. 104.  [13] *Ibid.*, p. 108.

[14] Eva Broido, *Memoirs of a Revolutionary*, trans. and ed. Vera Broido (New York and Toronto, 1967), p. 74. The organization here referred to is the Organization of Workers of Balakhany and Bibi-Eibat, the Social-Democratic group led by the Shendrikov brothers in 1904–1905. This group is discussed at length below.

[15] Arkomed, p. 122.

Social Democrats, whose small organization could not hope to lead such a massive undertaking. The socialists attempted to bring a degree of order into the strike by forming a strike committee, but, though it issued leaflets daily in several languages, it could not direct the energies of the workers into supporting a single list of demands.[16] About fifty thousand workers had left work at the height of the strike, and they were encouraged by the simultaneous outbreak of strikes in Tiflis, Batum, and Poti.[17] Negotiations began with the Council of the Congress of Oil Industrialists, which recognized the workers' right to contractual relations with the owners of the industry. Declaring, however, that the present strike should not be considered as a strike but simply as violence, the Council rejected all the demands of the workers.[18] The strike failed. Nevertheless, an important principle for future worker–manager conflicts had been laid down, the first article of what became known as the *mazutnaia konstitutsiia* ("Crude Oil Constitution"). The effects of the Baku strike were immediately felt throughout southern Russia in the general strike of that summer, "in which the Baku workers played, as it were, the role of pioneer."[19]

As the workers of Baku struck for higher wages, the leadership of the Russian Social Democrats was gathering for the Second Congress of the RSDRP. Lenin and the *Iskra* "hards" came out for a narrow definition of a party member, a seemingly innocuous formula that ultimately led to a schism between the Bolsheviks and the Mensheviks. The original causes of the split are less important than the consequent formation of the two factions, during which rival outlooks were formulated. Each local committee was fought over, and victories claimed by both

[16] *Ibid.*, pp. 124–125.     [17] *Ibid.*, p. 131.
[18] *Ibid.*, p. 125.
[19] L. Martov *et al.* (eds.), *Obshchestvennoe dvizhenie v Rossii v nachale XX-go veka* (St. Petersburg, 1909–1914), I, p. 209.

sides. The Baku Committee took the "conciliationist" position of Leonid Krasin, a prominent Social Democrat then working in the local electrical power-plant, and invoked a "plague on both houses." Within the year arrests and desertions gave the Mensheviks control of the Committee, but by mid-1904 the old committee was disbanded and a new one formed under Bolshevik management.[20]

The factional struggles within the Baku Committee consumed the energies of the committeemen to the detriment of the labor movement. A Menshevik attack that the Committee had lost its way in a maze of bureaucratism, that its intellectuals had lost touch with the workers, hit a sensitive spot. The Committee dismissed several agitators sympathetic to the Menshevik opposition, and by so doing unleashed a massive trade-unionist movement which nearly swamped Bolshevism in Baku.

Among those expelled were two brothers, Lev and Ilya Shendrikov, who had expressed their interest in organizing workers on the periphery of Baku separately from the Committee.[21] Within months the brothers Shendrikov had formed their own labor group, the Balakhany and Bibi-Eibat Workers' Organization, which competed with the Baku Social Democrats for the loyalty of the workers. The Shendrikov Organization worked in the oil-fields, which

[20] For additional information on the Baku organization after the Second Party Congress see M. N. Liadov and S. M. Pozner (eds.), *Leonid Borisovich Krasin ("Nikitich"): Gody podpol'ia. Sbornik vospominanii, stat'i i dokumentov* (Moscow–Leningrad, 1928), *passim.*; N. I. Bukharin, V. I. Molotov, and I. I. Skvortsov-Stepanov (eds.), *Leninskii sbornik,* x (Moscow–Leningrad, 1929), pp. 135–138; A. Stopani, "Iz proshlogo nashei partii 1904–1908 gg.," *Iz proshlogo: stat'i i vospominaniia iz istorii bakinskoi organizatsii i rabochego dvizheniia v Baku* (Baku, 1923). This collection was the first of two issues of articles on the Baku labor movement and Social Democracy. Hereafter they will be cited as "*Iz proshlogo*" with the date of publication.

[21] *Tretii s"ezd RSDRP, Aprel'–Mai 1905 goda: Protokoly* (Moscow, 1959), p. 611.

had been neglected by the Social Democrats. They rejected work in the underground in favor of agitation
among the workers.[22]

The tactics of the Shendrikovs in their first months of
activity were simple and effective: to gain a real base of
support among the workers by articulating their purely
economic demands. Along with this, the Organization itself was to be democratic in the broadest sense in order to
draw the workers into a Western-style labor movement.[23]
Their success was immediate and dramatic; meetings were
well attended, and by the end of 1904 the Shendrikovs
could claim four thousand members as against the three

[22] For a Menshevik account of the "Shendrikovshchina," see Solomon M. Schwarz, appendix 6, "The Baku Strike of December, 1904:
Myth and Reality," in his *The Russian Revolution of 1905: The
Workers' Movement and the Formation of Bolshevism and Menshevism* (Chicago, 1967), pp. 301–314.

Both Bolshevik and Menshevik writers on the Shendrikovshchina
link that movement with the Mensheviks—the Bolsheviks in order
to incriminate the Shendrikovtsy, and the Mensheviks to take credit
for the successes of the Organization. Although Ilya Shendrikov
himself was sympathetic to the Mensheviks, it only confuses matters to identify the Shendrikov Organization with Menshevism in
Baku while associating the Baku Committee with Bolshevism. In
fact, the Baku Social Democrats, both Mensheviks and Bolsheviks,
were still in 1904–1905 members of one organization. ("Perepiska N.
Lenina i N. K. Krupskaia c Kavkazskoi organizatsiei," *Proletarskaia
revoliutsiia*, no. 5 [40] [May 1925], pp. 6–7. These letters were
introduced and edited by A. M. Stopani and M. Leman.) Not until
the fall of 1907 were there two separate party organizations. Both
factions uneasily coexisted within the party, while the Shendrikov
Organization existed outside the party. The Shendrikovs rivaled the
whole of Social Democracy in Baku, though ideologically they were
a direct threat to the Bolsheviks alone. Non-Bolshevik elements
within the party gravitated to the Shendrikovs, further weakening
Menshevik expression in Social-Democratic circles. The Shendrikov
Organization had no formal ties with the Menshevik leadership
abroad until the departure of Ilya Shendrikov for Geneva in
April 1905.

[23] E. L. Keenan, "Remarques sur l'histoire du mouvement révolutionnaire à Bakou (1904–1905)," *Cahiers du monde russe et
soviétique*, III, 2 (April/June, 1962), p. 243.

hundred adherents to the Baku Committee.[24] A. Rokhlin, then a member of the Baku Committee, admitted years later: "From the end of 1904 until the beginning of 1906, the Shendrikovtsy actually led the Baku masses, and we, with all our political influence, had to fall in line (at least, in the area of the economic struggle) along their front."[25] The Baku Committee realized its mistake in concentrating its organizational efforts almost exclusively in the center of the city, and, in order to counter the mushrooming influence of the Shendrikovs, began to work more energetically in the oil-fields, especially among Moslem workers whom the Russian-oriented Shendrikovtsy ignored.[26]

In December 1904 the Shendrikovs called a general strike affecting the oil-fields and refineries, the shipyards and workshops. It was the largest labor manifestation Baku had yet seen. Not to be left out, the Baku Committee reversed an earlier decision and agreed to participate in the strike.[27] A strike committee was formed, on which the Bolsheviks Dzhaparidze, Stopani, and Fioletov sat with Lev and Ilya Shendrikov and representatives of the Hnchak party.[28]

[24] *Ibid.*, p. 242.

[25] *Iz proshlogo* (Baku, 1924), p. 79.

[26] A. M. Raevskii, *Bol'sheviki i Men'sheviki v Baku v 1904–05 godakh* (Baku, 1930), pp. 100, 146.

[27] *Ibid.*, p. 113.

[28] *Ibid.*, p. 114. Prokofiia Aprasionovich Dzhaparidze ("Alesha") (1880–1918) spent his entire life in the Social Democratic movement, becoming a Bolshevik shortly after the Second Party Congress. He worked in Baku from 1904 until his death, except for periods of arrest and exile. Second only to Stepan Shaumian in the Baku Commune, Dzhaparidze was usually in the moderate wing of the Bolshevik Party. He was executed as one of the Twenty-six Commissars.

A. M. Stopani (1871–1932) had been a participant in the Second Congress of the RSDRP (1903) and was a member of the Baku Committee in the years 1904–1907. He was to participate in the Fifth Congress of the Party (1907); he returned to Baku in 1909. While carrying on revolutionary work, he also was involved in consumer cooperatives. In 1917 he was the chairman of the Baku Provincial Food Supply Committee. He left Baku in 1918 to be-

The differences between the Baku Committee and the Shendrikovtsy survived their pragmatic alliance during the strike. The goals of both groups were ostensibly the same: victory for the strikers, and political revolution if possible. But their rivalry over tactics continued. The Bolsheviks sought to turn the economic strike into a political protest directed against the autocracy by means of peaceful demonstrations. Such demonstrations were in fact held during funerals of workers killed by the Cossacks or the police, but the Shendrikovtsy criticized them for endangering the lives of the participants. The Armenian political community too was split on this tactical matter. The Hnchaks aligned themselves with the Bolsheviks, favoring a peaceful demonstration, while the Dashnaks hesitated to join any demonstration not well armed.[29]

The December alliance of the Social Democrats and the Shendrikov organization came to a sudden end when the latter began advocating economic terror and sabotage as a means of intimidating the capitalists into accepting the workers' demands. The Social Democrats opened their own negotiations with the industrialists separately from the Shendrikovtsy. They soon came to an agreement on terms for ending the strike. The strike did not end, however, until the Shendrikovtsy themselves carried on negotiations with results similar to those achieved by the Bolsheviks.[30] Despite the division among the labor leaders, it was this strike that achieved the first labor contract in Russian his-

---

come the Commissar of Labor and Industry in the Terek People's Soviet.

Ivan Timofeevich Fioletov (1884–1918) was born in a peasant family in Tambov Province, emigrated to Baku with his parents, and at the age of 16 joined an S.D. circle. In 1904 he became a member of the Baku Committee. Active in trade unions, Fioletov was elected chairman of the Union of Oil Workers after the February Revolution. During the Commune he was head of the Baku Council of People's Economy, and on September 20, 1918, he was killed along with the Twenty-six Commissars.

[29] *Ibid.*, p. 116.       [30] *Ibid.*, p. 125.

tory and a great victory for the workers. They were promised an eight-to-nine-hour day, sick pay for up to three months, pay for the period of the strike, and substantial increases in wages. Several articles had been added to the *mazutnaia konstitutsiia*, though the promises made had still to be fulfilled.

When the news of Bloody Sunday reached Baku, the Social-Democratic Committee decided that a peaceful demonstration would be an appropriate response. The workers, however, demanded to be armed, and when the Baku Committee confessed that it was impossible to secure arms immediately, the workers chose to attend meetings organized by the Shendrikovtsy rather than risk the fate of their Petersburg counterparts.[31] The Shendrikovtsy issued their own call for an armed insurrection, but the workers did not respond.[32] Instead, at this critical point pent-up emotions erupted in four days—February 6–9—of looting and killing by bands of Azerbaijanis and Armenians. The Azerbaijanis, alarmed by rumors that the Armenians were arming, attacked first, as the police and soldiers refused to protect Armenians. The Armenians under Dashnak leadership were merciless in their retaliation. The Social Democrats and the Shendrikovtsy were joined by the liberals in denouncing the massacres and the inaction of the governor of the city.

The Baku oil industrialists, fearing the dislocations that accompanied strikes and violence, sought to create a sense of mutual interest between the Social Democrats and the liberal factory-owners. During the massacres, Armenian industrialists subscribed to the demands of the Baku Committee, and Social-Democratic resolutions were passed at mass meetings made up of both workers and nonworkers.[33] During the general strike in May, the Council of the

[31] *Ibid.*, p. 140; *Tretii s"ezd . . . : Protokoly*, pp. 140–141.
[32] A. L'vov, "1905 god v Baku (Kratkii obzor sobytii)," *Novyi Vostok*, nos. 13–14 (1926), p. 133; Raevskii, p. 141.
[33] *Ibid.*, p. 188.

Congress of Oil Industrialists telegraphed Saint Petersburg expressing its hope that the workers would be given
freedom of speech and assembly, as well as the right to
form unions and to strike. While the workers were deprived of means to express themselves legally, every strike
and demonstration escalated into a revolutionary act.[34] The
"liberal" attitude of the industrialists was well expressed
when the oil magnates petitioned the government to allow
workers' delegates to attend a conference called by the
Ministry of Finance to discuss the crisis in the oil industry.
The ministry agreed, and the stage was set for the elections of the first labor delegates to participate in a state
conference.

The Shendrikovtsy welcomed the possibility offered by
the conference, but the Baku Committee was fearful of
side-tracking the revolution. The Shendrikovs answered
their critics: "The *komitetchiki* think that by sending
delegates we are forgetting about the struggle, rejecting
the revolution. On the contrary, by this means we are
fighting, we are organizing ourselves in battle and go the
true way to revolution. It will not be accomplished by revolutionary appeals alone."[35] The Shendrikov campaign for
participation in the conference gained momentum in the
late summer. In August the Armenians and Azerbaijanis
began another round of their perennial feud. The mobs
moved from the city to the oil-fields, setting fire to wells
and leaving many workers without homes or jobs. According to one Bolshevik analyst present in Baku, the result-
ant unemployment decided many workers to vote for participation in the conference.[36] The Baku Committee was
further weakened at this crucial moment by the arrest of
the entire Bolshevik *aktiv*. A week later elections resulted
in a decisive Shendrikov victory.[37]

[34] *Ibid.*, p. 189.          [35] *Ibid.*, p. 190.
[36] M. N. Liadov, *Iz zhizni partii v 1903–1907 godakh (Vospominaniia)* (Moscow, 1956), p. 86.
[37] *Ibid.*, p. 87; Raevskii, p. 192.

The five delegates who traveled to Saint Petersburg included two workers, a merchant, a member of the Hnchak party, and Lev Shendrikov. For several weeks in October the conference deliberated over the complaints of the workers as well as those of the industrialists. At the end of the month, the workers' delegation returned to Baku satisfied that they had secured promises to establish days of rest, to end overtime without pay, to equalize pay in certain categories, and to create *kamery soglasheniia* (mediation boards) in factories.[38] The delegation had failed to have pay for Persian workers raised to the level of the workers of other nationalities, and efforts by the Azerbaijani liberal Topchibashev to have the industrialists agree to equal pay for equal work had likewise been fruitless.[39] But the crowning achievement of the workers' delegation had been the industrialists' recognition of the factory committees which had first appeared in May 1905.[40] Although the Bolsheviks were unenthusiastic about factory committees, the Shendrikovtsy visualized them as "that rock on which can be built free institutions in Russia."[41]

Although serious tactical differences had kept the Shendrikovtsky and the Baku Committee from allying in joint action from May to November 1905, the events of October—the political demonstrations, the tsar's manifesto of October 17, and the clashes in the streets of Baku between workers and the Black Hundreds—led to reconsideration by both organizations of projects for unification.

[38] Raevskii, p. 206.
[39] *Ibid.*, p. 208. Ali Mardan bey Topchibashev (1862–1934) was a Baku lawyer, editor of *Kaspii*, a founder of the Moslem party "Ittifag al-Muslimin," deputy in the First and Second State Dumas (he signed the Vyborg Manifesto protesting the dissolution of the First Duma), and a prominent liberal.
[40] *Ibid.*; D. D. Gadzhinskii, "Vozniknovenie v Baku promyslovo-zavodskikh komissii i ikh deiatel'nost' v 1905 g.," *Izvestiia Akademii nauk azerbaidzhanskoi SSR, Seriia obshchestvennykh nauk*, no. 7 (1961), p. 19.
[41] Raevskii, p. 208.

The Shendrikovtsy, in contrast to the Tiflis Mensheviks, had declared their opposition to participation in the new State Duma proposed by the tsar, as had the Bolsheviks. More importantly, a movement toward the reunification of Social Democracy was under way throughout Russia. On November 19 a united executive commission of the Baku Committee and the Union of Baku Workers was formed. The union was incomplete and did not involve unconditional adoption of either group's program. Rather, a degree of vagueness affected the public image of the Baku labor leaders. Outside the party the Shendrikovs maintained their energetic activities, but within the organization the Bolsheviks held fast.

On November 17, 1905, the Shendrikovtsy called a meeting of representatives of the factory committees to discuss the distribution of wages for the period of the August pogrom. When 173 representatives gathered, the meeting unexpectedly declared itself a Soviet of Workers' Deputies, in imitation of the already well-known soviets in Saint Petersburg and Moscow. Lev Shendrikov was elected chairman; and shortly afterwards his brother became the editor of the *Izvestiia* of the soviet, which unlike any other such newspaper in Russia appeared six times legally. The Bolsheviks at first disapproved of the soviet as a mass, non-party organization, but soon insisted on more elections in order to increase the number of Social Democrats. The Bolshevik delegation in the soviet remained small, however, not many more than eleven, and no Bolsheviks were elected to the bureau of the soviet.[42] To the disgust of the Bolsheviks, the Shendrikovtsy led the soviet into an almost exclusively economic struggle with the oil industrialists. The single political action taken by the soviet was to call a general strike on December 14, which was a miserable failure. The soviet could hardly arouse enthusiasm for the strike, much less hope to emulate the Moscow workers

[42] *Ibid.*, pp. 218–220.

then engaged in an armed insurrection.[43] The labor leadership was unable to rally the workers for a political demonstration in the wake of the economic gains made in the last year. The more extreme tactic of the Bolsheviks, calling for an armed insurrection, was supported neither by the moderate Shendrikovtsy nor by those intermittent terrorists, the Dashnaks and the Socialist Revolutionaries.[44] By the end of the revolutionary year, the Baku workers were among the most apolitical in Russia; only their comrades in Odessa approached them in their lack of interest in political demands.

Although the Shendrikovtsy had attempted to save the general strike by allying with the liberal Union of Unions and with the Union of Engineers, once the strike collapsed they as its leaders were exposed to the censure of the other parties in the soviet. On January 19 soviet deputies charged that the Shendrikovtsy were in the pay of the capitalists, an unfounded allegation but one effective in removing the last supports of the soviet leaders.[45] The fall of the Shendrikovtsy was even more rapid than their rise. From the beginning of 1906 the Social Democrats, despite the Menshevik–Bolshevik in-fighting, were once again the dominant force in the Baku labor movement.[46] Shendri-

[43] *Ibid.*, p. 230. Lev Shendrikov later defended the Baku soviet's rather passive attitude at the height of the revolution: "At that time when, in Petersburg, Moscow, and Rostov-on-Don, the Soviets of Workers' Deputies, overestimating their strength, called for a revolutionary seizure of the eight-hour day, threw out other violent slogans, and, pushing aside the bourgeoisie, at that moment tore itself from the working masses, in Baku the Soviet of Workers' Deputies, under the leadership of L. N. [Shendrikov], directed its efforts to organizing the working masses and attracting broad strata of society to the liberation movement" (*ibid.*, p. 231).

[44] *Ibid.*, pp. 230–231.   [45] *Ibid.*, p. 234.

[46] On June 4, 1906, the Baku organization again expelled Lev Shendrikov from the party (Iu. Larin, *Rabochie neftianogo dela* [*iz byta i dvizheniia 1903–1908 gg.*] [Moscow, 1909], p. 35n.). Shortly afterwards, Lev died, and Ilya left Baku, not to figure again significantly until 1917, when Kerensky appointed him provisional commissar in Turkestan.

kovism as an organized movement was dead, but the enthusiasm for economic improvement that had marked it remained characteristic of Baku workers. The lessons of 1904–1905 were clear to the Social Democrats: organize the workers around economic demands, do not neglect the workers of the outlying districts, maintain closer contact between the underground party and the mass labor organizations. Degrees of emphasis divided Bolsheviks from Mensheviks, but both factions were clearly impressed by the potency of the economic struggle.

To a stranger arriving in Baku from other parts of Russia in 1906, the city presented a picture of exceptional freedom from police persecution and of flourishing independent workers' organizations and legally appearing labor newspapers inconceivable in the rest of the empire.[47] In addition to the Union of Workers of Mechanical Production, run by the Mensheviks (M. Kol'tsov, Iu. Larin, Vainshtein, Ezhov, and later Bogdan Knuniants), a rival Union of Oil Workers was set up in September 1906 by the Bolsheviks with V. Tronov as chairman and Dzhaparidze as secretary.[48] The Menshevik union, characterized by later Menshevik writings as an infirm organization tending toward "economism," catered to Russian workers,[49] while the Bolshevik union had its headquarters in Balakhany and was predominantly Moslem in its membership.[50] The factory committees created in 1905 continued to operate, and occasionally met with representatives of both the oil industry and the city government to discuss grievances. In 1907–1908, while the rest of Russia slept under police rule, a veritable "workers' parliament"

[47] Larin, pp. 5–6.
[48] Stopani, "Iz proshlogo . . . 1904–1908 gg.," *Iz proshlogo* (Baku, 1923), p. 18n.
[49] I. Jordania (Zhordaniia) and L. Zhgenti, "Rabochee dvizhenie v. Baku i bol'sheviki" (unpublished manuscript, Columbia University, New York), p. 24; Larin, p. 22. Sixty-seven percent of the Union's members were Russian, 9% Armenian, 21% Moslem.
[50] Larin, p. 22.

was meeting in Baku, the result of a state-initiated campaign to bring labor and the oil industry together in a conference.[51]

On May 12, 1907, the viceroy's agent in Baku, General Dzhunkovskii, proposed that elected representatives of the workers meet with the industrialists to discuss a new labor contract. Oil prices at the time were high, and both government and industry feared new strikes that would lead to further destruction of the oil-wells. They were quite willing to make concessions in order to maintain peace and production. The workers, on the other hand, were divided between those who wanted to negotiate directly with the industrialists in a state conference and those who favored a strike. The division within the working class was reflected in the positions of the various political parties. The Mensheviks were unequivocally in favor of the conference. The Socialist Revolutionaries and Dashnaks were equally adamant in their opposition to the conference. The Bolsheviks held the balance, but at this critical moment their ranks were in disarray. A left wing within the organization, led by "Koba," was for boycotting the conference; the rest of the Bolsheviks were more sympathetic to participation, but some insisted that preconditions be set down before the workers should agree to join.[52] At first the party came out for boycott, but as the feasibility of organizing another general strike dwindled, a majority of Bolsheviks coalesced around the middle position, "the conference with guarantees," which demanded that a council of workers' plenipotentiaries meet simultaneously with the conference to discuss the reports of worker delegates.

[51] The best account of the campaign for the conference is in Larin, *passim*.

[52] Iosif Vissarionovich Dzhugashvili ("Koba," "Stalin") (1879–1953) worked in Baku from 1907 to 1910, primarily in the underground party organization. For a fuller account of his activity in Baku, see T. Akindinova, "Iz istorii bakinskoi organizatsii bol'shevikov (1907–1909 gg.)," *Proletarskaia Revoliutsiia*, no. 4 (1940), pp. 64–97.

For nearly a year the debate on the conference filled the pages of *Gudok* ("Factory Whistle") and other labor newspapers. Meanwhile the labor leaders persuaded Dzhunkovskii to permit open agitation among the workers for and against the conference. Thus the campaign for a worker–industrialist conference in Baku, like that in Saint Petersburg for the elections to the Shidlovskii Commission in early 1905, helped immeasurably in the education and organization of the working class.

Elections were finally held to a council of workers' plenipotentiaries in January 1908. The council was designated to meet periodically during the conference as the representative of the workers. Thirty-five thousand workers voted for the four hundred plenipotentiaries, two-thirds of whom were either Social Democrats or Social-Democrat sympathizers. The council began its meetings on March 30 with an opening speech by Dzhaparidze reminding the audience that Baku alone of Russia's cities had such an open workers' council.[53] On April 26, after a series of fruitless sessions, the council voted 199–124 for participation in the conference with the industrialists. The Socialist Revolutionaries and Dashnaks walked out of the meeting, the former calling for a general strike instead of a conference, the latter promising to return when the demands made on the industrialists were to be debated.[54] This vote marked the latest in a series of triumphs for the Social Democrats, particularly for the Bolshevik faction. It also marked the most complete submersion to date of the Bolsheviks' concern for party affairs in the day-to-day struggles of the mass labor movement.[55]

[53] P. A. Dzhaparidze, *Izbrannye stat'i, rechi i pis'ma, 1905–1918 gg.* (Moscow, 1958), pp. 46–47.

[54] Larin, pp. 136–137.

[55] The issue of the conference aided the Bolsheviks in solidifying their position within the labor movement and the Baku organization. Throughout 1907 the Bolsheviks seemed to be outstripping the Mensheviks both inside and outside of the party. The Menshe-

Just as the success of the campaign for a labor–industry conference seemed inevitable, the industrialists and the government lost interest. The underlying reason for the change may be found in the new crisis that the oil industry underwent in 1908. Whereas in 1907 prices of oil had steadily risen, making increases in costs tolerable to the industrial managers, in 1908 a steady and rapid decline in prices made it impossible for the industry to consider wage-increases or the amelioration of working conditions without substantial losses for the investors.[56] Even more suggestive as to the causes for the change of heart by the government is the letter from Stolypin to Vorontsov-Dashkov of April 11, 1908, deploring the permissive policy of the Transcaucasian administration vis-à-vis the revolutionaries and the labor leadership.[57] Stolypin was concerned with a discernible rise in "terrorism" in Transcaucasia, which had accounted for 3,060 individual acts (1,732 were robberies) during the year 1907. "In Baku daily tens of murders and expropriations occur openly and the guilty remain free."[58] Stolypin rejected

viks, according to Larin, had concentrated their activities in small political meetings, while the Bolsheviks, after the rude lesson they had learned from the Shendrikovtsy, did not miss a strike. The influx of new members into the party, which occurred simultaneously with a decline in membership of the trade unions, aided the Bolsheviks. In the fall the Bolsheviks demanded the reshuffling of the Baku Committee to reflect their majority in the organization. When the Mensheviks hesitated to comply, the Bolsheviks set up their own Baku Committee. The Mensheviks then changed the name of their committee to "Leading Collective," and the Baku organization continued with two independent and often conflicting centers. An official schism of the two factions was prevented by the attitude of the workers, who were consistent advocates of party unity. (Jordania and Zhgenti, p. 34; Larin, p. 85.)

[56] *Ibid.*, p. 138.

[57] P. A. Stolypin and I. I. Vorontsov-Dashkov, "Bor'ba s revoliutsionnym dvizheniem na Kavkaze v epokhu Stolypinshchiny (Iz perepiski P. A. Stolypina s gr. I. I. Vorontsovym-Dashkovym)," *Krasnyi arkhiv*, no. 3 (34) (1929), pp. 187–202.

[58] *Ibid.*, p. 195.

Vorontsov-Dashkov's analysis of the strikes as purely economic, for the activity of Socialist Revolutionaries and anarchists ("some of whom are Jews") was designed, he said,
to lead to an armed uprising.[59] Stolypin made it clear to
the viceroy that he believed the disorder in Transcaucasia
stemmed from the inertia of the local police, and he demanded a change in policy.[60]

In May Dzhunkovskii and the oil industry suddenly announced that the trade unions would not be permitted to
participate in the organizational committee which was to
arrange the elections of delegates from the council of
plenipotentiaries to the conference.[61] This slight issue initiated a series of actions by the government that eliminated the possibility of a conference. Shortly afterwards,
the government announced it would take no initiative in
convening the organizational committee. The next day
Dzhaparidze was arrested.[62] May 1908 marks the beginning of the "reaction" in Baku.

Baku's labor movement, from its inception through the
stormy years to 1908, had always been characterized by an
apolitical approach to the resolution of conflicts between
workers and management. In 1905 there had been but
five "political" strikes; in 1906 only four. Besides the tra-

[59] *Ibid.*, p. 196.
[60] Count Illarion Ivanovich Vorontsov-Dashkov (1837–1916) became in his later years an exceptionally liberal administrator. Immediately after the assassination of Alexander II (1881), Vorontsov-
Dashkov had helped organize the *Sviashchennaia druzhina* (Holy
Host), a band of pro-government enthusiasts who set out to hunt
down and destroy revolutionaries. From 1881 to 1897 Vorontsov-
Dashkov was minister of state domains. With his appointment to
the viceroyalty of the Caucasus in 1905, a tolerant policy toward
the Armenians was adopted, and Armenian church properties
seized in 1903 were returned to the Armenians. Vorontsov-Dashkov
was interested in initiating liberal economic reforms and extending
the institution of *Zemstva* into the Caucasus. He opposed the trials
of the Dashnaks in 1912. For Vorontsov-Dashkov's personal assess-
ment of his administration, see his *Vsepoddanneishii otchet za
vosem' let upravleniia Kavkazom* (St. Petersburg, 1913).
[61] Larin, p. 139.              [62] *Ibid.*, p. 140.

ditional May Day Strike, the other 1906 political strikes had been caused by the murder of a worker by a soldier (August 8–9), by the exiling of strikers (August 25–26), and by the prosecution of eleven sailors who had supported the strikers (September 4–5). In 1907 only one strike could be considered political and that was a local work-stoppage in Bibi-Eibat to protest the murder of the Social Democrat Khanlar.[63] While in 1907 not even May Day had been properly observed, in 1908 there was a demonstration in which 72 percent of the workers were said to have participated—but again this was the sole political act of the Baku proletariat in that year.[64]

Its concentration on economic concerns, however, in no way diminishes the achievements of the labor movement in Baku up to the "reaction." Except for the year of revolution, 1905, the economic strikes in Baku had occurred more often, lasted longer, and been on the average more successful than those in any other Russian city.[65] The campaign over the labor–management conference had demonstrated a sense of organization which the Baku workers had painfully developed since their first major strikes in 1903. The Social-Democratic intelligentsia had by 1908 firmly established ties with the workers; these ties broke down at times under the pressure of the tsarist police, but their frequent renewal seems to indicate that the Social Democrats had at long last earned a certain affection and loyalty from their chosen constituents. The second decade of Social Democracy in Baku began in the dark days of 1908 when the gains of the past seemed to have disappeared forever. In June 1908 the number of days lost by striking workers was cut to one-tenth of that of the previous month, and the figure continued to decline for several months.[66]

[63] *Ibid.*, p. 39.
[64] V. I. Frolov, *Zabastovki bakinskikh neftepromyshlennykh rabochikh v 1908 godu* (Baku, 1909), p. 58.
[65] Larin, p. 55.     [66] Frolov, p. 60.

With the decline of the strike movement and the increase of police pressure, both the trade unions and the party suffered losses of members and influence. The unions, never as strong in Baku as the party or the factory committees, had through 1907 been challenged by the latter, which refused to coordinate their strike activities with the unions. The factory committees were meanwhile attempting to gain recognition by the industry of their right to veto decisions on the hiring and firing of workers; and some 30 percent of the economic strikes in 1907 had included demands for such recognition, implicitly a threat to the prerogatives of the trade unions.[67] The two largest unions in Baku had also been hurt by their competition within the same labor group, namely, the oil workers. Despite repeated attempts throughout 1907–1908 by the Bolsheviks to unite the two unions into one organization, the Menshevik leadership of the Union of Workers of Mechanical Production refused to consent to a merger with the larger union.[68] By the beginning of 1909 the Menshevik union could count only 450 active members; the two unions together had a membership of less than a thousand.[69]

To the collapse of the unions and the mass labor movement, the Baku Social Democrats responded either by abandoning work in the organization altogether or by concentrating efforts in the still-existent party underground. The retreat to the underground was necessitated as much by the intensified police persecution of labor leaders as by the surprising unwillingness of the workers themselves to assist or to be helped by the Social Democrats. Shaumian wrote to his old comrade Mikha Tskhakaia in April 1909: "The conditions of the workers, dear Mikha, have become terribly difficult. They literally crucify us, spit on us from

[67] Larin, pp. 41, 48.
[68] Ibid., p. 125; Jordania and Zhgenti, p. 58.
[69] Larin, pp. 147, 149.

all sides, humiliate us. Besides this, each day the reaction among the workers (the internal reaction) is being strengthened; sometimes the best comrades among the workers abandon us. But we don't lose heart."[70] Just as Baku had lagged behind the rest of Russia in experiencing "reaction," so too the city did not participate in what Soviet historians call the "new revolutionary upsurge" until well into 1913. In all of Transcaucasia there were only thirty strikes in 1909, with 9,771 participants; the next year, which marks the beginning of the "upsurge" in Russia, Transcaucasia's strike activity slowed down to only thirteen strikes and 1,006 strikers. Eleven of those strikes, five of which can be considered successful, were in Baku. The strikes of this period were defensive in nature, i.e., they were efforts by the workers to protect gains they had made in the earlier years. Few strikes actually called for higher wages, whereas several were provoked by the industrialists' taking away holidays or increasing the hours in the working day. May Day, 1910, was the first May Day since 1901 not to be celebrated by the calling of a general strike.[71] In 1911 there was again a decline in the number of strikes in Transcaucasia (only ten occurring in that year), as well as in the number of strikers (434). Six of those strikes took place in the oil capital.[72] Even after the shootings at the Lena gold-fields, an event which galvanized workers in most of the empire, the Baku workers remained passive. A few protest meetings were held, but nothing more.[73] May Day, 1912, attracted only 360 strikers; and the factory inspection reported that, of all categories of workers striking in 1912, the oil workers were in last place.[74] Not

[70] S. G. Shaumian, Pis'ma, 1896–1918 (Erevan, 1959), p. 154. Hereafter this collection will be cited as "Pis'ma."

[71] G. A. Arutiunov, Rabochee dvizhenie v Zakavkaz'e v period novogo revoliutsionnogo pod"ema (1910–1914 gg.) (Moscow–Baku, 1963), pp. 147–149.

[72] Ibid., p. 147.     [73] Ibid., pp. 222–223.

[74] Ibid., p. 228.

even the sizable printers' strike in December 1912 can be used as the watershed between the "reaction" and the "upsurge" in Baku, for in the first four and a half months of 1913 not one strike was recorded.[75]

The passivity of Baku workers from 1908 until the summer of 1913 can be explained by the continuing depression in the oil industry. The industrial upsurge in Russia after 1909, which correlated with the revival of labor activity, was reflected in most industries in Transcaucasia—except the oil industry of Baku. Each year brought the unhappy statistics of declining production. In 1911 output fell 11.1 percent from the previous year; in 1912 it fell by 1.5 percent; in 1913 by 6.8 percent; and in 1914 by 7.8 percent. The figures for 1913 represent an output of two hundred million poods of oil less than for 1901. The decline in oil-drilling affected the refineries. From 1910 to 1913 no fewer than 20 of the 84 refineries closed down, and only 30 worked full-time.[76]

For decades the oil industrialists had neglected to innovate technologically as foreign producers had done. The

[75] *Ibid.*, pp. 229–230. In 1912 there were only 2,790 strikers in the whole of Transcaucasia (*ibid.*, p. 12).

Even as this crisis in the labor movement continued, the Baku Social Democrats achieved two significant political victories. The first occurred in December 1911, when Meshadi Aziz ogly Azizbekov, who for years had participated in the Bolshevik underground and been a member of Hummet while working legally as an electrician, was elected to the Baku city duma (Mamedi Kaziev, *Meshadi Azizbekov* [Baku, 1966], p. 62). Even more notable was the campaign run by Ina Zhordaniia (Jordania), the Russian wife of Noi Zhordaniia, to elect M. I. Skobelev, the son of a wealthy flour-miller, to the Fourth State Duma from the Russian curia in Transcaucasia. Skobelev was victorious over the incumbent, Timoshkin, a member of the reactionary Union of the Russian People, and in the fall of 1912 he joined the Social-Democratic faction in the duma (Jordania and Zhgenti, pp. 85–86). When in 1913 the S.D. faction split into Menshevik and Bolshevik groups, Skobelev entered the Menshevik group.

[76] I. A. Guseinov *et al.* (eds.), *Istoriia Azerbaidzhana* (Baku, 1959–1963), II, p. 675.

foreign market for Baku oil had shrunk accordingly, and Baku began to depend on domestic sales. With the support of the government, and high tariffs which kept out foreign competition, the oil industry used its domestic monopoly to its own advantage by keeping prices high. From 1910 to 1914 oil prices rose almost 200 percent. Profits rose correspondingly, while an "oil hunger" developed in Russia. Demand for oil was rising while supply of oil declined, and prices and profits accelerated upward. The "oil hunger" led the Fourth State Duma to protest the rise in oil prices, but to no avail.[77] The industry was favored by the government, which not only permitted the rise in prices but, after 1908, through its police and the law effectively limited the activity of labor.

After five years of relative inactivity and of isolation from the Social Democrats, the Baku workers in the second half of July 1913 suddenly reactivated their economic struggle with the oil industry. The strikes began insignificantly on July 16 with 774 workers from the Rothschild fields leaving work in Balakhany-Sabunchiny. As workers from other companies joined the strikers, a strike committee, led by Mensheviks, began to operate, calling a general strike on July 25.[78] The strike had been started by the drillers, "the least conscious element of the Baku workers," and only afterwards had the factory workers joined them.[79] By the end of July, 19,075 workers from 88 different firms had joined the strike.[80] Significantly, workers of all nationalities, including migrant Azerbaijanis from northern Persia, united in the common effort to

[77] Ibid., p. 676.

[78] S. E. Sef, "Iz istorii bakinskogo rabochego dvizheniia (otchet bakinskogo gradonachal'nika Martynova o vseobshchei stachke 1914 g.)," Proletarskaia revoliutsiia, no. 7 (54) (July 1926), pp. 236–237.

[79] Severnaia Pravda, no. 5, August 6, 1913; A. N. Guliev, Bakinskii proletariat v gody novogo revoliutsionnogo pod"ema (Baku, 1963), p. 94.

[80] Ibid., p. 145; Arutiunov, p. 310.

secure higher wages and decent living conditions. The Social Democrats, who for several years had been powerless to initiate any labor activity in Baku, now drew up a list of demands for the workers—demands which differed little from those of the strike of December 1904 and those of the campaign for a labor–management conference in July 1907.[81]

Support for the workers came from Saint Petersburg. Two Menshevik deputies in the State Duma arrived in Baku to head off a confrontation between the workers and the police. Skobelev and Chkheidze prevailed on the military governor of Baku not to interfere in the purely economic struggle between labor and management. The Mensheviks sought, on the one hand, to limit workers' demands to economic concessions and, on the other, by keeping the labor movement apolitical, to prevent the government from intervening and repressing the strikers.[82] Skobelev and Chkheidze were successful in their mission: the confrontation was avoided. The summer strike of 1913, however, succeeded in resurrecting the labor movement in Baku. In that year altogether 490,735 worker-days were lost, a figure not equaled since 1907.[83] The workers were volatile, not to be restrained. The Mensheviks' desire to restrict the movement to economic issues was soon to be frustrated.

In 1914 the number of strikes in Baku reached the 1905 level.[84] But the Bolsheviks, who now dominated the Baku Committee, were not impressed. On his return to Baku in the spring of 1914 from exile in Astrakhan, Shaumian reported to Lenin on the underdeveloped "consciousness" of the Baku workers:

[81] Guliev, p. 102.
[82] Ibid., pp. 120–121.
[83] Frolov, p. 1; in 1907, 667,867 worker-days had been lost; in 1908 the number had been reduced to 368,718.
[84] Guliev, p. 156.

In general the workers here are a terribly mercantilistic group. The rapaciousness of the oil industrialists has affected them. They are thinking and talking about a new economic strike in order to snatch another greasy piece and to increase "bonuses." It is good that this comes easily, but there is not the slightest interest in politics, not the slightest care about the creation of an organization, about the strengthening of the union, etc. I would be glad if it could be shown that I exaggerate, but at the moment the impression is bad.[85]

The Bolsheviks wanted no part of a purely trade-unionist movement as promoted by the Menshevik-Liquidators. Their appetites were aroused only when economic discontent developed into political rebellion.

The year 1914, however, held surprises for Shaumian. A month and a half after his pessimistic report to Lenin, Shaumian witnessed a political demonstration in which ten thousand workers marched to mark May Day. Shortly afterwards, the Nobel workers responded to a call in the Bolshevik newspaper, *Pravda*, and walked out to celebrate the Day of the Labor Press.[86] Some political consciousness did exist among the Baku workers, as well as a sense of solidarity with workers in other parts of the empire, though political interests were limited to only a small part of the Baku proletariat. The "economism" of the Baku workers was never overcome by the Bolsheviks, but at times—most notably in 1914 and 1917—the Social Democrats were able to direct that energy into an organized activity and even supply political overtones.

In May 1914 the workers of the oil industry were preparing another massive strike. As the military commander in Baku, Colonel Martynov, reported to Vorontsov-Dashkov, the excitement of the workers had not abated at the end of the 1913 strike. The complaints of labor centered

[85] *Pis'ma*, p. 40.  [86] *Ibid.*, p. 47.

on the usual issues: late payment of wages, intolerable living conditions, administrative arbitrariness, low pay, excessive overtime, etc.[87] Delegates elected by the workers met with members of a hastily formed strike committee, dominated by Bolsheviks. Discussions about a list of common demands were carried on for several weeks, while the workers impatiently awaited the call to strike. Shaumian wrote to Lenin of his difficulty in restraining the strikers in order to give the movement a semblance of organization:

> Already for nearly a month, meetings of plenipotentiaries from the workers have taken place at which the common demands have been discussed; the workers long for a strike and did not even want to wait for the drafting and publication of their demands. With difficulty our worker-comrades held them back.
> Finally the demands were ready. On Monday the 26th [of May] in the evening, there was a meeting of plenipotentiaries in agreement with the preliminary decision of the Baku Committee, to present the plants with the demands on Tuesday and to strike on Wednesday. And that is how it all happened.[88]

The anxious workers, barely restrained by the strike committee, struck at six in the morning May 28, first at the Mirzoev Plant in Balakhany and then throughout the city. By the end of the day 18,917 men had walked out.[89] The strike committee issued a leaflet in which the common demands were spelled out: recognition of the factory committees, a contract with the oil industry to ensure that the gains would be kept, the removal of workers' homes from the oil-fields and factory districts to separate settlements, improved housing to be supervised by sanitation committees controlled by workers, and recognition of a council

[87] *Proletarskaia revoliutsiia*, no. 7 (54) (July 1926), p. 246.
[88] *Pis'ma*, pp. 46–47.          [89] Guliev, p. 179.

of workers' plenipotentiaries to negotiate with the industry.[90] Supplementary demands were suggested by workers' meetings held during the strike. The workers wanted fulfillment of promises made by the oil industrialists in 1913, as well as dozens of specific economic concessions, such as a shorter work-day and two rest days a week. The preponderance of the demands were economic, but the city administration considered the recognition of factory committees, a labor contract, and the council of plenipotentiaries to be political in nature.

The oil industrialists of Baku replied to the workers' demands with an ultimatum of their own. They categorically refused to consider additional increases in wages, pay for the strike period, or money for housing. They warned the workers that if they did not return to their jobs within three days they could consider themselves unemployed. The tsarist government, in the person of Goremykin, the chairman of the council of ministers, fully supported the position of the oil industry and declared the strikers' demands unacceptable.[91] Both the industry and the government were prepared to resort to repressive measures rather than concede to the workers. At the end of May troops were already beginning to arrive in Baku. It was generally thought that they would be used to put down the strike. The argument for suppressing the strike gained strength meanwhile when the strikers began to attack nonstrikers. Colonel Martynov requested reinforcements from Tiflis, emphasizing that the strike was not "of local origin, but organized from without, most probably from Petersburg."[92]

By June 2, thirty thousand men were on strike.[93] In the first weeks of the month some three thousand returned to work, probably in response to police pressure, but yet

---

[90] *Ibid.*, p. 181.  [91] *Ibid.*, pp. 193-194.
[92] *Proletarskaia revoliutsiia*, no. 7 (54) (July 1926), p. 256.
[93] Guliev, p. 198.

other thousands joined the strikers. This instability in the mass of strikers led to outbreaks of violence and to attacks on strike-breakers and on the property of the oil companies. The Socialist Revolutionaries on the strike committee called for terrorizing the administrators of the oil firms, and when the committee refused to endorse such a tactic the Socialist Revolutionaries called for rejection of the strike leadership.[94] The Social Democrats opposed individual acts of violence, and the strike committee emphasized the need for unity and friendship among all workers. Fortunately for the strikers, national differences among workers were subordinated to the common struggle against the industrialists. No outbreaks of friction between nationalities occurred, but, as Colonel Martynov reports, the various nationalities showed different degrees of commitment to the strike: "The most zealous strikers are the Armenians, the most conscious and organized; as for the Tatars, they in their mass are indifferent to the strike and would be ready to return to work immediately, especially those among them that work in small companies, if they were promised a monetary bonus; the Russians in part would like to start to work, in part they are for the strike."[95] From mid-June the workers' districts took on the aspect of an armed camp. Cossack and police patrols were scattered through the area. The trade unions of the oil workers were suppressed and members arrested. The police drove striking workers from their homes, which were owned by the oil companies. A protest demonstration was ordered for June 20. Twenty thousand marched. Some of the demonstrators headed for the city but were cut off by Cossacks and dispersed.[96] Arrests and evacuations of workers continued. Baku was in a state of siege.

The very dimensions and duration of the strike quickly

[94] *Ibid.*, p. 203.
[95] *Proletarskaia revoliutsiia*, no. 7 (54) (July 1926), pp. 256–257.
[96] Guliev, p. 214; A. Badayev (Badaev), *The Bolsheviks in the Tsarist Duma* (New York, n.d.), pp. 167-168.

raised it from an event of merely local importance to a matter of interest to the whole nation. A shortage of oil affected industry. Workers in other large cities read the labor press—particularly *Pravda*, which had a "Baku department"—and gave moral and monetary support to their colleagues in Baku. On July 1 meetings and sympathy-strikes were held in Saint Petersburg. A few days later, at the Putilov works, twelve thousand workers listened to speakers tell about conditions in Baku; at the close of the meeting the police fired into the crowd, killing two, wounding fifty, and initiating the most serious crisis in Russia since 1905.[97] The strike in Baku, and the wide coverage given to the clashes between the workers, their women, and the police, were the immediate stimuli of the wave of strikes which shook the empire in the months before the First World War. The strike, begun with purely economic aims, had in its course taken on a political significance unknown since 1905 in the Baku labor movement.

Of 51,900 oil workers in the city and the surrounding districts, 38,830 participated at one time or another in the strike. In the last week of June and the first week of July the number of strikers fell rapidly; by July 10, only 19,730 men still refused to return to work. Ten days later the number had dropped to 9,595.[98] The reasons for the decline in the number of strikers in July must include the arrival of General Dzhunkovskii, sent with full civil and military powers to bring the strike to a halt. His plan was to cut off Baku from the rest of Russia. The newspapers were forbidden to write about the strike; money collected for the strikers in other parts of the empire was confiscated by the police; telegrams from Baku were censored.

[97] For a recent Western discussion of the social crisis on the eve of the First World War, see Leopold Haimson, "The Problem of Social Stability in Urban Russia, 1905–1917," *Slavic Review*, XXIII, 4 (December 1964), pp. 619–642, and 1 (March 1965), pp. 1–22.

[98] Guliev, p. 288.

These police measures had a dampening effect on the workers' morale, and the ranks of the strikers were further depleted.

The failure of the strike cannot be attributed exclusively to Dzhunkovskii's measures. The movement had been declining even before the general's arrival, though he did effectively curtail the resources available to the strikers. Material hardships forced many strikers to return to work. But the ultimate cause of the strike's defeat was the preparation for war. Mobilization was declared, and able-bodied men were conscripted into the army. By the end of July the strike leaders were forced to admit defeat, as arrests, mobilization, and a patriotic mood reduced the strikers to about seven hundred men.

The Baku Strike of 1914 was a major manifestation of labor discontent and a potentially revolutionary event. Yet the war changed Baku from a seat of rebellion into a docile supplier of the precious fuel which lubricated the war machine. Social-Democratic activity in Baku came to a standstill. The organization had been penetrated by police spies, and by the end of the year arrests ended all organized activity. Meetings between Social Democrats continued only on an individual basis or in small groups.[99]

In October 1915 Shaumian reported on the confusion among the working masses and the impotence of the Social-Democratic organization in Baku. In the midst of the crisis, however, he managed to write optimistically about future prospects and observable trends.

> In Baku the organization is growing now there are about sixty active members, but respectable work goes on in legal organizations: 1) the Union of Tailors,

[99] *Krasnyi arkhiv*, no. 4 (77) (1936), pp. 83–84. In August 1914 the Bolshevik duma deputy, Badaev, made a secret journey to Baku to confer with his comrades. He was unable to move freely in Transcaucasia because of police surveillance, but urged the Baku Bolsheviks to form an underground center to keep in touch with Petrograd. (*Ibid.*; Badayev, pp. 202–203.)

2) the Union of Printers, 3) the Union of Office Workers, 4) over fifteen cooperatives, 5) the Committee to aid Refugees, which is organizing a Labor Exchange, etc. Everywhere our friends are the most influential. With the slightest weakening of the reaction it will be possible to turn out great work, but now it is difficult.[100]

Few old Bolshevik professionals remained in Baku after 1915. By the end of the following year Shaumian himself had been arrested and exiled to the Volga region.

The Transcaucasian Social Democrats divided sharply over their position on the war. In October 1914 N. N. Iakovlev arrived in Baku with the text of Lenin's theses calling for Russia's defeat and the transformation of the world war into a civil war.[101] Although the theses were reprinted in many copies and distributed both in Baku and Tiflis, no decision was taken by the organization on its attitude toward the war. The Bolsheviks followed the general line of their leadership and boycotted the elections to the workers' groups of the War-Industry Committees. The Mensheviks, on the other hand, participated in these groups, which were created with the help of Gvozdev from Petrograd.[102] The initial enthusiasm for the war among the Armenians and Georgians, and the general fear of a Turkish victory, made it difficult for any Social Democrat to adopt Lenin's open advocacy of a Russian defeat.

Besides the "defeatist" position three other attitudes were open to the Social Democrats. Plekhanov had come out in favor of Russia's war against imperialist Germany and was labeled "defensist" by his opponents. He was opposed by the so-called "internationalists," like Trotsky,

[100] *Pis'ma*, pp. 185–186.
[101] M. S. Iskenderov *et al.*, *Ocherki istorii kommunisticheskoi partii Azerbaidzhana* (Baku, 1963), p. 185. Henceforth this work, the closest thing to an "official" history of the Communist Party of Azerbaijan, will be referred to simply as "*Ocherki.*"
[102] *Ibid.*, p. 182; Guseinov *et al.*, II, p. 766.

Martov, and Tseretelli, who advocated peace "without annexations and contributions," but refused to support either
side in the war. The veteran of Georgian Menshevism,
Zhordaniia, adopted the moderately "defensist" position of
men like Potresov, who opposed "civil peace" while the
war was raging. Considering the government incompetent
to carry on the war, Zhordaniia, Potresov in Petrograd, and
the group that published *Samozashchita* in 1916 envisaged
revolution as the means to victory in the war.

For the first year of the war most Social Democrats in
Transcaucasia adopted an internationalist position. They
opposed the war but were unwilling to sabotage the war
effort. At the beginning of October 1915 Shaumian wrote
to Lenin and reviewed the line-up on the war issue in code:

> The behavior of Uncle George [Plekhanov] was
> incomprehensible, and the escapades of his Petersburg
> followers (Ior. and the others) [N. I. Iordanskii] were
> distasteful and disturbing. Our whole clan agreed with
> me, and even those close to George are decisively against
> him and in agreement with us, and that continues
> up to this time.
>
> In general, George has not been successful in the
> Caucasus; An. [Zhordaniia] is his only well-wisher [sic].
> He came here and bent only one person to his side (the
> fat Pl.; Sl. knows him). [Pl. is unknown; Sl. is V. M.
> Kasparian], but this ended sadly for the latter. For
> making such a move his friends drove him from their
> midst in scandal.[103]

[103] *Pis'ma*, p. 49. In Georgia, according to Uratadze, the opinion
of the duma faction expressed in the declaration of July 26, 1914,
was dominant among the Social Democrats. The war was opposed
and unity of the people with the government was explicitly denied. Zhordaniia's "defensism" was rejected by the *Oblastnoi
komitet* and he was not permitted to publish his articles in the
committee's newspaper, *Tanamendrove Azri* ("Modern Thought").
With the permission of the Georgian Menshevik leadership, Uratadze and Zhordaniia brought out another newspaper, *Akhvai Kvali*,

Early in October 1915 the Mensheviks in Transcaucasia met in an illegal conference in Guria, while the Bolsheviks gathered in Baku. Up to this time Zhordaniia had not been able to convince the antiwar *Oblastnoi komitet* to adopt his position supporting the bourgeoisie in its efforts to make a revolution in order to win the war. In Guria, however, the conference was dominated by delegates from the small towns of western Georgia, and Zhordaniia was able to swing the fifteen participants toward his brand of "defensism." Strikes and demonstrations were advocated in support of the bourgeoisie and the duma, as well as full support of the war effort.[104]

Shaumian chaired the Bolshevik conference in Baku. Only five delegates attended: three from Baku, one from Tiflis, and one from the workers of Kutais. In a letter to his fellow-Bolshevik Shklovskii, Shaumian revealed how this conference reached its decision on the war issue without clearly understanding the various positions of the socialist parties:

> We do not understand very well what is going on generally in Europe, even what is going on in Petersburg and Moscow. The slogans of Petersburg [comrades] were sent to us in the following form: 1) The Bolsheviks demand a constituent assembly, peace at any price, and are against participation in any organization connected with the war. This is supposedly the Leninist tactic, and 2) the Mensheviks (Martov, Dan, and the others)

---

in Kutais, in which Zhordaniia's position on the war was aired. Eventually the *Oblastnoi komitet* forced a second editor, unsympathetic to the newspaper's position, on Zhordaniia. He and Uratadze subsequently quit the paper. (Uratadze, pp. 403–415.)

For a complete treatment of the various Social-Democratic positions on the war issue, see B. Dvinov, *Pervaia mirovaia voina i rossiiskaia sotsialdemokratiia* (Inter-university Project on the History of the Menshevik Movement, Paper no. 3, New York, August 1962).

[104] *Pis'ma*, pp. 183–184.

also are for a constituent assembly, peace at any price, but are for participation in all organizations including the war-industrial committees, 3) the Duma factions are for a constituent assembly to resolve the question "of war and peace," 4) the Socialist Revolutionaries are for a constituent assembly to organize a victory over the enemy.

The slogan "peace at any price" was met with bewilderment and opposition. I and one other Baku delegate . . . (he himself a worker) proposed the formulation of the faction, one insisted on "peace at any price." As you can see from the resolution, a middle position was adopted. In general the mood is depressed in view of the absence of interest in the broad masses, the inertia and confusion of the workers. We attribute little significance to our resolution.[105]

The resolution, written by Shaumian and adopted by the Bolshevik conference, stated that peace could be achieved only by the people in its constituent assembly and that such an assembly could be convened, neither by the duma nor by the tsar, but only after a victorious revolution. In the meantime no support should be given the war effort.[106]

The war had a generally deleterious effect on the population of Baku. The rise in prices in Russia during the war years was reflected locally. Between September 1914 and January 1917, the price of bread rose 100 percent, sugar 51 percent, milk 205 percent, and eggs 292 percent.[107] Wages, too, rose steadily, but lagged behind the price increases. On the average, wages rose 218 percent in that period, but the cost of 90.499 calories of food had risen 256.3 percent. The greatest increases in prices came in

[105] *Ibid.*, p. 185.

[106] S. G. Shaumian, *Izbrannye proizvedeniia*, I: 1902–1916 gg. (Moscow, 1957), p. 489. Hereafter this collection of articles and letters will be cited as "Shaumian, I."

[107] V. V. Pokshishevskii, *Polozhenie bakinskogo proletariata nakanune revoliutsii (1914–1917 gg.)* (Baku, 1927), p. 31.

1916, and the rate of increase rose as the year went on.[108] Real wages declined steadily.

The war at first had a stimulating effect on the oil industry. The decline in output was reversed, and military requirements brought about an increase to slightly above the 1912 level by 1916. This was accomplished in the face of decreasing labor productivity through more intensive exploitation of existing oil-fields and the opening of new ones. Work-days were lengthened, and more days added to the work-week.[109] After an initial fall in prices in 1915, due to the beginning of the war with Turkey and the subsequent loss of Black Sea shipping lanes, the price of oil began a steady climb from 42.24 kopeks a pood of raw oil in 1915, through 46.1 in 1916, to 68.7 in 1917. At the beginning of 1915 consumers asked for the establishment of price-controls on oil, but the oil-producers opposed them and were supported by the influential viceroy of the Caucasus. The ministers of communications and of trade and industry prevailed, however, and on December 31, 1915, a fixed price of 45 kopeks for sixteen kilograms of raw oil was established.[110] This price made oil the most economical fuel for most consumers, but in view of the rising costs of obtaining oil (resulting from the shortage and high cost of materials, increased wages, and the decline in labor productivity) the incentive to drill was reduced, thus sharply lowering the amount drilled.[111] For a while there was no loss of profit, since the fixed price had been three kopeks higher than the average 1915 free price, but as inflation continued through 1916 the squeeze was felt by the industry as well as by the workers. By mid-1917, small companies especially faced serious declines in profits.[112]

The strikes of 1915 in Baku were small, and strictly economic in their demands; most frequently they involved

[108] A. Dubner, *Bakinskii proletariat v gody revoliutsii* (*1917–1920 gg.*) (Baku, 1931), pp. 2–3.

[109] Pokshishevskii, pp. 13–15.    [110] *Ibid.*, pp. 15–18.
[111] Dubner, p. 24.    [112] *Ibid.*, p. 25.

small factories outside the oil industry. The only strike of any magnitude took place at the Tagiev textile mill at the beginning of September, when the workers demanded a raise in wages and a shortening of the work-day from eleven to ten hours.[113] In mid-February 1916 eleven hundred men walked out at the Caspian–Black Sea Company. In contrast to the 1914 general strike, a significant number of Moslem workers joined in the demands for additional subsidies in this and subsequent strikes during the war.[114] Russian workers who, unlike the Moslems, were potentially subject to the draft refrained from strikes.[115] In a sense, these strikes can also be viewed as largely defensive efforts by the workers to hold their own against the rising cost of living or to regain the shorter hours they had enjoyed before 1908.

Together with the fall in real wages, an acute food-supply shortage hit Baku in the war years. As early as August 1914 the Baku city administration had become aware of serious dislocations in deliveries to the city because of the demands of the army, and had petitioned military authorities to alleviate the situation.[116] The irregularity in the flow of goods continued, however, and from February 14 to 16, 1916, the women of Baku, most of them Russian, carried out a *bab'ii bunt*, looting shops for whatever they could find.[117] For three days crowds roamed the streets, tearing shops apart and smashing the largest flour-mills, until nine people lay dead and fifty-seven were wounded.[118] Only with the arrival of armed reinforcements were the local police able to put down the riot. Soldiers stationed in

[113] Pokshishevski, p. 49.

[114] *Ibid.*, pp. 50, 53.

[115] S. E. Sef, *Kak bol'sheviki prishli k vlasti v 1917–1918 gg. v bakinskom raione* (Baku, 1927), p. 45.

[116] Pokshishevskii, p. 24.

[117] *Ibid.*, p. 27; S. E. Sef, *Bor'ba za Oktiabr' v Zakavkaz'i* (Tiflis, 1932), pp. 9–10.

[118] Sef, *Bor'ba . . .* , p. 13.

Baku had either unenthusiastically aided the police or actively sided with the women.[119]

In June similar *bab'ie bunty* erupted in Tiflis, Sukhumi, and the smaller towns of Georgia. By the end of 1916 the newspapers were filled with the ominous warnings of the nearness of catastrophe, but the myriad food-supply commissions and cooperative organizations were powerless in the face of the general disorganization in the nation. The liberal intelligentsia, as well as the Menshevik leadership of Georgian Social Democracy, reacted to the women's agitation with suspicion, even going so far as to theorize that the movement had been inspired by the police.[120] The parties of the opposition did not attempt to manipulate the discontent, but the liberal bourgeoisie, as a result of the disorder in the cities, drew further away from the imperial administration which stood above the municipal authorities and actually hindered their efforts to alleviate the crisis. The imperial officials, acting through the police, allowed speculators to carry on their operations with impunity. Discontent was general and diffuse. Even without political guidance it was turning against the government of Nicholas II.[121]

In 1916 altogether sixteen thousand workers struck in Baku, over half of them in the last three months of the year.[122] These last strikes differed from the earlier ones in that they were directed against larger companies which paid the workers higher wages.[123] At the same time the local authorities attempted to stifle the strikes by ending the draft exemption for oil workers and conscripting the strikers. The workers reacted by protesting through semipolitical strikes, demanding the release of arrested or drafted comrades. Thus, with the more skilled workers becoming involved in strikes and political protests in late 1916, and

---

[119] *Ibid.*, p. 25.
[121] *Ibid.*, p. 6.
[123] Pokshishevskii, p. 59.

[120] *Ibid.*, pp. 2, 22–23.
[122] Guseinov *et al.*, II, p. 769.

the government pursuing a policy of inducting strikers, the labor movement assumed a political overtone—especially notable in the last important strike before the revolution, the January strike at the Nobel Plant.[124]

On the eve of the February Revolution Baku was calm. The shortage of supplies and the collapse of Russia's military efforts added to the general gloom. Discontent with the way the war was being handled was evident. As early as 1915 troops began to show reluctance about being sent to the front. The British vice-consul in Baku witnessed women lying on the rails to prevent the trains from leaving for the front. Soldiers refused to remove them and the regrettable task had to be turned over to the Cossacks.[125] Yet the workers did not protest the war, and, if anything, tended to restrain their more volatile comrades from engaging in strikes. What strikes did occur were centered on immediate economic issues. Only the protests against the arrest of strikers can be viewed as semipolitical, guided as they were by feelings of solidarity within the labor movement.[126]

[124] On January 2, 1917, the administration of the Nobel Company in Baku rejected the demands of its workers for a raise in basic wages, an increase in the wartime subsidy, the end of overtime work, and improvement in housing conditions. Eleven days later the workers declared a strike. A small group of Bolsheviks, led by G. Sturua, who had returned to Baku late in 1916, had carefully prepared the ground for the strike. Shortly after the strike broke out, Sturua and other leaders were arrested. The workers demanded their release. When that demand was granted on January 22, the strike ended, only to begin again four days later when some of the most active strikers were drafted. Finally the Nobel administration telegraphed Tiflis requesting the release of all those arrested and drafted. The strike ended, and the economic demands were quietly forgotten. (Dubner, pp. 11–17.)

[125] Ranald MacDonell, *"And Nothing Long"* (London, 1938), p. 175.

[126] Several Soviet historians emphasize the rising tempo of the strike and protest movement in the last months before the February Revolution. Dubner, for example, writes: "January and February are characterized by an uninterrupted growth in the strike movement. The February Revolution in Baku occurred in the midst

The First World War had a peculiar effect on the composition of the Baku proletariat, so that the workers who manned the barricades during the revolution were significantly different from those who had for long years struggled in the labor movement. Some 20–22 percent of Baku workers were drafted up to 1917. This is a smaller percentage than in other industrial regions, such as the Donbass or the Urals, but slightly more than in Petrograd where about 17 percent were mobilized.[127] But the call-up did not affect all categories of workers in the same way. The Russians and the Armenians were affected but the Azerbaijanis were exempt from military service. A much larger proportion of unskilled workers fell victim to the draft than of skilled workers. The age-group most affected included those who had come to Baku in the four years immediately preceding the war—those who had been initiated into the labor movement during the so-called "new revolutionary upsurge" (1910–1914).

A kind of "generation gap" was created. Three groups of workers may be distinguished—those hired up to the end of 1909, those hired from 1910 to the beginning of the war, and those hired during the war—of which the middle group suffered most from mobilization: so that by the time of the revolution the Baku proletariat was divided between an older, experienced group of factory workers and the younger, less experienced workers of the fields. The former group, called in Russian *sluzhashchie*, made up about 10

---

of a great upsurge of the working masses" (p. 17). But, in fact, the January strike at the Nobel Company was the last strike of any significance until the beginning of March. Pokshishevskii also believes that the strike movement, although weak and disorganized, was indicative of a "hidden consolidation of proletarian strength" (p. 77). This thesis that there was a crescendo of strikes and protests before February is consistent with the Soviet reading of that same period in Petrograd and Moscow and has been upheld in recent "official" histories of Baku (*Ocherki*, p. 204).

[127] S. S. Aliiarov, "Izmeneniia v sostave rabochikh Baku v gody pervoi mirovoi voiny," *Istoria SSSR*, no. 2 (1960), p. 51.

percent of the working class and was considered a kind of labor aristocracy. Besides highly skilled workers this group included office workers, foremen, and petty bureaucrats. Their experiences and attitudes differed greatly from those of the *chernye* workers of the oil-fields. The more skilled workers, particularly those in the Railroad District and those employed by Nobel, tended towards trade-unionism and Menshevism.

The First World War accelerated the influx of semiproletarian elements into the oil-fields. It was these men on whom the Bolsheviks had to rely for support. Baku, like other newer industrial districts, never developed a hereditary working class on the scale of the older industrial regions, such as Saint Petersburg, the Urals, the Baltic area, or the central industrial district.[128] Baku's proletariat, at least in the outlying districts, remained transient, rootless, divided, provincial in its outlook, and physically miserable. These workers, unlike the new recruits in other parts of Russia, were notably passive, uninterested in strikes or revolutionary activity.[129] Consequently, in the months before the February Revolution Baku did not rise to the same pitch of activity as Petrograd and Moscow. When the revolution came to Baku the workers acknowledged it as a welcome import from the north.

[128] *Ibid.*, p. 58.

[129] S. S. Aliiarov, "K voprosu o sostave bakinskogo proletariata nakanune oktiabr'skoi revoliutsii," *Izvestiia akademii nauk azerbaidzhanskoi SSR*, 1961, no. 9, p. 15. During the war most of the new recruits were peasants from Caucasian Azerbaijan. While the number of southern Azerbaijanis (immigrants from Persia) and Volga Tatars dropped, the number of northern Azerbaijanis in the working class rose by 61.2% in the war years until they made up 13.3% of the proletariat. The southern Azerbaijanis made up 23.6% of all workers on the eve of the revolution. The number of Russian workers rose by 4.1% during the war, while the number of Armenian workers rose by 17.4%. The Daghestani contingent rose by 33.2%. (S. S. Aliiarov, "Chislennost' . . . ," p. 33.)

# 3

## The New Order and the Old Parties

STEPAN SHAUMIAN heard about the revolution in exile in Saratov. From the Volga town he set out immediately to join his family in Baku. From the other parts of Russia, from Siberian exile, from the Caucasian and Western Fronts, Shaumian's comrades and political rivals also hurried back to continue their revolutionary pursuits that had been interrupted by arrests and the World War. Prokofiia Dzhaparidze returned from Trebizond to Tiflis, where he boarded a train for Baku. Perhaps the story is apocryphal, but it is reported that, when asked by a fellow-passenger why he was going to Baku, Dzhaparidze replied, "To make a revolution." The perplexed traveler observed that the revolution had already been made, but "Alesha," not in the least put off by his companion, added in confidence that there would be another.[1]

The first revolution of 1917 might be called the "unanimous" revolution in the sense that it was supported by almost all social groups and political parties in the country. Within Baku this unanimity was expressed in the first days of the new order in the meetings of workers and politicians, in the declarations of political parties, and in the amorphous pronouncements of the new organs of power. Baku received word of the events in Petrograd from Tiflis on March 2, the day of the tsar's abdication. The telegram, identical to the one sent from Petrograd to all major cities, called for calm and reminded municipal officials that the

---

[1] Valentin, "Dalekoe," *Pamiati 26. Materialy k istorii bakinskoi kommuny 1918 g.,* ed. Mikhail Lifshits and P. Chagin (Baku, 1922), p. 111.

country was still at war and that discipline was required in the rear:

> In view of the various rumors circulating, we report that in Petrograd events have taken place which called for the change of the highest governing persons and that at the present time tranquillity has settled over the capital.
>
> The forces of the Caucasian Army are victoriously advancing toward a juncture with our valiant allies, the English.
>
> The observance of complete peacefulness on the part of the population of the Caucasus is absolutely indispensable to secure victory for the army as well as for the uninterrupted supplying and provision of foodstuffs for the population.[2]

By the early morning of March 3, workers were calling strikes in support of the revolution. Crowds filled the streets and squares to read the telegrams published in the newspapers. Kerensky's full amnesty for political prisoners added to the euphoria of the moment. Good will reigned, and little hostility was displayed toward the men of the old order. Only Admiral Kliupfel, the commandant of the Baku garrison, and two particularly noxious police officials were arrested by the new authorities.[3] That evening the workers in the electrical power-plant returned to their posts so that Baku could continue its celebration in light. The theaters played to capacity audiences, and the spectators stood for the playing of the Marseillaise.[4]

At noon on the 3rd citizens gathered in the courtyard of the city hall and proposed electing an executive committee to govern the city temporarily.[5] The meeting was

---

[2] *Kaspii*, no. 50, March 3, 1917.

[3] A. L. Popov, "Revoliutsiia v Baku: Ocherk pervyi, Fevral'–Oktiabr' 1917 g., *Byloe*, no. 22 (1923), p. 280.

[4] *Baku*, no. 50, March 5, 1917.

[5] *Ibid.*

chaired by Vasili Il'ich Frolov, who in the first days of the revolution found himself in the center of events, attempting to rescue order out of chaos.[6] Frolov met with workers' representatives who discussed the means of electing the executive committee. The workers feared that the Stock Exchange Committee would have decisive influence over the new administration. This antagonism toward the big bourgeoisie led the workers to turn to leaders they trusted, like the Bolshevik Stopani and the nonpartisan Social Democrat Mandel'shtam (Liadov).[7] That evening, as the duma met downstairs in the city hall, representatives of the unions and cooperatives met upstairs under the chairmanship of Stopani. From downstairs the news came that the duma had disapproved the formation of the executive committee, and the anxious workers sent Stopani down to investigate. He reported that only the Stock Exchange Committee had disapproved, along with the Council of Oil Industrialists—the duma had not taken their position.[8] For the workers the executive committee represented their first entrance into the public decision-making processes in the city, and therefore was not to be sacrificed.

At the same time as they planned to join the old elite

[6] Vasili Il'ich Frolov was an economist and statistician. He was trusted both by the workers, whom he had represented in negotiations with the oil industrialists, and by the industrialists, for whom he had prepared statistical outlines of the strike movement in Baku. He wrote for the newspaper of the Council of the Congress of Oil Industrialists, *Neftianoe delo* ("Oil Business"). Politically he stood close to the Menshevik-Defensists; later in 1917 he became the leader of the Baku organization of Plekhanovites, Edinstvo ("Unity").

[7] M. N. Mandel'shtam (Liadov) (1872–1947) had been a Bolshevik from 1903 to 1907. Then he joined the Menshevik faction. He came to Baku in 1905 and finally settled there in 1911. As a "nonfactional Social Democrat" Mandel'shtam worked in the executive committee of the Baku soviet. In September–October 1917, he became its chairman. During the Baku Commune he was assistant to the chairman of the Baku Sovnarkhoz. When the Turks took the city, he was arrested and exiled to Tiflis. Later he worked in Sverdlov Communist University and as the director of Glavnauk.

[8] *Baku*, no. 50, March 3, 1917.

in the executive committee, workers throughout the city were electing plenipotentiaries to a specifically workers' gathering at the city hall, a gathering which set up the machinery for electing a soviet of workers' deputies.[9] The confusion and profusion of meetings on March 3 ended in the embryonic formation of two bodies which between them would share power for the next nine months: the executive committee and the soviet. *Dvoevlastie* was as real in Baku as it was in Petrograd.

Orders from the Provisional Government in Petrograd had gone out to provincial cities to form executive committees which would act as local organs of the new central government. On March 4, members of the city government met with representatives of professional organizations, the workers, the war-industry committee, and the cooperatives to establish such an executive committee. The city mayor, L. L. Bych, chaired the meeting and announced that the city duma had decided on the composition of the executive committee. No elections took place. It was simply assumed that the duma was the heir to the old imperial government and had the legal right to make such a decision. When Bych said that the executive committee should decide on pressing matters but not organize meetings and discussions, he was reminded that the limits on the committee's prerogatives should be decided by the duma. Thus, the authority of the duma over the executive committee was taken for granted by the old municipal authorities.[10]

The Executive Committee of Public Organizations (*Ispolnitel'nyi Komitet Obshchestvennykh Organizatsii*, or IKOO) soon made it clear that it would not be the creature of the duma. For the duma was the representative of the *tsentsovoe obshchestvo*, the ruling classes of the *ancien régime*,

[9] *Izvestiia* (of the Baku soviet), no. 1, March 30, 1917.
[10] *Bakinets*, no. 13, March 6, 1917; *Kavkazskii telegraf*, no. 13, March 6, 1917.

and had been elected under notoriously undemocratic electoral laws. The IKOO, on the other hand, personified the new order of the February Revolution, the collaboration of all classes in the population. In this collaboration was the initial attraction of the IKOO and its eventually fatal flaw. With members representing every class and national group in the city, the council of the IKOO was unable to take decisive action. By mid-March it had seventy-five members, too many for a body of men with nothing but geography in common.[11] The social composition of the council made it a poor rival for municipal leadership against the old city duma and the new and vociferous workers' soviet.

Leadership in the IKOO fell largely to men of liberal sympathy who had worked in public positions before the revolution. Frolov was chairman. A. K. Leontovich, a lawyer and a Kadet, became the head of the municipal police. Other professional men were put in charge of the city's services. V. V. Likhachev from the cooperative movement directed the post and telegraph office. Ia. N. Smirnov was to keep public order. The Bolshevik Stopani, because of his wartime experience in the cooperatives, was entrusted with the Provincial Supply Committee and became assist-

[11] Sitting in the council were: one representative from the Armenian community, one from the Moslems, one Georgian, one Jew, a Molokan, and a Pole; one each from the lawyers, doctors, engineers, teachers, and city employees; twelve from the Soviet of Workers' Deputies; five from the trade unions; five from the cooperatives; five from the Soviet of Soldiers' Deputies; three from the Soviet of Officers' Deputies; two from the city government (*gorodskaia uprava*); five from the city duma; three from the council of the Congress of Oil Industrialists; two from the Stock Exchange Committee; one from the Union of Cities; two from the food-supply conference; one from the Board of Small Tradesmen (*meshchanskaia uprava*); three from commercial and industrial organizations; one from the press; one from the international cultural and educational organizations; two from the merchant marine; three representatives of political parties (Dashnak, S.R., and S.D.); and one priest. (Popov, p. 282.)

ant chairman of the IKOO. The liberals were nominally in charge, but soviet deputies were continually being added to the IKOO until the council seemed to many to be no more than a mouthpiece for the workers. At the same time the Left in the soviet viewed the IKOO as the personification of the bourgeoisie in Baku. In any case, with its faults and its few virtues, the IKOO was the Provisional Government in Baku.[12]

On March 6, fifty-two delegates, said to have been elected by 52,000 workers (about half of the Baku proletariat) met in the building of the Armenian Humanitarian Society in the historic first session of the Baku Soviet of Workers' Deputies. Grigorii Gustavovich Aiollo, a Menshevik who had worked in Baku for over a decade, opened the meeting at about nine in the evening; it proceeded to the election of officers. The delegates cried for "Comrade Stepan" to be named chairman, and Shaumian was elected *in absentia*. Mrs. Shaumian and her small son, Lev, received the congratulations of the delegates, while her husband read of his election days later on the train from Saratov.[13] Shaumian's election in no way reflected Bolshevik dominance of the new body—only nine Bolsheviks were present at this first session. It was his own personal popularity and his activity

[12] The legal hierarchy through Tiflis to Petrograd remained intact. On March 9, Prince Lvov signed the order creating the *Osobyi Zakavkazskii komitet* (Ozakom), which was to act as the Provisional Government's agent in Transcaucasia. Its members were: V. A. Kharlamov (a Russian Kadet), M. I. Papajanov (an Armenian Right Kadet), M. Iu. Jafarov (Azerbaijani, nonparty, later a Musavatist), K. G. Abashidze (who was later replaced by his fellow Georgian, A. I. Chkhenkeli, a prominent Menshevik), and P. N. Pereverzev. The Ozakom never had much power in Transcaucasia; in Tiflis the local soviet, controlled by the Mensheviks, wielded the only effective power. But the Ozakom represented a court of appeal for Baku when local disagreements between governmental bodies could not be locally resolved.

[13] This description of the first session of the Baku soviet was related to the author by Lev Stepanovich Shaumian, who had been present, in an interview held on January 10, 1966.

during the 1914 strike that led the delegates to proclaim him their chairman.[14]

The first session of the soviet continued briefly with questions being put by the delegates to V. I. Frolov, but the sharpness of the criticism implied in the questions led Aiollo to cut off the debate.[15] Although the soviet at this time had no idea of taking power into its own hands, and would not consider such an idea for another six months, evident from the first days of the revolution in Baku was the inherent antagonism between the workers and the propertied classes. Nevertheless, in the spring of 1917, this antagonism was subordinate to the greater desire for harmonious relations between the workers and the other classes.

In the first flush of enthusiasm for the revolution, the Baku soviet echoed the appeals of its constituent parties for order, unity, and peace. The soviet declared itself in favor of cooperation with the IKOO and chose five representatives to sit on its council. Shaumian and Mandel'shtam were elected soviet delegates to the executive committee, thus solidifying the tie between the workers and the rest of the population.[16] When Shaumian took his place in the IKOO, L. L. Bych, who had served as mayor of Baku while Shaumian had been arrested and exiled, greeted the Bolshevik with a speech commending him for his sufferings under the tsarist regime.[17] Bych's attitude, as well as Shaumian's, reflected perfectly the mood of cooperation and solidarity which marked the February

[14] The first presidium of the new Baku soviet reflected the peaceful interparty relations at the time: chairman Shaumian (Bolshevik), Vasin (S.R.), Mandel'shtam (nonfactional S.D.), Aiollo (Menshevik), Arakelian (Dashnak). The soviet's executive committee (IKS) consisted of the full presidium plus one S.D., one S.R., and three elected from the soviet at large—Fioletov (Bolshevik), Kaprielian, and Sochnev. (*Izvestiia*, no. 1, March 30, 1917.)

[15] Popov, p. 287.

[16] *Kaspii*, no. 56, March 10, 1917.

[17] *Baku*, no. 57, March 11, 1917.

Revolution at its inception. No party in Baku at that time opposed cooperation with the bourgeoisie and its organs of power, although the Social Democrats had warned that the bourgeoisie was organizing and that "its representative organs, if not today then tomorrow, will begin an economic struggle with the proletariat."[18]

Politically the most disruptive issue in the early days of the revolution, in both Baku and Petrograd, was the question of the war. In the capital the first major political crisis was already looming, over foreign policy. The soviet balked at foreign minister Miliukov's attempt to retain the tsarist war aims, which included the annexation of Constantinople and the Straits. On March 14 the Petrograd soviet adopted a resolution opposing "the policy of conquest of its ruling classes" while pledging the defense of Russia against "the bayonets of conquerors."[19] Two days later the Baku soviet adopted the position of the Petrograd soviet and sent "greetings to the revolutionary army," bidding "them to stay at their positions to guard freedom from counterrevolutionary attempts from within and without."[20] A similar resolution was passed by the First Congress of Transcaucasian Soviets held in Tiflis later that week. Like the Petrograd soviet, the congress called on the Austrian and German workers to overthrow their monarchs as the first step to peace.[21] Where governments had failed with weapons, the soviets hoped to succeed with direct appeals

[18] *Dok.*, pp. 7–8.

[19] Rex A. Wade, *The Russian Search for Peace, February–October 1917* (Stanford, Calif., 1969), p. 16.

[20] *Kaspii*, no. 63, March 18, 1917. The only dissonant note was the resolution of the Baku's soldiers' soviet (March 21), which called for "war until a victorious conclusion," the usual formulation of the rightist parties, but the resolution continued with the phrase "without seeking conquests." The imprecision of the language was understandable in the early weeks of the revolution (*Baku*, no. 67, March 22, 1917.)

[21] TsGA Arm. SSR, f. 119, op. 1, d. 26, 1917, 1. 19.

to the people. In the euphoria of the revolution diplomacy seemed an irrelevance. Within a week the vague statements of the various soviets were given more precise meaning by the emerging leader of the Petrograd soviet, Irakli Tseretelli. On his return from Siberian exile the veteran Menshevik convinced the soviet it should adopt his formula of "revolutionary defensism": defense of the country while simultaneously working toward a general peace without annexations or indemnities. This became the position of most socialists, but not the Bolsheviks. In both Petrograd and Baku, revolutionary defensism found an immediate positive response from local workers and soldiers.

The new revolutionary institutions were desperately in need of leadership. The relatively spontaneous genesis of these institutions had resulted in a haphazard assortment of members which did not accurately represent the political sympathies of their constituents. The IKOO, as well as the soviet, was irregularly elected, and while it could claim the allegiance of the city's population there was no guarantee that it would express the aspirations of the politically articulate. The IKOO was in the hands of the old professional class. The soviet was in the hands of the old revolutionary elite—those Socialist Revolutionaries, Dashnaks, and Social Democrats who happened to be in Baku, in prison or free, at the time of the February Revolution. The soviet majority and its executive body reflected the more conservative socialist tendencies. More extreme revolutionaries had not yet made their presence felt. The Bolsheviks were not yet organized into an effective faction, and for the first four months of the revolution continued to work within an ostensibly united Social-Democratic organization. The Moslems and their principal political spokesmen, the Musavatists, were largely excluded from the sessions of the soviet until well into the summer of 1917. The political complexion of the Russian and Armenian workers was itself confused in the first months of the revolution. They seemed to be waiting for their traditional leaders to make decisions, while the leaders of the various parties were themselves attempting to sort out their political programs.

The Baku organization of the Kadet Party had to accommodate itself to a revolution the very first manifestations of which had outrun the plans for a constitutional monarchy that the liberals had envisaged as the fitting solution to the crisis in the Russian Empire. At one of the first meetings after the revolution, the Baku Committee adopted a resolution in favor of a republic, with only a few diehards holding that the question should be left open until the Constituent Assembly could decide it. Committed to a liberal, democratic republic, the Kadets were faced with the discouraging fact that the hitherto disenfranchised and inarticulate masses of the city and its surrounding industrial regions were predominantly socialist in political complexion. The Kadets, supported by the commercial and industrial leaders of Baku, represented the only alternative to socialism. It was, thus, natural that the necessary funds for printing the party newspaper, *Narodnaia svoboda,* and for organizing meetings and classes to popularize liberal ideas came from the propertied class in the city.[22]

The first shock of revolution depleted the party of several influential members. L. L. Bych, for instance, who had in 1912 run for the duma as a Kadet, suddenly became one of the "March socialists" who embraced the slogans of the new order eagerly. Later in the year the chairman of the party, K. A. Iretskii, announced that he considered himself left of the Kadets and would join the Plekhanovite "Edinstvo" group, and Prince I. I. Dadiani

---

[22] Boris Baikov, "Vospominaniia o revoliutsii v Zakavkaz'e (1917–1920 gg.)," *Arkhiv russkoi revoliutsii* (Berlin), IX (1923), p. 99.

joined the nationalistic Georgian Social Federalists.[23] As the revolution moved to the left and national tensions grew, the Kadets found themselves isolated among the more popular socialist and nationalist parties.[24] With no support in the industrial districts at all and with the absence of *zemstva* in Transcaucasia, the Kadets could hope to gain support only in the city proper. Whereas in other Russian cities the Kadets made themselves felt in the reelected municipal dumas, in Baku the discredited *tsentsovaia* duma was not reelected until *after* the October Revolution.

The Kadet leadership consisted largely of professional men rather than of the very richest and most powerful oil magnates of the city. The chairman of the Baku Committee and the editor of the party newspaper, Pavel Makarovich Kara-Murza, listed himself as a "doctor of philosophy." The finest orator of the party, Mikhail Frolovich Podshibiakin, was a lawyer, as were other leading members, Boris Lvovich Baikov, Aleksei Petrovich Delytsin, and Viacheslav Nikolaevich Klement'ev, all of whom had important posts in the judicial structure. Khristafor Avakumovich Vermishev, the publisher of *Baku* and a Kadet member of the city duma, had served as mayor of Tiflis until August 1905 when he had resigned in the scandal following the violent and bloody routing of a workers' gathering in the city hall. His newspaper consistently followed the Kadet line, and Vermishev carried on a personal polemic with the Bolshevik leader, Shaumian. To Vermishev and his colleagues raised in the legal or journalistic profes-

---

[23] *Ibid.*, pp. 95, 99.

[24] Many Armenians were associated with the Baku Kadets through the local branch of the Armenian National People's Party. This party was founded by Hambartsum Arakelian, editor of the Tiflis Armenian newspaper, *Mshak* ("Toiler"), in 1914. In mid-July 1917, a section of this Kadet-inspired party was established in Baku with the statement that it differed from the Kadets only in its special interest in Armenian affairs. The "populists," as they were sometimes called, were never very influential.

sions, the Bolsheviks represented the enemies of law and order, the harbingers of anarchy.[25]

While the Party of People's Freedom, as the Kadets were officially named, was largely made up of professional men —lawyers, teachers, civil servants, along with a few army officers—its style and outlook were considered "bourgeois" by its socialist opponents. The Kadets in turn were disturbed by the extralegal political behavior of masses of the people. Baikov wrote later of the socialists' tactics: "In the pursuit of their goals, under the slogan of deepening and strengthening the conquests of the revolution, the socialists, seeing in the Russian revolution the elements of social revolution, actively carried on the organization of the broad masses, more accurately the social dregs."[26] When the Bolsheviks proposed annexing the outlying industrial districts to the city proper for the purpose of elections and administration, the Kadets bitterly fought the suggestion. Such a move would have added vast numbers of socialist voters to the city rolls, thus further reducing what little influence the Kadets had. As the year unfolded workers from the outlying districts began to engage more energetically in city politics. But by that time the Party of People's Freedom had ceased to play any role in Baku but that of convenient scapegoat.

The moderate socialist parties (the Socialist Revolutionaries, the Dashnaktsutiun, and the Menshevik wing of Social Democracy) benefited from the defensist mood of the population and the relative calm in Baku during the first months of the revolution. They supported the *dvoevlastie*, as did the Bolsheviks until late spring. By June the Socialist Revolutionaries could boast the largest faction in the Baku soviet, particularly in the soldiers' section. The Mensheviks were also secure, with fifty-six delegates.

[25] *Baku*, no. 246, November 2, 1917; *Narodnaia svoboda* (Baku), no. 33, July 13, 1917, no. 34, July 14, and no. 36, July 16.
[26] Baikov, p. 101.

The Bolsheviks could count only twenty-five.[27] The Dashnak faction remained, considering its fixed constituency,
influential. The Musavat was unrepresented. While the
Socialist Revolutionaries and Bolsheviks did have some
Moslem support, until October the soviet represented primarily the Russian workers and soldiers and part of the
Armenian community.

Despite the overwhelmingly proletarian composition of
the "revolutionary democracy" of Baku and its environs,
the "party of the peasantry," the Socialist Revolutionaries,
exercised considerable influence in the city, rivaling the
Social Democrats for the dominant influence within the
soviet. The Baku Organization of Socialist Revolutionaries
had been established in 1903, three years after the party
came into existence in Russia. Competing with the Social
Democrats for the workers' support, the Socialist Revolutionaries usually had held out for a more radical, insurrection-
ary tactic. From 1905 to 1908 the Socialist Revolutionaries
had consistently rejected the industrialists' proposal to hold
a conference of worker and industrial representatives to
discuss a labor contract, while the Social Democrats had
eventually agreed to such a conference. Working both in
the city and in Balakhany, the Socialist Revolutionaries
had managed to keep their organization intact through
the "reaction" of the Stolypin period; during the World
War, however, the organization had collapsed; they had
revived it in the fall of 1916, but on the eve of the revolution they had suffered several arrests.[28]

On March 5, 1917, in the Baku city hall, the Socialist
Revolutionaries held their first meeting since the revolu-

27 Additional elections were held in April to increase the number
of deputies in the Baku Soviet from 52 to 113. The number of
Bolsheviks rose from 9 to 25. When the workers' and soldiers'
soviets were merged on May 10, the Bolshevik faction did not increase: the soldiers were predominantly S.R. (Guseinov *et al.*
[eds.], *Istoriia Azerbaidzhana*, III, pp. 9, 24.)

28 *Ocherki*, p. 206; Oliver H. Radkey, *The Agrarian Foes of
Bolshevism: Promise and Default of the Russian Socialist Revolutionaries, February to October, 1917* (New York, 1958), p. 129.

(81)

tion, at which they decided to build the broadest possible coalition of political forces in the city.[29] These calls for unity, however, seemed somewhat insincere to the would-be allies of the Socialist Revolutionaries, particularly to the Social Democrats who were shouted down by Socialist Revolutionaries at election meetings for soviet deputies in March and April.[30] Socialist-Revolutionary orators promised that if they came to power every citizen would receive 37½ desiatins of land. To the Social Democrats such a promise seemed demagogic. Nevertheless, the two parties did join with the Dashnaks in a bloc for the elections to the city food supply committees in May. After the Bolshevik–Menshevik split in July, the Socialist Revolutionaries formed a firm alliance with the Mensheviks based on coalition with the bourgeoisie and the principles of "revolutionary defensism." A common list of candidates to the city duma was drawn up.[31] The Dashnaks, who wanted desperately to ally with their ideological compatriots, the Socialist Revolutionaries, were not considered seriously socialist by many of these, and so the formation of a three-party socialist bloc was delayed until the fall of 1917.

The Baku Socialist-Revolutionary center was less consistent than its Menshevik ally in its support of the coalition with the bourgeoisie, and on several occasions came out for soviet power. As early as the First Congress of Soviets in Petrograd in June, Sako Sahakian, the most influential of Baku's Socialist Revolutionaries, took on Lenin in a dispute about the current situation and surmised that perhaps at the next congress the question of the soviets' taking power could be posed.[32] The Baku So-

[29] *Baku*, no. 53, March 7, 1917.
[30] *Bakinskii rabochii*, no. 2, April 26, 1917.
[31] *Izvestiia*, no. 80, July 9, 1917.
[32] *Pervyi Vserossiiskii s"ezd sovetov rabochikh i soldatskikh deputatov, 3–11 iiunia 1917 goda: Stenograficheskii otchet* (Moscow–Leningrad, 1930), p. 184.
Sako Sahakian became the leader of the Right S.R.s in Baku. He was chairman of the IKS in May–June 1917, a member of the

cialist Revolutionaries stood between the Bolsheviks and the Mensheviks in their political line, voting generally with the latter but able on occasion to cooperate with the former. The party found its base of support in the Russian working class, among soldiers (at least until the late summer of 1917), and among the sailors of the Caspian Fleet. On March 13, the Socialist Revolutionaries organized a meeting of the sailors of the commercial fleet to discuss the re-establishment of the sailors' union.[33] Ten years before, such a union had operated as an adjunct of the Baku Socialist-Revolutionary organization. Socialist-Revolutionary interest in the affairs of the merchant marine and the military fleet was matched by expressions of loyalty from sailors. In 1917 the sailors' union, Tsentrokaspii, was led by the Socialist Revolutionaries, and, despite some wavering, remained loyal to them long after the Baku garrison had gone over to the Bolsheviks.

Many writers on the Baku Socialist Revolutionaries see the organization as the Russian national equivalent to the Dashnaktsutiun and the Musavat.[34] Its appeals, while not specifically nationalistic, were sufficiently patriotic to attract Russian loyalists. Eventually both Moslem and Armenian Socialist Revolutionaries formed their own sections with their own newspapers in their native languages.

The Dashnaktsutiun continued to meet in secret after the revolution, unable to free itself from its conspiratorial

---

Soviet's committee of revolutionary defense in March–April 1918, and closely connected with the Dictatorship of Tsentrokaspii. Despite his critical attitude toward the Bolsheviks, Sahakian survived the revolution to work in Moscow and Berlin in the Soviet trade agency, Vneshtorg. (This information comes from L. S. Shaumian.)

[33] *Delo naroda* (Petrograd), no. 7, March 22, 1917.

[34] S. E. Sef, *Kak bol'sheviki prishli k vlasti v 1917–1918 gg. v bakinskom raione* (Baku, 1927), p. 5. In this symposium Ratgauzer agrees with Sef that the S.R.s were a Russian national party. He pointed out that 60–70% of skilled workers were Russian and that many of them supported the S.R.s. (*Ibid.*, p. 45.)

past. On March 26 the party met to vote its support of the Provisional Government and of the war effort "until victory would bring freedom and democracy to small nations."[35] For the first half-year of the revolution, the party was not active in the day-to-day governing of the city. Its attention was turned, rather, to the formulation of its basic political demands. In April a Caucasian conference of Dashnaks put forth the party's minimal program: local languages in all judicial and administrative bodies, and changes in the administrative divisions of the Caucasus.[36] Besides a national program, the conference asked for arbitration courts for workers, the lowering of land rents, and the creation of national schools.

When the Armenians of Baku organized a National Bureau in Baku and a fifty-man council to direct community affairs, the Dashnaks sent seventeen delegates to the council. Of the rest, seven were Social Democrats, six Hnchaks, and twenty nonparty.[37] A Dashnak, O. Kachaznuni, was elected chairman of the council, which became the spokesman for the Armenians in Baku. The Dashnaktsutiun, through the Armenian National Council, through its unions and worker organizations, and through the newspaper, *Arev*, effectively dominated the Armenian national community in the city, although its willingness to defer to the other socialist parties in the IKOO and the soviet reduced its significance in the administration of the city itself.

The Dashnaktsutiun was the only major political party which did not respond tactically to the radicalization of the workers and soldiers in the late summer of 1917. The Armenian leadership continued to advocate unity of the national community and, on the all-Russian scale, coali-

[35] *Arev*, no. 64, March 28, 1917.
[36] *Baku*, no. 87, April 22, 1917.
[37] *Baku*, no. 132, June 16, 1917.

tion government. They remained defensist. Their principal fear was that an end to the war might leave the Armenians in Turkey at the mercy of their oppressors. In Baku the Dashnaks remained close to the Right Socialist Revolutionaries and voted consistently with the Right socialist bloc. Early in October the Armenians of Russia met in Tiflis in a national congress to work out their program for the Constituent Assembly. The Dashnaktsutiun dominated the congress, and the program adopted reflected the federalist notions of the Dashnaks.[38] Like the Musavat, and the Georgian Mensheviks, the Dashnaktsutiun at this time did not conceive of independence as the goal of its people. Rather, like the other nationalist parties in Transcaucasia, the Dashnaktsutiun favored national cultural autonomy within a Russian federal union. The great strength of the party came from its influence in the Armenian national regiments which operated on the Caucasian Front and which would eventually defend Baku from the Turkish advance in 1918.

The Musavat Party did not enjoy the same predominance in the Moslem community as the Dashnaks did in the Armenian. Neither Musavat nor the Social Democratic Hummet could be considered the spokesman for the more than thirty Moslem organizations in Baku or for both the Moslem workers and the Moslem bourgeoisie. The Moslem peasantry was almost completely without political organization. Within the community ethnic and sectarian differences divided Azerbaijanis from Persians, Daghestanis from Volga Tatars. With the revolution each group organized its own council or committee to defend its inter-

---

[38] *Baku*, no. 220, October 3, 1917; *Kaspii*, no. 249, November 14, 1917. For accounts of the congress see: S. Masurian, "Rusahayots Azgayin Hamagumare," in *Mayis 28* (Paris, 1926), pp. 4–22; Richard G. Hovannisian, *Armenia on the Road to Independence, 1918* (Berkeley and Los Angeles, 1967), pp. 88–92.

ests before the authorities.[39] In order to unify the Moslem community and create a single authoritative voice for all the Moslems of Baku, Azerbaijani leaders held several meetings in March to discuss the formation of a Moslem Council. Early in April the Council was formed and elected a provisional committee to lead it.[40]

At its inception the Moslem National Council had no political program other than support for the democratic republic and unity for the Moslems. A few weeks later Moslem students in Baku adopted a resolution calling for "national territorial autonomy" for Transcaucasian Azerbaijanis, for Daghestan, and for the Moslem areas of central Asia, to be based on a decentralization of state power.[41] The federalist ideal was strongly advocated by the new Turkish Party of Federalists created in Elisavetpol.[42] Resul Zade, the Musavat leader in Baku, introduced the federalist plank into the debate at the All-Russian Moslem Congress in Moscow in May, and by the summer of 1917 all of Russian Islam had settled on federalism as its national political goal.[43] The Musavat further expressed its federalist sympathies by merging with the Elisavetpol Turkish

[39] The Volga Tatars on April 9 elected a council which in three weeks claimed that its society's membership had grown to three thousand. (*Kaspii*, no. 79, April 5, 1917; no. 112, May 24, 1917.) Soon a leftist organization, Birlik, was formed by the Volga Tatars, which worked together with Hummet. The Persians too had their leftist group, Adalet, also affiliated with the Azerbaijani Hummet. Hummet, in turn, decided not to merge with the Baku Organization of Social Democrats but keep its organizational autonomy. (*Dok.*, p. 5.)

[40] *Baku*, no. 75, April 6, 1917.

[41] *Kaspii*, no. 82, April 8, 1917.

[42] At the First All-Caucasian Moslem Congress, which met in Baku from April 15 to 20, 1917, the federalist resolution of the Musavatists and Turkish Federalists was passed. The Azerbaijani millionaire, Tagiev, objected to the word "Azerbaijan" in the resolution, on the grounds that it would frighten the Provisional Government, and it was removed. (S. M. Dimanshtein, ed., *Revoliutsiia i natsional'nyi vopros*, III [Moscow, 1930], pp. 337–339.)

[43] *Ibid.*, pp. 294–295. Resul Zade's resolution was passed by a vote of 446–271.

Federalist Party in June.[44] Such major points of contention as the solution to the agrarian question were submerged in the enthusiasm for a joint federalist stand.

Adoption of a minimal political program was an inadequate basis for achieving real unity among the Baku Moslems. Within the Moslem National Council three sharply divided groups could be distinguished: the group of Hummetists and Left Socialist Revolutionaries, the Musavatists, and the liberals led by men of wealth like Topchibashev and Tagiev. By the summer of 1917 pressure from the Left and the Musavatist center led to the reelection of the Council's directing committee and to the inclusion of more "democratic" elements.[45] Still divisions plagued the Council: Hummet wished to limit the role of the national organization to cultural and communal affairs, while the Musavat saw the Council as a potentially powerful political force. In disgust at its own failure to reduce the role of the Moslem National Council, Hummet decided to end its participation within the body and to engage in agitation from the outside.

The Musavatists were strengthened by the walkout of Hummet, and sought to attract the Council away from the conservative forces to collaboration with the democratic and socialist parties. M. G. Gadzhinskii called for the Moslem Council to "go hand in hand with those groups and political parties which do not know any kind of national tendency or feelings and which appear to be the true friends of the Moslem masses."[46] Although this formula-

44 *Kaspii*, no. 135, June 20, 1917. The new central committee of the hybrid Turkish Federalist Party (Musavat) included four representatives from Baku—Resul Zade, M. H. Gadzhinskii (chairman of the Moslem National Committee), M. Rafiev, and M. Vekilov— and four from Elisavetpol (Ganja)—N.-bek Usubekkov, G.-bek Agaev, Sh.-bek Rustambekov, and Mirza Mamed Akhundov. The Federalists from Elisavetpol were more conservative than the Baku Musavatists. Resul Zade represented the left wing of the new party.

45 *Bakinskii rabochii*, no. 16, June 21, 1917.

46 *Kaspii*, no. 142, June 28, 1917.

tion would specifically have excluded a national political party like the Dashnaktsutiun, it would conceivably have allowed for cooperation with the Socialist Revolutionaries, the Mensheviks, and the Bolsheviks.

The Musavat campaign bore fruit in the elections to the Moslem National Committee which took place on July 12. The newspaper *Kaspii* remarked that the elections signaled the entrance of the "democratic intelligentsia" into the Committee.[47] The new Committee adopted a municipal program which envisioned the city duma as having full control over the city's affairs. The main task of the duma was to be "the creation for the dispossessed classes of the population of easier living conditions, satisfaction of their material demands, and the guarantee to develop their spiritual forces."[48] Government was not to be a matter for class organs, like the soviet, but rather for democratically elected representatives of the whole society. As for national goals, the program called for schools in the national languages with curricula which reflected the mores of the nationalities. As for economic reforms, the program was moderate, calling for a labor exchange and housing improvement. A graded tax on all classes except the poorest was to be the basis for the financial policy of the new duma. Private initiative in the economy was not to be discouraged, notwithstanding the city government's participation in the supplying of food to the city. The government would merely

---

[47] *Ibid.*, no. 156, July 15, 1917. Among the twenty-two elected were: Kasim Kasimov, Beibut-khan Dzhevanshir (a personal friend but not a political ally of Shaumian), Topchibashev, Musa bei Tagiev, Khan-Khoiskii, Mamed Hasan Gadzhinskii, Aga Husein Tagiev, Kiazym Zade, and Resul Zade. Among the six elected to represent the workers and peasants was M. G. Vezirov, later a leader of the Left S.R.s in Baku. Topchibashev was elected chairman of the committee, with Vezirov as secretary and Gadzhinskii and Resul Zade as assistant chairmen. (*Ibid.*, no. 157, July 16, 1917.)

[48] *Ibid.*, no. 171, August 2, 1917.

act as the largest seller of produce, working with cooperatives. The program began and ended with affirmations of peace between the nationalities.[49]

The first task for Social Democrats in March was to resurrect their moribund organization. On March 10, two days after Shaumian had returned to Baku, a temporary Social-Democratic committee was elected. While it is difficult to gauge at this point the relative strength of the Bolsheviks and the Mensheviks, there are indications that the Mensheviks could more effectively make their support felt—their followers being located within the city proper, whereas Bolshevik support was largely confined to the outlying industrial districts. In any case both wings of the party had to bow to an overwhelming desire on the part of all workers, expressed in resolutions adopted at local meetings, for unity among the revolutionary parties. Very few of the Baku Bolsheviks, any more than their party comrades elsewhere in Russia, called for a definite break with the Mensheviks at this point.[50]

In this spirit of reconciliation the Social Democrats

---

[49] *Ibid.*

[50] The Baku Social-Democratic Party organization was badly in need of rapid and thorough reorganization. The first issue of *Bakinskii rabochii*, on April 22, 1917, reported: "In the Soviet of Workers' Deputies the Social Democrats are not organized; agitation and lectures are not organized; the listing of members is going on unsatisfactorily; there is no definite line; and the main thing is that the 'apparatus,' uniting and tying together the members of the party, has been badly set up." From the new provisional Baku Committee, a bureau of nine (five Bolsheviks) was chosen to act as the committee's contact with its agitators and the general public. Elected were: A. Dzhaparidze, Aiollo, Naneishvili, Kasashvili, G. Sturua, V. Kasparova, Kalmin, Okinshevich, and Ansheles.

Another organizational matter was the publication of a party newspaper, *Bakinskii rabochii*. The editorial board included Shaumian (editor-in-chief), Gurevich, Dzhaparidze, Rokhlin, and Ansheles. An Armenian-language newspaper, *Sotsial-Demokrat*, was also brought out. The young Anastas Mikoyan served on its staff.

gathered on April 10 for a city-wide conference. Shaumian proposed the adoption of a resolution branding the Russian bourgeoisie "objectively counterrevolutionary" and calling for class struggle rather than civil peace.[51] At once the mood of collaboration was disturbed by the factional differences between the Social Democrats. The Menshevik Rokhlin attempted to soften the condemnation of the Provisional Government by having the term "counterrevolutionary" eliminated. The conference adopted this correction by a 23-vote majority, but the compromise was unacceptable to a Menshevik minority, led by Aiollo, who considered the resolution unnecessarily hostile to the new government.

The position adopted by the Baku Social-Democratic conference was close to that of the Stalin-Kamenev center Bolshevik group, then in ascendency in Petrograd. Their attitude toward the Provisional Government was cautious. They accepted the *dvoevlastie* but saw the soviet as a watchdog against the Provisional Government's potentially counterrevolutionary behavior. At the same time leftist Bolsheviks argued for a more hostile line toward the bourgeois government. Shaumian belonged to this latter group: he was opposed to collaboration with the bourgeoisie and, like Lenin, was convinced that Russia was on the threshold of a socialist revolution. In his resolution adopted on April 10 Shaumian wrote:

> The crisis of capitalism, having ripened already before the war, has deepened in the course of the last three years so much that the outburst of social revolution in Europe seems as unavoidable in the near future as was the inevitable explosion of revolution we have lived through in Russia.

[51] *Bakinskii rabochii*, no. 1, April 22, 1917; S. G. Shaumian, *Izbrannye proizvedeniia*, II: 1917–1918 gg. (Moscow, 1958), pp. 7–9 (hereafter this work will be cited: Shaumian, II).

> The Russian Revolution, although bourgeois-democratic
> in its content, is the prelude to the social revolution in
> Europe under whose influence it will gradually turn into
> a social revolution.[52]

Shaumian here expressed the notion of a "continuous revolution" (*nepriryvnaia revoliutsiia*), the gradual metamorphosis of the bourgeois revolution into the socialist revolution.

Bolshevik cooperation with the Mensheviks and acquiescence in the soviet's support of the Provisional Government died hard, in both Petrograd and Baku. Only after Lenin's arrival at the Finland Station was the line of the Bolshevik faction clarified. Lenin declared that all power should be handed over to the soviets, the only true representatives of Russian "democracy." No collaboration with defensist Mensheviks or with the bourgeois Provisional Government was acceptable. In Baku the *April Theses* were received with some confusion. The Social-Democratic newspaper published them, but with a disclaimer that they had not yet been discussed by the local party membership. Shaumian continued his attack on the collaborationist tactics of the Mensheviks when in May Mensheviks and Socialist Revolutionaries joined the bourgeois parties in a coalition government.[53] It was only a matter of time before the divergent tactics of the Bolsheviks and Mensheviks in Baku would tear the united organization apart. But the final break was delayed until June and came only after pressure had been applied from the Bolshevik center in Petrograd.

By the first two weeks in May two delegates from the April conference of Bolsheviks in Petrograd arrived in Tiflis. Mikha Tskhakaia and Filip Makharadze, both old friends of Shaumian and Bolsheviks since the first split in the party, told their local comrades to follow Petrograd's

---

[52] *Ibid.*
[53] *Sotsial-Demokrat*, no. 2, May 7, 1917; Shaumian, II, pp. 13–15.

lead and break with "collaborationist" Mensheviks immediately.[54] They further urged the local Bolsheviks to unite only with the Menshevik-Internationalists, who, like the Bolsheviks, opposed the coalition government. This prescription fitted the situation in Petrograd, where the coalition was already becoming unpopular among soldiers and workers; but in Baku and other provincial cities the Provisional Government *was* the revolution, and opposition to it was tantamount to counterrevolution. What is more, the workers of Baku had expressed repeatedly in the local committees of the RSDRP that they wanted party unity and a guarantee that the minority within the party could express its point of view freely.[55] An open break with the Mensheviks was impossible with the feelings of the workers as they were. Nevertheless, from April on the Bolsheviks met separately in a group of ten or twelve and impatiently awaited the opportunity to set up their own organization.[56]

Such an opportunity developed in mid-May at the second city-wide conference of the Social-Democratic organization. Shaumian introduced two resolutions, one opposing the coalition and the other denouncing the loan floated by the government to continue the war. Both were adopted by the pro-Bolshevik majority.[57] The conference, however, did not vote on the question of a full transfer of power to the soviets. Instead the conference called for eliminating the "imperialist" classes from government, and for turning the government over to the proletariat and "other democratic classes," which could then bring the war to a close.[58] In other words, the Baku conference had adopted the solution, midway between soviet power and the

[54] Anastas Mikoyan, "Bakinskaia organizatsiia bol'shevikov v 17–18 gg.," *Iz proshlogo* (Baku, 1923), p. 30.
[55] *Bakinskii rabochii*, no. 3, May 2, 1917.
[56] Mikoyan, p. 30.
[57] *Sotsial-Demokrat*, no. 4, May 28, 1917.
[58] *Pravda* (Petrograd), no. 77, June 22, 1917.

coalition government, of a government of the whole democracy (what would eventually be called *odnorodnoe demokraticheskoe pravitel'stvo*, "homogeneous democratic government"). Dissatisfied Mensheviks left the conference, and the remaining delegates immediately chose a new temporary Baku Committee, almost entirely Bolshevik in composition. They decided to call another conference of Bolsheviks and Menshevik-Internationalists to form a new Social-Democratic organization.[59]

Through May the small Bolshevik group in the soviet ran into stiff resistance to its criticism of the coalition government in Petrograd. When the military soviet merged with the workers' soviet on May 11, the joint body of 211 members elected a Socialist Revolutionary, Sako Sahakian, chairman.[60] Shaumian, still an influential delegate (a week later he was elected to the First Congress of Soviets along with Sahakian, Sadovskii, and Bekzadian), continued his attacks on the Provisional Government, which he contended could not solve the basic question of the moment, the question of war and peace. But in Baku the mood of the workers and of the soldiers was clearly "defensist," and propaganda deemed harmful to the war effort was barely tolerated. On May 16 Shaumian failed to have the soviet adopt his resolution expressing no confidence in the Government. Instead, by a vote of 166 for and 9 against, with 8 abstaining, a Menshevik–Socialist-Revolutionary–Dashnak resolution was passed which stated that the inclusion of members of the Petrograd soviet into the Provisional Government had been necessary in order to defend the revolution.[61] Later in the month the Bolsheviks were again defeated when they proposed a resolution calling

[59] *Ocherki*, p. 218.

[60] *Znamia truda* (Baku), no. 6; S. N. Belen'kii and A. Manvelov, *Revoliutsiia 1917 g. v Azerbaidzhane (Khronika sobytii)* (Baku, 1927), p. 47.

[61] *Pravda* (Petrograd), no. 77, June 22, 1917; *Dok.*, pp. 20–21; Shaumian, II, pp. 19–20.

for a break with "Russia's Octobrist-Kadet bourgeoisie" and a struggle for peace by workers of all nations.[62]

Yet another issue which divided the Baku Bolsheviks from the Mensheviks and Socialist Revolutionaries was the tactic toward the "nationalist" parties. The Bolsheviks were disturbed by a polemic which broke out between the *Izvestiia* of the soviet and the *Izvestiia* of the Council of Moslem Organizations. *Bakinskii rabochii* did not reproach the editors of the soviet's *Izvestiia*, Mandel'shtam and Ter-Arakelian, but insisted that it was the soviet itself that was responsible for the paper's line, which attacked Moslem nationalism specifically without mentioning the nationalism of local Armenians, Jews, and even Russians:

> The newspaper is indignant that the Moslem congress came out for the rebuilding of the state on federalist lines. We are sharply opposed to the demands of the Moslem congress. But we cannot silently ignore the fact that, before the Moslems demanded federation, it was advocated by the Georgian and Armenian nationalists. Isn't it clear that this is not a matter of Moslem, Georgian, or Armenian nationalism, but of nationalism in general?[63]

The Bolsheviks alone of the socialist parties were sensitive to the mood of isolation and growing alienation which hung over the Moslem politicians. While the Bolsheviks felt unable to collaborate with the Moslem National Committee because of its "bourgeois" and nationalist composition, they did remain, through Hummet, in touch with a part of the Moslem "democracy" throughout 1917.

The disagreements between Bolsheviks and Mensheviks in Baku on the questions of the war, of coalition with the bourgeoisie, and of the nationalities strained the frail bonds of party unity. But even more serious than these

[62] *Bakinskii rabochii*, no. 5, May 28, 1917; *Dok.*, pp. 24–25.
[63] *Bakinskii rabochii*, no. 13, June 14, 1917.

issues was the fact that the Bolshevik faction in other parts of Russia had already responded to Lenin's call for schism. The Tiflis Committee of Bolsheviks had announced on June 6 that it had terminated its organizational association with the Menshevik-Defensists.[64] The Baku Bolsheviks could not act effectively while linked with the Mensheviks, and faced isolation from their own party if they continued collaboration. Even before the formal break, separate factions of Bolsheviks and Mensheviks appeared in the soviet. Early in June, three Mensheviks left the editorial board of *Bakinskii rabochii* over the Bolshevik line of its editors.[65] On June 11 the first issue of the Menshevik newspaper, *Sotsial-Demokrat*, appeared. Finally, elections were held within the party to choose delegates to the June conference which would decide which faction would control the organizations.[66]

The elections were held but not the conference. Before a joint meeting of all the delegates could be held, factional conferences took the matter into their own hands. The Mensheviks acted first, calling a conference for June 24. They protested the actions of the Baku Committee and arranged for an all-party conference to be held even if the Committee refused to call one. The Bolsheviks responded by accusing the Mensheviks of being the real *"raskolniki"* (splitters):

> Our inter-district conferences were chaotic and disorderly. Finding themselves in the minority, the Menshevik-Defensists did not want to subordinate themselves to the decisions of the organization and actually long ago deviated from it. Leaving the conference they formed their own independent organization, formed their own group of leaders, split

[64] *Kavkazskii rabochii* (Tiflis), no. 67, June 6, 1917.
[65] I. S. Ansheles, S. M. Gurevich, and A. V. Rokhlin left the editorial board (*Bakinskii rabochii*, no. 8, June 4, 1917).
[66] *Ibid.*, no. 5, May 28, 1917; *Dok.*, pp. 28–29.

the faction in the Soviet of Workers' Deputies, and called a conference of Menshevik delegates for Saturday, June 24. The inter-district conference recognized that we are not on the same road as the Menshevik-Defensists, that a single organization is possible only with the Menshevik-Internationalists of the Martov type, with the Menshevik-Internationalists who adopted the resolution of the inter-district conference in Petrograd of Bolsheviks and Menshevik-Internationalists.[67]

A few days later the Bolsheviks met to set up their own factional organization. Three Mensheviks interested in preserving unity came to the Bolshevik conference uninvited, but their pleas fell on deaf ears. Some speakers declared that the organization had been in fact split since the Menshevik walkout from the May Conference. The conference adopted a resolution to form a joint Bolshevik–Menshevik-Internationalist party organization.[68]

The Mensheviks responded to the Bolshevik creation of a separate committee by joining with all non-Bolshevik Social Democrats. On July 2, Ansheles opened a meeting of eighty-six delegates who represented 1,660 party members.[69] Like the Bolsheviks, the Mensheviks claimed that the other faction had forced the schism. Neither faction wished to appear before the workers with the onus of

[67] *Bakinskii rabochii*, no. 18, June 25, 1917; *Dok.*, p. 43.

[68] The Internationalist Baku committee included Shaumian, Dzhaparidze, Piatakov, Tsintsadze, Amirian, and P. M. Okinshevich, with Gabrielian as a candidate member. On June 27 a bureau of the Baku Committee of RSDRP(b) was elected: Dzhaparidze, Shaumian, V. Naneishvili, K. Tsintsadze, Piatakov, and Efendiev, with Basin and Sturua as candidate members. (*Bakinskii rabochii*, no. 22, July 5, 1917.)

[69] *Izvestiia*, no. 75, July 4, 1917. The joint Menshevik–Jewish-Bund–Armenian-Social-Democratic organization formed a united committee: Ansheles, Aiollo, Bagaturov, Anabekov, Druzhinin, Ziablikov, Choniia, Khachiev, Krishtal', Kolakov, Churaev, Ramishvili, Ebanoidze, and Landiia.

responsibility for the final break. Unity, however, had in fact been out of the question once the Bolsheviks had adopted the militant Leninist position. Social Democracy was at last split into two separate and antagonistic parties after fourteen years of conflict. The oldest issues—dominance by workers versus dominance by intellectuals; an open labor movement versus a conspiratorial underground —had been superseded by the immediate questions of the revolution: whether to form a coalition with the bourgeoisie and how to end the war.

Once the break had been made with the Mensheviks the possibility was provided for the Bolsheviks to become an extremely radical alternative to the moderate socialist parties; and yet in Baku the Bolsheviks hesitated to isolate themselves from the mood of the workers as they interpreted it, and from the other political parties. The brunt of the Bolshevik polemic was directed against their former comrades, the Mensheviks, and, by August, against the Socialist Revolutionaries, too, who were branded "conciliators." The alliance with the bourgeoisie was consistently attacked. Nevertheless, the Bolsheviks maintained their representatives within the IKOO and in the city duma, an arrangement which Lenin would have considered impermissible. The Baku Bolsheviks were also quite cautious in their dealings with the national parties, the Dashnaktsutiun and the Musavat, which they generally refrained from attacking until October 1917.[70] This general caution on the part of the Baku Bolsheviks may in part have been a consequence of their years of work in the mass labor movement and their acquired sensitivity to the moods of the masses, which, in this case, they read correctly. For the "revolutionary democracy" in Baku was not prepared as early as were the workers and soldiers in Petrograd and

[70] Ia. A. Ratgauzer, *Revoliutsiia i grazhdanskaia voina v Baku*, I: 1917–1918, p. 9.

Moscow to discard the Provisional Government and seize power.

In mid-May Shaumian wrote: "The revolution is not finished,—it is continuing. No one can argue with this, except the counterrevolutionaries."[71] For Leninists, indeed, the revolution had not ended with the establishment of the *dvoevlastie* or the coalition government. No compromise could be imagined by the Bolsheviks between the government of the bourgeoisie and the soviets of the workers, peasants, and soldiers. All power, said Lenin and Shaumian, must be transferred to the soviets. The dilemma of the Bolsheviks in the first months of the revolution, both in Petrograd and in Baku, arose from the unwillingness of the soviets themselves to challenge the coalition and take power into its own hands. The soviets in both cities still supported the coalition government and the war effort.

Historians of the revolution in Baku have been hard put to explain the hegemony of the Menshevik and Socialist-Revolutionary parties in the soviet from March to October, in view of the rise of the Bolsheviks after 1907 and their maintenance of a predominant position through the years of "reaction" to the 1914 strike. Ia. Ratgauzer, a prolific writer on Baku themes, wrote on the tenth anniversary of the revolution:

> The fact that the Soviet of Workers' Deputies in Baku, where in the prerevolutionary period the Mensheviks and S.R.s had not enjoyed any influence among the workers, consisted almost exclusively of S.R.s and Mensheviks is explained by the destruction of labor organizations during the war and by the massive mobilization in the first year of the war. In the place of the old cadres of the proletariat appeared new elements, recently emergent from the villages. When deferment from military duty

[71] *Sotsial-Demokrat* (Bolshevik Armenian organ in Baku), no. 3, May 14, 1917; Shaumian, II, p. 16.

was established, those who wanted to be saved from the draft, among whom were few old workers, came to Baku. These circumstances gave the conciliatory parties the opportunity to develop.[72]

Recently an Azerbaijani scholar, S. S. Aliiarov, has been working on the general problem of the composition of the Baku proletariat on the eve of the revolution. In a series of articles Aliiarov has established that significant changes did take place in the population of Baku, particularly among the workers. In the war years the total population of Baku rose by 14.2 percent, while the number of workers rose by only 8–10 percent.[73] The greatest number of newcomers probably consisted of soldiers stationed in the city and of Armenian refugees fleeing from the Turks. Among the workers, the portion of the working class made up of *mastery* (highly skilled workers) increased from 20.5 to 22 percent.[74] The rate of increase for other workers declined with the level of skill. Thus, the Baku proletariat during the war was becoming increasingly more skilled, better educated. The very groups from which the Bolsheviks had recruited their most vehement followers during the great strikes in the past were diminishing. In the oil-fields southern Azerbaijanis were leaving for Persia; Volga Tatars and unskilled Armenians and Russians were being drafted. To take their places at the drilling sites came the

---

[72] Ratgauzer, *Revoliutsiia i grazhdanskaia voina* . . . , p. 3. Ratgauzer's hypothesis that the change in the composition of the working class explains the change in party loyalty was challenged by his colleague, Semen Sef, who pointed out that in Baku only some Armenian and Russian unskilled workers were subject to the draft. Most Moslems and skilled workers were exempted from military service. Therefore, Baku's working class underwent less of a change than in other industrial areas. (Sef, *Kak bol'sheviki prishli k vlasti v 1917–1918 gg. v bakinskom raione* [Baku, 1927], p. 61.)

[73] S. S. Aliiarov, "Chislennost', professional'nyi i natsional'nyi sostav bakinskogo proletariata v period pervoi mirovoi voiny," p. 73.

[74] *Ibid.*, p. 79.

poorest Azerbaijani peasants with no experience in the labor movement and intimate ties to the villages. Moslems accounted for 74 percent of the unskilled labor in Baku.[75]

Higher skills, literacy, and permanence of residence became the new hallmarks of the workers of the city proper, while in the oil-fields the overwhelming majority were Moslems with only a thin proletarian veneer. And the elite workers continued to respond more readily to Menshevik appeals than to Bolshevik ones. The Bolsheviks were forced to turn anew to the semiproletarians who had emigrated to Baku during the war, but in 1917–1918 they had to contend with the rival appeals of the Musavatists and Moslem nationalists. In one sense the revolution in Baku can be seen as a struggle for the mind of the Moslem poor. To the victor in Balakhany and Sabunchiny belonged the spoils of the center city.

Another factor aiding the moderate socialists in the soviet was the disproportionate representation of skilled workers, particularly Russian workers. The center city was represented more heavily than the outlying districts and the Moslem workers, and as long as this remained true the Bolsheviks had little chance to increase their influence in the soviet. And most importantly, the soviet was made up not only of workers, but of soldiers and their officers, who until the fall of 1917 tended to be "defensist" in their attitude toward the war. The soldiers were primarily Socialist-Revolutionary in sympathy, and were responsible for the removal of Shaumian from the chairmanship of the merged soviets in May. Where workers voted alone, as in the factory committees, they were more receptive to Bolshevik appeals. While they might not be prepared to follow the Leninists against the coalition government or the war effort, the workers were attracted by Bolshevik energy and militance in dealings with the oil industry.

For the first months of revolution, to support the moder-

[75] *Ibid.*, part II, p. 35.

ate socialist parties was an affirmation of confidence in the *dvoevlastie*, in the Provisional Government, and in the class organ of the workers, the soviet. It was supporting the achievements of the February Revolution, the overthrow of the autocracy, the establishment of the new freedoms, and the defense of revolutionary Russia. Ratgauzer makes the point:

> After the February Revolution the defensist tendencies, the defensist ideals were not eliminated, probably because here the danger of an invasion by the Turks was more palpable, more concrete, and had an influence on a significant part of the Russian workers. . . . I attentively read the newspapers of 1917–1918 and became acquainted with almost all the resolutions which were published in *Bakinskii rabochii* and in *Izvestiia*, and I found very few resolutions directed against defensism. Such resolutions were carried at meetings of soldiers and not at meetings of workers.[76]

The strategy of the moderate socialist parties, based as it was on collaboration between classes and revolutionary defensism, proved untenable in Baku as the economic crisis deepened. The "defensist" workers supported the policies of the "conciliatory" parties on the war and the political order, but they began to vote with the Bolsheviks on the important issues concerning their economic life, because they wanted more aggressive champions of labor's cause. The shift in support from the Right socialists to the Left socialists by the late summer of 1917 occurred as economic despair brought men to believe that within the present alliance with the bourgeoisie meaningful improvement of conditions was impossible.

[76] Ratgauzer in Sef, *Kak bol'sheviki prishli k vlasti* . . . , p. 46.

# 4

## From Economics to Politics: the Revolution Moves Left

THE COALITION of the "revolutionary democracy" and the *tsentsovoe obshchestvo* (the old ruling classes and the bourgeoisie) on which the Right socialists based their strategy was steadily being eroded away in the summer of 1917. The tremendous pressures on the masses, caused by the war and its stepchild, hunger, drove them to more radical alternatives. Before the war Baku had received its food-supplies by ship from the Volga region and by rail from the north Caucasus. But the dislocations of the war had stopped the regular flow of goods into the city, and, with the outbreak of the revolution and the discrediting of local authorities, the peasants of the north Caucasus refused to sell grain to the city at the low fixed prices. They demanded a rise in the official prices, but the government feared that increases in prices would lead to further inflation. A spokesman from Kuba, a provincial city in eastern Transcaucasia, reported:

> The peasants refuse to give grain to the cities because the city robs the peasants. For all urban goods the peasants have to pay exorbitant prices. The peasants will not give grain to the industrialists who think up the prices, will not give to the workers who by their strikes raise the cost of goods. The city will give nothing to the village in exchange for grain.[1]

[1] *Izvestiia*, no. 114, August 19, 1917.

Efforts by the Baku consumer cooperatives to work with city food-supply organs came to nought. The city government refused to set up a government monopoly on food-supplies and yet discouraged the cooperatives from taking resolute action of their own.[2] The Baku soviet hesitated to get involved in the food question. By May, when the supplies dropped drastically, members of the soviet called for the establishment of a food-supply dictatorship to oversee and coordinate all activity in that field within the city, to stop speculation and hoarding.[3] On the suggestion of Shaumian, Dzhaparidze, and Mandel'shtam, the soviet on May 13 decided to "work out measures" to ease the food shortage.[4] This modest intervention into an area of municipal administration was the first step by the soviet toward assuming the prerogatives of the city duma. It would not be long before people in Baku would consider the institution which most effectively dealt with the food-supply question to be the *de facto* government of the city.[5]

[2] Besides the City Food Supply Commission, there was a Provincial Food Supply Commission, headed by A. A. Stopani. This latter body took a line left of the City Commission and by June 25 demanded that the soviets, as the only revolutionary democratic organs, should guide the food-supply committees. Stopani's commission was the most active governmental agency operating in the political vacuum of Baku Province, but was largely powerless before the local Azerbaijani landlords, who often had the local police "in their pockets" (*Baku*, no. 107, May 17, 1917; *Dok.*, pp. 19–20). The peasants in Baku Province remained unaffected by the revolution, except negatively. The absence of authority encouraged the appearance of bandits who pillaged and murdered with impunity.

[3] Stopani reported to the soviet that deliveries of grain to Baku had dropped from 350,000 poods of wheat in January and 423,000 in February to 210,000 in March, and 178,000 in April; and that for the first twelve days of May only 34,000 poods had been received (*Izvestiia*, no. 36, May 17, 1917). Normal deliveries for Baku were about 700,000 poods a month.

[4] *Ibid.*

[5] In May, elections to the local food-supply committees were held. Although only 49,525 votes were cast and irregularities were reported at the polls, the results are at least indicative of the rela-

While extending its own influence in the city, the Baku soviet continued to support the IKOO and the Provisional Government. Its loyalty to the *status quo* was displayed in the aftermath of the "July Days." The fall of the first coalition government in Petrograd on July 2 precipitated Bolshevik-led demonstrations by workers and soldiers calling for the transfer of all power to the soviets. Only the Bolsheviks and Martov's Menshevik-Internationalists sympathized with the demands of the crowds. Rumors spread that the Bolsheviks were attempting to seize power, that Lenin was a German agent. The Bolshevik leader was forced into hiding and his party was condemned by the soviet leadership. The crisis ended with the formation of a new coalition with Alexander Kerensky as prime minister, but the crisis for the Bolsheviks continued for another two months. July was the low ebb of popularity for the extreme Left.

In Baku the July Days were greeted with shock and dismay. The Socialist Revolutionary Bekzadian contrasted the milder Bolsheviks of Baku with the more dangerous

---

tive strength of the principal political blocs in the city on May 21. The totals were:

| | |
|---|---|
| Moslem list | 25,550 |
| Socialist Bloc (S.R., S.D., Dashnaks) | 20,573 |
| Mixed Socialist list | 1,379 |
| Kadets | 913 |
| Independents | 730 |
| Invalid votes | 380 |

(*Kaspii*, no. 115, May 27, 1917).

The elections made clear that the Kadets had been effectively eliminated from playing any role in Baku almost immediately after the revolution. More significantly, the socialists were faced by a strong national bloc, the Moslems, which would have to be considered in the future. This "lesson" of the elections, however, was not heeded by the socialists (with the notable exception of the Bolsheviks), who continued to treat the Moslems with condescension and to limit their political role in the soviet and duma as far as was possible.

(104)

Petrograd variety: "Here in Baku we still do business with a high-principled Bolshevism. But there along with Bolshevism go strange elements. They stir up the water, and someone, unknown as of now, is casting his rod into the water."[6]

Even the Bolsheviks were disturbed by the indications that the Petrograd organization might have attempted to seize power by an armed insurrection. Shaumian rose in the soviet to defend his party: "In the Petrograd events the Bolsheviks were not guilty. They could not hold back the revolutionary masses from a demonstration; this happened against the wishes and without the participation of the Bolsheviks. I am certain that our party did not wage this act. We Bolsheviks have always opposed premature, rash decisions and are against the seizure of power by force of arms!!"[7]

The socialist parties in Baku called a conference of their central committees to discuss the recent events. The Menshevik Bagaturov bitterly attacked the Bolsheviks and called for the transfer of all local power to the IKOO. A motion to that effect by Aiollo was carried, despite strong protests by Bolshevik and Hummet delegates.[8] Attempts to reconcile the majority with the Bolsheviks were futile. The Menshevik Ramishvili's assurance that Lenin, "a fanatic in this matter," is "a man of unusual pride but an honest fighter" fell on deaf ears. Shaumian concluded that no common language existed between the Left and Right socialists: "Either we are traitors or you are counterrevolutionaries. The petty bourgeoisie is already dragging along counterrevolution. We do not hide our views and will not

[6] *Izvestiia*, no. 79, July 8, 1917.

[7] *Ibid.*; Shaumian, II, p. 25. For a thorough discussion of the Bolshevik role in the July Days, see Alexander Rabinowitch, *Prelude to Revolution: The Petrograd Bolsheviks and the July 1917 Uprising* (Bloomington, Ind., 1968).

[8] *Izvestiia*, no. 86, July 16, 1917.

hide them. We are ready for your repressions. But I do not know if your police will be as noble as the police of the Romanovs."[9]

Two days later the soviet adopted the resolution of the socialist conference establishing a local "dictatorship of the revolutionary power" to be exercised by the IKOO.[10] Sentiment among the deputies was heavily anti-Bolshevik. Meetings among workers and soldiers throughout the city had already denounced the demonstrations in Petrograd. In the soviet the Menshevik leader, Sadovskii, minced no words: "The servants of reaction, German agents, hooligans, etc., hurried to appear as anarchists and Bolsheviks in order to carry out their dark work without risk."[11] Shaumian maintained in the face of such indictments that the Petrograd events had been spontaneous and that the Bolsheviks had never meant to overthrow the Provisional Government: "If it were proven that the Bolsheviks consciously prepared an armed conspiracy, I would be the first to leave them and say that this is a party of adventurists."[12] He was greeted by jeers and shouts. Dzhaparidze attempted to explain to the soviet that the Bolsheviks did not intend to carry the revolution immediately into a socialist phase but did insist on the necessity of taking power away from the counterrevolutionary bourgeoisie. He too was shouted down.[13]

Paradoxically, the Baku soviet, like the Petrograd soviet and the Central Executive Committee, refused to take

[9] *Ibid.*, no. 85, July 15, 1917.
[10] *Baku*, no. 157, July 16, 1917.
[11] *Izvestiia*, no. 89, July 20, 1917.
[12] *Ibid.*, no. 90, July 21, 1917; Shaumian, II, p. 40.
[13] *Ibid.*, no. 88, July 19, 1917; Dzhaparidze, pp. 166–167. Though the Baku Bolsheviks were disturbed by the accusations against their party, they did not go as far as the Tiflis Bolsheviks, who expressed confidence in the Central Executive Committee of the Soviets on July 7 and joined other socialist parties in protesting "any unsanctioned demonstration, armed or unarmed" (S. E. Sef, *Bor'ba za Oktiabr' v Zakavkaz'i* [Tiflis, 1932], pp. 56–57).

power formally just when real power was falling into its hands. After the July Days it rejected the only political parties that advocated soviet power, and the Bolsheviks for their part dropped the slogan "All Power to the Soviets." These developments on both the national and the local scenes complicated greatly the question of where power would lie in Baku. For most of 1917 Baku experienced not only *dvoevlastie*, but in effect a tripartite administration. The soviet, the duma, and the IKOO all claimed to have the prerogative of the supreme governing body. None of the three could be said to be "democratic," or even representative, except in a formal sense. The duma was six years old, and by the spring of 1917 a "great tiredness" was felt within it. Members rarely attended, and, as we have seen, a quorum could often not be gathered.[14] Just a few days before the outbreak of the February Revolution, the duma had voted to petition the viceroy of the Caucasus for new elections. Discussion had been held about increasing the number of Moslem members to correspond with the preponderance of Moslems in the local population.[15]

IKOO had never been directly elected by the population and had been conceived as an interim executive to govern only until democratically elected bodies could be convened. Shortly after its creation, the IKOO had ceased to act as if it were subordinate to the duma and in fact, it increasingly became the mouthpiece of soviet policies. By increasing its membership in the IKOO the Baku soviet managed effectively to dominate the local "provisional government."

Even the soviet could not pretend to represent the population of the city but only its workers and soldiers. Moreover, the Moslem poor were hardly represented in the soviet until the fall of 1917. The soviet was, however, the only body in Baku to represent the workers of the oil-field

14 *Kaspii*, no. 43, February 23, 1917.

15 *Ibid.*; by law the Moslems were not permitted to hold more than half the seats in the duma. Moslem liberals and Musavatists had agitated for years for an increase in Moslem representation.

districts and, therefore, to be interested in having those districts officially incorporated into the city.

In the spring and summer of 1917 most politically-minded residents of Baku, including the majority of the socialists, hoped that sometime in the future their city would be governed by a democratically elected duma. The Bolsheviks and Menshevik-Internationalists alone wanted power to be transferred to the soviet. Yet the former prospect met innumerable obstacles as the preparations for elections were carried out. The question which divided the old duma from the soviet was whether the oil-field districts should be incorporated into the city before or after the elections. The soviet approved early incorporation, and authorized two of its deputies to the First Congress of Soviets, Shaumian and Sahakian, to petition the Provisional Government to issue such a decree.[16] The soviet also decided that, until the duma elections, deputies from the soviet should be sent to the duma equal in number to the present duma membership.[17] Although this resolution was not implemented until late summer, it insured soviet influence inside the duma, the same kind of influence as it had achieved in the IKOO.

The city duma, on the other hand, opposed incorporation of the oil-fields before the elections. The Kadet leadership of the duma joined with Moslem leaders in opposition to the soviet proposal.[18] The Moslems feared that incorporation would break the "natural" bond which they imagined existed between the Moslems of the oil-fields and the Moslem peasants of the neighboring villages. The Kadets were more pragmatic in their reasoning. Incorporation would mean more votes for the socialist and national parties and few for the Kadets. The Kadets' only hope of maintaining even their minimal authority in the

[16] *Bakinskii rabochii*, no. 8, June 4, 1917.
[17] *Izvestiia*, no. 51, June 4, 1917.
[18] *Baku*, no. 130, June 14, 1917.

duma was to exclude the workers of the oil-fields. Vermishev joined the Moslem National Committee in asking for the creation of a special administration for the oil districts and the thirty-three villages of the Baku area.[19]

The Bolsheviks had initiated and led the campaign for incorporation. They maintained that close economic ties existed, not between the outlying villages and the oil-fields, but between the fields and the city proper. Azizbekov, the Bolshevik member of the duma, argued that the oil-fields must be incorporated into the city or they would be governed as in the past by the oil industrialists.[20] The Bolsheviks were anxious to have the workers of the oil-fields represented in the duma for the obvious reason that they expected support from these voters.

On July 26, the IKOO joined the soviet and the conference of factory committees in sanctioning the incorporation.[21] The Kadets protested to no avail. Shaumian's motion to send a commission to Tiflis to lay the matter before the Ozakom was adopted by the IKOO three days later. Vermishev's application to go to Tiflis to explain the liberal point of view was rejected.[22] Both Shaumian and Vermishev did go to Tiflis, however, the latter on a mandate from the duma, and argued for their respective positions.[23] A final decision was not made until September 7, and even then it was a compromise. The oil-fields were to be incorporated—but after the elections. Elections for duma representatives from the oil-fields were to be held at a later time.[24]

Two clear effects of the controversy over incorporation are evident. The first was the defeat of the Moslems and Kadets who wished to keep the villages and the oil-fields

[19] *Kaspii*, no. 200, September 7, 1917.
[20] *Ibid.*, no. 172, August 3, 1917.
[21] *Baku*, no. 167, July 28, 1917.
[22] *Bakinskii rabochii*, no. 34, August 2, 1917.
[23] *Baku*, no. 172, August 3, 1917.
[24] *Izvestiia*, no. 131, September 10, 1917.

unified; the second, a victory for the soviet, particularly for its Bolshevik deputies, who had championed incorporation without the villages. The long-range effect of the controversy was to delay the elections until their results would be largely insignificant. The duma had not only lost the campaign against incorporation but, even more important, it had lost time. In most other large cities the elections to the duma had already been held, and in some the liberals had not done badly. But in Baku the "democratic" duma would not be elected, for technical reasons, until the end of October, after the Bolshevik revolution.

The authority of all three governing bodies disintegrated in the summer of 1917. Law and order broke down, and the response of the authorities was inadequate. The police chief, Leontovich, resigned early in the summer after his force had been crippled by the loss of former officers now accused of abuses under the old regime. Even ordinary functions of the city government, such as sanitation, had to be taken over by voluntary organizations. One such group, "Tsentrodom," headed by Leontovich, Ia. N. Smirnov, and M. Ia. Shor, ran hospitals and shelters for orphans and aided the consumer cooperatives.[25] A power vacuum existed in Baku, with no institution willing and able to assert its authority. The threat of hostilities between Armenians and Azerbaijanis hung over the city, and rumors spread that one or the other nationality was arming.

The summer of 1917 witnessed not only a breakdown of law and order and a worsening of the food shortage, but also the first massive appearance of the Moslem poor on the revolutionary stage, in the protests against the food shortage. Hunger, even more than the struggle for a living wage, galvanized the Moslems into mass action.

---

[25] Boris Baikov, "Vospominaniia o revoliutsii v Zakavkaz'e (1917–1920 gg.)," *Arkhiv russkoi revoliutsii* (Berlin), IX (1923), pp. 96, 118.

As early as April a system of rationing by card had been adopted by the City Food Supply Commission.[26] But price-controls had not been put into effect, and speculation continued. The poorer classes suffered most from the inflation, and the psychological result of the crisis was to personalize its causes, to blame the situation on specific groups or individuals, even though the underlying causes were connected with the growing isolation of Baku from its sources of food. Workers began to feel that the chaos resulted from the voracious appetites of merchants who raised prices or of rich people who hoarded food. On June 1, a crowd of about one thousand Azerbaijanis gathered at the city hall, entered the building, and attacked an official whom they mistook for a member of the City Food Supply Commission. Army units had to aid the police in dispersing the angry crowd, which demanded an increase in the grain ration. That same day several thousand Persian citizens stood outside the Persian consulate asking for either an increase in the ration or transportation back to Persia.[27]

In August the Food Supply Commission of Baku Province decided that the grain ration must be cut by one-quarter and that official searches for grain hoards should be organized. The soviet responded favorably to these suggestions, but before it could act the population of the city undertook its own efforts to alleviate the hunger in the city. On August 19, the day the grain ration was cut by a quarter, groups of workers began roaming the streets, invading the homes of those they suspected of hoarding grain.[28] The unorganized searches were the spontaneous reaction of one segment of the poorer classes to the latest and most severe crisis in supplies, but they took on an anti-Moslem tone when most of the searches were carried out

26 *Izvestiia*, no. 16, April 22, 1917.
27 *Kaspii*, no. 120, June 2, 1917.
28 *Baku*, no. 189, August 24, 1917.

against Moslems. On August 24, a meeting of three thousand Moslems at the Tazar-Pir Mosque adopted a resolution condemning the searches and protesting the discrimination against the homes of Moslems.[29] That same day the leaders of the political and labor organizations of the city met with workers to discuss the unorganized searches. A clear disagreement between the leadership and the volatile elements among the workers broke into the open. Workers called for the setting-up of a committee to supervise the searches, but the soviet delegates and political leaders opposed all such searches. Workers shouted from the floor, "You have all become completely bourgeois!"[30] Petrukhin, a worker and a former Socialist-Revolutionary who called himself the "representative of the hungry section," shouted: "They tell us to organize. Here we organized and came here hungry. And who has brought us to starvation? the authorities!"[31]

No decision was taken by the meeting, though all parties from the Bolsheviks to the Musavatists rejected the spontaneous searches. The Bolsheviks could not condone this "anarchistic" manifestation of discontent, and Shaumian in *Bakinskii rabochii* begged the workers to take more "conscious" action and protest against the war, which was the cause of their unhappiness.[32] But the transmutation of undirected discontent into political protest had only begun in August, and it would take the threat of counterrevolution in the *Kornilovshchina* and the general strike in September, as well as the worsening of the food situation, to convince the workers of Baku that they should advocate the seizure of power by their own class organs, the soviets.

News of the Kornilov threat to Petrograd and the formation of a military-revolutionary committee in the capital

[29] *Kaspii*, no. 190, August 25, 1917.
[30] *Izvestiia*, no. 120, August 26, 1917; *Baku*, no. 191, August 26, 1917.
[31] *Ibid.*
[32] *Bakinskii rabochii*, no. 44, August 25, 1917.

reached Baku on August 28. Immediately the representatives of the socialist parties met in a closed special session with the executive committee of the Baku soviet.[33] Without hesitation the meeting resolved to form a Bureau for the Struggle against Counterrevolution.[34] The Bolsheviks were wary of joining the Bureau, fearing that in the future it could be turned against deviants on the left as well as on the right; nevertheless, they joined. On the 30th the Baku soviet met to discuss the measures taken against the danger from the right. Under the pressures of the moment a dramatic shift to the left took place. Mandel'shtam, who considered himself a nonfactional Social Democrat, urged that the soviet "should revolutionize the masses."[35] The Bolsheviks, along with some Socialist-Revolutionary supporters, offered a resolution to transfer power to a special bureau of IKS members and representatives of the socialist parties. This bureau, unlike the one formed to fight counterrevolution, would operate independently of the IKOO as an arm of the soviet. The soviet members voted to accept this resolution.

The passage of the resolution was the first important political victory of the Bolsheviks in Baku, and the first demonstration of the new alliance between the Bolsheviks and the emerging Left Socialist Revolutionaries, who opposed their party majority on the questions of the coalition government and the war. The socialist Right, which had unquestionably controlled the soviet up to this time, was startled by the sudden turn of events, and impulsively retired the executive committee of the soviet and the two-day-old Bureau.[36]

[33] *Izvestiia*, no. 123, August 30, 1917; *Baku*, no. 195, September 1, 1917. The executive committee of the Baku soviet will be referred to by its initials, IKS (*Ispolnitel'nyi Komitet Soveta*).

[34] The Bureau had fifteen members: seven from the IKS; two each from the S.R.s, Bolsheviks, and Mensheviks; one Dashnak; and one from the trade unions (*ibid*).

[35] *Kaspii*, no. 195, September 1, 1917.

[36] *Baku*, no. 195, September 1, 1917.

While the significance of the Bolshevik victory was considerable, it should not be exaggerated. Of the 180 members of the soviet, only 69 were present on August 30 (23 workers' deputies, 46 soldiers'). The session had difficulty achieving a quorum, and the decision to retire the IKS was rash in view of the small number of deputies at the meeting.[37] This difficulty in attracting its members to meetings—from which the soviet had been suffering for some months—is significant in itself, however: enthusiasm for the soviet had reached a low point by late August. Bolsheviks blamed this deflation of interest in the soviet on the "conciliationist" line of its majority. In the short run the Bolshevik victory was unimportant, for two days later the soviet reversed its earlier decision, accepted the resolution of the old IKS, and reestablished the Bureau for the Struggle against Counterrevolution. But in the long run the split in the Socialist Revolutionary Party and the defection from the soviet majority of the workers' sympathy presented new opportunities to the Left.

By September the near-starvation of the poorer classes combined with their frustrations at inconclusive negotiations with the oil industrialists to create an explosive situation in the city. As the undirected searches for food turned against Moslem homes, crowds of angry Moslems took to the streets. On September 3, three thousand people in Sabunchiny gathered to protest against the food shortage, and in their resolutions they linked the crisis with the ineffectual policies of the IKOO, the duma, and the soviet and its executive committee. New elections to the soviet were specifically demanded.[38] A week later a crowd of Moslems terrorized the Balakhany food-supply committee.[39] In the soviet the next day a speaker reviewed the situation for the deputies:

[37] *Ibid.*
[38] *Bakinskii rabochii*, no. 49, September 6, 1917.
[39] *Izvestiia*, no. 132, September 10, 1917.

The population of Baku and the industrial districts feels extremely nervous about the supply problems. An intelligent attitude is noticeable among only a few. The dark forces are not sleeping and are using the situation being created to carry on hooligan agitation. Daily at the supply centers excited crowds gather, led by a few constantly active agitators, provoking the crowd to violence. Such phenomena are noticed in the industrial region. Crowds of uninformed Moslems appear with reproaches that no one cares about them. Behind them appears a crowd of similarly uninformed Russian women, claiming that it is mostly the Moslems about whom [the authorities] care.[40]

Once again hunger and economic stress had brought the national communities of Baku to the brink of racial war. No matter how complex or diffused the causes of the material crisis, the nationalities expressed their anger and frustration in the traditional hostility toward their ethnic enemies. Nationalism was the form that the expression of ill-understood economic and social problems took. When the blame was pinned on an Armenian or Russian or Azerbaijani, problems which had seemed rootless and eternal became comprehensible and capable of simple solution. The irony, of course, was that national animosity was not a solution at all but part of the problem. Baku was the victim of its own geography, its ethnic diversity, and the class divisions and hatreds bequeathed to the city in the decades of capitalist industrialization.

Spontaneous as these disorders were, it was impossible to distinguish the mood created by the food shortage from the disgust at the failure to negotiate the labor contract. Just as the hunger was indiscriminate in its victims, so the struggle for a contract had repercussions beyond the oil workers and their families. By September the whole city

[40] *Baku*, no. 204, September 13, 1917.

was in turmoil; the causes had faded into the past, and the authorities had lost control of the population. In a telegram to the Provisional Government, the Congress of Oil Industrialists described the general mood in the city:

> Starvation threatens the population of Baku and the oil-field districts with all its consequences. . . . In the oil-fields separate strikes have begun; workers demand bread, although the organization of the oil industrialists is completely uninvolved in the business of supplying food. The mood of the masses is threatening. Because of the hunger, not only is a full stoppage of work in the fields inevitable, but excesses and wrecking which will paralyze the whole industry for a long time. The moment is catastrophic in the full sense of the word.[41]

The industrialists pleaded for governmental intervention, especially for pressure on the north Caucasian authorities to send badly needed food to Baku.

The political shift to the Left which almost all political groups in Baku experienced in September and October was a response to the evident change of mood of the urban masses from reliance on the soviet leaders to spontaneous and often violent action. While hunger lay at the base of this new mood, the growing impatience of the workers with the industry's delay in signing a labor contract was another contributing factor. The labor movement had never been inactive in Baku, even in the dark years of the war, although labor organizations and professional leadership had almost disappeared after the 1914 strike and the subsequent arrests. With the February Revolution, the workers had first turned to setting up committees of representatives in each of their factories or oil-fields, reminiscent of the factory committees the workers had enjoyed up to 1908. Only after these local committees had sprung up

[41] *Izvestiia*, no. 134, September 13, 1917.

were the trade unions resurrected. On March 24, representatives of nonindustrial unions formed a Council of Trade Unions ("Sovprof," sometimes referred to as the Central Bureau of Trade Unions). This organ represented about thirty-two small unions and was under the influence of the Socialist Revolutionaries and Mensheviks.[42] Within the oil industry the workers were once again weakened by the formation of two separate unions: the Union of Oil Workers and the Union of Employees of the Oil Industry. (The latter union was formed sometime in March by office workers in the Nobel Plant in Black City, who thought it unwise to join with the workers of the plants and oilfields.)[43] The unions tended to concern themselves with local problems, at least until the September strike, and the Union of Oil Workers suffered from its constituents' belief that the factory committees satisfied their needs better than the unions.[44]

Besides the relatively weak trade unions, two other working-class organizations existed in the city as potential leaders of the economic struggle: the soviet and the conference of factory committees. Soviets were still a new phenomenon and their precise competence was still undefined. Trade-unionists resented soviet interference in economic affairs and argued that the soviet should restrict its activity to political matters.[45] In Baku, however, the soviet almost immediately engaged in the field of labor relations by setting up courts of conciliation (*primiritel'nye kamery*), to mediate minor labor–management disputes, and an arbitration commission (*soglasitel'naia kommissiia*), to which the soviet would send workers' representatives and IKOO would send representatives of the industrialists to

[42] A. Dubner, *Bakinskii proletariat v gody revoliutsii* (1917–1920 gg.) (Baku, 1931), p. 18.

[43] A. Nikishin, "Promyshlovo-zavodskie komitety i profsoiuzy v 1917–18 gg. v. Baku," *Iz Proshlogo* (Baku, 1924), pp. 57–59.

[44] *Ibid.*, p. 60.

[45] *Izvestiia*, no. 1, March 30, 1917.

negotiate disputes which otherwise might develop into strikes.[46]

Through these commissions the soviet kept its hand in the economic struggle. Reports filtered in from the local courts of conciliation on the principal areas of dissension within the labor community.[47] Workers felt that promises to pay wartime subsidies and bonuses had not been fulfilled. The engineers, as well as the workers, were disgusted with the failure to implement factory legislation to insure safety and improve the general conditions of work. The sometimes brusque treatment of employees by administrators was also resented.[48] These problems, and the difficulties caused by the fall in real wages, were taken up by a soviet commission to work out a project for a labor contract.

The soviet warned the workers not to enter into separate agreements with the industrialists as they had done in the past, since a "collective agreement," a labor contract for all of Baku, would be negotiated. The drillers, oppressed by their unbearable conditions, were especially likely to grasp at the straw of a separate strike or a separate agreement with the owners.[49] Yet another threat to unified action was the workers' old habit of accepting individual subsidies

[46] *Ibid.*, no. 3, April 1, 1917. Sahakian, Shaumian, and Aiollo were elected by the soviet to participate in the arbitration commission. The first meeting recognized the recently established courts of conciliation and approved the introduction of factory committees in the Baku oil districts. (*Ibid.*, no. 11, April 14, 1917.)

[47] The arbitration commission split over the question of the eight-hour day. The industrialists agreed to introduce it only in Baku district, not in the oil-fields, and the ship-owners rejected it as impractical. The IKOO then announced that it had accepted the eight-hour day in principle, though for the duration of the war overtime would be compulsory. (*Izvestiia*, no. 14, April 18, 1917.)

[48] *Ibid.*

[49] A special section of the soviet commission was formed to investigate the particularly noxious conditions of the workers in sixty-two drilling enterprises. They had demanded that their wages be raised to the level of the better-paid refinery workers. (*Ibid.*, no. 11, April 11, 1917.)

from their employees, rather than insisting on a general salary increase.

On May 22 Dzhaparidze went before the soviet to comment on the decisions of the commission to work out the labor contract. Wage demands, the commission had decided, were to be based on the 1914 level with increases to be made proportional to the rise in the cost of living. The soviet then elected a new commission to negotiate with the managers on the labor contract.[50] Pressure from a series of small strikes at the end of May reinforced the soviet's determination to carry through the labor contract. Printers, boiler-makers, tobacco workers, and the merchant marine struck for economic reasons, some specifically for the introduction of an eight-hour day which their bosses refused to grant.[51]

The new commission to negotiate a labor contract met on June 16 under the chairmanship of V. I. Frolov. From industry came representatives of the Union of Oil Industrialists, the Zafatem group (the Union of Plant, Factory and Technical Workshop Owners), and the smaller associations of industrialists. The workers were represented by soviet deputies, the Union of Oil Workers, the Unions of Employees and of Sailors, and the Central Bureau of Trade Unions. Before substantive matters could be discussed, the industrialists challenged the right of the soviet deputies to participate. The workers' delegation replied that, in view of the present weakness of the trade unions, the soviet had been forced to take on the negotiations for the labor contract. The industrialists reluctantly recognized the soviet as the spokesman for labor.[52]

Two weeks later, with few concrete decisions taken, the negotiations broke down completely. The Union of Kero-

---

[50] *Izvestiia*, no. 41, May 24, 1917.

[51] S. N. Belen'kii and A. Manvelov, *Revoliutsiia 1917 g. v Azerbaidzhane* (Baku, 1927), pp. 56, 58–59; *Izvestiia*, no. 51, June 4, 1917.

[52] *Izvestiia*, no. 73, July 2, 1917.

sine Factory Owners, along with the Ship Owners and Drilling Contractors, refused to participate in a general labor contract. The workers' delegation walked out of the meeting. The next day the soviet heard Dzhaparidze on the failure of the negotiations. He pointed out that the industrialists themselves were divided. The First Union of Oil Industrialists had agreed in part to the soviet proposition to raise all wages to 375 percent of their 1914 level, but the Second Union, made up of the smaller and more vulnerable companies, had rejected the rates proposed. The Second Union was joined by the drilling contractors and other plant-owners.[53] In the city the workers' excitement was reaching fever pitch. In Balakhany they arrested the director of the Caspian Company, and the soviet had to despatch three men to secure his release. Within the soviet a split developed between the more radical elements, who wanted the nationalization of the oil industry or at least a demonstration-strike, and the moderate elements who talked of appealing to the government in Tiflis or Petrograd to mediate the conflict. The soviet finally resolved to call a conference of factory committees and have that body decide on the question of a strike.[54]

The Unions of Baku Oil Industrialists shared the viewpoint of the moderates, like Ramishvili, and telegraphed Prince Lvov and the minister of labor, Skobelev, in Petrograd. They explained that the smaller firms could not satisfy the wage demands of their workers and continue to operate at a profit.[55] That same day (July 5) Ramishvili telegraphed Skobelev: "The negotiations for the labor contract between the workers and the entrepreneurs have been broken off. The entrepreneurs refuse to negotiate. A general strike is foreseen which is undesirable in view of the national significance of this industry. . . . Intervention

[53] *Ibid.*, no. 76, July 5, 1917.
[54] *Bakinskii rabochii*, no. 22, July 5, 1917; *Dok.*, pp. 48–49.
[55] Belen'kii and Manvelov, p. 75.

by the government is necessary."[56] Not until the end of the month did Ramishvili receive word that Skobelev was leaving for Baku.[57] By that time the situation had been complicated by actions taken by the factory committees.

As requested by the soviet the first conference of factory committees was held on July 6. These committees, the successors to the factory committees that were first set up in May 1905, had reappeared immediately after the February Revolution. Workers at the Nobel Plant, at A. I. Mantashev, and at S. M. Shibaev and Company were the first to elect plant commissions (*zavodskie komissii*). This simplest form of workers' organization spread until all of Baku and the industrial districts were organized in industrial plant commissions (*promyslovo-zavodskie komissii*). Every twenty-five workers elected one representative to the committee. The committees were uniquely responsive to workers' moods and desires because of the frequency of elections to them and their physical proximity to the workers. Not surprisingly, the Bolsheviks were energetic supporters of the factory committees, and the support of many workers, particularly in outlying districts for the Bolsheviks was reflected in the election of Bolsheviks to committee chairmanships. Shortly after the revolution the central factory committees in both Black City and White City, old Menshevik strongholds, elected Bolshevik chairmen.

As in central Russia, the factory committees in Baku mirrored the radicalization of the masses months earlier than the soviet. Their conferences that began in July were the most important forum for the Bolshevik party regulars. At the very first conference Dzhaparidze reported to the 607 delegates that the industrialists had been given three days in which to answer the workers' demands for resumption of negotiations for the labor contract. So far the industrialists had called the system of calculating the

56 *Ibid.*, p. 76.
57 *Izvestiia*, no. 102, August 2, 1917.

wage-rate increases unfair. The Second Union stated that it would agree to a rise in wages only if oil prices were raised. Overestimating the radical temper of the conference, Dzhaparidze called for a one-day work stoppage to show that the workers stood behind the soviet negotiators.[58] The Bolshevik resolution was defeated, and a milder Menshevik–Dashnak–Socialist-Revolutionary resolution— to have the labor contract put into effect by decree of the soviet and, if the oil industrialists did not respond, for the Provisional Government to decree a minimum wage—was adopted. The conference wished to resort to a strike only when all other means of struggle had been tried and proved unsuccessful.[59] Dzhaparidze in fury announced that the Bolsheviks would abdicate all responsibility for the labor contract in view of the victory of the "conciliatory" policy of the other socialist parties. He demonstratively announced his departure from the commission that was to negotiate the contract.[60]

At this point an energetic attack on the activity of the soviet and the role it was assuming was launched by the Council of Trade Unions, the conference of factory committees, and groups of workers. The Trade Union Council, led by Mensheviks and Socialist Revolutionaries, asserted on July 7 that all economic policy should be formulated by the council with the soviet acting only as a revolutionary and political instrument.[61] At the second conference of factory committees, the Bolshevik Melnikov said that the soviet was being distracted from its main task by involvement in the small problems of the economic

[58] *Ibid.*, no. 80, July 9, 1917.
[59] *Ibid.*, no. 79, July 8, 1917; *Baku*, no. 50, July 8, 1917.
[60] *Izvestiia*, no. 80, July 9, 1917.
[61] Belen'kii and Manvelov, p. 77. This Menshevik bid to increase the power of the trade unions vis-à-vis the soviet coincided with the Bolsheviks' effort to take the direction of the economic struggle away from the soviet, probably with the factory committees as the beneficiary. Similar conflicts among soviets, trade unions, and factory committees occurred in other parts of Russia.

struggle. He felt these matters could be dealt with by the Central Bureau of Trade Unions. Ivan Fioletov, a leading worker-Bolshevik, agreed with Melnikov and suggested that the soviet become either a purely trade-unionist body or a purely political organ, but not both.[62] Dzhaparidze, despite his recent display of disgust with the factory committees, made the radical suggestion that the conference of factory committees, not the trade unions, assume the leadership of the economic struggle:

> The Soviet is an organ of the whole revolutionary democracy, but the working class needs a class organization. In peaceful times this need is satisfied by trade unions, but a revolutionary time arbitrarily gives rise to new organizations. Such [an organization] is the conference [of factory committees], which ought to lead the economic struggle of the whole Baku proletariat. Such a conference already exists in Petrograd.[63]

The Mensheviks, aware of the strength of the Bolsheviks within factory committees, preferred the trade unions. Sadovskii suggested that factory committees enter trade unions as the basic cells and lead the economic struggle within the union movement. He feared that the conference of factory committees would support the Bolsheviks against the soviet line, as had already happened in Petrograd. The working class, he predicted, would be fractionalized, with some adhering to the soviet and others to the factory committees. The Bolsheviks, at this point, supported taking the economic struggle out of the hands of the soviet, but they were undecided whether to prefer the trade unions or the conference of factory committees. In the agitation for the labor contract it was the conference of factory committees that assumed the most im-

[62] *Izvestiia*, no. 83, July 13, 1917.
[63] *Ibid.*

portant role, while most of the actual negotiations were taken over by Ramishvili and Skobelev. Success, however, would elude all negotiators until the conference itself, led by Dzhaparidze, turned into the strike committee and led the workers against the oil industry.

Ramishvili's attempts to find an agreement acceptable to both the workers and the managers led him to initiate a commission specifically empowered to find a coefficient of the rise in the cost of living on which the wage-rates could be based.[64] The commission was given two weeks to complete its work. After calculations by both sides, the industrialists proposed to raise wages 50 percent. The workers, however, decided that, to keep pace with the cost of living, wages should immediately be doubled.[65] Ramishvili reported to the conference of factory committees on July 21 that the cost of living had actually risen 475 percent since 1914. Since it had been determined that wages had increased much less than half as much as the cost of living (by September 1917, wages had increased only 178 percent over 1913 for the Nobel workers, probably the highest-paid group in the city), even the workers' demand was conservative and would not quite raise the real wage of even the best-paid workers to the 1914 level.[66] As negotiations dragged on and prices continued to rise, the proposed wage-increases became daily less advantageous to the workers.

Nevertheless, two weeks later the commissar of labor announced to the public that the commission had decided on the 50 percent increase. The labor leaders were, indeed, making most modest demands. At the same time Ramishvili called for more time to negotiate with the industrialists, for the original time-limit had long run out. The

---

[64] *Ibid.*, no. 82, July 12, 1917; Ia. A. Ratgauzer, *Bor'ba bakinskogo proletariata za kollektivnyi dogovor 1917 g.* (Baku, 1927), p. 41.
[65] Belen'kii and Manvelov, p. 83.          [66] Dubner, p. 24.

conference stormed against the proposal, and delegates called for taking the matter to the masses.[67] Their patience had worn thin. But after the initial excitement subsided, the conference resolved to let Ramishvili's commission continue its work. Even the Bolsheviks favored negotiations rather than an immediate strike at this point. All parties stood committed to negotiations for the time being.

On July 26 negotiations resumed, and the meeting continued far into the night. At four in the morning the delegates dispersed with no agreement. The First Union of Oil Industrialists expressed its willingness to recognize a labor contract effective from April 1 and to pay a two-month advance on the basis of the 50 percent increase, but only if oil prices were raised. The Second Union and the drilling-contractors refused to introduce a labor contract until the price-raise had been effected.[68] On receiving the news of the stalemate, the IKS telegraphed Petrograd to send a delegation with full powers to settle the dispute.[69] A conference of workers from the oil-fields could hardly be kept under control by Ramishvili, who struggled to keep them from striking and to confine their energies to telegraphing Petrograd for intervention.[70]

In the face of the industrialists' obstinacy, the Bolsheviks met on July 30 to analyze their tactic vis-à-vis the general line of the soviet and the conference of factory committees. The Baku Bolsheviks feared that the "reactionary trend" that was gripping Petrograd, where the Bolshevik leaders were under arrest if not in hiding, would soon reach Baku. They were, therefore, notably cautious in their proposals. A Left minority called for short demonstration-strikes but was disregarded. Fioletov

---

[67] *Bakinskii rabochii*, no. 31, July 26, 1917.
[68] *Izvestiia*, no. 96, July 27, 1917.
[69] *Bakinskii rabochii*, no. 32, July 28, 1917.
[70] *Kaspii*, no. 167, July 28, 1917.

reasoned that intervention by the central government was the only solution. Petrograd, he argued, should "syndical-ize" the small and large companies, or simply create a state monopoly over the whole industry.[71] But Shaumian's moderate proposal was adopted by the conference as the tactic for the party: to reject calls for a strike, in view of the unfavorable political and economic situation, and to call on the most "advanced" workers to explain the situa-tion to the others. In the event of a spontaneous strike, however, the Bolsheviks should take the most active part in it in order to give the movement an organized charac-ter. This two-pronged approach in effect became the tactic of the Bolsheviks in Baku in August and September, the period of the most rapid expansion of their popularity and influence. Bolshevik success in these months was the result of the coincidence of the party's tactical stance and the interests of the workers. The hope of the Right so-cialists lay in the success of the negotiations carried on by the government. Once these failed, a strike was in-evitable, and equally inevitable was Bolshevik leadership of that strike.

Matvei Ivanovich Skobelev (1885–1930?), minister of labor in the first coalition government, arrived in Baku as trouble-shooter for the Provisional Government. He was determined to stem the tide toward a general strike. For five furious days (August 4–9) he rushed from conference to meeting to private conversation, taking a middle po-sition between two sides with irreconcilable points of view. He tried to identify with the workers but came down heavily on the side of the industrialists. He told the con-ference of factory committees: "In the spring of 1912 I left the city of Baku as a newly elected member of the Social-Democratic faction of the Fourth Duma. When a few days ago I approached Baku, I wanted to feel myself, not a representative of the government, but as your com-

[71] *Bakinskii rabochii*, no. 34, August 2, 1917; *Dok.*, pp. 76–78.

rade working with you in the name of the revolution."[72] His solution was simply to adjourn the negotiations to Petrograd and there calmly settle the matter.

Skobelev told the workers that the country was fast approaching a financial crisis, one of the causes of which was the drop in productivity of labor. In his view to ask for higher wages at this time would be inflationary and harmful.[73] To the soviet and the IKOO he explained that he would make sure that the workers received at least the minimum necessary for their existence and promised that the price of oil would not be raised unless the rise in wages was so great as to warrant it. Skobelev soon realized that the workers were firmly committed to receiving an increase of at least 50 percent and could not be easily dissuaded. By the end of his stay in Baku he came out in support of that figure.[74] Meanwhile the industrialists had agreed to raise wages according to that figure if oil prices were raised. A basis for agreement seemed at hand.

Besides wages, agreement over the issue of authority over hiring and firing remained a key to the final agreement, and here Skobelev was notably sympathetic to the managers' viewpoint:

> The entrepreneur will bear the responsibility for the correct operation of the enterprise. . . . He answers not only before the authorities but also before third persons for losses and disorder. It is natural that it is his inalienable right to hire, fire, and transfer employees and workers at his own discretion. . . . The right to hire without any limitations ought to remain with the employer. . . . The government stands firmly on this. . . . The worker has one means to fight the employer—to

---

[72] *Izvestiia*, no. 108, August 11, 1917.
[73] *Ibid.*, no. 104, August 6, 1917; *Baku*, no. 175, August 6, 1917; *Kaspii*, no. 175, August 6, 1917.
[74] Belen'kii and Manvelov, p. 95.

leave work, and this, in its turn, is the inalienable right of the worker. . . . The labor contract can not take away anyone's private or public rights.[75]

The workers' representatives had earlier decided that hiring and firing, although the prerogative of the owners, should be carried out with the participation of the trade unions and factory committees, which should have the right to reject those hired without their consent. Skobelev addressed himself to this demand of the workers by arguing that, while such an arrangement is desirable, it would be difficult to require that the employers hire only from the unions. On August 9 the conference of factory committees accepted Skobelev's plan to adjourn the negotiations to Petrograd, and that same day the minister left for the north.[76] This seemed to be the only remaining alternative to a strike.

Hopes were raised for an early settlement of the conflict, which was now entering its sixth month, but tensions within the industry had reached the breaking-point and there was no way to restrain individual strikes by groups of workers. In August workers from the Nobel plants, the Neft Company, and the Zafatem enterprises left work. Dock workers, munition workers, more workers from the Zafatem group of firms walked out in the first two weeks of September. With Mandel'shtam's return to Baku the final rounds of negotiations began. They too soon ground to a halt. The oil industrialists balked at relinquishing their complete control over the hiring and firing of employees.[77]

[75] *Ibid.*, p. 94.

[76] *Izvestiia*, no. 108, August 11, 1917. Mandel'shtam, of the workers' soviet, made the trip to Petrograd also, but the industrialists hesitated and then refused to send a plenipotentiary. The discussions took place in the capital, nevertheless, with the government and officials of the oil companies resident in Petrograd.

[77] *Ibid.*, no. 143, September 26, 1917. After agreeing to sign a contract in Petrograd, the oil companies had the price of oil raised

On September 16, a conference of factory committees met jointly with the executive committee of the soviet and listened to a report on the breakdown of the negotiations. Many of the audience called for an immediate strike; others shouted that systematic terror should be directed against the industrialists. Fioletov, speaking as a member of the arbitration commission, cautioned the workers against the use of terror and was shouted down. Angrily he replied: "To whom are you shouting, 'Down!'? For fifteen years I have defended the interests of the workers, and, except for becoming a cripple, have received nothing for it. Against whom will you carry on terror? Here in Baku live only the directors of the plants, the owners are abroad."[78] The Bolsheviks opposed a strike at this time, since the industry had large stocks of oil to fall back on and the workers could not carry on a lengthy walkout.[79] The conference ended by deciding to continue the negotiations until September 22, at which time an ultimatum would be issued and the industrialists given five days in which to accept it or face a strike. The gauntlet had been thrown down.

Each of the major political parties viewed the impending strike as a potential disaster in view of the economic condition of the city, but the wave of spontaneous strikes and the violence expressed in speeches by workers at the conferences indicated to the political leadership of the "democracy" that the alternative to economic suicide would be political suicide. The Dashnaks opposed an immediate strike, but conceded that after all efforts had failed a strike was inevitable.[80] The Mensheviks and Socialist Rev-

---

from September 1, not from the day of the final signature. Thus it was in their interest to delay the final signing of the contract, which no longer had any effect on the price of oil.

[78] *Baku*, no. 208, September 19, 1917.
[79] *Kaspii*, no. 208, September 19, 1917.
[80] *Izvestiia*, no. 141, September 23, 1917.

olutionaries were also cautious but ready to accede to the pressure from the workers.[81] Even the Musavat was prepared to support the strike. The Bolsheviks took the line that a strike would be a disaster, and that a suitable alternative would be the immediate nationalization of the oil industry by government decree. But if the workers decided on a strike, the conference should lead it. Dzhaparidze feared that "the masses will go past us," and on September 21 he proposed that the conference be declared a strike committee. The proposal was adopted by a large majority.[82]

The strike began at seven in the morning of September 27, 1917. Of the 610 firms that were affected, the workers in 554 (numbering 52,920) struck specifically because the industrialists had refused to sign the labor contract. Another 12,355 workers struck because of the refusal of their administrations to pay the two-month advance or for other reasons.[83] The strike lasted six days, causing the loss of 405,623 worker-days, and was carried on with exemplary order. Gegechkori assured the strike leaders that the legal parts of the labor agreement could be decreed into law by the Ozakom.[84] After three days of the strike a delegation of industrialists left Baku for Tiflis and discussions with the Ozakom on the labor contract.[85]

By October 1 the main items of the labor contract had been accepted by the industrialists, particularly a scale of

[81] *Ibid.; Baku*, no. 211, September 22, 1917.

[82] *Izvestiia*, no. 141, September 23, 1917. On September 22, the conference, now calling itself the strike committee, set the strike for September 27 (*ibid.*, no. 142, September 24, 1917).

[83] Dubner, p. 30. The conference decided that during the strike the army, the fleet, and all cities would be supplied with oil. Although the great majority of the workers rallied around the conference's call for a strike, the port workers, the Caspian fleet, a meeting of regimental committees, the Cossacks, the Union of Engineers and Technicians, and the railroad workers opposed it. (*Kaspii*, no. 214, September 26, 1917.)

[84] *Bakinskii rabochii*, no. 59, September 29, 1917.

[85] *Kaspii*, no. 219, October 1, 1917.

minimum wages ranging from 4r. 35k. to 11r. 75k. a day for the various categories of workers. Many workers wanted to continue the strike until all thirteen points of the workers' ultimatum had been secured, but the moderates appealed for an end to it. Ramishvili pleaded:

> With great joy I came to this meeting; I wanted to congratulate you on your victory, although you have beaten not only the capitalists but me too who was all the time against the strike. But I hear here speeches which dim my joy. Not all of you consider the victory enough. It's not necessary to dissipate our strength, it's not necessary to continue the strike out of blind stubbornness; now it is necessary to end it. That's how true warriors of the working class should act.[86]

The conference decided that local meetings should decide on the question of stopping the strike and that their decisions would be considered at the next meeting. Dzhaparidze summed up the nature of the workers' victory:

> Our first and principal victory is our organization. This strike proved that we are strong because of our being well organized. There's a famous saying—give me a fulcrum and I will overturn the whole world. It can be paraphrased: give me an organization of workers and I will overturn the whole capitalist world. ... Our second victory is the recognition of a single labor contract for all workers and employees.[87]

On October 2 the industrialists finally agreed to accept the preliminary conditions for the labor contract, and the conference-turned-strike-committee announced the end of the strike. In the euphoria that greeted the victory the workers wildly cheered Ramishvili's efforts in the negotiations, as well as Dzhaparidze's leadership of the strike

[86] *Izvestiia*, no. 150, October 3, 1917.
[87] *Ibid.*

committee. The Bolsheviks greeted the victory as a decisive defeat for the conciliatory policy of their political rivals. The strike had indeed changed forever the balance of political power in Baku. A more radical and uncompromising working class faced a hostile and discredited bourgeoisie, a bourgeoisie—it should be emphasized—whose power survived only as long as it was tolerated by the revolutionary parties.

The political response of the soviet to the continuing crisis was, on the whole, inadequate, and in turn, tended to worsen the situation. The workers looked for new leadership in the factory committees and in the strike committee. The political orientation of Baku had made a complete about-face since July, when Bolshevik orators were shouted down at street meetings. In early September Bolshevik resolutions were passing easily in the factory committees and other workers' gatherings. Whereas in July workers had wanted unity in the ranks of the "revolutionary democracy," by September there were suggestions that the "conciliatory" tactic of the Right socialists was at the root of the crisis. The Bolsheviks hoped to have this new mood of the workers reflected in the soviet, and called for elections. Early in September Shaumian wrote in *Bakinskii rabochii*:

> Our soviet is perishing! It must be treated and cured. It is necessary to demand new elections. . . .
> We do not propose this because we think that our party can constitute at present a majority. It's true that there is a significant shift to the left in the ranks of the workers. The collapse of the defensist and conciliationist policy of the Mensheviks and S.R.s, the treacherous character of the slander on the Bolsheviks, and, finally, the Kadet–Kornilov counterrevolutionary conspiracy could not but act on the minds of the

workers. The influence of the Bolsheviks and S.R.-Internationalists grows rapidly. But we would prefer in the interests of our party not to hurry and to wait yet a little longer. However, the terrible picture of demoralization and disintegration to which misters Mandel'shtam, Aiollo, and their followers have led the soviet demand the most immediate and decisive measures for its cure.[88]

On September 6, Shaumian proposed a plan by which every five hundred workers or soldiers would elect one deputy, and the soviet approved the formation of a commission to work out procedures for the new elections.[89] The lack of popular confidence in the old soviet was recognized by its members, who now hoped that the organ of the "revolutionary democracy" could be revitalized through new elections.[90]

While the Baku soviet responded to the radicalization of the masses with notable caution, with no more than a call for new elections, the conference of factory committees, then deeply engaged in the struggle for a labor contract, adopted a Bolshevik resolution which condemned the "conciliatory" tactic of the Right socialist parties. The resolution also demanded the transfer of all power to the

[88] *Bakinskii rabochii*, no. 43, September 3, 1917; Shaumian, II, pp. 84-85.

[89] *Izvestiia*, no. 130, September 7, 1917.

[90] In earlier elections to the soviet every ten officers had been allowed to elect one deputy, and consequently the military was overrepresented, especially the officer corps. In making the elections more equitable, the Bolsheviks hoped to have the leftward trends in the electorate more accurately reflected in the soviet. Even in the old soviet this trend was somewhat evident. At the September 6 session the deputies elected two Left S.R.s (Sukhartsev and the soldier Abramovich) to the forthcoming Democratic Conference in Petrograd. The three remaining delegates to the conference were chosen by the IKOO, since the duma had not yet been "democratically" elected. They were Shaumian, Belavin (Left S.R.), and Kagramanian (Menshevik-Defensist). (*Izvestiia*, no. 130, September 7, 1917; *Bakinskii rabochii*, no. 50, September 8, 1917.)

revolutionary democracy, the end of the war, the arming of the people, the liberation of all Bolsheviks and Internationalists arrested in central Russia, and the abolition of the death penalty. In connection with the financial debacle, the conference of September 18 called for the abolition of private property, workers' control over industry, and the nationalization of large industry. Mandel'shtam and the Mensheviks criticized the resolutions, but to no avail. The conference was the most Bolshevized organ in the city of Baku.[91] Evident in its decisions was the leftist trend in which the workers of Baku had been caught up, a trend to which each of the political parties in the city had to accommodate itself.

Shaumian described the general radicalization of the "revolutionary democracy" in a letter to *Rabochii put'*:

> The Bolshevization noticeable in all of Russia
> has appeared in the widest dimensions in our oil
> empire. And long before the *Kornilovshchina*. The
> former masters of the situation, the Mensheviks, are
> not able to show themselves in the workers' districts.
> Along with the Bolsheviks the S.R.-Internationalists
> have begun to get stronger. They have become so
> strong that they have topped the defensists in their
> own party, and have formed a bloc with the Bolsheviks
> in the Soviet of Workers' Deputies and in the districts.
> The Mensheviks are completely isolated. It must be said
> that after the Bolsheviks tossed them off, only the
> most right-wing, definitely Kadetist elements remained
> in the ranks of the Mensheviks.
>
> Even the sharp turn made by the Tiflis Mensheviks
> headed by Zhordaniia, expressing themselves
> unanimously opposed to any kind of coalition with the
> bourgeoisie and for the immediate end of the war and

[91] *Bakinskii rabochii*, no. 55, September 20, 1917; *Izvestiia*, no. 139, September 21, 1917.

the taking of power together with the S.R.s in the Caucasus, has not had any effect on the Baku Mensheviks.[92]

The leftist position of the Tiflis Mensheviks, supporting a government of all socialist parties (including the Bolsheviks), was the only feasible alternative to a Bolshevik seizure of power.[93] The Baku Mensheviks, however, made no leftward adjustment in their political program until the eve of the October Revolution. They remained the most conservative socialist party throughout 1917 and on the right wing of Russian Menshevism. As late as October 19, after the Transcaucasian congress of Men-

[92] *Rabochii put'* (Petrograd), no. 10, September 14, 1917.

[93] The Tiflis soviet, the Territorial Center of Transcaucasian Soviets, and the *Oblastnoi Komitet* of the RSDRP, all controlled by the Georgian Mensheviks, had been drawn steadily to the left by the events of the spring and summer of 1917. The first divergence between the followers of Zhordaniia and the Menshevik leadership in Russia occurred in May, when Zhordaniia denounced the decision of the Russian Mensheviks to join the coalition government. Later that month, at the First Congress of Soviets of Transcaucasia, Zhordaniia said:

> The entrance into the Coalition ministry is a great mistake for the proletariat. . . . As representatives of the proletariat, the socialist ministers cannot refuse to put through the social demands presented to them by their class; otherwise it will turn away from them. But, by putting them through, they push the bourgeoisie into the camp of the counterrevolution. Entering the ministry puts the socialists before an insoluble dilemma. (S. E. Sef, *Bor'ba za Oktiabr'* . . . , pp. 37–38.)

But Zhordaniia went on to say that, since the coalition was already an accomplished fact, the Transcaucasian Mensheviks would support it as long as it followed the "path of democracy" (*ibid.*, p. 38). In September, Zhordaniia proposed that an end be put to the collaboration with the bourgeoisie and that power should be given to a government made up of the "revolutionary democracy" from the Populist Socialists to the Bolsheviks (*Bakinskii rabochii*, no. 50, September 8, 1917). By the time the Democratic Conference met in Petrograd on September 14, a near-majority of Mensheviks opposed coalition in any form, and a large majority opposed coalition with the Kadets (Noi Zhordaniia, *Maia Zhizn'* [Stanford, Calif., 1968], pp. 77–78).

sheviks had adopted Zhordaniia's resolution to form a government of the "revolutionary democracy" and deny confidence to the present coalition, the Baku Mensheviks were unable to rally around Zhordaniia's position. Sadovskii held out for the old policy of supporting the coalition, while I. Ramishvili and A. Khachiev called for acceptance of the congress's resolution, bolstering their argument with citations of poor attendance at Menshevik preelection meetings. There was no doubt that the Mensheviks' rigidity in refusing to break with the coalition government even as it was being discredited in the eyes of the "democracy" was responsible for the rapid falling-off in Menshevik influence among the workers. Only on October 23 did the Baku Committee of Mensheviks vote (8–5, with one abstention) to accept Zhordaniia's strategic principle.[94] The lateness of the hour was apparent to all, and the subsequent events in Petrograd so altered the political order that the Mensheviks in Baku reverted soon after to their former position supporting collaboration with the Right.

The Socialist Revolutionary Party too suffered an internal crisis as a result of the leftward trend of the workers. On September 2, the day after the soviet readopted the Socialist-Revolutionary–Menshevik–Dashnak resolution on the current movement, the Bibi-Eibat local committee of the Socialist-Revolutionary organization resolved to support the Bolshevik resolution of August 30, and called for new elections to the soviet and the establishment of a firm democratic authority in Baku based on the soviet. Although the committee supported the Provisional Government as well, the tenor of the resolution was clearly far to the left of the Socialist Revolutionary majority and close to the Bolshevik position.[95] Later in the month the

[94] Belen'kii and Manvelov, p. 175.
[95] Izvestiia, no. 128, September 5, 1917.

Baku council of Socialist Revolutionaries met to elect a new party committee. At that meeting the council could not form a majority to support a resolution of the Central Executive Committee of Soviets, another indication of the leftist strength within the Socialist-Revolutionary organization. At this point, however, the Left Socialist Revolutionaries could not get the organization to adopt their resolution.[96]

Throughout Transcaucasia the Socialist Revolutionaries were by September losing their predominant position among the Russian soldiers. At the First Congress of Soldiers in Transcaucasia, the Socialist Revolutionaries had managed to have their plank on "socialization of land" adopted and gained control of the territorial council of the Congress.[97] But by September the Tiflis garrison was no longer a Socialist-Revolutionary stronghold and was turning into a Bolshevik one. Only the soldiers at the front were free from Bolshevik influence, thanks to the restrictions on Bolshevik agitators established by the Tiflis authorities. In Baku the soldiers had been meeting regularly on Freedom Square since July, listening to anyone not afraid to take the podium. The meetings started in the heat of the afternoon and went on until midnight. Most popular of the speakers was the young commandant of Baku, Osip Avakian, a nonfactional Social Democrat who in the course of the summer gravitated closer to the Bolsheviks. The oratorical battles on Freedom Square were as decisive as any other part of the political struggle in Baku, for they would ultimately decide which party would win the support of the Baku garrison. Earlier in the year the soldiers were overwhelmingly defensist and supported the Socialist-Revolutionary position. But by September

[96] The S.R. committee included Ter-Oganian, Maria Sundukiants, Mitskevich, Belavin, Nikitin, Tobel'berg, Israfil'bekov, Kasparov, Pavlov, Liaia Loiko, Velunts, Sukhartsev, Krestovskii, and Afanas'ev (*ibid.*, no. 134, September 13, 1917).

[97] Sef, *Bor'ba za Oktiabr'* . . . , pp. 39–40.

Avakian and his audience were responding sympathetically to the Bolshevik slogans. Only the officer corps and the
Armenian volunteer bands continued to support the war.[98]
More representative of the majority of the soldiers was
the Baku United Socialist Military Organization, now the
chief mouthpiece of the soldiers apart from their elected
soviet deputies. On September 10, the Military Organization, which was left of the soldiers' section of the soviet,
called a meeting of soldiers on Freedom Square which
adopted a series of Bolshevik resolutions.[99] The soldiers
demanded an immediate break with the bourgeoisie, the
purging of the military command of counterrevolutionary
elements, the abolition of the death penalty (which Kerensky had reestablished), "All Power to the Soviets," the transfer of land to the peasantry, and a "decisive struggle for
bread and peace for suffering, laboring humanity." The
next day the Organization asked the IKS to allow agitators
from all revolutionary groups free access to the military
ranks to spread their programs.[100] By the end of September
Avakian could assure the Bolsheviks: "The soldier is on

[98] A poll taken at the end of September among the officers of the
Caucasian Army revealed the following declarations of party allegiance. Of the 13 generals, 95 staff officers, and 1,248 other officers who answered the poll, there was only one who called himself
a Bolshevik. The rest answered as follows:

| Kadets | 336 |
|---|---|
| Mensheviks | 263 |
| S.R.s | 227 |
| Plekhanovites | 201 |
| National parties | 152 |
| Trudoviki | 86 |
| Monarchists | 16 |
| Maximalists | 2 |
| Nonpolitical | 75 |

(*Izvestiia*, no. 150, October 3, 1917).

[99] *Bakinskii rabochii*, no. 52, September 13, 1917.

[100] The decision of the Military Organization referred to a controversy which had arisen shortly after the Kornilov affair. The
soviet had appointed the officer Melnikov commissar of the Baku
garrison, and the new commissar drew up a list of conditions to
insure discipline in the army. Melnikov declared that the soldiers

the outside a Socialist Revolutionary, but inside he is a Bolshevik."[101]

Even after losing their hold over the garrison, the Socialist Revolutionaries managed to maintain their influence in the Caspian Fleet, despite Bolshevik inroads. The sailors' newspaper, *Volna*, was edited by the Sukhartsev, a Left Socialist Revolutionary, but Right Socialist-Revolutionary influence was strong in the sailors' union and its executive, Tsentrokaspii. The chairman of Tsentrokaspii was the Georgian naval doctor, Turkiia (S.R.), who, along with his lieutenant Nadzharov (S.R.), was extremely popular among sailors of the commercial fleet. The Bolsheviks enjoyed support among the dock and arsenal workers particularly, and the military fleet wavered between the Socialist Revolutionaries and the Bolsheviks.[102]

The Moslem leaders too had reached the end of their patience with the soviet majority that had consistently demonstrated its willingness to underrepresent the Moslem citizens of Baku. The Musavatist newspaper, *Achizsoz*, blamed the socialists for not securing representation of the Moslems more energetically:

The leftist parties, having taken in their hands the organization of the revolutionary government, have in their first moves made a great mistake. This mistake is

---

had had enough of meetings and politics, that the time had come to end the disruptive influence of Freedom Square. These ill-considered remarks led to an attack on Melnikov by Shaumian. Even before the Bolshevik attack was published, Melnikov was removed from his position and transferred to a less controversial post in the Food Supply Commission. (*Bakinskii rabochii*, no. 49, September 6, 1917.)

101 *Ibid.*, no. 61, October 4, 1917.

102 Baikov, p. 105. A disturbing anomaly for the Left socialist parties in Baku was the Naval Aviation School, which served as a base for monarchists and Kadets, as well as for refugees from the defeated Kornilov forces. It remained a center of counterrevolution until the fall of Baku to the Turks. (N. N. Lishin, *Na kaspiiskom more: Gody beloi bor'by* [Prague, 1938], p. 7.)

the lack of attention paid to the local population,
in this case the Moslems who make up the majority.
This is expressed in the absence of representatives
of Moslems in significant local organizations, like the
IKOO, the Soviet of Workers' Deputies, etc. In some
organizations which have less importance Moslem
representatives have entered in a meaningless minority,
and in the more important have not entered at all.[103]

Both Topchibashev, a Kadet, and the Musavatist Resul
Zade denounced the Kornilov mutiny and linked it with the
policy of the soviet leadership, which "has made great
mistakes by giving in on important questions to reactionary circles."[104] On September 8, the executive committee
of the Baku soviet denied the Musavat a seat in the Bureau for the Struggle against Counterrevolution, thus
further alienating the Moslem leadership from the socialist majority. It is not surprising then that at this time the
Musavatists began to move closer to the Bolsheviks both
on the issue of the war and on the question of Moslem
rights.[105]

[103] Reprinted in *Kaspii*, no. 117, May 30, 1917.
[104] *Ibid.*, no. 197, September 3, 1917. Although the Moslems supported the Provisional Government, they had on a number of occasions made known their dissatisfaction with its handling of
Moslem affairs. In July the Baku Moslem National Council had
protested the creation of a commissariat of Caucasian affairs in
Petrograd, headed by a Russian, Vladimir Nabokov, assisted by an
Armenian, Evangulov. (*Ibid.*, no. 154, July 15, 1917.) They also requested that General Averianov, governor of Turkish Armenia, be
given a Moslem assistant (B. Ishkhanian, *Hakaheghapokhakan
sharzhume Andrkovkasum* [*Bagvi aryunahegh antskeri aritov*]
[Baku, 1918], p. 46).
[105] The Moslem Council was being pressured by its worker constituents to democratize itself. On September 4, G.-bek Akhundov
reported that Moslem workers had demanded thirty-five places in
the Council. (*Kaspii*, no. 199, September 6, 1917.) But the next day,
when the elections for the Council's executive committee were held,
workers did not participate. Narimanov protested and asked for the
postponement of the elections. But the Council accepted the motion of Resul Zade to the effect that the committee should later be

Midway through 1917 the Moslem leadership in Baku shifted from supporting the military effort made by the Provisional Government to a radical criticism of the war. In May the Committee of Baku Moslem Public Organizations had issued a proclamation which reluctantly admitted that "we cannot yet stop the war." Although all wanted peace, it said, with the enemy in their land they could not lay down arms.[106] As for Moslem participation in the war and in all future wars, the First All-Russian Moslem Congress had called for the establishment of national Moslem military units with Moslem officers.[107] The proposal was also adopted by the Moslem Military Congress in Kazan in July;[108] but the Provisional Government did not approve the formation of such units until well into October. Until August Moslem leaders, except for the Hummetists, supported the war, as did the Mensheviks, the Socialist Revolutionaries, and the Dashnaks. But by September the Musavat had reversed its position and forcefully expressed its displeasure with the war: "This failure, without a doubt, lies in the lack of boldness to recognize frankly that Russia is already not in a condition to continue this aimless war. This realization is not the fruit of faintheartedness and the closing of eyes to the interests of the country, but comes from the most active and real interests of the revolution, the republic, the motherland,

---

enlarged to include representatives of the workers and peasants. (*Ibid.*, no. 200, September 7, 1917.) The thirty-five-man committee elected that day included all the prominent liberal and Musavat leaders, Topchibashev, Resul Zade, Khan-Khoiskii, Dzhevanshir, Gadzhinskii, etc., but lacked the left wing of the Moslem community, the Hummet and Birlik parties. These groups favored the disbanding of the Moslem National Council and an alliance of the Moslems with the multinational "democracy." (*Dok.*, pp. 125–126; *Hummet*, no. 11, September 12, 1917.)

[106] *Kavkazskii telegraf*, no. 29, May 23, 1917.

[107] S. M. Dimanshtein (ed.), *Revoliutsiia i natsional'nyi vopros*, III (Moscow, 1930), p. 299.

[108] *Ibid.*, pp. 313–314.

and democracy."[109] This change in attitude made the Musavatists the natural allies of the Bolsheviks on the war issue, though the nationalist rhetoric of the Moslems discouraged the Bolsheviks from close cooperation with Resul Zade and his followers. What was less clear at this moment, but would emerge in a few months as the principal component in Musavat policy, was the party's renewed commitment to an alliance not with the antiwar socialists but with the Ottoman Turks. Freed from their wartime Russian orientation, the Musavatists in the last months of 1917 reasserted the traditional Ottoman orientation which in the prewar years had marked the formation of Azerbaijani nationalism.

Musavat was attracted by the Leninist slogan of "self-determination for all nationalities" and saw in it a basis for cooperation with the Bolsheviks. At the October congress of their party, the Musavat leader Resul Zade reiterated his interest in autonomy for Moslems.[110] The conflict between the Marxist notion of class warfare and the nationalist ideal of the unity of all classes of one nationality was underplayed. Musavat believed that self-determination in eastern Transcaucasia could lead only to Moslem dominance, since the Azerbaijanis were the vast majority of the population; so if the Bolsheviks kept their pledge, then it would be Musavat which would tolerate the Bolsheviks and not vice versa. As long as the Bolsheviks

[109] From *Achiz-soz*, the Musavat newspaper in Baku; reprinted in *Kaspii*, no. 208, September 19, 1917.

[110] M. D. Guseinov, *Tiurkskaia demokraticheskaia partiia federalistov "Musavat" v proshlom i v nastoiashchem*, I: programma i taktika (Tiflis, 1927), p. 30. The outstanding issue between the old Turkish Federalists of Elisavetpol and the Baku Musavatists—the agrarian question—was finally resolved at the October congress in favor of the Federalists. The Federalists favored government purchase of private estates for distribution to the peasants, while the Musavatists wanted outright expropriation of land. The tensions between the Right and the Left in the new Musavat party continued to be felt through the period of the Azerbaijani Republic (1918–1920).

advocated national self-determination and were committed to ending the war, a tacit understanding between the RSDRP(b) and Musavat kept mutual criticism at a minimum.

While remaining the most radical political party in Baku, the local Bolsheviks were more moderate than the Leninists in Petrograd. Shaumian's caution may have been rooted in fears that the launching of a civil war in Baku would trigger off interethnic hostilities. Or he may have carefully calculated the resources of the Baku Bolsheviks and concluded that without a majority in the Soviet and support from the local garrison a seizure of power was unthinkable. In any case, his caution was not shared by all the members of his party. A. Karinian, then a member of the Baku organization, remembers:

A small group of "leftists" that existed in the Baku organization often criticized the leaders of the organization for excessive caution and insisted on taking more "decisive" measures. The most brilliant opponent of this group was always Comrade Dzhaparidze, who referred to the fact that the civil war in Baku, in view of the disorganization of the proletariat and the presence of national units, will inevitably take on a national tone and in this way slow down the tempo of the workers' movement.[111]

Dzhaparidze was Baku's chief delegate to the Sixth Congress of the RSDRP(b), held in Petrograd from July 26 to August 3. There he opposed Stalin's suggestion that the party withdraw the slogan "All Power to the Soviets." Stalin, as Lenin's spokesman in this case, argued that the Central Executive Committee of the Soviets had joined the counterrevolution and that a peaceful transfer of power to

111 S. G. Shaumian, *Stat'i i rechi, 1902–1918 gg.* (Baku, 1924), introductory article by A. Karinian, pp. 25–26.

the soviets was now impossible. Only armed insurrection could assure the establishment of the dictatorship of the proletariat and poor peasantry. Dzhaparidze countered with an argument based on experience in Baku:

> If earlier the provincial soviets expressed the views of the TsIK, now they do not reflect its attitudes. For instance, in Baku, despite the fact that we are not able to win elections, despite the fact that in a soviet of three hundred workers' and military deputies there are only 20–25 Bolsheviks, all our resolutions passed and we actually dominated until July 3–5. This shows that the line recommended by our TsK was brilliantly carried out and served the function of sobering the masses.[112]

The congress did drop the slogan, and Baku Bolsheviks stopped speaking about the transfer of power to the soviets and instead spoke about the need for the proletariat to change the soviets from without. Basically, however, the Bolshevik tactic in Baku did not change. Through pressure on nonparty delegates the Bolsheviks continued to have resolutions passed within the soviet on specific local issues, though they could not bring the soviet around to accepting the Bolshevik analysis of the current situation. Early in September the Bolsheviks succeeded in convincing the soviet that new elections were imperative. The soviets would be reformed by their constituents.

Once the radicalization of the workers and soldiers had become apparent, the Baku Bolsheviks did not hesitate to echo their comrades in the capital and call for a seizure of power by the "revolutionary democracy." On September 12, Dzhaparidze told a conference of Bolsheviks: "If up to this time we have talked about the transfer of power into the hands of the revolutionary democracy, from now on

[112] *Shestoi s"ezd RSDRP (bol'shevikov). Avgust 1917 goda: Protokoly* (Moscow, 1958), p. 125.

we are going to speak of conquest."[113] Two weeks later the Bolsheviks adopted a resolution which read: "The transfer of power to the democracy cannot be accomplished without a struggle, for which the party should be preparing."[114] The Bolsheviks were confident that their increased influence could be translated easily into political power. At the First Congress of Bolshevik Organizations of the Caucasus, which met at the beginning of October, Shaumian clarified the new militancy of the Bolsheviks:

> After July 3–5, it was possible to speak only of the conquest of power, not of its transfer.
> The new government created real anarchy; we cannot remain calm in such a situation. Recognizing that the influence of the Bolsheviks is gaining in many soviets, that even the peasantry is being Bolshevized, that the Ukrainians and even the headquarters of the Mensheviks—Transcaucasia—are expressing themselves against the coalition, finally that unrest is growing everywhere, and land is being seized, etc., our task is to stand at the head of the revolution and to take power into our own hands. . . .
> Despite all the responsibility we will take on ourselves, not fearing the difficulties and complexities of the work, [we must] go forward boldly toward our tasks which life has given us, and having taken power into our hands carry the revolution to its victorious end. (stormy applause)[115]

The Baku Bolsheviks, like most of the other leading political parties in the city, had been stimulated by the new radical stance of the masses to shift to a more militant position. In September and October they called for a

[113] *Bakinskii rabochii*, no. 54, September 18, 1917.
[114] *Ibid.*, no. 61, October 4, 1917.
[115] *Kavkazskii rabochii* (Tiflis), no. 170, October 11, 1917; Shaumian, II, pp. 101–102.

seizure of power by their party. Yet within the city their deeds did not match their words. If their tactics were measured by what they did, then the Baku Bolsheviks, like most of Lenin's comrades in the Central Committee, remained more moderate than Lenin. Despite the radical rhetoric of September and October, Shaumian and his comrades continued to act as if they sought a peaceful transfer of power to the soviets. Their hesitation to use the Bolshevized garrison in September and October to take power delayed the Bolshevik seizure for six months.

# 5

# October in Baku

WHILE IN THE NORTH Lenin was writing frantic letters
to his Bolshevik Central Committee urging it to seize
power in Petrograd, the Bolsheviks of Baku were cau-
tiously maneuvering the local soviet into a declaration of
soviet power. Shaumian managed in the space of one
month to reelect the soviet's executive committee (with
himself as chairman once again), expand the soviet's
membership by introducing delegates from the Bolshevized
conference of factory committees, and eliminate two rivals
of soviet power—the newly formed Committee of Public
Safety and the IKOO. In this way the Bolsheviks achieved
predominance in the local soviet without ever winning a
majority in elections, and persuaded the soviet to declare
itself sovereign in the city without firing a shot. Shaumian's strategy of "peaceful transition" to socialism appeared briefly to be bearing fruit.

The working class, which had demonstrated exemplary
organization and energy in the September strike, began
after October to betray disinterest and lethargy. Whereas
during the first period of the revolution—February to October—the workers had rallied around the soviet and the
strike committee in the united effort to win a contract,
in the period from October to January those workers who
had benefited most from the labor contract began to lose
their interest in radical political change. During the last
months of 1917 it was not the oil workers as a group but
the Moslem poor who most often took to the streets to
protest the failure of the municipal authorities to relieve
the food shortage.

The labor leaders of Baku had proclaimed the victory of the September strike once the industry had been brought to sign the "preliminary agreement" on October 2. The struggle seemed to have closed with an unconditional surrender on the part of the industrialists, and the need to go beyond collective bargaining toward nationalization seemed to have disappeared. The workers were prepared to work within the capitalist system for the time being, rather than risk upsetting the structure which provided them with their livelihood. However, the owners of the industry were unwilling to implement the conditions to which they had agreed, and began a series of delaying moves which prevented the drawing-up of a final edition of the contract. Questions of salary for certain categories of qualified workers, the eight-hour day, and rights over hiring and firing still had to be decided.[1]

[1] The Baku strike committee insisted that the labor contract be issued as a legal decree by the Ozakom, and had secured an assurance from Gegechkori and Bekzadian that Tiflis would oblige. But the Ozakom balked at the suggestion and sent the matter to Petrograd. The conference of factory committees protested the delay and despatched Dzhaparidze and Fioletov to Tiflis to press for the decree. (*Izvestiia*, no. 157, October 11, 1917.) Meanwhile the Provisional Government also refused to act and threw the ball back to Tiflis. With all exits blocked, the Ozakom issued the decree which set the rules for hiring and firing. Until the creation of a labor exchange in Baku (in February 1918) employers were to hire and fire at their discretion but were supposed to give preference to candidates suggested by the trade unions. Factory committees, as well as the unions, had the right to protest individual firings, and conflicts were to be referred to a court of conciliation. Workers could not be laid off without a two-week notice, and mass layoffs had to be channeled through a special control commission. (*Bakinskii rabochii*, no. 66, October 15, 1917.) The factory-owners in Baku energetically resisted these limitations on their prerogative. The Unions of Oil Industrialists, along with the Union of Drilling Contractors and of the Zafatem, declared that the Ozakom's decree had put the industry in "an impossible position" and petitioned Petrograd to reexamine and invalidate the decree. When a few days later the Provisional Government fell, the Ozakom lost its authority and the Baku industrialists simply ignored the decree. (S. S. Aliiarov, "Primenialsia li fakticheski kollektivnyi dogovor bakinskikh rabochikh 1917 g.," *Istoriia SSSR*, no. 1 [1966], p. 113.)

Despite these delays, individual agreements between managers and workers, based on the norms of the labor contract, raised wages for most workers by the end of October. This first appreciable result of the labor contract was soon wiped out by the rapid rise in prices. But basing wages on the labor contract did reduce the differentials among workers originating in the system of payment that had characterized the Baku proletariat from its formation.[2]

Negotiations between the industry and the workers continued in the sessions of the editing commission. The industry, Fioletov reported to the soviet on November 24, had retracted its agreement to pay according to the new rates and had decided to wait until the new government in Transcaucasia would permit a rise in the price of oil.[3] Deputies, angered and frustrated by the industry's arbitrary actions, called for sterner measures, for the arrest of capitalists, for throwing them into the Caspian. Fioletov clarified the conflict by pointing out that once again it was the smaller companies which refused to raise wages, not Nobel and the companies of the First Union. The IKS had sent a telegram to Tiflis requesting that the price of oil should not be raised without consent from the Baku soviet. Fioletov concluded by threatening that "If the oil industrialists do not agree to our demands, then we will take the operation of the industry into our own hands. If it turns out that we do not have the money to pay the workers, then we shall turn to Petrograd, to the Council of People's Commissars, and they will send us money."[4] The soviet responded to the Bolsheviks' militancy by issuing a three-day ultimatum to the industrialists, threatening a new general strike unless the labor contract were signed.[5]

Confidently the industrialists rejected the soviet's ultimatum. The central strike committee, instead of following

2 *Ibid.*, pp. 117–119.
3 *Kaspii*, no. 258, November 25, 1917.
4 *Ibid.*
5 *Izvestiia*, no. 195, November 28, 1917.

through on the soviet's threat, resolved to hold the workers back from striking.[6] The committee sought to sidetrack the capitalists and appealed to the new soviet government in Petrograd to speed up the decision to nationalize the oil industry and shipping. The committee also threatened with arrest industrialists unwilling to sign the contract, and called for "control over production." The majority of the strike committee, by voting against a strike, in effect deprived the workers of their most powerful weapon against the industrialists. A minority, led by the Bolshevik Sahak Ter-Gabrielian, disagreed with Dzhaparidze and proposed a one-day demonstration-strike. Dzhaparidze feared disorganization within the ranks of the workers, and on December 11 he managed to convince the "broadened" soviet to support the majority in strike committee. At that session the soviet unilaterally issued the labor contract in its own edition, turned the central strike committee into a central control committee, and authorized that committee and the IKS to implement the labor contract even if it meant using force. The soviet also joined the central strike committee in recommending to the Sovnarkom that nationalization of the oil industry be seriously considered as the ultimate solution.[7]

Although the contract was now law, the industrialists refused to recognize the soviet's edition. The First Union supported its own version of the contract. The soviet's writ did not run through all classes in Baku. Nevertheless, by the end of 1917, workers in individual factories and fields had themselves established an eight-hour day and forced the management to recognize the rights of the factory committees in hiring and firing. Conflicts remained, but for all practical purposes the workers had taken what they had won in the September strike. Baku delegates to

[6] *Ibid.*, no. 198, December 1, 1917.
[7] *Ibid.*, no. 208, December 14, 1917; *Bakinskii rabochii*, no. 106, December 14, 1917; *Dok.*, pp. 218–219.

the First All-Russian Congress of Trade Unions could affirm that the eight-hour day and the powers of the factory committees had been realized.[8]

While it may have been true that wages were more often than not paid according to the rates agreed to in the labor contract, the steady rise of prices made real wages decline. The contract had specified a rise of 50 percent, but food prices alone rose 125 percent in 1917.[9] Dubner estimates that real wages in January 1918 were only 30–35 percent of prewar wages, and that by March they had fallen to 15–20 percent. Companies frequently failed to pay workers at all because of the chronic shortage of banknotes in the city. In February a series of one-day strikes broke out to protest both the lack of bread and the absence of paper money.[10] Once wages had been brought into line with the norms of the labor contract, by January 1918, the rate of the decline in real wages increased, so that in the first months of 1918 the workers' condition deteriorated at a rapid rate. Simultaneously the food shortage, now a permanent feature in Baku's economic life, was making the strains on the workers as unbearable as they had been in September 1917. The brief stabilization of the workers' condition had ended by January, and a new period of economic distress and political turmoil began.

The victory of the workers in the September strike coincided with the breakdown of legal authority within Baku. No organ in the city, not even the soviet, could exercise control over the population. The duma had not yet been democratically reorganized and so was left to deliberate about the forthcoming elections. The IKOO had witnessed the steady loss of its prerogatives to the soviet, which either acted independently of it or determined IKOO

[8] Aliiarov, "Primenialsia li fakticheski . . . ," p. 115.
[9] A. Dubner, *Bakinskii proletariat v gody revoliutsii (1917–1920 gg.)* (Baku, 1931), p. 52.
[10] *Ibid.*, p. 53.

policy through its majority there. The first political shake-up to follow the strike revealed the true nature of the IKOO as a façade for soviet actions. On October 4, two days after the industrialists agreed to the oil workers' terms, the Council of Baku Public Organizations met to discuss the retirement of V. I. Frolov, chairman of the IKOO. During the strike Frolov, a Plekhanovite Social Democrat, had taken it upon himself to publish a series of articles opposing the September strike as a crime against the motherland in a time of national danger. Frolov had affirmed that class interests should be subordinated to state interests.[11] The soviet leaders who had supported and directed the strike were determined to use this opportunity to get rid of Frolov, who on numerous occasions had expressed concern at the soviet's increase in power. At the council session, Frolov rose to defend his actions:

> Today marks exactly seven months since in the city of Baku the first revolutionary act after the overthrow [of the tsar] was accomplished. Seven months ago in Baku the first revolutionary official was appointed, replacing the local mayor. And that official was I, Frolov. And today I, appointed later the chairman of the IKOO, am forced to announce my retirement. The cause of retirement is not fatigue, not illness, not any such cause. No, I must say that I do not go willingly into retirement, rather I have been retired. Who retired me? The Soviet of Workers' and Soldiers' Deputies, its executive committee, and other democratic organizations. This is all the more surprising since in the past these same organizations gave me full confidence and support.
> ... The history of these relations [of the soviet to the IKOO] is a history of a "million torments." The responsibilities placed on the chairman by society were

11 *Baku*, no. 216, September 28, 1917; *Ibid.*, no. 220, October 3, 1917.

great, but in reality he was powerless. He was only a
veil behind which hid the soviet of deputies, in the most
unceremonious way usurping the rights of the IKOO.
The IKOO alone considered itself a government and, in
fact, it was no such thing.[12]

Frolov had been angered by arrests of people by committees not duly authorized by the IKOO. Mandel'shtam of the
soviet executive committee defended these arrests of, as
he put it, "spies and police agents," who could not be
turned over to the courts on which the revolutionary
democracy had no representation.[13] Mandel'shtam's defense of supralegal means to enforce a notion of class
justice expressed one of the basic assumptions of the Left
that Frolov could not share. Frolov preferred the legal
standards of the liberals, by which duly constituted authority must be obeyed, while the socialists, who based
their understanding on the Marxist axiom that law and
legal institutions themselves were reflections of the class
structure of a society, felt little obligation to turn over
class enemies to organs of enemy classes.

Mensheviks and Socialist Revolutionaries, as well as
Bolsheviks, attacked Frolov and voted for his replacement
by A. P. Nikitin, an engineer. The dismissal of Frolov
inevitably raised the central question of where power
should lie in Baku, and Dzhaparidze exploited the moment
to call for "All Power to the Soviets" and for a government
of the working class. Frolov, he said, was the ideologue
of the coalition government. And the Socialist Revolutionary Sahakian supported the Bolshevik suggestion that the
soviets should establish some kind of government, though
he remained vague on the specifics of how that could be
accomplished.[14] The conclusions of the Bolsheviks and the
Socialist Revolutionaries thus diametrically opposed those

[12] *Ibid.*, no. 223, October 6, 1917.
[13] *Ibid.*
[14] *Izvestiia*, no. 153, October 6, 1917.

of Frolov, of the Kadets who supported him but kept silent, and of the Mensheviks. The Left wanted to establish a soviet hegemony in Baku, while the Right feared rule by the socialists alone.

To establish soviet power in Baku the soviet itself had first to want to take power. In a word, the soviet had to be "Bolshevized." In contrast to the Bolsheviks in Petrograd and Moscow, who succeeded in gaining majorities in the local soviets, the Bolshevik party in Baku, while enjoying a disproportionate influence, could not win a numerical majority. Only extraparliamentary techniques could achieve what elections had failed to bring. On October 13, after several hours of waiting for a quorum, Mandel'shtam opened the session of the soviet to discuss the composition of the executive committee (IKS). Both the IKS and its presidium had demanded the dismissal of the deputy Avakian for his "antirevolutionary" and disruptive activities among the soldiers.[15] Shaumian seized the opportunity to call for the retirement of the IKS, and the soviet followed his lead and voted to dismiss its leadership. Mandel'shtam, furious at the turn of events, declared that he was walking out of the soviet. That same evening a meeting of "socialist parties and democratic organizations" elected a temporary executive committee

[15] Avakian was a militant revolutionary, not a member of the Bolshevik Party at this time, who in the fall of 1917 frequently made speeches on Freedom Square condemning the "conciliatory" leadership of the Baku soviet. Mandel'shtam accused Avakian of changing "fronts," at one time embracing General Sokolovskii, the commander on the Caucasian Front, and later cursing him. The newspaper *Baku* systematically attacked Avakian. When in the soviet debate Shaumian rose to defend Avakian, Mandel'shtam blurted out: "Comrade Shaumian kissed General Sokolovskii." With the debate reduced to this personal level, Shaumian answered: "Yes . . . I had the pleasure of kissing General Sokolovskii. This was on the holiday of the revolution. He gave such a revolutionary speech that I thought—what is left for me to say after his words. After my speech the general came up to me and kissed me. I could not knock him off the platform. But, suppose, that I myself had kissed him. What of it? Does this constitute counterrevolution?" (*Kaspii,* no. 231, October 13, 1917.)

with Shaumian as chairman.[16] Thus, in a matter of hours, the Bolsheviks had brought about the retirement of the old executive committee and had elected a new one, all on the seemingly insignificant issue of Avakian's participation in the old IKS.

Two days later ninety-nine soviet deputies met with members of district soviets, factory committees, and military organizations, altogether 371 delegates. Shaumian announced that a quorum for a valid soviet session had not been reached and that the conference would have to decide if it considered itself entitled to elect delegates to the forthcoming congress of soviets. The Menshevik Sadovskii opposed such a move, but the Left Socialist Revolutionary Sukhartsev declared: "We don't have a soviet, but the pitiful remnants of one. I recognize that our conference is sufficiently authoritative and competent to elect and send delegates."[17] The vast majority of the conference voted to elect the delegates, with only fifteen delegates opposed. The conference then went on to censure the Democratic Conference in Petrograd and adopted, by a vote of 238–55, Shaumian's resolution to the effect that power now rested with the counterrevolutionary bourgeoisie and should pass into the hands of the soviets in order that a constituent assembly might be called.[18] Thus, ten days before the seizure of power in Petrograd, the Baku "conference of the broadened soviet" had voted for the transfer of all power to the soviets, and this had been accomplished in a body which did not have a Bolshevik majority. The new "broadened" soviet had given the Baku Bolsheviks their single greatest political triumph since the revolution began. After months in political limbo

---

[16] The temporary executive committee included S. Frolov (Menshevik), Vasin (S.R.), and Arakelian (Dashnak) from the workers' section. Semenov (Bolshevik), Iaryshev, and Iashkevich represented the soldiers' section. Representatives of the political parties and nine delegates from the United Socialist Military Organization were added to the committee. (*Ibid.*)

[17] *Izvestiia*, no. 162, October 17, 1917.     [18] *Ibid.*

Shaumian and his comrades had managed to harness the energies of the workers and soldiers of the city and identify them with the slogans of the Bolshevik party. The Bolsheviks alone of the major political parties offered an alternative to the impasse out of which the coalition was incapable of leading the country. Baku's resolution was aimed not just at a political solution for local conditions but at dealing with the crisis which gripped the entire country. At no time, however, did the soviet support the Bolsheviks in attacking what Lenin saw as the source of that crisis, namely the war.

The Bolsheviks enjoyed a rare feeling of great confidence after the soviet session of October 15. But their hopes for a Bolshevik majority were dashed quite soon in the elections to the soviet held on the 22nd. The results were inconclusive, except in so far as they indicated overwhelming and previously unsuspected support for the Musavat. In all industrial districts, except Zabrat, the Musavat won a plurality, outdrawing the Bolsheviks.[19] The only published results of the elections are far from complete, but they reveal the following totals:

| Musavat | 8,147 |
| Socialist Revolutionaries | 6,305 |
| Dashnaks | 5,289 |
| Bolsheviks | 3,883 |
| Mensheviks | 687[20] |

The Bolsheviks responded by refusing to recognize the elections as valid, claiming that there had been many infractions of the election laws.[21] The "broadened" soviet continued to meet; the Musavat victory was canceled; and arrangements were made to hold new elections.

In the weeks before the Bolshevik coup in Petrograd,

[19] *Kaspii*, no. 239, October 25, 1917.
[20] *Ibid.*; *Izvestiia*, no. 170, October 27, 1917; S. N. Belen'kii and A. Manvelov, *Revoliutsiia 1917 g. v Azerbaidzhane* (Baku, 1927), p. 171.
[21] *Bakinskii rabochii*, no. 71, October 27, 1917.

the likelihood of an insurrection against the Provisional Government was felt both in the capitals and in Transcaucasia. The Bolsheviks made no secret of their intentions, though the precise time of the insurrection was not known even to Shaumian and Dzhaparidze.[22] On October 19, Shaumian spoke about the coming insurrection:

> We must be prepared for all circumstances. Tomorrow
> or the day after tomorrow it is possible we may read
> telegrams that in the streets of Petrograd revolutionary
> seizures are taking place. . . .
> We must support our comrades in the center, and
> when they take power in the center, in the capital, we
> ought to take power in the provinces. And this we can
> do only by leaning on the workers and soldiers. We
> could take power here now. We only have to blow, and
> all these chairmen of various committees, commissars,
> commissions, etc., will disappear. But we must wait for
> the seizure of power in the center, since without this
> the seizure of power in the provinces would be worthless.
> And for this we must be prepared.[23]

At that same meeting Avakian assured the Bolsheviks that the Baku garrison was ready to follow them. The military, as well as the most active elements in the working class, had been radicalized to the point where they were willing to follow the Bolsheviks to a seizure of power in the name of the revolutionary democracy.

The news of the Bolshevik-led insurrection in Petrograd was relayed to Baku on October 26. The new temporary executive committee of the soviet met with the committees

[22] Shaumian, as a member of the Central Committee of the RSDRP(b), had attended several of its meetings in September in Petrograd, including the meeting of September 15 at which Lenin's letters calling for an armed insurrection were discussed. But he had left Petrograd before the October 10 meeting at which a majority had voted for preparing the insurrection. (*Protokoly tsentral'nogo komiteta RSDRP[b]. Avgust 1917–Fevral' 1918* [Moscow, 1958], pp. 55, 85–86.)

[23] *Baku*, no. 236, October 21, 1917.

of socialist parties, the strike committee, and the trade unions, and was joined by other "democratic" organizations.[24] Shaumian opened the meeting at 11 p.m. and declared that the executive committee was opposed to the formation of any new organ to fight "counterrevolution." The Bolshevik Zevin tried to have the question transferred to the conference of the "broadened" soviet for resolution, but the assembled representatives voted down his proposal by a 26-vote majority, with only fourteen voting for the Bolshevik proposal.[25] Shaumian recognized the danger his executive committee faced from the Right socialists, but he refused to relinquish any of its rights. The executive committee, he claimed, was responsible only to the "broadened" soviet. Shaumian's position was challenged by Mitskevich, speaking for the Socialist-Revolutionary–Menshevik–Dashnak bloc, who claimed that the temporary executive committee was competent only in questions of reelections to the soviet and minor trade-union and organizational questions. The leading political role, he declared, should be played by a committee to be organized to work with the IKOO against counterrevolution. Several resolutions were put before the meeting: among them were a Bolshevik resolution to support the new government in Petrograd and expand the rights of the Baku soviet, and the resolution of the three united socialist parties, to support revolutionary order, fight counterrevolution, and guard the gains of the revolution, by forming a new revolutionary organ. The Bolshevik resolution was defeated by a vote of 13 for and 18 against with 4 abstentions, while the Dashnak–Menshevik–Socialist-Revolutionary motion passed, 21–12. A Committee of Public Safety was formed with representatives from the soviet, the political parties, the trade unions, Tsentrokaspii, etc.[26] Its purpose ostensibly was to

[24] *Kaspii*, no. 241, October 27, 1918.

[25] *Izvestiia*, no. 173, October 31, 1917.

[26] The presidium of the Committee of Public Safety included Shaumian (Bolshevik), Denezhkin (S.R.), Bekzadian (S.R.), and

keep order in the city and establish control over all public and governmental bodies. Its real purpose was to prevent a Bolshevik take-over of Baku.[27]

The temporary setback for the Bolsheviks was reflected in the soviet the next day. The socialist parties feared the outbreak of civil war, and though Dzhaparidze tried to reassure them that "there will be no civil war here," the Baku "broadened" soviet voted (248–166 with 3 abstentions) to accept the socialist bloc's resolution calling for the "peaceful liquidation" of the October Revolution. This was the second rebuff dealt to the Bolsheviks by the socialist bloc, and, as Shaumian pointed out, it completely reversed the October 15 decision of the "broadened" soviet calling for a transfer of power to the soviet. The insurrection in Petrograd had frightened the Baku soviet and forced it to reconsider its earlier commitment to the transfer of power to the soviets. Ramishvili stated: "We, Mensheviks and Socialist Revolutionaries, never were opposed to what our comrades, the Bolsheviks, demanded, but we always affirmed that their demand was placed too early."[28] This setback to the Bolsheviks proved to be of short duration. On the last day of the month the discussion of where power should lie in Baku again divided the conference of the "broadened" soviet. Over thirty resolutions were offered from the floor. Chairman Shaumian proposed that instead of voting on all of them the Bolshevik resolution rejected on October 27 be reconsidered. The conference voted 279–25, with 58 abstentions, to accept the Bolshevik position: "Supporting the newly reformed government on an all-Russian scale, in opposition to the bourgeoisie and the Kaledinites, the 'broadened' Baku soviet finds it imperative to put before itself the task of widen-

---

Rabinovich (Menshevik). Shaumian never served on the committee despite his appointment. (*Ibid.*)

27 *Ibid.*; *Baku*, no. 245, November 1, 1917.

28 *Baku*, no. 242, October 28, 1917.

ing the power of the soviet in the Baku district right up to the transfer of all power into its hands."[29] The Baku soviet, after accepting and then rejecting the notion of soviet power, had once again recognized the principle; the indecisiveness was the result of the wavering within the large Socialist-Revolutionary faction and among the nonparty deputies. The reality of soviet power in Baku had yet to be achieved. Yet the Bolsheviks by the end of October had revealed that they were the single most influential party in Baku. It was only a matter of time before that influence would be turned into political power, for the Bolshevik constituency was one that could make its small numbers felt even more effectively than its opponents in the majority. The Bolsheviks by the end of October were the undisputed masters both of the conference of factory committees and, more significantly, of the Baku garrison. Victory at the polls, however, continued to elude them.

In the midst of the crisis over soviet power in Baku, the scheduled elections to the city duma, so long delayed, were held. Once again the results of the voting did not correspond with the actual balance of political power within the city.

| party | votes | % of total |
|---|---|---|
| Moslem National Parties | 18,384 | 25.25 |
| Socialist Bloc (Mensheviks & Socialist Revolutionaries) | 17,523 | 24.05 |
| Armenian National Parties | 13,120 | 20.17 |
| Bolsheviks | 11,202 | 15.37 |
| Kadets | 4,172 | 6.06 |
| Jewish National Parties | 2,393 | 3.25 |
| Total | 72,808 | 94.15[30] |

[29] *Izvestiia*, no. 175, November 2, 1917; *Dok.*, p. 183; Shaumian, II, pp. 109–110.

[30] *Kaspii*, no. 263, December 1, 1917. Of the 104 duma members elected, thirty-eight were Armenian, thirty-one Moslem, nineteen Russian, twelve Jewish, three Polish, and two Georgian (*Baku*, no.

The Bolsheviks, as in the earlier elections to the soviet, retained 15–16 percent of the vote, but in the absence of any other party having a clear majority or even a significant plurality the Bolsheviks emerged as a significant faction within the city duma. No single party had won as many votes as the Bolsheviks, though three blocs had achieved higher totals. The Bolshevik faction of nineteen delegates was the largest in the "democratically elected duma." But the elections reveal a more significant phenomenon, and one later to be confirmed in the elections to the constituent assembly: the extent of Bolshevik support among the soldiers. Of the 3,093 soldiers who voted, 2,675 voted Bolshevik. Avakian's boast about the Baku garrison's being on the side of the Bolsheviks had not been an idle one, and this fact made the outcome of the struggle for power in the city less dependent on the results of elections than on the disposition of physical strength. It was not how many supported a party, but who they were.

The crisis in the soviet did not end at the October 31 session with the defeat of the Right socialists and the disbandment of the Committee of Public Safety. When, at the "broadened" soviet's next session on November 2, Shaumian raised the question of how the transfer of power to the soviets could be practically arranged, the Right socialists dramatically demonstrated their opposition by walking out of the soviet[31]—an act that paralleled the

---

246, November 2, 1917). Of the final duma membership, twenty-five were professionally employed as agronomists, statisticians, etc.; twenty-three were lawyers, twelve were engineers and chemists, eleven were doctors, eleven more were members of other professions; ten were teachers, seven were industrialists and merchants; and six were journalists (*ibid.*). The duma, thus, was overwhelmingly made up of professional men, of the technical and legal intelligentsia.

[31] Speaking in the name of the Mensheviks, Right S.R.s, and Dashnaks, the Menshevik deputy N. Atebekov read the following resolution.

1. The performance of the Bolsheviks and the seizure of power by the Petrograd Soviet and garrison, carried out against the will

walkout of their party comrades from the Second Congress of Soviets in Petrograd a few days before.

The socialist bloc refused to recognize the legitimacy of the "broadened" soviet, which was completely dominated by the Bolsheviks and Left Socialist Revolutionaries. The next day their protest took organizational form when the Committee of Public Safety was recreated, this time without the Bolsheviks, and began to publish its own newspaper.[32] The Bolsheviks, disturbed but not daunted by the turn of events, proceeded immediately after the walkout to reconstitute the soviet. Of 468 deputies present at the beginning of the November 2 session, 344 remained after the walkout. The party breakdown was as follows:

---

of the majority of the organized revolutionary democracy, we consider harmful and destructive for the revolution and the cause of the working class. This act ought to be liquidated as soon and as painlessly as possible.

2. The Congress of Soviets, after the walkout by the whole delegation from the Front and the representatives of all the socialist parties except the Bolsheviks, is not considered by us to be a Congress of Soviets but rather a conference of the Bolshevik members of the Congress.

3. In so far as the Temporary Executive Committee of the Baku Soviet of Workers' and Soldiers' Deputies began to execute a seizure of power here in Baku, the [three] parties, not wanting to bear the responsibility for the consequences of this disastrous step, recall their representatives from the Temporary Executive Committee and its organs and propose to the members of our organizations not to join such [organs].

4. We demand that the Central Electoral Committee, having recognized that the elections to the Soviet of Workers' and Soldiers' Deputies were legal, immediately call the newly elected Soviet into session and concern itself with the carrying-out of elections in those districts where elections have not yet been held.

5. We propose to all members of our party organizations to walk out of this meeting immediately.

(*Izvestiia*, no. 177, November 4, 1917; Belen'kii and Manvelov, p. 187.)

[32] *Kaspii*, no. 248, November 4, 1917.

Bolsheviks
| | |
|---|---|
| Worker Bolsheviks | 91 |
| Sympathizers | 47 |
| Soldier Bolsheviks | 31 |
| Sympathizers | 62 |
| Total | 231 |
| Left Socialist Revolutionaries | 84 |
| Menshevik-Internationalists | 6 |
| Dashnak | 1 |
| Nonparty workers | 8 |
| Nonparty soldiers | 14[33] |

The rump "broadened" soviet declared itself legitimate, and set about electing a new executive committee of seven Bolsheviks, six Left Socialist Revolutionaries, ten soldiers, and four sailors.[34] The reelected chairman, Stepan Shaumian, spoke about the need to concentrate all military power in the soviet with the barely tolerable IKOO playing only an economic role. He welcomed the "purging" of the soviet of the coalitionist elements, envisioning a future with less resistance from the moderates in the "revolutionary democracy."

Perhaps among us there are less intellectual workers than among those running away from us, but to make up for it we have a more healthy sense, knowledge of the real people's life, the ability to resolve problems of the moment from the practical side, which demands less waste of strength and means and gives the most positive results in a given situation. The direct and definite democratic policy which the Soviet undertakes today, free from obstacles and obstructions, I hope, will arouse the spontaneous activity of the members of the Soviet and of those masses of the population which

[33] *Bakinskii rabochii*, no. 80, November 9, 1917.
[34] *Izvestiia*, no. 177, November 4, 1917.

(163)

invested them with their confidence. The slight loss of *rabotniki* [here, party workers] will be made up by the general inspiration, by the awakening of selfless activity of those healthy and powerful creative forces of the lower classes [*narodnye nizy*] that up to this time have slumbered because they did not have room to make their appearance.[35]

By the second week of November the attempt by the socialist bloc to set up an authoritative organ to counter the soviet had come to nought. The Committee of Public Safety was not immediately dissolved, but the worker members of the Right socialist parties themselves opposed the walkout from the soviet and the schism in the democracy. The Right socialists had indeed suffered a decisive defeat, for they had lost control of the soviet in October and lost the possibility of establishing another revolutionary center to oppose the now Bolshevized "broadened" soviet. The Socialist Revolutionaries had also precipitated a crisis within their own party which led within a few months to the defection of the left wing. The Socialist Revolutionaries and Dashnaks by the end of the year recognized the inevitable victory of soviet power. The Mensheviks, on the other hand, moved farther to the right and joined the Kadets in supporting the city duma as the legitimate government of Baku.

Although factional difficulties had been evident within the Socialist Revolutionary Party long before they were manifested in public debates in August, the Baku organization had managed to retain a degree of organizational unity. But with the October Revolution and the walkout of the socialist bloc from the soviet, the Left Socialist Revolutionaries, no longer willing to submit to party discipline, remained within the soviet. The Baku Committee of Socialist Revolutionaries declared on November 4 that

[35] *Ibid.*, no. 178, November 5, 1917; Belen'kii and Manvelov, p. 187.

it could take no responsibility for the "broadened" soviet and recalled its representatives in that body. But on the same day the Council of the Baku Organization took the opposite position: that a return by the Socialist Revolutionaries to the soviet was imperative.[36] While the committee was in the hands of the older party members who stood on the right of the party, the majority of the council was on the left.

The Baku Socialist Revolutionaries met to resolve their internal differences in November 1917 only to discover that the party was split in three. About half the organization sympathized with the achievements of the October Revolution and could be considered Left Socialist Revolutionaries. Another group was sympathetic to the leftists but wished to prevent a party schism; and a small minority maintained its anti-Bolshevik posture.[37] On November 14 the Left Socialist Revolutionaries issued a call for a separate party on the Petrograd model.[38] On December 1 an organizational meeting was held by the leftists, and within a week the rump council of the Socialist Revolutionaries officially expelled Sukhartsev, Tumanian, and their comrades.[39]

Other groups within the city sided with the Bolshevized soviet against the Committee of Public Safety. The pro-soviet Bolsheviks and Left Socialist Revolutionaries were joined by the small group of Menshevik-Internationalists, who denounced the Committee of Public Safety and called for all parties to recognize the soviet as the "representative of the will of the revolutionary socialist democracy." But the Menshevik-Internationalists did ask their Bolshevik comrades to work for the unity of all socialist parties willing to break with the bourgeoisie; and, in their appeal

[36] Belen'kii and Manvelov, pp. 190–191.
[37] Ia. A. Ratgauzer, *Revoliutsiia i grazhdanskaia voina v Baku*, I: 1917–1918 gg. (Baku, 1927), p. 108.
[38] *Izvestiia*, no. 184, November 14, 1917.
[39] *Ibid.*, no. 203, December 8, 1917.

of November 5, they did not explicitly recognize the Soviet government in Petrograd, nor did they call for all power to the soviet in Baku.[40]

More significant for the Bolsheviks was the meeting of the council of the Musavat Party held on November 7, which adopted a resolution that allied the Musavat with the extreme Left in Baku. Beginning with a critique of the foreign policy of the Provisional Government, which had served only to prolong the war, and of its policy toward the nationalities, which could not satisfy the democratic aspirations of the national minorities, the Musavatists listed their proposals for dealing with the present crisis.

1. The government ought to be purely democratic and made up from the representatives of the revolutionary democracy without differentiation by nationality or party in accordance with the real strength of each party.

2. The liquidation of the conflict which has arisen within the Baku democracy by means of the crushing of Bolshevism is a most harmful step for the goals and tasks of the whole democracy.

3. To recognize as inexpedient the tactic of a part of the democracy directed at the isolation of the Bolsheviks, and the walkout of this part of the democracy from the Soviet of Workers' and Soldiers' Deputies.

4. To arrange for the immediate elections of a new Soviet by means of a general, equal, direct and proportional casting of votes.

5. The party Musavat, finding the peaceful solution of the conflict essential, calls the whole democracy to join in the tactic of the conciliation and, recognizing the form of action of the "Revolutionary Committee of

[40] *Ibid.*, no. 179, November 7, 1917.

Public Safety" as harmful for the policy of conciliation and agreement, declares that it cannot possibly participate in this committee.[41]

The First Congress of Delegates from the Caspian Fleet, which met from November 3 to 8, held a surprise for the Socialist Revolutionaries, who had enjoyed the predominant influence within the fleet. After speeches by Sahakian for the Socialist Revolutionaries and by Zevin in the name of the Bolsheviks, the congress adopted the Bolshevik resolution to transfer all power to the Baku soviet and to press all deputies who had walked out of the soviet to return immediately.[42] The sailors were in the same conciliatory mood as the Musavat and the Menshevik-Internationalists, and considered the Right socialists' walkout a schismatic and dangerous challenge to the unity of the "revolutionary democracy." Even so un-Bolshevik an organization as the Council of Trade Unions found it impossible to justify the action of the Right socialists, and, on November 3, the council refused to send a delegate either to the Committee of Public Safety or to the executive committee of the soviet, which was no longer a coalition organ. The council called for unity of the socialist parties and the reconstitution of Baku soviet to reflect the political will of the masses.[43]

On November 3–4 leaflets appeared in the city claiming that the Bolsheviks were preparing an armed seizure of power in Baku. Some were signed: "Committee of Public Safety." The executive committee of the soviet warned the population not to believe these charges: "In the city sinister people are spreading deliberately false and provocative rumors about an alleged uprising being

[41] *Bakinskii rabochii*, no. 82, November 14, 1917.
[42] *Izvestiia*, no. 178, November 5, 1917; *ibid.*, no. 179, November 7, 1917.
[43] Belen'kii and Manvelov, p. 189.

(167)

prepared by the Bolsheviks, Dashnaks, and other revolutionary organizations. The Executive Committee of the Soviet of Workers' and Soldiers' Deputies decisively denies these rumors and calls on the population to be completely calm and proclaims that persons spreading these provocative rumors will be answerable."[44] An investigation by the soviet discovered that, although some of the leaflets had been printed by the Committee of Public Safety, a number of the more provocative ones were the handiwork of the Kadet Party.[45] The Soviet met on November 5 to deal with the problem of provocation in general and the Committee of Public Safety in particular. The Right Socialist Revolutionaries arrived at the session, declaring that their walkout had been only a demonstration of protest. Also joining the soviet for the first time were the Musavatists. The meeting rejected a motion to negotiate with the committee and resolved by a vote of 409–25 to disband the committee by force if it did not dissolve itself within two days.

The committee lingered on for a few more weeks, but with its support dwindling it posed no threat to the soviet. By the end of November, the committee had disappeared and its members returned to a soviet now wholly in leftist hands.

The Baku soviet (which at this point was more accurately referred to as the "conference of the broadened Baku soviet," to indicate that elected deputies to the soviet met together with representatives of factory committees, soldiers' committees, trade unions, etc.) was still in the throes of the struggle with the Committee of Public Safety, and trying to deal with the printers' strike, when it also met a serious challenge from the IKOO. Nikitin, the chairman of the IKOO, engaged Shaumian in a dispute over the printing of the soviet's *Izvestiia*. Nikitin had insisted on the publication of the Committee of Public

[44] *Izvestiia*, no. 178, November 5, 1917.
[45] *Ibid.*, no. 179, November 7, 1917.

Safety's *Izvestiia* on the soviet's press. At the November 12 session of the soviet, Shaumian demanded the dismissal of Nikitin and the abolition of the IKOO, and he coupled this with an ultimatum to the owners of the printing-houses to accept all the demands of the workers by the next morning or face nationalization of their presses.[46] The soviet accepted Shaumian's suggestions, as well as a Bolshevik resolution which placed all local power in the executive committee of the soviet until new elections to the soviet could be held.[47]

The authority of the IKOO had essentially come to an end with the resignation of Frolov in October, but its formal powers were kept intact until the final thrust from the soviet came on November 12. Four days later the soviet forces occupied the IKOO's printing house.[48] A final meeting of the Council of Public Organizations, for which the IKOO had acted as an executive, was held on November 21. The Bolsheviks insisted on the dismissal of Nikitin, while the Mensheviks, Socialist Revolutionaries, Kadets, and members of national groups defended him. The final vote was close, 24–23, against Nikitin, and the meeting elected Dzhaparidze the new chairman. The question of liquidating the Council was raised, and even Nikitin argued that its function had ceased once a democratic duma had been elected. The Mensheviks and Socialist Revolutionaries called for the transfer of the powers of the Council to the new duma; the Bolsheviks maintained that all power should pass to the soviet, and their resolution was adopted by the Council which then ceased to exist.[49]

46 *Ibid.*, no. 184, November 14, 1917; *Dok.*, pp. 201–202.
47 The Musavatists joined the Bolsheviks and Left S.R.s to vote 269–101, with 16 abstentions, for this resolution. A resolution proposed by the socialist bloc for the establishment of a new temporary authority to govern until the elections was defeated decisively, receiving only 101 votes. (*Ibid.*)
48 *Kaspii*, no. 263, December 1, 1917.
49 *Bakinets*, no. 60, November 22, 1917.

October and November 1917 were the months in which the class collaboration which had marked the February Revolution ended. The old moderate socialist leadership, discredited in the months before the September strike, was swept out of the IKS. The IKOO was dissolved, and the forces for coalition between the "democracy" and the bourgeoisie gathered around the city duma, the only meaningful opponent of the soviet. Soviet power had been declared in Baku, but it could not be implemented. Five months would pass before Baku would have its own "October."

The Bolsheviks of Baku did not have the unqualified success of their comrades in Petrograd and Moscow, yet even without a numerical majority they maintained a political hegemony over the soviet for five months until the internal civil war gave them military victory and nearly undisputed power. In those five months the struggle to dominate the other parties and the vacillating rank and file was constant, and the greatest attraction of the Bolsheviks was their identification with soviet power. Not the party, but the party's role as the most articulate voice of the local soviet, guaranteed Bolshevik power in Baku as the organs in competition with the soviet fell for lack of support. Most importantly, the issues of soviet power and unity with central Russia became inextricably fused after the October revolution. The choice between soviet power and any alternative also involved a choice between recognition of the central Russian government and separation from Russia and, perhaps, from the revolution.

# 6

## From Politics
## to Armed Insurrection

BETWEEN THE DECLARATIONS of soviet power in October and November 1917 and the final conquest of power in March 1918, the soviet, all the while determined to establish its own sovereignty by creating a military force, could do no more than tolerate rival political authorities within the city. In that period all the major political parties, with the exception of the Kadets and the Mensheviks, recognized the local soviet as the highest governmental body in the city, yet the city duma continued to function as if it were sovereign. The national councils of the Moslems and the Armenians, as they gained armed support, likewise attempted to intervene in the governing of the municipality. The danger of an armed conflict became imminent. In December the tacit alliance between the Bolsheviks and the Musavat disintegrated as Shaumian and his comrades turned from "defeatism" to "defense of the revolution." In the first months of 1918 a common interest developed between the Armenians and the Bolsheviks based on common opposition to the threat posed by the Turkish advance and the Moslem counterrevolution centered in Elisavetpol and the north Caucasus. In Transcaucasia generally and in Baku particularly the revolution had turned from a struggle between classes into a war between hostile nationalities. The year 1917 ended with each nationality organizing itself for the battle at hand.

The reaction throughout Transcaucasia to the Bolshevik

insurrection was one of shock and dismay.[1] When the news reached Tiflis the Territorial Center of Soviets quickly passed the following resolution expressing its complete opposition to the Bolsheviks' action:

> The action of the Bolsheviks in Petrograd, either in the case of their temporary success or the immediate crushing of it by force of arms, leads to the triumph of counterrevolution and the destruction of the freedoms gained. The interest of the revolution dictates the peaceful liquidation of the uprising on the basis of an agreement from the whole revolutionary democracy in the spirit of democratizing the government, with the condition of calling the Constituent Assembly in the set time. Declaring this, the Territorial Center asks everyone to preserve revolutionary order and the unity of the revolutionary democracy.[2]

The Georgian Mensheviks, as well as the Socialist Revolutionaries in the Tiflis soviet and the Territorial Center, tried to wish away the Bolshevik takeover without proposing any positive resistance to it, hoping for the "peaceful liquidation" of the unfortunate event. In Baku the Mensheviks, Socialist Revolutionaries and Dashnaks immediately subscribed to the Tiflis resolution, fearing that the Bolshevik insurrection might lead to a response from the counterrevolutionary Right.[3]

The October Revolution drove a lasting wedge between

[1] Even before the insurrection in Petrograd the Transcaucasian Center of Soviets had tightened its control over local affairs hoping to prevent a Bolshevik coup in Tiflis. On October 20, the Center adopted a plan for the organization of an agency to replace the Ozakom. Four days later it proposed that all soviets form committees of public safety to fight against "anarchy, pogroms, and counterrevolution." (Belen'kii and Manvelov, p. 177.)

[2] A. L. Popov, "Iz istorii revoliutsii v Vostochnom Zakavkaz'e (1917–1918 gg.)," *Proletarskaia revoliutsiia*, no. 5 (28) (1924), pp. 16–17.

[3] *Kaspii*, no. 243, October 29, 1917.

Tiflis and Baku. On October 31, the Territorial Center announced the formation of a Committee of Public Safety, made up of all political parties with the significant exception of the Bolsheviks. The Tiflis Committee of Public Safety set as its task the formation of a strong central power in Transcaucasia which would resist the Bolshevik "mutiny" in Petrograd.[4] In November the struggle with the Bolsheviks began in earnest. The Menshevik leadership decided that the single source of Bolshevik strength in Tiflis, the garrison, must be neutralized. Although they met with protests both from the Tiflis Socialist Revolutionaries and from the majority at the garrison, the Mensheviks ordered the garrison to disperse, and armed their guard with the weapons the soldiers had left. The workers' guard, newly armed, became the military support for the local soviet. The threat of a Bolshevik coup in Tiflis had been dispelled.[5]

On November 15 the defunct Ozakom was replaced by

---

[4] *Izvestiia*, no. 173, October 31, 1917. On November 11, 540 representatives of political parties and organizations met in Tiflis to decide on the nature of the new Transcaucasian government. The Bolshevik Filip Makharadze asserted that the only real power in the territory was the power of the soviets which recognized the Petrograd government. Then the Bolsheviks left the meeting, which subsequently adopted the resolution of the S.R. Donskoi:

> (1) until the completion of the elections to the Constituent Assembly of delegates from Transcaucasia and the Caucasian Front, the administration of the territory [should be] transferred to the Committee of Public Safety . . .
> (2) on the completion of the elections to the Constituent Assembly in the territory and at the Front, a provisional government [should be] organized . . .

The provisional government was to operate until a legitimate Russian government was formed by the Constituent Assembly. The Transcaucasian S.R.s and Mensheviks were not yet committed to separation from Russia. (Popov, "Iz istorii . . . , pp. 18–19; Belen'kii and Manvelov, pp. 201–202; *Izvestiia*, no. 184, November 14, 1917.)

[5] Noi Zhordaniia, *Maia Zhizn'* (Stanford, Calif., 1968), pp. 80–81.

a new organ, the Transcaucasian Commissariat (*Zakav-kazskii Komisariat* or Zavkom). Its twelve members were all from the "revolutionary democracy."[6] The organization of Zavakom was the first step toward the separation of Transcaucasia from Russia, a declaration of local auton-omy which within five months would lead to a declaration of independence. But at the time this first step was not seen in terms of separation, but rather as the establishment of a non-Bolshevik variant of soviet power. The real power in Tiflis was the soviet and the Territorial Center, but the Mensheviks and the Socialist Revolutionaries were prepared neither to recognize the Bolshevik government nor to ally themselves with the bourgeoisie. Zhordaniia stated his "third" position most clearly on November 2 at a session of the workers' section of the Tiflis soviet:

> The position taken by the Caucasus is . . .
> completely clear and definite. . . . In its attitude
> toward this event [the Bolshevik revolution] Russia has
> fallen into three camps: the camp of the bourgeoisie,
> the camp of the Bolsheviks, and the camp of all the
> rest of the democracy from the Internationalists to the
> Bolsheviks of *Novaia zhizn'* inclusive. We have attached
> ourselves to the third camp. Our sole task is: to unite
> the democracy, to liquidate the schism within it, a
> schism which is aiding the victory of the counter-
> revolutionary camp.[7]

Tiflis's actions following the October Revolution made conciliation with the Baku soviet impossible. Shaumian

[6] The membership of the Zavkom was as follows: Mensheviks—Gegechkori (chairman), Ter-Ghazarian, Chkhenkeli; S.R.s—Donskoi, Neruchev; Dashnaks—Oganjanian, Sarkisian; Moslems—Khan-Khoiskii, Dzhafarov, Melik-Aslanov, Khasmamedov, Gaidarov; and the Georgian Social Federalist Alekseev-Meskhiev (*Kaspii*, no. 250, November 15, 1917).

[7] Popov, "Iz istorii . . . ," p. 16. Zhordaniia's position was essen-tially that of the Menshevik-Internationalists, who by this time formed the majority of the Menshevik party in Russia.

denounced the effort of the Mensheviks and Socialist Revolutionaries to form a new government in Transcaucasia:

When they received the news of the October Revolution in Petrograd, the Tiflis S.R.s threatened the Bolsheviks with "blood and iron." The Mensheviks did not go that far but considered the "act of the Bolsheviks" the greatest misfortune and dreamed of its suppression without "blood and iron." The union of these two defensist parties, enlarged by the addition of the nationalist parties of the Armenians, the Moslems, and the other tribes and nations, uniting actually all classes and castes of the Caucasus, cannot create a *revolutionary* power. It can give us only a government of *order*, a government of struggle with the revolution, a government of "salvation" from the revolution. And it is not surprising, of course, that the party of the revolutionary proletariat—the Bolsheviks —refused to participate in such a government.

The Caucasus is a petty-bourgeois country. The petty-bourgeois parties of Mensheviks, Dashnaks, and others have always played a dominating role among us. Industrial Baku has always stood to one side with its predominantly Bolshevik proletariat. Petty-bourgeois attitudes, on one hand, and nationalism, on the other, are the causes for our political backwardness in the Caucasus.[8]

From November 26 to 28 the elections to the Constituent Assembly were held throughout Transcaucasia. In Baku and the industrial districts the 161,963 eligible voters were offered fifteen separate lists of candidates, each drawn up by a political party, each to be accepted or rejected in full with no substitutions of candidates possible.[9] The Dashnaks campaigned most actively, using

[8] *Bakinskii rabochii*, no. 86, November 18, 1917; Shaumian, II, pp. 117–118.
[9] *Izvestiia*, no. 182, November 11, 1917.

automobiles to speed their agitators about the city, and the Moslems were second only to the Dashnaks in their campaign efforts. Clashes between Musavatists and Islam in Russia, and between the Moslem socialist bloc and a group of Hummet Mensheviks, were reported, but there were no serious infractions of the law during the three days of voting. The turnout in the city averaged about 52 percent of the electorate, while in the oil districts it averaged 75 percent. Among soldiers, too, about 75 percent voted, and, as had been the case in the elections to the soviet a month before, they voted overwhelmingly for the Bolsheviks.[10] The breakdown of the 111,050 votes cast was as follows:

| | |
|---|---|
| Bolsheviks | 22,276 |
| Musavat-Federalists | 21,752 |
| Dashnaktsutiun | 20,214 |
| Socialist Revolutionaries | 18,789 |
| Kadets | 9,062 |
| Islam in Russia | 7,850 |
| Mensheviks | 5,667 |
| Zionists | 2,081 |
| Armenian People's Party | 1,508 |
| Moslem Socialist Bloc | 903 |
| Georgian Socialist Federalists | 456 |
| Georgian National Democrats | 245 |
| Hummet-Mensheviks | 128 |
| People's Socialists | 116 |
| Moslems of Transcaucasia | 3[11] |

[10] *Ibid.*, no. 195, November 28, 1917. Of 10,877 soldiers' votes, 7,699 were cast for the Bolsheviks, 1,541 for the S.R.s (Belen'kii and Manvelov, p. 214).

[11] M. Lifshits and P. Chagin (eds.), *Pamiati 26. Materialy k istorii bakinskoi kommuny* (Baku, 1922), pp. 150–151; S. N. Belen'kii and A. Manvelov, *Revoliutsiia 1917 g. v Azerbaidzhane* (Baku, 1927), p. 219. The first list has a few insignificant differences from the latter; the higher numbers were always chosen.

A further analysis reveals that in the city proper the Dashnaks had the largest number of votes, 12,157, followed by the Musavat and then the Bolsheviks. Kadet strength was almost completely located within the city, while the Socialist-Revolutionary votes were divided evenly between the city and the districts. In the districts the Musavat had the most support, followed by the Socialist Revolutionaries, the Dashnaks, and the Bolsheviks in that order. Without the votes they received from the soldiers, the Bolsheviks, instead of being the leading party in Baku, would have trailed the Musavat, Dashnaks, and Socialist Revolutionaries.[12] The Bolsheviks, it is interesting to note, did very well in the "prisoners'" vote, winning 186 votes out of 198 cast.[13] A more ominous note for the "internationalist" parties was that a little over half of the voters cast their ballots for parties representing their nationality. 30,636 Moslems had voted for the Moslem lists, and 22,260 Armenians had voted for Armenian lists.

Outside of Baku, but within Baku province, the overwhelming majority of the Moslem peasantry voted for Musavat. In Lenkoran *uezd*, out of 64,183 votes cast, the Musavat received 53,910 votes and Islam in Russia 7,625; no other party came close. The Socialist Revolutionaries took 848 votes, the Bolsheviks 789. In Geokchai *uezd* the Musavat took 27,046 votes out of 48,799 cast, while Islam in Russia received 14,518.[14] In Baku *uezd*, which comprised the Apsheron Peninsula, the Musavatists made no showing at all, while Islam in Russia gained a spectacular

12 Belen'kii and Manvelov, p. 214.

13 *Kaspii*, no. 262, November 30, 1917.

14 *Izvestiia*, no. 213, December 20, 1917; Belen'kii and Manvelov, p. 237. "Islam in Russia" or "Ittihad" was a nationalist party which advocated a democratic, federal republic and "freedom for all Moslems from European capitalism and imperialism." Its candidates were professional men (doctors, teachers, etc.), whose politics were liberal rather than socialist. (*Kaspii*, no. 259, November 20, 1917.)

victory, receiving 19,812 votes out of a total of 25,748.[15] The city of Baku was an island of Russian and Armenian socialist parties in a sea of Moslem nationalism.

The elections in Baku were an isolated example of Menshevik defeat in Transcaucasia. When the figures for the elections throughout the area are considered, the singularity of Baku is clearly seen. A total of 2,455,274 votes were cast:

| | |
|---|---|
| Mensheviks | 661,934 |
| Musavat-Federalists | 615,816 |
| Dashnaks | 558,400 |
| Moslem Socialist Bloc | 159,770 |
| Socialist Revolutionaries | 117,522 |
| Bolsheviks | 93,581 |
| Hummet-Mensheviks | 84,743 |
| Islam in Russia | 66,505 |
| Georgian National Democrats | 25,733 |
| Kadets | 25,673 |
| Georgian Socialist Federalists | 22,754 |
| Armenian People's Party | 15,180 |
| Zionists | 7,018 |
| People's Socialists | 570 |
| Moslems of Transcaucasia | 71[16] |

Their strong showing in Georgia gave the Mensheviks eleven seats from Transcaucasia, the bulk of the Menshevik faction in the Constituent Assembly. The Musavat received ten seats, the Dashnaks nine, the Moslem Socialist Bloc two, and the Bolsheviks, the Socialist Revolutionaries, the Hummet-Mensheviks, and Islam in Russia one seat each.[17] The Socialist Revolutionaries made their best showing in the voting among the soldiers on the Caucasian Front. Although figures are not available, four

[15] *Kaspii*, no. 279, December 21, 1917; Belen'kii and Manvelov, p. 238.

[16] *Arev*, no. 52, March 23, 1918. These figures from the Baku Armenian newspaper are the most complete I have seen.

[17] *Ibid.*

Socialist Revolutionaries (Donskoi, Berezov, Pyzhev, and Tumanov) were elected along with one Bolshevik (Aleksei Grigorevich Badaev) as delegates to the Constituent Assembly.[18] Radkey explains the lack of Bolshevik success: "The Socialist-Revolutionary leadership of the soldiers' soviets, strongly in favor of national defense, had used its authority to throttle Bolshevik agitation on the front, even denying to that party representation on electoral information committees, and had gotten away with its one-sided policy because of remoteness from the hearth of revolution."[19] The vote on the Caucasian Front had no effect on the soldiers' "voting with their feet" in November and December by demobilizing and drifting northward.

With the dissolution of the IKOO in mid-November the Baku city duma alone remained as a rival to the Baku soviet. For two months its authority, owing to its recent election, was great enough to challenge seriously its competitor.[20] The sizable Bolshevik faction decided to partici-

---

[18] *Kavkazskii rabochii* (Tiflis), no. 231, December 30, 1917. In O. H. Radkey, *The Election to the Russian Constituent Assembly of 1917* (Cambridge, Mass., 1950), the author writes that there were five S.R.s and one Bolshevik elected from the Front.

[19] Radkey, p. 37; Belen'kii and Manvelov, pp. 124, 159; S. E. Sef (ed.), *Revoliutsiia 1917 goda v Zakavkaz'e* (Tiflis, 1927), pp. 84–86, 221–222, 272, 345.

[20] The number of seats alloted to the various parties after the October elections was as follows:

| | |
|---|---|
| Socialist Bloc | 25 |
| Bolsheviks | 19 |
| Dashnaktsutiun | 17 |
| Musavat–Moslem Committee | 14 |
| Moslem Clericals | 11 |
| Kadets | 6 |
| Union of State Employees | 5 |
| Edinstvo | 4 |
| Jewish Social Organizations | 3 |
| Armenian Democratic Party | 3 |
| Russian Cultural-Democratic Organizations | 2 |
| Total | 109 |

(Belen'kii and Manvelov, p. 181).
At the first session of the "democratic" duma, Fataly Khan-Khoiskii

pate in the duma sessions, at a time when their comrades in central Russia were disbanding local dumas.[21] But the tactic of the Baku Bolsheviks was to gain control of the duma through the forthcoming elections in the oil-field districts. At the first sessions of the duma, Bolsheviks insisted that the duma presidium be considered temporary pending the elections in the outlying districts. The duma agreed to this stipulation. Even as they worked within the duma the Bolsheviks made clear in their factional declaration of November 14 that their participation was based on expediency, that their first loyalty was to the soviet:

> The fraction of Social-Democrats–Bolsheviks points out the great political significance which the city government ought to have in the process of revolution and especially in the sharp period of crisis we are living through.
>
> The City Duma, if it is on the watch for the interests of the people and the revolution, ought to demand together with all of democratic Russia the immediate ending of the war. The parties of the proletariat and the urban revolutionary democracy, as well as the parties of the peasants in the *zemskie samoupravleniia* (rural organs of self-government), should demand that state power in the center and in the provinces be given to the revolutionary classes—the proletariat and the peasantry.
>
> The city government, as an organ uniting all classes of the population, revolutionary classes and reactionary classes, cannot be an organ of power in the revolutionary period. While the revolution is not yet finished, and so that it may be victoriously concluded,

---

(Kadet) was elected chairman and the S.R. Sahakian deputy chairman (*Baku*, no. 249, November 14, 1917).

[21] In December 1917 the dumas in Moscow, Petrograd, Saratov, and Kaluga were dispersed, and in January seven others in large cities were forced to end their meetings.

power in the country must belong exclusively to the
revolutionary classes. Our revolution has already
created organs of revolutionary power in the form of
Soviets of Workers', Soldiers' and Peasants' Deputies.
Power ought to belong to these Soviets. . . .

There is no way to return to the old order, and all
delay in recognizing the new government signifies
a continuation of the civil war, death and destruction
for the country.[22]

The Bolshevik tactic of radicalizing the duma from within
by passing Bolshevik resolutions and increasing the number of leftist delegates depended on rallying some socialists, who together with the Bolsheviks would form a clear
majority in the duma, behind Bolshevik programs. On
November 18, Shaumian raised the time-worn issue of
the incorporation of the oil-fields and the elections in those
districts. In the voting, forty-four Bolsheviks, Mensheviks,
Socialist Revolutionaries, and Dashnaks carried the resolution for incorporation, reversing the sense of the old
duma, against twenty-four Moslems, Plekhanovites, and
Kadets who abstained.[23] The Moslem faction left the
duma in protest.

Clearly there was no anti-Bolshevik bloc in the city
duma. The socialist bloc could cooperate with the Moslems
and the Kadets only on such issues as drawing up a
protest against the dispersal by the Bolsheviks of the
Moscow city duma.[24] But more often than not they were
forced to vote with the Bolsheviks on local issues. The possibility of forming a community of interests between the
bourgeoisie and the "revolutionary democracy" had long
ceased to exist, and yet only on this basis could a conciliatory policy toward the bourgeoisie be justified. The Bolsheviks, on the other hand, were willing to promote the

[22] *Izvestiia*, no. 191, November 23, 1917.
[23] *Ibid.*, no. 190, November 19, 1917.
[24] *Ibid.*

interests of one part of the population at the expense of another, since they recognized a deep conflict of interest between them.[25]

Feeding the soldiers, running the food-supply committees, and reestablishing public education put unbearable strains on the financial solvency of the duma. At the December 5 session, the Dashnak delegate, Zarafian, proposed that the only way to fill the empty treasury, in view of the refusal of the local banks to lend money to the duma, was a compulsory loan to be levied on the city's moneylenders. The Bolsheviks supported Zarafian's proposal, and it passed, 34–31.[26] The Kadet Vermishev explained that the bankers of Baku would not extend the duma credit because they had already witnessed the fate of the Petrograd and Moscow city dumas at the hands of the Bolsheviks.[27] The duma, though it was now the only representative of the bourgeoisie in the state structure, received no cooperation from the fearful men of property. Without money and military or police power the duma was condemned to steady decline. In December it lost its prerogatives of law-enforcement to the soviet and its newly constituted military-revolutionary committee, and along with that it lost the allegiance of many of its former supporters.

The soviet and the duma competed rather than cooperated in their efforts to supply Baku with food. The City Food Supply Commission was unwilling to create a monopoly in the grain trade and was therefore forced to deal with speculators. The conference of factory committees,

[25] The Bolsheviks limited their participation in the city duma to the sessions of the whole duma and did not participate in the *gorodskaia uprava* (city board). Shaumian announced that the Bolsheviks could not sit on the city board with the Right socialists who "already in no way differ from Kadets, and we do not want to be responsible for their policies." (*Izvestiia*, no. 198, December 1, 1917.)

[26] *Ibid.*, no. 203, December 8, 1917.

[27] *Ibid.*

early in October, called for prohibition of private purchases of grain, but little was done to implement the resolution.[28] On November 12, Dzhaparidze reported to the
"broadened" soviet on the desperate situation and persuaded the deputies to create a central food-supply committee to control and plan the activities of all other supply
committees.[29] Again the effect of this resolution was merely to create one more competitive organ to complicate an
already chaotic situation. The duma, the conference of
factory committees, and the soviet were none of them
at this time able to subordinate all local committees to
their authority and create a state monopoly of the
purchase and distribution of foodstuffs. Any efforts short
of these drastic steps were bound to fail once civil war
cut Baku off from the north Caucasus.

Situated on the desolate and unfruitful Apsheron Peninsula, the city of Baku had always depended on areas to
the west and north for foodstuffs. The three-cornered
civil war in the north Caucasus—between Cossacks,
mountain tribes, and pro-soviet urban workers—had effectively cut Baku off from its principal sources of food.
At the same time, Tiflis was reluctant to divert supplies
to Baku when the Baku soviet was pursuing a policy of
encouraging the pro-Bolshevik forces in the north Caucasus. Baku naturally felt betrayed by Tiflis. On November 24 the Baku soviet decided to send a delegation to
Grozny in the north Caucasus to bring about a peaceful
conclusion to the fighting between the Chechen mountaineers and the urban population.[30] The soviet also en-
dorsed the resolution to seek intervention by Tiflis and
decided to despatch agitators to convince the north Caucasian peasants they should sell to the public food committees servicing Baku, instead of to the speculators.

28 *Ibid.*, no. 156, October 10, 1917.
29 *Ibid.*, no. 184, November 14, 1917.
30 *Ibid.*, no. 195, November 28, 1917.

Baku's interest in the north Caucasus was both economic and political. The city needed grain from the north, as well as political allies in the coming civil war. If the north fell to the anti-Bolsheviks there would be no land route connecting central Russia with Soviet Baku.

The food crisis deepened. The grain ration was cut to a half-pound. Angry workers in Sabunchiny and Balakhany refused to accept the reduced ration and stayed home from work. As in the past the food shortage was felt most acutely by the Moslems. On November 29 a crowd of Moslems attacked the City Food Supply Commission, demanding an increase in the grain ration. They were dispersed only when soldiers, sailors, and an artillery platoon arrived on the scene.[31] On December 12, Baku received a crushing blow from Tiflis—a telegram notifying the city that all shipments from the north Caucasus had been stopped.[32] Local measures would have to be taken to avoid catastrophe.

As the fighting around Grozny intensified, meetings were held in Baku to decide what steps should be taken to keep the railroad lines open to the north. On December 3, about seven hundred railroad workers heard a report by a member of the Grozny city soviet. The Bolsheviks proposed that the meeting adopt a resolution declaring "merciless war" on the anti-soviet Cossacks and mountaineers and calling for united action with the central Russian government. But this resolution was rejected, and the Menshevik-oriented railroad workers adopted the milder alternative proposed by the Socialist Revolutionaries

[31] *Kaspii*, no. 262, November 30, 1917.

[32] *Izvestiia*, no. 206, December 12, 1917. Bitterness against Tiflis was great. On January 25, the chairman of the Baku soviet's food-supply committee accused Tiflis of wanting "to force us to recognize the Caucasian Commissariat by starving us. . . . We sent a delegation to Tiflis asking . . . them to give us the right of autonomy to buy grain, but they would not give this to us, and the grain coming now through Novorossisk does not reach us." (Ratgauzer, *Revoliutsiia i grazhdanskaia voina . . .* , p. 115.)

(184)

and Mensheviks—to collect a fund for the workers of the Grozny and Vladikavkaz railroads and to issue a call for an end to the fighting.[33] In direct contrast to the mood of the railroad workers, a large meeting of sailors, soldiers, and Cossacks, held two days later, protested against what it took to be collaboration by the Transcaucasian Commissariat with the counterrevolution in the north Caucasus and southern Russia.[34] On December 8, the executive committee of the Baku soviet decided to send aid, arms and supplies to the Grozny soviet.[35]

The decision by the Baku IKS to aid the pro-soviet elements in the north Caucasus sharply defined Baku's new attitude of insubordination to Tiflis. Still dependent on the Georgian capital for its food-supply, Baku nevertheless separated itself from the growing anti-Bolshevik trend evident there. Tiflis, the north Caucasus, the Ukraine, and the Don Region had, by declaring themselves autonomous regions, created centers for anti-Bolshevik activity, and Baku was already dedicated to the eradication of these separatist tendencies. By sending a military force to assist in the fighting around Grozny, the Baku soviet had taken the first of a series of military actions which directly engaged the city in the civil war on the side of the Bolshevik government in Petrograd.

Its first military campaign was not a great success and held dire consequences for the internal situation in Baku. Dzhaparidze wrote to Shaumian, who was then in Tiflis, on the matter:

> First of all, one must realize that the Karaulovs and Kaledins in the same way strive to cut off completely the Caucasus and Transcaucasia and not allow the fire of revolution to spread here. The detachment sent by us was not strong enough to offer

[33] *Kaspii*, no. 267, December 6, 1917.
[34] *Bakinskii rabochii*, no. 102, December 9, 1917; *Dok.*, p. 213.
[35] *Izvestiia*, no. 205, December 10, 1917.

the necessary resistance, and today the station Gudermes is completely cut off. Comrades sent to Chechen villages report that nothing is to be gained through words; all arriving comrades insist on help in the form of real force, otherwise in Transcaucasia starvation is inevitable.

There is no possibility to restore order on the railroad, neither at Grozny nor up to Gudermes.

In general, all draw a picture close to catastrophe. The soldiers are losing heart as a consequence of their small number and poor armament. We are sending another detachment, but it too is small, though we want it to hold a part of the railroad until reinforcements arrive.

We received the last wagons of grain; in two days there will be hunger among us, unless extraordinary measures are taken. A strong detachment must be sent immediately. . . .[36]

While the Baku soviet had decided to intervene in the civil war in the north Caucasus, in Tiflis authorities were divided as to the proper course to be taken. The principal element in Tiflis's policy toward the autonomous north Caucasian governments was concern not to disrupt the supply of foodstuffs from that region to Transcaucasia. From that concern emerged a policy of accommodation toward the anti-Bolshevik authorities. As early as November 11, Donskoi had outlined the attitude of the Transcaucasian leadership toward the north Caucasus: "In relation to food-supply, Transcaucasia depends on the north Caucasus, which, in its turn, is interested in the Caucasian Front's standing at its post, which will allow for peaceful life in the territory. This mutual dependence will be the link by which we will promote, once we have

36 *Kavkazskii rabochii* (Tiflis), no. 220, December 14, 1917; P. A. Dzhaparidze, *Izbrannye stat'i, rechi i pis'ma, 1905–1918 gg.* (Moscow, 1958), p. 211.

an authoritative government, the establishment of local contacts with our neighbors who have already created their local government."[37] Those favoring a proclamation of autonomy for Transcaucasia were understandably sympathetic to such declarations in other parts of Russia, especially since they were clearly directed against the central Bolshevik government. In so far as its soviet reflected Bolshevik policy, Baku opposed the movement toward local autonomy which in that city could aid only the Moslems. Tiflis continued to encourage the anti-Bolshevik movement in the north Caucasus, and further antagonized Baku. Shaumian accused Tiflis of sending arms and other supplies to the Cossacks in the north, and on this issue managed to rally support from the other socialist parties in Baku for a resolution attacking the Zavkom.[38]

In December, as in September, hunger brought the people into the streets. Goods were seized by soldiers, and theft was the general rule in the city. The executive committee of the soviet called an emergency meeting on December 12 with representatives of the regimental committees of the Baku garrison to discuss the restoration of order in the city and the deployment of military force to Mugan in Baku Province to end the activities of local bandits. The general breakdown in order called for drastic measures, and the IKS decided to create a military-revolutionary committee with "the broadest powers to reestablish revolutionary discipline and order."[39] Both the civilian population and the military were to be subordinate to the committee, and a revolutionary court was set up to try infractions of the new order.[40]

[37] *Dokumenty i materialy po vneshnei politike Zakavkaz'ia i Gruzii* (Tiflis, 1919), p. 5.
[38] *Bakinskii rabochii*, no. 102, December 9, 1917; Shaumian, II, pp. 120–123. *Kavkazskii rabochii* (Tiflis), no. 218, December 12, 1917; Shaumian, II, pp. 124–126.
[39] *Izvestiia*, no. 208, December 14, 1917.
[40] *Ibid.* The chairman of the committee was I. Sukhartsev (Left S.R.) (*Izvestiia*, no. 60 [282], March 30, 1918).

The city did not find out about the new revolutionary authority until two days after its formation. In the meantime, on December 13, thousands of Moslems, angered by the excesses committed by soldiers in the city, marched to the Ismailie Building, a national center, and protested the lack of protection for Moslem citizens. They demanded Moslem policemen in Moslem quarters.[41] In the face of the municipal authorities' failure to protect them, the Moslems were prepared to organize their own self-defense. Later that same day five Moslem representatives—Topchibashev, B. Ashurbekov, Resul Zade, I. Gaidarov, and M. G. Gadzhinskii—met with the military-revolutionary committee, but a serious difference in interpretation of the causes of the current mood of the Moslems was apparent.[42] Topchibashev attributed it to an indifference toward the Moslems on the part of the revolutionary parties, until the Moslem "silence" became a "scream." Dzhaparidze contended that the political leadership had not ignored the Moslems—it was simply that they were culturally more backward than the rest of the population and revolutionary groups had no influence over them.[43]

An extraordinary session of the duma was called for December 15 to discuss the military-revolutionary committee. The debate turned into a consideration of the organization of power in the city. The mayor of Baku, Iliushkin, refused to subordinate himself to the new committee and asserted that the city board was the highest executive authority in the city. Varshamian, the head of the militia, wanted to know if he was to obey the rash of orders emanating from the committee, which ranged from instructions for the arrest of all people provoking interethnic strife to those for the enforcement of curfews on taverns and for the prohibition of sales of alcohol.[44] Dzhaparidze defended the actions of the IKS and the military-revolution-

[41] *Kaspii*, no. 273, December 14, 1917.
[42] *Izvestiia*, no. 209, December 15, 1917.
[43] *Ibid.*        [44] *Ibid.*, no. 211, December 17, 1917.

(188)

ary committee and asked the duma members to recognize that, in fact, both in Baku and in Tiflis power was in the hands of the soviets, even though the Bolsheviks were in the minority. Order, he claimed, could be established only by supporting a monopoly of power by the local soviet. At this point each party in the duma enunciated its position on the organization of power in Baku. The Kadets, Edinstvo, and the city board supported the exclusive power of the City Duma. The Mensheviks wanted the formation of a new government made up of representatives of all revolutionary and democratic organizations: this was essentially the position of the Tiflis Mensheviks. The Dashnaks sought a coalition of the duma, the soviet, representatives of the national councils, and other democratic organizations—a throwback to the concept of the old IKOO. The Musavat and Islam in Russia supported a similar coalition government, while the Socialist Revolutionaries envisioned a simple coalition of the duma and the soviet. These new positions, particularly those of the Socialist Revolutionaries and the Musavat, indicate a significant shift in the space of one month from support of soviet power to a more equivocal relationship to the soviet, which had not yet been reconstituted by meaningful elections. The voting was erratic. The Bolsheviks collected eleven votes for soviet power, while twenty voted for duma power. Eleven Socialist Revolutionaries and Mensheviks voted for a soviet–duma coalition, but the greatest number of votes—twenty-nine—went for a grand coalition of duma, soviet, peasant union, national councils, etc. After a short conference the Mensheviks also came to support this last proposal, and the duma accepted by the final vote of 47–24 the resolution to form a coalition government of the city of Baku.[45]

45 The Mensheviks had shifted to a position, new for them, permitting the participation of the national councils in the local government (*Kaspii*, no. 276, December 17, 1917; Belen'kii and Manvelov, p. 232).

Soon afterwards the political parties of Baku, with the exception of the Bolsheviks, gathered to form a supreme organ of power for the city in line with the duma's decision of December 15. A body of nine members was decided on: one from the workers' soviet, one from the soldiers', one from the peasants, one from each of the three national organizations (Moslem, Armenian, and Russian), and three from the city government (the duma and the city board).[46] The Bolsheviks, in accordance with their allegiance to soviet power, refused to participate in this new organ of government.[47]

The challenge to the soviet by the city duma may seem to have been presumptuous, since the duma had no real basis on which to found their authority within the city, while the soviet, through the military-revolutionary committee, was proving that it alone could handle disorders there. But at the time, in December 1917, the duma could still depend on powerful allies among the Kadets and Right socialist parties who were not yet committed to soviet power. The duma was confident enough to believe that declarations of power equaled power, and this belief might have been borne out had not the soviet regained its own self-assurance and begun to build a military base of support. For in December the Baku garrison, the keystone of soviet power in Baku, was rapidly dwindling away, and would have to be replaced by a new armed force.

Even the opponents of the military-revolutionary committee were soon forced to admit that its extraordinary measures had secured a minimum of essential order inside the city of Baku. On December 20, the Socialist-Revolutionary organization resolved that competence on matters dealing with the struggle against anarchy and disorder

[46] *Izvestiia*, no. 214, December 21, 1917.
[47] *Baku*, no. 279, December 21, 1917. This "government" never functioned.

belonged to the soviet, a patent recognition that only that
body which controlled the military could end the violence
in the streets.[48] The effectiveness of the soviet was in large
part responsible for the strategic shift to the left by the
Socialist Revolutionaries and their Armenian allies, the
Dashnaks, at the end of December.

At the first joint session of the workers' and soldiers'
sections of the newly elected soviet on December 31, a
new distribution of political allegiances emerged.[49] The
Left in the soviet had been enlarged in the December
elections, and the Right, while still maintaining the larger
bloc, was neither as unified as the Left nor committed to
any single way out of the impasse in which the question
of political sovereignty was caught.

Each party in turn made a definite statement of its position on the crucial question of power, local and central.
The Bolsheviks and Left Socialist Revolutionaries once
again reiterated their commitment to exclusive power in

[48] Belen'kii and Manvelov, p. 236.
[49] The elections to the Baku soviet were held on December 12–16.
The results are difficult to determine, for different sources give
different totals. Issue no. 52 of *Znamia Truda*, the Baku S.R. organ,
gives the following totals, according to Belen'kii and Manvelov,
p. 233:

| | |
|---|---|
| S.R.s | 85 |
| Bolsheviks | 48 |
| Dashnaks | 36 |
| Musavatists | 18 |
| Mensheviks | 13 |
| | 200 (workers' section) |

Guseinov *et al.* in the official Soviet history of Azerbaijan give the
following figures on page 83:

| | |
|---|---|
| Bolsheviks | 51 |
| Dashnaks | 41 |
| Left S.R.s | 38 |
| Right S.R.s | 28 |
| Musavatists | 21 |
| Mensheviks | 11 |
| | 190 (workers' section) |

the hands of the soviets, both in the provinces and in the central, to a recognition of Lenin's government, and to support of the Constituent Assembly only if it agreed to support the "interests of the people." The Dashnaks and Right Socialist Revolutionaries declared that in the present power vacuum the Baku soviet was the only organ of the organized democracy. They decided therefore that they would not protest against the transfer of all power to the local soviet, and promised to participate actively in the work of the soviet, but reserved their support of the Constituent Assembly in the center. Resul Zade stood to speak for the Musavat and affirmed that his party was in principle for soviet power but that, in view of the "undemocratic" nature of the Baku soviet (in which the local peasantry was unrepresented), the Musavat declined to support the transfer of power to it or to work in its executive committee. The Mensheviks maintained their former position: for the Constituent Assembly in the center and for a duma–soviet coalition in Baku. Only on this basis would the Mensheviks consent to enter the IKS.[50]

The Baku soviet voted for the position formulated by the Bolsheviks and Left Socialist Revolutionaries: all power to the soviets, locally and in the center.[51] The Bolsheviks had indeed succeeded in Bolshevizing the soviet. Yet the

[50] *Izvestiia*, no. 1 (223), January 1, 1918.
[51] *Ibid*. The soviet elected a new executive committee to which only parties recognizing the transfer of power to the local soviet would be admitted. This eliminated only the Mensheviks, for, despite Resul Zade's declaration, the Musavat decided to participate in the work of the IKS.
The composition of the IKS was as follows: Bolsheviks—Dzhaparidze, Basin, Zagarian, Israilbekov, Golubev; Left S.R.s—Sukhartsev, Tumanian, Botov, Bairamov; Dashnaks—Melik-Eolchian, Ter-Ghazarian, Avalian, A. Arakelian, A. Nurijanian; Right S.R.s—Denezhkin, Vasin, and one unknown; Musavatists—Velikov, Mamedov-ali (*Arev*, no. 2, January 3, 1918); Soldiers—Raskoniuk, Mitenkov, Smolenskii, and two unknowns. P. A. Dzhaparidze was elected chairman of the IKS (*Izvestiia*, no. 2 [224], January 4, 1918). This new IKS continued to be led by the Left socialist parties, like the old one which operated from October.

soviet itself was unable to secure a monopoly of power within the city. The duma remained its rival, though an increasingly weaker one. And the soviet and its Bolshevik leadership were unable to secure total commitment of the workers and their representatives to the notion of soviet power throughout Russia. For many the Constituent Assembly seemed to be the only legitimate arbitrator of Russia's future.

The Constituent Assembly represented for the moderate socialist parties in Transcaucasia the only alternative to the Bolshevik government, the legal authority in revolutionary Russia, and the real expression of the people's will. When the Bolsheviks refused to allow the assembly to reconvene after its first long session of January 5 and 6, 1918, the anti-Bolsheviks in Tiflis reacted decisively and undertook the legal separation of Transcaucasia from Russia. In Baku, however, the only protests came from a large meeting of post-office and telegraph workers (January 12) and from a conclave of railroad workers, both groups sympathetic to the Mensheviks.[52] The local committee of the soviet in the Railroad District, a Menshevik stronghold, also adopted a resolution opposing the dissolution of the Constituent Assembly.[53] On January 22, after the Bolsheviks and Left Socialist Revolutionaries had failed to put through a motion to remove the issue of the Constituent Assembly from the agenda, the central Baku soviet undertook a detailed discussion and evaluation of the events in Petrograd. But after each party had made its factional statement, the soviet voted 98–76 in favor of the resolution of the Bolsheviks and Left Socialist Revolutionaries to support only a constituent assembly which recognized the soviet government and to accept the decisions of the Third

[52] *Bakinskii Rabochii*, no. 12 (128), January 17, 1918.
[53] This committee also protested the exclusion of railroad workers from the Red Guards. Evidently the organizers of the Red Guards sought to eliminate anti-Bolshevik elements from the ranks (*Izvestiia*, no. 23 [245], January 30, 1918).

Congress of Soviets.[54] The Musavat voted with the Bolsheviks although earlier they had condemned the dispersal of the assembly.[55] A motion of the Right Socialist Revolutionaries to reconvene the Constituent Assembly received only sixty-eight votes, while the Menshevik resolution—"that the character of our revolution demands from the proletariat, not the creation of their own class state organs, but an independent class policy in organs of the whole people organized on the basis of general, direct, equal, and secret elections"—received only forty-eight votes. The Dashnaks gathered forty-five votes for a simple protest against the dispersal.[56] The result revealed once again that the mood of the soviet majority was clearly pro-Bolshevik and on the side of the central Soviet government.

In Georgia the reaction to the dispersal of the Constituent Assembly was demonstrably anti-Bolshevik. With the Assembly gone, the Mensheviks considered the last legal tie to central Russia broken. In Tiflis the Georgian leadership used the occasion of a meeting of the elected delegates to the Constituent Assembly to discuss the convocation of an autonomous legislature for Transcaucasia. The Dashnaks and Socialist Revolutionaries opposed the creation of a local Seim, but the Moslem delegates sided with the Mensheviks, forming a majority of two votes. The Dashnaks tried to have a resolution adopted by which the delegates to the Constituent Assembly from Transcaucasia themselves would constitute a temporary Seim, but they failed to win a majority.[57] The Seim met on February 23, after the Socialist Revolutionaries and Dashnaks agreed to participate in the new parliament. Each party was given delegates in proportion to the number of votes it had received

54 *Ibid.*, no. 22 (244), January 28, 1918.

55 B. Ishkhanian, *Hakaheghapokhakan sharzhume Andrkovkasum (Bagvi aryunahegh antskeri aritov)* (Baku, 1918), p. 62.

56 *Izvestiia*, no. 22 (244), January 28, 1918.

57 *Ibid.*, no. 30 (252), January 21, 1918; *Baku*, no. 28, January 6, 1918.

in the elections to the Constituent Assembly.[58] Transcaucasia, except for Baku, no longer recognized itself as
subordinate to the central Russian authority.

The general disintegration of the Russian Army in 1917
had been evident on the Caucasian Front only since the
summer. Allen and Muratoff in their study of the Caucasian Front write that the military successes of Yudenich's
army had brought about a situation in which "it is clear
that the outbreak of the Russian Revolution in the spring
of 1917 alone saved the Turks from complete military
disaster in Asia Minor."[59] But the ultimate victory was not
grasped, because of faulty intelligence reports and the
effects of the revolutionary events within the army. The
Caucasian Army disintegrated from the rear forward: "the
Cossacks and the border regiments and many long-service
soldiers in the ranks remained little affected, but the crack
dragoon regiments proved to contain some of the elements
politically more unreliable, while the rear services were
widely affected."[60] By June the Caucasian Army was in
the throes of disintegration, though it was a more gradual
disintegration than on the Western front.[61] That month
Yudenich resigned, exasperated by interventions by revolutionary committees, and was replaced by General Przhevalskii. In July the Provisional Government's commissars
in the Caucasian Army reported that units refused to engage the enemy or to obey orders to move.[62] Regiments
on leave in the rear refused to return to the front.[63] By
September the murder of officers was becoming common,

[58] *Baku*, no. 29, February 7, 1918.
[59] W. E. D. Allen and Paul Muratoff, *Caucasian Battlefields. A
History of the Wars on the Turco-Caucasian Border, 1828–1921*
(Cambridge, 1953), p. 438.
[60] *Ibid.*, p. 447.
[61] *Ibid.*, p. 449.
[62] N. E. Kakurin (comp.), *Razlozhenie armii v 1917 godu* (Moscow, 1925), pp. 106–107.
[63] *Ibid.*, p. 129.

(195)

and Tiflis barred Bolshevik agitators from the front.[64] A "kind of informal armistice" kept the Turks from advancing, even though by November discipline had disappeared and Russian soldiers were spontaneously demobilizing.[65]

On November 21 General Przhevalskii informed the Zavkom that he had received a proposal for armistice from the Turkish Commander, Ferik-Vehib Pasha. That same day the Zavkom resolved that:

> taking into consideration the absence in Russia of a single central government recognized by all, and having in mind that the staff of the Supreme Command has already been destroyed by civil war . . . and also considering the general political situation in Russia . . . , the Commissariat recognizes that it is opportune to welcome the proposal of the Turkish Command and to propose to him immediately to stop military actions along the entire Caucasian Front with the *sine qua non* that no strategic regroupings take place which could hurt the English Army in Mesopotamia.[66]

The next day Przhevalskii informed the British and French consuls in Tiflis that he had accepted an armistice with the Turks, excusing himself to his allies by claiming that if he had not so acted the Bolsheviks would have gained control of his troops.[67]

As the soldiers moved to the rear, the responsibility for their well-being, shelter, and provisions fell on Baku and Tiflis. At the same time armed forces within these cities posed serious political problems for the municipal governments. Tiflis was as reluctant to tolerate a Bolshevik garrison as Baku was to house Cossack regiments. Shaumian telegraphed Tiflis in November:

[64] *Ibid.*, pp. 132–133.
[65] Allen and Muratoff, p. 457.
[66] Popov, "Iz istorii . . . ," p. 20.
[67] Richard Ullman, *Anglo-Soviet Relations, 1917–1921: Intervention and the War* (Princeton, 1961), p. 51.

Cossack units are arriving in Baku. In view of the
absence of shelter and the food-supply difficulties we
cannot accept them. They will wait in the trains. I
request that you immediately telegraph about sending
them further to the North Caucasus.

For the future we declare: No military units may be
sent to Baku without the consent and agreement of the
Executive Committee of the Soviet of Workers' and
Soldiers' Deputies. In any other case we will place the
responsibility for the consequences on you.[68]

Gegechkori agreed in talks with Shaumian that no soldiers
returning from the front would be directed toward Baku.

On November 13 the soldiers' section of the Baku soviet
made a series of decisions which formed the basic military
policy of the soviet. A resolution was passed approving the
executive committee's decision to send troops to protect
the inhabitants of Dzhevat, Shemakhin, and Kuba from
armed bands.[69] By this measure the Baku soviet sought to
reestablish order in the province as well as its own authority in the outlying areas. The session went on to deal
with the question of the demobilizing soldiers, and, on the
motion of the Bolshevik Zevin, decided not to allow the
retiring soldiers to leave Baku with weapons and to form
with the weapons acquired from them a local unit of
Red Guards. An international workers' brigade was to replace the disintegrating Russian Army and defend the
revolution.

Before the Red Guards could be organized, the Armenians, Georgians, and Moslems of Transcaucasia began
forming their own national military units for self-defense.
With no Russian army between Transcaucasia and the
Turkish forces, the Armenians and Georgians felt the
necessity to organize their own defenses against the Turks.
The Azerbaijanis, on the other hand, feared the armed

[68] *Kavkazskii rabochii* (Tiflis), no. 207, November 24, 1917.
[69] *Kaspii*, no. 250, November 15, 1917.

Christians and sought to link up with their Ottoman brothers. The likelihood of Moslem treachery convinced the Armenians and Georgians that national units were preferable to the multinational Red Guards urged by the Bolsheviks. In December Turkish Armenian leaders elected General Andranik (Ozanian) to command their forces.[70] Within Baku Armenian soldiers were regrouped into national units under Dashnak auspices. Georgian units and a national corps were also organized in December. The Moslems, on the other hand, who had agitated for permission to form their own national units since the spring of 1917, were denied equipment. Before the fall of the Provisional Government Kerensky had authorized the formation of Moslem units, but no measures were taken to supply them. But despite resistance from the local authorities, Moslems in Transcaucasia began organizing military units in December; for arms they looked to returning Russian soldiers.[71]

The tacit understanding which had allowed the Musavatists and Bolsheviks to unite in their opposition to the war was breaking down by December 1917. Even more than the internal conflict between the Baku soviet and local Moslems, events in the city of Elisavetpol acted to accentuate the irreconcilable differences between the two parties. On December 17 Moslem forces fought the 219th Regiment, which was Bolshevik in sympathy, when the latter refused to disarm itself.[72] A series of robberies and

[70] Eghishe Geghamiants, *Tajiknere Kovkasum ev Bagvi ankume* (Baku, 1919), pp. 19–21.

[71] *Izvestiia VTsIK* (Petrograd), no. 228, November 17, 1917. On November 15 Stalin permitted the formation of national units within the ranks of other military units, but the Soviet government did not sanction independent national units.

[72] S. E. Sef writes about the forced disarming of the 219th:

The regiment observed and maintained discipline, and . . .
the local organizations in Elisavetpol, including the Executive
Committee of the Elisavetpol Soviet, never allowed the disarming
of the regiment, since they were completely capable of protecting

the pillaging of villages around Elisavetpol followed, and armed bands effectively disrupted the railroad ties with Baku. Rumors of warfare spread to Baku and brought the military-revolutionary committee into session.[73] The causes of the disturbances remained obscure to the soviet, and speculation that the fighting had been started by a Moslem military unit known as the Savage Division (*Dikaia divisiia*) was ended only by information from Tiflis. Nevertheless, the military-revolutionary committee, meeting with the representatives of the political parties, pressed forward with the plan to form a Red Guards' unit in Baku.[74] On December 24 the Baku soviet decided to end the reign of anarchy on the Baku–Elisavetpol railroad by sending armed units, agitators, and representatives of the Moslem parties to the afflicted areas.[75] The disorders committed by Moslem bands and the disarming by the Moslems of Russian soldiers both had the effect of placing the Bolsheviks and the Moslem parties in opposing camps. The tensions between the Musavat and the Bolsheviks were aggravated in January 1918 by the tragic and confused events at Shamkhor, where in the process of disarming troops leaving the front one thousand Russian soldiers

---

the city. But, under the pressure of the Moslem National Council, on December 14, 1917, an order was sent from the General Staff of the Caucasian Front to surrender weapons and all military equipment to the Tatar regiment being formed. Despite the fact that this order was canceled by the local commander, General Mdivani, the Moslem National Council carried out the disarmament by force, and the operation was marked by massive pillaging. Everything down to their underwear was taken from the soldiers, who were then sent to the railroad station. (*Bor'ba za Oktiabr'*, p. 71.)

Thus, one month after the Mensheviks had neutralized the Bolshevik armed forces in Tiflis by seizing the arsenal, the Moslem leadership in Elisavetpol had done the same by disarming and dispersing the Russian garrison there.

[73] *Izvestiia*, no. 214, December 12, 1917.
[74] *Kaspii*, no. 279, December 21, 1917.
[75] *Bakinskii rabochii*, no. 116, December 24, 1917.

were killed. Shamkhor shocked Baku, embarrassed Tiflis, and strengthened the Transcaucasian Moslems, who had proven that they had the single most effective military force in the area.

In the face of the danger from the Moslem bands around Baku and the hostility of the Tiflis authorities, the soviet rejected Tiflis's suggestion that the garrison be dispersed so that national military units could be formed, and instead decided to form international units made up primarily of reliable workers. A class principle was being counterposed to the national principle. Even the head of the Dashnak faction in the soviet, Melik-Eolchian, agreed that international units alone should operate within Baku and that Armenian national units should be sent to the front.[76]

The arrival of the Military-Revolutionary Committee of the Caucasian Army in Baku in January further shifted the balance of local power toward the Bolsheviks. With its chairman, Korganov, came several echelons of loyal soldiers and stores of ammunition and weapons, all of which were placed under the authority of the Baku Committee of the RSDRP(b). The Military-Revolutionary Committee worked energetically to form a unit of Red Guards for the soviet, and the Bolshevik officer Solntsev directed a school for the training of a command apparatus.[77] With these additions from Tiflis, the Red Guards soon surpassed in number the experienced troops of the Armenian National Council and the few raw recruits of the Moslem National Council.[78] Though the old Baku garrison with its Bol-

[76] *Izvestiia*, no. 5 (227), January 9, 1918.

[77] N. N. Kolesnikova, *Iz istorii bor'by za sovetskuiu vlast' v Baku (Avgust 1917 g.—iiul' 1918 g.): Vospominaniia* (Baku, 1958), p. 69.

[78] Although the Military-Revolutionary Committee of the Caucasian Army had been formed at the Second Congress of the Caucasian Army (December 10–23) in Tiflis, once it moved to Baku it became a strictly Bolshevik agency. The committee had been forced to leave Tiflis when the Menshevik and Right S.R. minor-

shevized soldiery had disbanded, the soviet could now rely on the newly formed workers' army. And the city duma, with no military of its own, continued to exist only as long as the soviet chose to tolerate it.

Early in 1918 the party newspaper of the Socialist Revolutionaries published an editorial which posed and answered the question of where power lay in Baku. The central thesis of the editorial was that power no longer meant legal authority but rather real force, particularly military force, by which orders could be implemented in a city without any clearly recognizable, fully sanctioned government.

We ask, who now actually has power in its hands—the Soviet of Workers' and Soldiers' Deputies or the Duma? It seems to us that even the [duma] delegates ought to realize that power does not lie with the Duma, which is supported by no one. It is not enough just to pass a resolution that power belongs to the city government, and thus settle everything. The Duma cannot even force the landlords to light lanterns outside their homes, those same landlords for whom representatives in the Duma are fighting for the transfer of power to the city government. . . . And whom does the city government think supports it when it effects some measure or other, let's say, of a political character? Isn't it the national regiments? They tell us that the Soviet is supported by no one, that there are no soldiers in the garrison and that the power of the Soviet is a self-delusion. It is possible that this is so, but nevertheless the Soviet has a workers' army which

---

ity on the Territorial Council of the Army seized the offices of the council by force. Soldiers in Tiflis made no move to assist the legitimate leaders of the council, the Bolsheviks and Left S.R.s, and Korganov soon took his authority with him to Baku. (*Izvestiia*, no. 4 [226], January 6, 1918.)

recognizes it as its higher organ, which subordinates itself to it, and on which, consequently, [the soviet] may lean.[79]

The editorial concluded with the declaration that, given the composition of the local duma and the conditions in the Caucasus, political power should at present belong to the soviet. Both Russian nationalism and pragmatism demanded support of the soviet. Only the soviet could enforce law and protect the city from the Moslem menace. The Socialist Revolutionaries thus broke with the Mensheviks, who continued to insist on the principle of democratic representation of all classes and therefore supported the Baku city duma.

By the end of January the situation was indeed desperate for the city duma. Of the socialist parties, only the Mensheviks and the insignificant Edinstvo group supported duma power, and they were joined on the Right by the Kadets, the Moslem National Council, and the Armenian National Democratic Party.[80] The Mensheviks, having been deserted by the Dashnaks and Socialist Revolutionaries on the issue of local government, had reluctantly allied with the right wing of the duma. Their principal concerns remained unity of the organ of power and legality. But within the duma no faction could rally a majority to support either soviet power or a duma government. Divided hopelessly, the duma made no decision on this matter, and several parties, including the Dashnaks, Islam in Russia, and the Armenian National Democrats, expressed their hopes that the Seim which was to meet in Tiflis would decide on the nature of the new government.[81]

While the city duma disintegrated into warring fac-

[79] *Znamia truda*, no. 9; cited in Ia. A. Ratgauzer, *Revoliutsiia i grazhdanskaia voina v Baku*, I: 1917–1918 gg. (Baku, 1927), p. 110.
[80] *Baku*, no. 23, January 30, 1918.
[81] *Ibid.*

tions, the soviet acted with renewed authority. The Red Guards were formed in mid-January. At the end of the month a revolutionary tribunal was created to enforce the new unwritten law against counterrevolutionary acts, and this tribunal replaced the existing courts.[82] The soviet was creating an apparatus by which it could act as a government. It sent commissars to all local banks to oversee their operation; the bank-directors resisted the commissars, provoking the soviet to send armed men to remove the directors.[83] The soviet meant to enforce its will with arms if necessary.

In the atmosphere of mistrust and suspicion in which the Armenians and Moslems of Baku lived, efforts to secure arms for coreligionists were inevitable. The uneasy armistice that had subsisted between Moslems and Armenians in the city was breaking down under the pressure of constant reports from other parts of Transcaucasia of clashes between these two groups.[84] Moslems within Baku felt an urgent need to arm themselves in view of the presence of Armenian military units in the city. While leftist Moslems, like the Socialist Revolutionary Vezirov, urged Moslem workers to join the Red Guards, Moslem workers felt that the soviet did not have confidence in the Moslems.[85] Within the executive committee of the soviet the Musavatist leader, Resul Zade, argued for the formation by the Moslem National Committee of military units. Resul Zade admitted that these units were financed by rich Moslems but considered them necessary for the reestablishment of order in the provinces.[86] Like other Moslem leaders, Resul Zade suspected that the soviet was

[82] *Izvestiia*, no. 15 (237), January 20, 1918; *ibid.*, no. 24 (246), February 14, 1918.

[83] *Ibid.*, no. 32 (254), February 23, 1918.

[84] *Arev*, no. 28, February 19, 1918.

[85] *Ibid.*, no. 30, February 21, 1918.

[86] *Izvestiia*, no. 27 (249), February 17, 1918; Shaumian, II, pp. 181–182.

arming only Russians and Armenians.[87] The executive committee of the soviet attempted to resolve the conflict by issuing an order to arm workers who were members of the Musavat party on the recommendation of local soviet organs.[88] The order notwithstanding, three separate military forces were formed during February and March in Baku: the Red Guards of the soviet, and the units of the Moslem National Council and the Armenian National Council.

The most formidable military rival to soviet power in Baku was the Armenian forces, loosely gathered under the authority of the Armenian National Council and the Dashnaktsutiun. These forces included seven hundred men of the Second Armenian Regiment, a partisan regiment of eight hundred under the command of Amazasp, a Dashnak detachment of fifty men, and several thousand Armenian soldiers who had been sent from the Western Front to complete the Armenian Corps being formed to defend the Caucasus.[89] Although these troops were heavily influenced by Dashnak and Armenian nationalist ideas, the Baku Bolsheviks did not consider them as a threat. After all, the Dashnaktsutiun in Baku had recognized soviet power, was willing to subordinate its troops to that power, and identified the counterrevolution, as did the Bolsheviks, with the separatist Seim and the Moslem federalists. While Dashnaks in Tiflis were cooperating with the Georgian Mensheviks in their efforts to negotiate with the Turks, the Dashnaks of Baku were condemning the policies of separation from Russia. The Dashnaktsutiun in Baku remained pro-Russian in its orientation and therefore was committed to the Bolshevik position. Shaumian was cautious in dealing with the Armenian nation-

---

[87] *Izvestiia*, no. 32 (254), February 23, 1918.

[88] *Ibid.*

[89] Gen. G. Korganoff, *La participation des arméniens à la guerre mondiale sur le front du Caucase* (*1914–1918*) (Paris, 1927), p. 175.

alists, as is indicated in a letter to Stalin in which he wrote: "Concerning the weapons for the Dashnaks, I ask that you deal with the affair so that the final resolution of the question depends on me here. Looking at the situation we will decide it here. I do not expect a change in their policy, but it is better if they depend on us here. . . ."[90] Mutual interest brought the Bolsheviks and the Dashnaks closer together, but ideological differences kept them from ever becoming close political allies.

Toward the end of February the sensitivities of the national parties, the Dashnaks and Musavatists, were offended by the tone of several articles in the soviet's *Izvestiia*, and the parties' factions walked out of the soviet.[91] The Dashnaks accused the Bolsheviks of having turned the *Izvestiia* into a party organ. The Bolsheviks attacked the walkout in a resolution adopted by the Soviet.

> The Soviet of Workers' and Soldiers' Deputies, having discussed the question of the walkout from the session of the Soviet of the Dashnak and Musavat factions, finds that at a moment when the forces of counterrevolution with each instant are becoming more threatening, when in the city hooliganism has begun to develop and killings and thefts are being committed, when between different representatives of national military units armed clashes are occurring—— at that moment when a revolutionary cohesion of all factions in the Soviet is essential—and, considering that this walkout was not necessary but might have been resolved peacefully (the question of the reorganization of the Editorial Board had already been put on the agenda) and that this is the continuation of the tactics of the struggle of the national-chauvinist minority of the Soviet against the internationalist

90 *Pis'ma*, p. 167.
91 *Arev*, no. 30, February 21, 1918; *ibid.*, no. 33, February 24, 1918; *Bakinskii rabochii*, no. 33 (149), February 24, 1918.

majority—states that by this split the bourgeois counterrevolutionaries are helped, and in the most sharp way condemns this walkout. . . .[92]

The Bolsheviks made no move, as they had in October of 1917, to take advantage of the walkout of the opposition parties, for in February 1918 they were more concerned about the risk of unleashing a disastrous national war which could easily work to their disadvantage. The Socialist Revolutionaries also condemned the walkout for its schismatic effect, but were more understanding than the Bolsheviks about the reasons for the Dashnak and Musavat actions.[93]

The relations between the soviet leadership in Baku and the Musavat Party reached breaking-point by February 1918. Once again events outside of Baku had worked even more strongly than local matters to bring about this situation. With Russian soldiers leaving the Caucasian Front, the Turkish command saw an opportunity to advance northward and secure victories badly needed for the morale of the army and the empire. The battles which ensued through February and March were in effect part of an Armeno-Turkish war, for the only real resistance to the Turkish advance came from the Armenian volunteer units. This ill-disciplined army often engaged in massacres of local Moslems in revenge for the systematic destruction of the Armenian nation by the Turks. The ferocity of the war on both sides had its repercussions in Transcaucasia and gave rise to a series of clashes between Armenians and Azerbaijanis. Resul Zade and his followers could not but deplore the violence while defending the Moslems. After almost a year of working with the soviet to achieve the reforms his party desired, the Musavat leader had concluded that a real federalist solution, autonomy for Azerbaijan, and power for the Moslem majority could better

[92] *Bakinskii rabochii*, no. 33 (149), February 24, 1918.
[93] *Ibid.*

be achieved by the anti-Bolshevik forces. Lenin's promise of national self-determination ceased to be meaningful for the Azerbaijani leadership. Resul Zade wrote:

> As it turns out for us, the Moslems, we cannot expect to have autonomy, for this is undesirable for the worker or for the noble-bourgeois class of Russia, and persistence in this matter will give us the biggest "pile of ruins"....
> Turkish Armenia receives a decree on self-determination, the Armenians approach their cherished dream, supported by the Dashnaktsutiun, but, for the Caucasian Azerbaijani federalists, the Baku Bolsheviks frighten them with "a pile of ruins."[94]

Shaumian answered Resul Zade by denying that the Bolsheviks discriminated in favor of the Armenians. Rather, he said, they were opposed equally to all nationalists and would not permit national self-determinaion if it meant control by the nationalists. But his arguments proved unconvincing.

The strategy of the Baku Bolsheviks based on winning power peacefully did not survive the "deepening of the revolutionary crisis" and the introduction of an overt nationalist challenge in 1918. The approaching civil war appeared to the Bolsheviks not only inevitable but desirable. They could already clearly identify, it seemed, the

[94] *Bakinskii rabochii*, no. 27 (143), February 17, 1918; Shaumian, II, pp. 182–183. Bolshevik policy was hampered somewhat by the rejection in October 1917 of Shaumian's proposal to the Caucasian congress of RSDRP(b) to divide Transcaucasia into three autonomous regions based on nationality. The congress considered this position to be too close to that of the Menshevik Zhordaniia. In his memoirs Mikoyan, who in 1917 voted against Shaumian's resolution, argues that if it had been adopted the Bolsheviks could have used the slogan of "National Autonomy" to attract peasant support. Not until the end of 1919 did the Communists adopt this position. (Anastas Mikoyan, "O dniakh bakinskoi kommuny [Iz vospominanii]," II, *Iunost'*, no. 12 [1967], p. 52.)

sources of the anti-Bolshevik counterrevolution: Tiflis, the north Caucasus, and Elisavetpol. In a speech early in the year, Shaumian distinguished between the tactic of civil peace and civil war and explained that they are based in the nature of the revolution:

> Tactics depend on whether a party considers the revolution bourgeois or socialist. For the Mensheviks it is bourgeois, but for us it is not bourgeois. The epoch of bourgeois revolutions has long passed the time when the bourgeoisie was revolutionary. In the epoch of finance capitalism and, tied with that, imperialism, the bourgeoisie as a class is reactionary all over Europe. Our bourgeoisie, being tightly tied to this reactionary bourgeoisie, cannot be revolutionary. In no bourgeois revolution was the proletariat opposed to the bourgeoisie as a special class with its own special self-consciousness and organizations and its special tasks. Meanwhile, here the proletariat exists as an independent organized force.[95]

Shaumian characterized the Russian revolution as "a transitory worker-peasant revolution which is taking decisive steps toward socialism and leading us to it."[96] He called for the destruction of the bourgeois state machinery, echoing Marx and Lenin on the Paris Commune, and for control by the workers of the economic order. Shaumian did not hide his views that this would mean civil war. On the contrary, he seemed to welcome it: "Civil war is the same as class war, in its aggravation and bitterness reaching armed clashes on the streets. We are supporters of civil war, not because we thirst for blood, but because without struggle the pile of oppressors will not give up their privileges to the people. To reject class struggle

[95] *Izvestiia*, no. (226), January 6, 1918. This speech has not been reproduced in any of the collections of Shaumian's works.
[96] *Ibid.*

means to reject the requirements of social reforms for the people."[97] He finished with the note that "the final triumph of the Bolsheviks, and, this means, socialism in Russia, is possible only if a revolution breaks out in Europe, the signs and objective reports of which are evident."[98]

Shaumian's tactical shift to overt declaration in favor of civil war meant in practical terms, first, an internal civil war within Baku against the anti-Soviet forces, and secondly, an external war against the centers of counter-revolution—Tiflis, Elisavetpol, and the north Caucasus. His optimism was great indeed as he urged his comrades in Baku to launch the final campaign against their enemies. In fact, he said, the Tiflis Mensheviks had already provoked the war by closing the Bolshevik newspaper, *Kavkazskii rabochii*, and by the dispersal under fire of a meeting of Bolshevik sympathizers in Tiflis on February 23, not to speak of their role (as conceived by Shaumian) in the Shamkhor events. Shaumian called for the overthrow of the Zavkom: "The Baku proletariat in this connection is called upon to play a special role. Our sacred task, comrades, is to go to the aid of the peasants and workers of all of Transcaucasia and help them overturn the criminal aristocratic-bourgeois Transcaucasian Commissariat."[99] On the first anniversary of the overthrow of the tsar, Shaumian spoke to a celebrating crowd in the soviet building using the image of the Paris Commune as the prototype for the Russian Soviet republic. He said, as had Lenin on numerous occasions, that soviet democracy was the historical successor to parliamentarism.[100] Thus, dismissing "liberal prejudices," Shaumian went on to em-

[97] *Ibid.*          [98] *Ibid.*

[99] *Bakinskii rabochii*, no. 45 (161), March 10, 1918; Shaumian, *Stat'i i rechi, 1917–1918 gg.* (Baku, 1929), p. 129. This particular article by Shaumian was not reprinted in the most recent edition of his selected works.

[100] *Izvestiia*, no. 49 (271), March 16, 1918; Shaumian, II, pp. 187–188.

phasize the need for a dictatorship of one class, of the proletariat, to carry out the long struggle for socialism. He saw Baku in the midst of a world-wide civil war and expressed great optimism about its outcome.[101] In a later speech Shaumian again reminded his audience of Baku's special position: "The Baku Soviet ought to become the main support and center in Transcaucasia of the civil war which the Soviet of People's Commissars has declared in Russia. It ought to carry the working people of Transcaucasia into the battle against the exploiters which will unquestionably end with the victory of the proletariat."[102] On March 5, Shaumian returned to Baku after two months' traveling around Transcaucasia. He met late that night with seven of his comrades to discuss the situation in Baku. Dzhaparidze and Zevin reported that the activity of the Military-Revolutionary Committee of the Caucasian Army in forming armed units was driving the "conciliatory" parties into the hands of the Kadets and Musavatists, from whom some kind of counterrevolutionary adventure could be expected. In opposition to this point of view, Fioletov, Azizbekov, Vasili Egorov, Arsen Amirian, and Kolesnikova argued that the counterrevolutionary movements required resolute action on the part of the committee. Shaumian sided with the latter group and held that conciliation with the anti-Bolshevik parties would be dangerous at this juncture. "Comrades, I am convinced that if it were not for the Military-Revolutionary Committee of the Caucasian Army and its decisive revolutionary activity, you all would have been arrested and the Baku Soviet dispersed. We do not want civil war, but the mobilizing counterrevolution is pushing us toward it and we must be prepared for it."[103] Shaumian's arrival marks the beginning of a more resolute Bolshevik policy vis-à-vis the anti-Bolsheviks both within Baku and without. Only prov-

[101] *Ibid.*, p. 188.
[102] *Ibid.*, p. 189.          [103] Kolesnikova, p. 66.

ocation by their adversaries was needed to begin the civil war.

Ten days passed and Shaumian spoke to the Baku soviet on the "Current Situation in Transcaucasia." He decried the separation of Transcaucasia from Russia, which he characterized as a turn from Europe to Asia. He called for revolutionary war against the separatists, and warned: "If [the Baku soviet] does not move against the counter-revolutionaries, then they themselves will come to us. After all, the Moslem nationalists dream of making Baku the capital of Azerbaijan."[104] The Baku soviet split on the issue of separation, with the Mensheviks and Musavatists abstaining in the vote on the Bolshevik resolution to censure the Seim. But the majority in the soviet, including the Dashnaks, were for the Bolshevik resolution (the vote was 121–16, with 32 abstentions), which, in part, stated: "The Baku Soviet considers it as its revolutionary duty to go to the aid of the fraternal working class and peasantry of the whole of Transcaucasia and together with them to overthrow this counterrevolutionary and criminal power of the Seim."[105] The Menshevik Aiollo attacked Shaumian for distorting the intentions of the Tiflis leadership. He asserted that Zhordaniia saw independence as an effort to unify the various nationalities. Better an independent Transcaucasia, he stated, than a protectorate of Turkey.[106] But the Right Socialist Revolutionaries, sometimes the ally of the Mensheviks, were not prepared to support separation from Russia. Sahakian stated he could not recognize the Seim, reversing his earlier position. The Bolshevik call for a crusade against Tiflis had been sanctioned by the soviet. It remained to be seen if that crusade meant a military campaign launched from Baku to win Transcaucasia for the soviets.

[104] *Izvestiia*, no. 51 (273), March 20, 1918; Shaumian, II, p. 192.
[105] *Bakinskii rabochii*, no. 51 (167), March 20, 1918; *Dok.*, pp. 316–317.
[106] *Izvestiia*, no. 53 (275), March 22, 1918.

The Bolshevik commitment to civil war necessitated the further strengthening of the military position of the Baku soviet and the unification of the military command in the Bolshevik-dominated Military-Revolutionary Committee of the Caucasian Army. Shaumian wrote to Stalin on March 16 requesting that money sent to Baku for military purposes be put directly under his control or that of the Military-Revolutionary Committee. The committee had been maintained, even though its original army had dispersed, in order to permit the Bolsheviks to control military matters without constant consultation with the other parties in the soviet.[107] In this way, military power for the Baku soviet had come to mean military power for the Bolshevik party. In March the soviet once again reduced the power of potential rivals by bringing the local militia under its authority and by reorganizing the Caspian Fleet. The soviet also decided to supplement the Red Guards with a regular Red Army.

Although revolutions follow no set patterns nor adhere to a fixed timetable, it is useful to ask the question why the October Revolution was delayed five months in Baku. Why could not the Bolsheviks in Baku seize power at the time their comrades did in Petrograd, Moscow, and elsewhere? The soviet in Baku, as in Petrograd, Moscow, Tiflis, and other cities, held the real state power long before October. The organ of the Provisional Government, the IKOO, was first tolerated, then converted into a "façade" for the soviet, and finally liquidated; but it never had autonomous power. The city duma, it is true, held formal power through 1917 and into 1918, but it was unable to carry out even rudimentary governing without the soviet. Real power was the monopoly of the soviet, yet it did not take power even when it claimed to be sovereign in the days *before* the October Revolution.

There were three elementary differences between Baku

[107] *Pis'ma*, pp. 165–167; Shaumian, II, pp. 194–195.

and Petrograd before "October." The Bolsheviks in Baku had no majority in the soviet; they lacked military force; and the Shaumian–Dzhaparidze leadership feared the outbreak of interethnic warfare. The Bolshevik faction in the soviet remained small throughout 1917, though their support among worker and soldier deputies was great enough for them to control the soviet from October on; nevertheless, the soviet wavered in the "October Days" and was not solidly committed to soviet power until the last day of December, when the Dashnaks and Right Socialist Revolutionaries joined the soviet Left in support of local soviet power.

By the time the soviet was "Bolshevized," i.e., committed to soviet power, the Bolsheviks, who in September and October had had overwhelming backing from the Baku garrison, had lost their military constituents. November and December were the months in which the armistice was signed and the Caucasian Army deserted. The local garrison dwindled, and the only military forces in the city were stranded Armenian units. Only in late January, with the arrival of Korganov's Military-Revolutionary Committee and the final formation of the Red Guards, did the Bolsheviks have the necessary muscle.

The Bolsheviks hesitated to seize power by force of arms in October because of fears that such action would lead to a renewal of the perennial Armeno-Azerbaijani feuds. Rather than provoke a civil war which would lead to a national war, Shaumian and Dzhaparidze continued applying the tactic of a peaceful transition to soviet power. This tactic was relatively successful, though a final consolidation of power could only be achieved after a military takeover had eliminated the duma and the power of the Moslem National Council. The Bolsheviks were assured of success in their battle against the bourgeoisie and the Moslems only if their alliance with the Armenian military and the Dashnaktsutiun held together. This alliance was flimsy and untested until the "March Days" of 1918.

# 7

## The "Baku October": The "March Days"

FEAR THAT THE REVOLUTION would degenerate into a national feud between Armenians and Azerbaijanis, like that of 1905, had a restraining effect on the political leadership in Baku. This fear had induced the Bolsheviks on numerous occasions to discount publicly rumors that they were about to seize power. The Dashnaks likewise denied that the Armenians were conspiring against the Moslems in league with any third group. As late as March 23, just a week before the "March Days," the central committee of the Dashnaktsutiun threatened to take the disciplining of such rumormongers into its own hands.[1] The proclamation was indicative of the tense atmosphere in which the population of Baku lived, cut off as it was by Moslems from Tiflis and the north Caucasus. Unexplained shootings occurred daily; and a duel between the Moslem forces, still weak and underequipped, and the well-armed soviet and Dashnak forces was expected to break out at any moment.

The fear knew no national bounds. The Armenians and other non-Moslems of the city feared the growing aggressiveness they perceived in Moslems outside of the city and expected it to spread to Baku. The Armenians knew that their national hero, General Andranik, had evacuated Erzerum on March 11 and that by the last two weeks of the month the Turkish army had pushed on to the 1914 Russo-Turkish border. The Moslems, on the other hand,

[1] *Arev*, no. 53, March 24, 1918; *Vesti Baku*, no. 14, March 25, 1918, *Baku*, no. 56, March 26, 1918.

feared that within Baku they were at the mercy of the armed Armenians. The soviet refused the Moslems the quantity of arms they had requested. In February the arrest of the commander of a Moslem division which had come to Baku intensified Moslem opposition to the Baku soviet and to the Bolsheviks in particular. The disaffection had deep roots, and the arrest of General Talyshinskii served as a catalyst to a demonstration and the closing of shops by Moslems.[2] The Musavat staged another walkout from the soviet.

At the end of February a massive emigration of Moslem families from Baku began.[3] This weakened the basis of Musavat support at the very time when the non-Moslems were being convinced that the Moslem leaders were engaged in a conspiracy to make Baku the capital of an autonomous Azerbaijan. The battle had already begun elsewhere. To the south of Baku in the rich grain district of Lenkoran, the perennial struggle between Russian settlers and Azerbaijani peasants had been temporarily settled by the armed establishment of a soviet government. The Moslems attempted unsuccessfully to overthrow the soviets and were forced to retreat. Part of the defeated forces fled by ship northward to Baku.

On March 30 the steamship *Evelina* arrived in Baku carrying the Moslem Savage Division (*Dikaia divisiia*). The Military-Revolutionary Committee of the Baku soviet sent a detachment to the docks to determine the purpose of the visit and the nature of the command. The division received the inspectors from the soviet with insults and gunfire. Several of the soviet agents were killed, several wounded.[4] Initiative then passed from the Military-Revo-

---

[2] S. E. Sef, *Bor'ba za Oktiabr' v Zakavkaz'i* (Tiflis, 1932), p. 136.

[3] A. L. Popov, "Iz istorii revoliutsii v Vostochnom Zakavkaz'e (1917–1918 gg.)," *Proletarskaia revoliutsiia*, no. 11 (1924), p. 154.

[4] *Izvestiia*, no. 62 (284), April 9, 1918; *Biulleten' komiteta revoliutsionnoi oborony*, no. 1, April 4, 1918. Hereafter this newspaper of the Committee of Revolutionary Defense will be cited simply as

lutionary Committee of the Baku soviet to the Military-Revolutionary Committee of the Caucasian Army, an all-Bolshevik organ with power over military units. The committee met with the executive committee of the soviet and demanded that those who had fired on the soviet agents be disarmed. Finally both the Moslem and Armenian National Councils agreed with the demands of the local authorities, and together they persuaded the men on the ship to give up their arms with no further incidents. At this point the conflict might have been "peacefully liquidated" had not the atmosphere in the city been saturated with the anxieties of the past months and the conviction that a national feud was overdue. During the night that followed the city was turned into an armed camp, with barricades going up in the Moslem quarter.[5]

On the morning of March 31 meetings were held throughout the city by Moslems opposed to the soviet's disarming of the Savage Division demanding the arming of the defenseless Moslem population.[6] Hummet, in its strategic position as a Moslem Bolshevik organization,

---

"*Biulleten'.*" S. E. Sef, "Bakinskii Oktiabr'," *Proletarskaia revoliutsiia*, no. 11 (106) (1930), p. 70. Sef notes that the Savage Division, like most other Moslem military units, were largely officered by Russians who sided with the Moslems against soviet Baku (pp. 73–74).

[5] The degree of spontaneity in the preparations for the coming battle is impossible to determine. The Bolsheviks at the time (like Soviet historians since) were convinced that the Musavat Party played the leading role in organizing the armed struggle against the soviet. The element of conspiracy is stressed. On the other hand, the arrival of the *Evelina* was not coordinated with the preparations for armed action. The barricades were thrown up only after the Savage Division was disarmed. Certainly the mood among the Moslems was conducive to an anti-soviet and anti-Armenian insurrection, and in the popular imagination Armenian and Bolshevik had become linked, if not synonymous, terms. Agitation by the Musavatists simply articulated the latent feelings of the Moslem community. The rising thus seems to have been largely spontaneous but kindled, shaped, and given a degree of organization by Musavatist activists.

[6] *Izvestiia*, no. 62 (284), April 9, 1918.

attempted to mediate the dispute between the soviet leadership and the Moslem nationalists, as it had done unsuccessfully a month before in the crisis which had followed the arrest of Talyshinskii. Hummet activists met with "some members of the Christian party" (probably the Dashnaks) and Shaumian in Narimanov's apartment. Narimanov pleaded with Shaumian that the civil war be delayed yet a little longer, for the danger still existed that it would turn into an interethnic feud. Hummet proposed that the arms taken from the Savage Division be transferred to the custody of the Hummet Party, an act which would have a tranquilizing effect on the Baku Moslems. Shaumian agreed to this solution and left the meeting with the understanding that the excited state of the Moslems would not be used as an excuse to initiate the civil war.[7]

At four in the afternoon a delegation from several Moslem parties appeared before the executive committee of the soviet and asked for arms for the Moslems. Dzhaparidze asked if their request could be considered an ultimatum, and the delegation declared that they had no other interest than to cool the passions of the Moslem masses who at that moment were in a state of great excitement. Dzhaparidze assured the Moslem leaders that he would take the matter to the Military-Revolutionary Committee of the Caucasian Army and support the granting of arms to the Moslems. But while Dzhaparidze consulted with the committee, reports that Moslems were firing on soviet troops in the streets came to their attention. The committee considered further discussion superfluous, and Dzhaparidze informed the delegation that their demands had been denied. The delegation left the soviet building to calm its countrymen, who were already digging trenches and firing on their supposed enemies.

The soviet leadership acted resolutely and rapidly to

[7] Nariman Narimanov, *Stat'i i pis'ma s kratkim biograficheskim ocherkom* (Moscow, 1925), p. 6.

head off the insurrection which threatened their power. In the early evening of March 31 a Committee of Revolutionary Defense was formed to act as the general staff for the operations against the rebel Moslems. The committee's membership included Shaumian, Dzhaparidze, Korganov, Sukhartsev, Sahakian, Melik-Eolchian, and Dr. Narimanov. In its first proclamation the new committee declared itself "the highest military-political organ" in Baku, accountable only to the soviet.[8]

As the Moslem rebellion against the soviet prepared its first move, the Armenian community dramatically declared its neutrality in the coming struggle. Clearly the side which could enlist the Armenian military units in its cause would have the preponderance of strength and could be assured of victory. The Musavat Party proposed a tactical alliance to the Dashnaks but received a rebuff. The Armenian National Council withdrew its forces to the Armenian parts of the city and limited its action to self-defense.[9] Thus before the actual shooting began it appeared that the conflict would not be a repetition of the Armeno-Azerbaijani feuds of the past but a civil war between the Soviets and the Moslems. But these expectations were not realized. Mysteriously, sometime on March 31, the Armenian leadership shifted its position and released its soldiers for service with the soviet.[10] The battle-lines were drawn. The soviet and Armenian forces stood from Parapet to the Boulevard, along the quay, and held parts of Armenian and Balakhany Streets from Stanislavskii. The rest of the city was held by the Moslems, as, at ten in the evening of March 31, the machine-gun and sporadic rifle fire intensified into a full-fledged battle.

[8] *Izvestiia*, no. 64 (286), April 11, 1918.
[9] *Arev*, no. 63, April 10, 1918; *ibid.*, no. 64, April 11, 1918.
[10] *Biulleten'*, no. 1, April 4, 1918. Baikov writes that the Armenian National Council had decided on neutrality, but that later the Baku committee of the Dashnaktsutiun decided to participate in the struggle against the Moslems. The Armenian soldiers in the city followed the lead of the Dashnaks. (Baikov, p. 121.)

The Committee of Revolutionary Defense issued a proclamation, probably on April 1, in which it set out its view of the events and their causes. The statement emphasized the anti-soviet aspect of the rebellion at the same time as it clearly put the onus for the Moslem action on the Musavat Party and the national leadership. The committee claimed that the insurrection was the result of a Musavat conspiracy and carefully laid plans:

> The enemies of soviet power in the city of Baku have
> raised their head. The malice and hatred with which
> they viewed the revolutionary organ of the workers
> and soldiers began recently to overflow into open
> counterrevolutionary actions. The appearance of the
> staff of the Savage Division, headed by the unmasked
> Talyshkhanov, the events in Lenkoran, in Mugan,
> and at Shemakh, the capture of Petrovsk by the
> Daghestan regiment and the withholding of grain
> shipments for Baku, the threats of Elisavetpol, and in
> the last few days of Tiflis, to march on Baku, against
> soviet power, the aggressive movements of the armored
> train of the Transcaucasian Commissariat in Adzhikabul,
> and, finally, the outrageous behavior of the Savage
> Division on the steamship *Evelina* in shooting comrades,
> —all this speaks of the criminal plans of the
> counterrevolutionaries grouped mainly around the Bek
> party Musavat and having as its goal the overthrow of
> soviet power, so hated by the bourgeoisie and landlords.[11]

Counterrevolution was identified as the efforts of the Moslem landlords and their political arm, the Musavat, to destroy soviet power in Baku and establish an autonomous Azerbaijani state. Clearly the soviet view did not emphasize the national aspects of the March Days but rather the anti-soviet thrust. But on April 1, when the Moslems were being beaten back and the Dashnak units took revenge for their

[11] *Dok.*, pp. 329-330.

national grievances, the submerged national content of the civil war in Baku became evident.[12]

The fighting spread rapidly to the oil fields. In the Balakhany-Surakhany districts an executive committee for the defense of the revolution was formed, and all armed forces in the area were put under its command.[13] In Balakhany and Romany the majority of Moslem workers stayed at their places, and the peasants were not moved to join the rebels. But in Surakhany the Moslems disarmed a small Red Guards unit, established their authority over the district, and organized a drive against Balakhany and Sabunchiny.[14] When on April 1 the Moslems attacked Sabunchiny, the combined forces of an armored car, front-line soldiers, and the Red Guards drove them back and destroyed them as a fighting force.[15] The Persian

[12] During and after the "March Days," the Baku Bolsheviks attempted to deemphasize the national character of the insurrection and play up its anti-soviet aspects. For Soviet historians the problem of whether the "Baku October" was a national or a class struggle has usually been resolved in favor of the latter. Western historians generally consider the event "a purely national clash" (Richard Pipes, *The Formation of the Soviet Union: Communism and Nationalism, 1917–1923* [Cambridge, Mass., 1957], p. 200). For the two years during which the Bolsheviks worked in the Azerbaijani Republic, they made several public admissions of the national character of the "March Days" (Sarkis, *Bor'ba za vlast': Opyt istorii bakinskoi organizatsii AKP.[b] za 1918–1920 gody* [Baku, 1930], pp. 39–40). Neither the Western nor the Soviet interpretations of the "March Days" are completely satisfactory. The counterrevolutionary thrust against the Baku soviet was made by the Moslems, aided by Russian officers, and they were defeated by a soviet–Dashnak alliance. But the national aspect of the struggle became overt only after several days of battle. Only then did Armenians begin to slaughter Moslems. And after the shooting and burning stopped, neither national group was in control of the city, but the soviet. It may be said most accurately that the soviet defended itself against the national counterrevolution with the aid of an opposing national group. The end result of this maneuver was to put the Left bloc in power and establish a soviet commune.

[13] *Bakinskii rabochii*, no. 62 (178), April 11, 1918.

[14] *Ibid.*; *Izvestiia*, no. 62 (284), April 9, 1918.

[15] *Ibid.*

workers remained passive all through the fighting, waiting for an end to the bloodshed, refusing to be drawn into someone else's battle.[16]

At ten in the morning on April 1 the Committee of Revolutionary Defense, sitting in the Hotel Astoria on Morskaia Street, decided that the situation called for the use of artillery against the Moslem quarter.[17] A leaflet was issued:

> In view of the fact that the counterrevolutionary party
> Musavat declared war on the Soviet of Workers',
> Soldiers', and Sailors' Deputies in the city of Baku
> and thus threatened the existence of the government
> of the revolutionary democracy, BAKU IS DECLARED
> TO BE IN A STATE OF SIEGE.[18]

The artillery-fire began almost immediately. The Moslems had not expected the heavy guns to be used, and with them against them the rebels could not hold out for long. At eleven in the morning the influential Moslem Ismail-Bek Safataliev telephoned Dr. Narimanov and pleaded with him to find a way to stop the fighting which now threatened to destroy the Moslem quarter and kill innocent bystanders.[19] An hour later out of the Moslem fortress in the center of the old city came Agu-Dzhafat with a similar plea, for the Moslems had run out of cartridges. "What did you hope for when you started this war?" asked Narimanov. Agu-Dzhafat answered: "It was a mistake."[20] Narimanov telephoned Dzhaparidze and relayed the pleas of the Moslems, but Dzhaparidze was unwilling to stop the shelling of the Moslem quarter until a delegation from the rebels appeared before the Committee of Revolutionary Defense.[21]

Early in the afternoon the Moslem delegation, led by

---

[16] Popov, "Iz istorii . . . ," no. 11 (1924), p. 157.
[17] Izvestiia, no. 63 (285), April 10, 1918.
[18] Dok., p. 332.
[19] Narimanov, p. 5.      [20] Ibid., pp. 5–6.
[21] Ibid.; Izvestiia, no. 63 (285), April 10, 1918.

Topchibashev, Ashurov, and D. Arutiunov, arrived at the Astoria. The committee presented them with an ultimatum and demanded that representatives from all Moslem organizations sign the document before the shelling stopped. The Moslems met separately in the building of the IKS and after some discussion decided to capitulate to the committee's demands. At about four o'clock the protocol was signed and the artillery bombardment halted. Individual shooting continued, however, during the negotiations. At five Dzhaparidze opened the conference between the committee representatives—Sahakian, Zevin, Fioletov, Dudin—and the Moslems, represented by Tagiev (Islam in Russia), Iliushkin (the mayor of the city), A. M. Topchibashev, the Mulla Haji Mir Mousum, Haji Hussein Tagiev, and Kazim Zade (Musavat). Also present were the Persian Consul in Baku; and Doctor L. Atabekian (S.R.) and Ter-Mikaelian from the Armenian National Council.[22] Dzhaparidze read the ultimatum of the committee with its strong anti-Musavat tenor. Kazim Zade protested the accusations directed at his party and maintained that the Musavat had not been in the trenches firing on soviet troops. The Musavat, he said, recognized soviet power in principle, though it had serious reservations about its technical operation. Nevertheless, the Musavat, the other Moslem groups, and the Armenian National Council agreed to the ultimatum; and the meeting closed at nine in the evening.

The ultimatum accepted by the Moslem plenipotentiaries on April 1, 1918, read as follows:

ULTIMATUM

presented by the Committee of Revolutionary Defense of the city of Baku and its districts to the Musavat party and other nationalist groups of Moslems which had begun the war against the Soviet.

We demand the immediate end of military activity

[22] *Izvestiia*, no. 63 (285), April 10, 1918.

opened against the soviet power in the city of Baku;
we demand the immediate surrender of fortified posts
and the destruction of trenches.

In order to avoid repetition in the future of such
acts, the Committee of Revolutionary Defense demands:

1. Open and unconditional recognition of the
power of the Baku Soviet of Workers', Soldiers', and
Sailors' Deputies and complete subordination to all its
orders.

2. The "Savage Division" as a counterrevolutionary
military unit cannot be tolerated within the
bounds of Baku and its districts. Other national
Moslem military units, as well as Armenian ones,
should be either led out of the city or subordinated
completely to the Soviet of Workers', Soldiers',
and Sailors' Deputies. The whole armed population
must be under the control and check of the Soviet
of Workers', Soldiers', and Sailors' Deputies.

3. We demand the acceptance of immediate
measures to open the railroads from Baku to
Tiflis and from Baku to Petrovsk.[23]

The ultimatum did not impose any penalties on the Musavat party and specifically did not exclude its members
from the soviet. Its purpose was to liquidate the armed
resistance to the soviet, not to isolate the Moslems in an
anti-soviet opposition. The attitude of the Committee of
Revolutionary Defense was quite conciliatory to the Moslems. There was an attempt to bring the Moslems back
into the fold of the "revolutionary democracy." But the
committee had no control over their allies, the Dashnaks
and the Armenian military units, whose actions on April 1
destroyed the possibility of reconciliation.

Before the ultimatum was signed the soviet forces advanced slowly, aided by artillery-fire, along Armenian

---

[23] *Dok.*, pp. 333-334.

Street, taking Vorontsov Street and the Metropole Hotel.
By midday the Moslem headquarters in the Ismailie Building on Nikolaevskaia Street were captured, and soviet
trenches had been advanced as far as Bazzar Street. Only
a strong wind, common in Baku in the spring and summer,
and sniper-fire from the roofs of buildings prevented a
more rapid advance. When the acceptance of the committee's terms by the Moslem delegates was announced,
shooting continued. The Armenian soldiers became more
brutal as resistance subsided, and for a day and a half
they looted, killed, and burned in the Moslem quarter.
They were indiscriminate in their vengeance, killing even
Moslems who were pro-Bolshevik. The Ismailie Building,
one of the finest examples of Moslem architecture in the
city, was burnt down. Tagiev's printing plant, where
*Kaspii* had been published, was set on fire.[24] Almost the
entire upper part of the city, from the Bazzar to Chembere-
kend, was burning by the afternoon of April 2, and the
battle continued on the mountain which rises in the center
of Baku.[25] Only toward the evening of April 2, after three
days of fighting, did the battle come to a close and the
looters take over the streets. In his report to the Sovnarkom
in Moscow, Shaumian estimated that more than three
thousand people had been killed during the three days
of fighting.[26]

When the shooting died down and the smoke cleared,
a totally new political order had come to Baku.[27] The

[24] *Biulleten'*, no. 3, April 6, 1918; Narimanov, p. 6.
[25] *Ibid.* Teams of high soviet officials rode through the city to explain that an armistice had been signed, but to little avail. Two
such officials, the S.R. leaders Levon Atabekian and Denezhkin,
were shot to death as they made their rounds. (*Arev*, no. 60, April
6, 1918; *ibid.*, no. 64, April 11, 1918.)
[26] Shaumian, II, p. 208. Richard Pipes accepts this estimate. Some
more lurid accounts claim that as many as 30,000 Moslems were
killed in the "March Days." See, for example, Essad Bey, *Blood and
Oil in the Orient* (New York, 1932), p. 111.
[27] The Baku committee of Kadets met secretly and decided to
halt its activities and hide its records (Baikov, p. 122).

Moslems, who hitherto had made up the bulk of the population, were now burying their dead and fleeing from the city *en masse*. Their political parties were not again to play a role until the Turkish army reinstated them. The Moslem National Council and Moslem military units simply disappeared.

The left wing of the Moslem community—the Socialist Revolutionaries and Hummet—emerged from the holocaust as the sole spokesmen for their countrymen, for the Musavat leadership had fled the city. Hummet's Israfilbekov opposed conciliation with the Musavat and demanded that that party be thrown out of the soviet. The Moslem workers, the Socialist Revolutionary Akhundov assured the soviet, had finally turned away from the Musavat. The Moslem Socialist Bureau, made up of Hummetists and Left Socialist Revolutionaries, appealed to the Committee of Revolutionary Defense to redress some of the grievances which had led the Moslem masses to such desperate actions. Specifically the Bureau requested: the dispersal of the Armenian National Committee, the subordination of its armed forces to the soviet or its removal from Baku, a Moslem Red Guards unit to defend the Moslem quarter, and more attention to be paid to the food-supply shortage in that quarter.[28]

The commissar of the Moslem Quarter appointed by the Committee of Revolutionary Defense, Azizbekov, appealed to his people not to leave the city, pledging them protection and justice.[29] But Elisavetpol and the north Caucasus seemed safer for the Moslems than Baku with its armed Armenians.

The response of the Committee of Revolutionary Defense was neither vengeful nor harsh. Rather, in the spirit of the ultimatum, soviet authorities sought an accommodation with the Moslems and regretted their desertion of the

[28] *Hummet*, no. 37, April 3, 1918; *Dok.*, p. 335.
[29] *Biulleten'*, no. 4, April 7, 1918; *Dok.*, p. 334.

city. In fact, on the day after the fighting stopped, an angry crowd of five thousand people, presumably made up largely of Armenians, gathered before the Astoria Hotel in protest against the lenient treatment of the Moslems.[30] Talking to representatives of the crowd inside the hotel, Dzhaparidze heatedly told them that their action was as bad as that of the "counterrevolutionary Baku bourgeoisie." The crowd dispersed after expressing confidence in the soviet, but a residue of ill-feeling remained. The soviet leadership had no wish to exchange its victory over the Moslems for a capitulation to the Armenians, and it set out to dismantle or neutralize the sources of Armenian strength in the city. The ultimatum had called for the dissolution of the Armenian National Council, but the Armenians chose not to fulfill their pledge until July 17. The Armenians could not be dealt with harshly since they represented a significant military force much needed by the soviet. Although most Armenian units were merged with soviet units, some purely Armenian units continued to exist. Within days of its victory over the "internal counterrevolution," the soviet faced a serious threat from Moslem bands from the north Caucasus.

The victory over the Moslem insurrection had been accomplished by a Bolshevik-led coalition with Socialist Revolutionaries and Dashnaks. The Mensheviks had played no role in the fighting, since the Military-Revolutionary Committee considered them anti-soviet and refused to give them arms despite their repeated requests.[31] In a letter to the Bolshevik leaders in Moscow, Shaumian analyzed the increased strength of their party within the Baku soviet:

> Here in Baku all parties have become peaceful; the Right S.R.s behaved themselves splendidly, fought and died together with us. Now the Mensheviks ask for weapons and promise their support. . . .

[30] *Biulletin'*, no. 2, April 5, 1918.
[31] *Izvestiia*, no. 63 (285), April 10, 1918.

After the victory gained by us in Baku, the Soviet
has finally been consolidated, and we are able to carry
through serious measures. . . .

Our influence, that of the Bolsheviks, was great before
but now we are the bosses of the situation in the full
sense of the word. Although the Dashnaktsutiun
supports us now in everything, do not promise and do
not give them anything yet. To strengthen them further
is wrong. . . .[32]

Power was at long last in Bolshevik hands.

On April 9 "bourgeois" newspapers were closed by order
of the Committee of Revolutionary Defense. In addition to
*Baku, Kaspii, Bakinets,* and *Vesti Baku,* the Menshevik
*Nash golos* was also shut down.[33] Two days later the
Committee of Revolutionary Defense began to function as
a peacetime government. Its members were each given a
specific area of competence. Shaumian dealt with the
food-supply; Dzhaparidze with transport, city affairs, and
sanitation, etc.; Sahakian was in charge of trade, industry,
and finance, and was assisted by Melik-Eolchian; Sukhartsev was responsible for security and justice, Narimanov
for welfare, and Korganov for military and naval affairs.[34]
This prototype of the Sovnarkom received complete sanction by the soviet.

The immediate tasks of the committee were to keep
workers from deserting their jobs and fleeing the city, and
to acquire money with which to pay them. Shaumian
called a meeting with representatives of the capitalists at
which he demanded payment of a fifty-million-ruble tax
within three days so that a military campaign could be
undertaken.[35] Sometime later the committee abolished the

[32] *Pis'ma,* pp. 66–67.
[33] *Izvestiia,* no. 62 (284), April 9, 1918. *Nash golos* was closed
for the duration of the period of martial law because the Mensheviks had published an article which purported that the "March
Days" had been a national bloodletting, not a civil war.
[34] *Ibid.,* no. 64 (286), April 11, 1918.
[35] *Bakinskii rabochii,* no. 65 (181) April 14, 1918.

right of private ownership of real estate in Baku, with the exception of buildings needed for industrial enterprises.[36] Small apartments were to be rent-free; those for the rich had to be paid for. The committee also disbanded the aristocratic Naval Aviation School, appointed commissars to assist in the direction of steamship companies, and, most importantly, on April 20 liquidated the last rival to the authority of the Baku soviet, the city duma. Shaumian and Korganov signed the decree, which read:

> In view of the fact that the composition of the current Duma is completely unrepresentative of the will and interests of the population of Baku and in view of the inability which the Duma has demonstrated to carry on the complex and responsible business of city government—the Baku City Duma is dissolved. The functions of government are transferred to the Soviet of Workers', Soldiers', and Sailors' Deputies, which founds a special department of municipal economy attached to itself. Until this department is formed, the Committee of Revolutionary Defense instructs the executive organ of the Duma—the *uprava*—to continue its work and all employees to remain at their posts.[37]

By this time the duma had been so discredited that no complaints were heard even from the Mensheviks, who had shortly before walked out of the duma because of its irresolute and ineffective policies.[38]

By mid-April the question of forming a permanent political structure to replace the Committee of Revolutionary Defense, the moribund city duma, and the ever-active Armenian National Council was raised in Bolshevik conferences and by the soviet. On April 19 the Bolsheviks decided to recommend the creation of a Council of People's Commissars (Sovnarkom) based on Lenin's governmental

[36] *Dok.*, pp. 354–355.     [37] *Ibid.*, p. 360.
[38] *Bakinskii rabochii*, no. 70 (186), April 20, 1918.

model. Debate ensued over whether the Bolsheviks, still a minority party, should form the government alone or join in a coalition, as in the present Committee of Revolutionary Defense. Dzhaparidze supported a coalition with the Left and Right Socialist Revolutionaries, but Shaumian proposed a narrow bloc of Bolsheviks and Left Socialist Revolutionaries alone. While Dzhaparidze found supporters among the *apparatchiki* of the executive committee of the soviet, Shaumian received the votes of the party workers. A compromise was finally reached whereby two Right Socialist Revolutionaries would be permitted to enter the government, but only on a personal basis, not as representatives of their party.[39]

Later that day Shaumian rose at the session of the soviet to propose the establishment of a Sovnarkom in Baku. As he outlined the history of the soviet's activities, the Bolshevik leader contrasted the relative conservatism and caution of Baku's program with the revolutionary developments in central Russia. The time had come, he said, for more radical reformation.

> The work of the Soviet and its executive committee has been only functioning as a city government and a police force. We only passed resolutions but did not wage the real struggle for the strengthening of soviet power. Our power has been bourgeois power. We did not work to improve the conditions of the workers, of the urban and rural poor. We did not even limit the rule of the exploiters. All this was so because we had no real force. Every government must have the necessary force, and recently, thanks to the efforts of the Military-Revolutionary Committee of the Caucasian Army, we have gained a military force. . . .
>
> Our government should not preserve the existing order; on the contrary, [it ought] to effect new social

[39] *Ibid.*

measures. Now we stand before the need to create a
new organ of power—a Council of People's Commissars.[40]

Shaumian envisioned the new government as ruling all
of Baku province and bringing the Moslem peasants into
full contact with soviet power. The reports from Azizbekov
had assured him that the Moslem peasantry in the province was no longer for the Musavat but had come around
to supporting the socialist organizations and local soviets.
Once again he hinted that the Caucasian Red Army would
"influence all of Transcaucasia." At the end of his speech
he rejected the pleas of the Right Socialist Revolutionaries
that "the blood of Denezhkin"[41] gave them the right to sit
in the new government as representatives of their party.

Dashnak and Right Socialist-Revolutionary speakers
stood up to challenge Shaumian. Melik-Eolchian claimed
that the "Armenian masses, especially the Dashnaktsutiun,
stand behind soviet power" and that their exclusion from
the government was indefensible. Sahakian attacked
Shaumian's motives:

> For me the interests of the Soviet are higher than the
> party. For Shaumian it is just the opposite. Shaumian
> thinks of the Soviet only as far as it is Bolshevik. If
> the interests of the Bolshevik Party sometime collided
> with the interests of the Soviet, Shaumian would be
> for the party against the Soviet. . . . Shaumian thinks of
> a government in the form of military force, but one
> cannot maintain power by the sword.[42]

Sahakian called for a coalition in this time of extended
danger. But the soviet rejected his proposal and approved
the Bolshevik resolution by a vote of 124–2 with 20
abstentions.

[40] *Izvestiia*, no. 74 (296), April 23, 1918; Shaumian, II, pp. 213–
214.
[41] See footnote 25.
[42] *Izvestiia*, no. 73 (295), April 21, 1918.

On April 25 the soviet met to approve the composition of the new government.[43] The Dashnaks and Right Socialist Revolutionaries refused to accept positions under the conditions set down by the Bolsheviks. Shaumian, on the other hand, refused to compromise with these parties until they agreed to recognize the central Soviet government. The Mensheviks joined the Dashnaks and Right Socialist Revolutionaries in abstaining from the vote approving the new Sovnarkom, but the soviet by a narrow margin approved the government of the Left bloc. A final list of the government consisted of the following members:

| | |
|---|---|
| Chairman<br>Foreign Affairs | Shaumian (B) |
| Internal Affairs | Dzhaparidze (B) |
| Military-Naval Affairs | Korganov (B) |
| People's Economy | Fioletov (B) |
| Municipal Economy | Narimanov (Hummet) |
| Public Education | Kolesnikova (B) |
| Justice | Karinian (B) |

[43] The composition of the Baku soviet in mid-April was as follows:

| | |
|---|---|
| Bolsheviks | 58 |
| Bolshevik sympathizers | 2 |
| Left S.R.s | 46 |
| Left S.R. sympathizers | 7 |
| Right S.R.s | 47 |
| Right S.R. sympathizers | 1 |
| Mensheviks | 28 |
| S.D. Internationalists | 3 |
| Dashnaks | 36 |
| Adalet | 1 |
| Anarchist | 1 |
| Polish Socialist | 1 |
| Musavatists | 23 |
| Leftist sympathizers | 2 |
| Nonparty or unknown | 52 |
| Total | 308 |

(*Bakinskii rabochii*, no. 64 [180], April 13, 1918). This was essentially the soviet elected in December 1917 with some additions.

| Transport, Posts and | |
|---|---|
| Telegraphs | Sukhartsev (Left S.R.) |
| Finance | Kireev (Left S.R.) |
| Control | S. Bogdanov (B) |
| Agriculture | Vezirov (Left S.R.) |
| Labor | Zevin (B)[44] |

The Bolsheviks preferred government by the Left bloc to a coalition of all the pro-soviet parties because they viewed the new Council of People's Commissars as the spearhead of a socialist reconstruction of the city and eventually of Transcaucasia. In their view the weaknesses of the soviet in the past had been rooted in coalition politics and the attempt to reconcile irreconcilable points of view on the nature of the revolution. Only by eliminating the Right socialist parties from the inner sanctum of decision-making could a radical program of social reform be created and carried out. The Bolsheviks were well aware of the advantages of bloc politics and had the successful example of the bloc that the Left Socialist Revolutionaries had formed with the Bolsheviks in Moscow to serve as inspiration. But they seem to have been less aware of the critical dangers of bloc politics. A narrow leftist government in Baku could survive only so long as the soviet majority and the military forces in the city acquiesced in its rule. Once the Right socialist parties could manifest a meaningful opposition to the leftist bloc, Bolshevik rule would end. The Bolsheviks, however, were optimistic about the extent of workers' and soldiers' support for their party and discounted the bitterness of the Right socialists who had been excluded from the government. And in fact Shaumian's estimate of the Bolshevik position immediately

[44] *Ibid.*, no. 76 (192), April 27, 1918; *Izvestiia*, no. 79 (301), April 28, 1918. Sef, in his article "Bakinskii Oktiabr'," demonstrates that the elections of the commissars were quite close. Dzhaparidze won by only one vote; Fioletov by five. Shaumian, however, won by nineteen votes. (p. 87.)

after the "March Days" was quite accurate. What he did not then realize, however, was that once the Bolsheviks became the government they would cease to be the spokesmen for the discontented. Instead they would then bear the brunt of the continuing dissatisfaction which the duma, the IKOO, and the "conciliatory" soviet had borne before them. Another danger of bloc politics stemmed from its very advantage. The narrowly based government could work out a distinct and energetic program of reform easily and rapidly, but such a program could not be put into effect without the agreement of the other parties. And such a program would, moreover, create social dislocations which would increase opposition.

# 8

# Socialism by Decree

In the months between April and July 1918, the bloc of Bolsheviks and Left Socialist Revolutionaries controlled the municipal government in Baku and sought to extend the power of the soviets over the whole of the Transcaucasian isthmus. This short-lived experiment in maximalist socialist administration has been called the "Baku Commune." Like the Paris Commune of 1871, Baku in 1918 was isolated and alone before its enemies. Like Paris, Baku underwent an intense social revolution while fighting for its existence against the more conservative forces opposing it. Baku had the experience of the first Commune to guide it, and its Bolshevik leaders sought to apply the lessons that socialist theoreticians had drawn from the failure of the original Communards. For socialists after 1871 Paris embodied the first proletarian revolution: the Commune was an ideal for the postrevolutionary organization of the state, as well as the testing-ground for tactical principles. It was this socialist image of the Commune, rather than the historical reality, which the Bolsheviks adopted as a guide to their party's actions. It was Marx's vision of the Commune, and later Lenin's, which was studied.[1]

With the formation of a soviet government on April 25, the Baku Commune came into formal existence. The local Sovnarkom in its first declaration to the people emphasized that it represented an integral part of the workers' and peasants' state which the October Revolution had introduced into Russia. The Russian Republic was a repub-

1 See Appendix.

lic of communes, each with its local prerogatives but inseparable from the center. The Sovnarkom took as its task "the implementation of all decrees and orders of the workers'—peasants' government of Russia, the Supreme Council of People's Commissars, as they correspond to local conditions." The last part of that phrase gave the local organ a degree of autonomy which only practice would more clearly define. At the same time as it determined its relation with the central Sovnarkom, the Bolshevik government outlined the internal political structure in Baku:

> The Baku Council of People's Commissars is not
> a local executive power, in the bourgeois sense of
> the word, in relation to the supreme organ of the
> Baku proletariat, the Soviet of Deputies. It does
> not appropriate for itself all executive power. The
> Baku Soviet of Workers', Soldiers', and Sailors'
> Deputies and its Executive Committee continues to
> exist, as before, as both the legislative and executive
> power. According to the principles of the new Soviet
> Socialist Republic the workers themselves legislate
> and rule through their deputies in the Soviet.
> The Baku Council of People's Commissars is only
> a technical organ which makes this task of legislation
> and rule easier. It will implement the decisions of
> the Soviet; it will legislate, publish decrees, etc.,
> but it will answer every minute and for every step
> before the Soviet of Workers', Soldiers', and
> Sailors' Deputies.[2]

Here ostensibly was the reincarnation of the Paris Commune as envisaged by Karl Marx and Lenin, the coexistence of legislative and executive powers in one body.

Before the Sovnarkom could effect any general economic or political reforms, the people's commissars had to

[2] *Izvestiia*, no. 81, May 1, 1918; *Dok.*, pp. 383–384.

develop sources of revenue in order to pay the soldiers of the Red Army. The fifty-million-ruble tax levied on the capitalists had not been paid, and force had to be applied. Mikoyan was sent with a small detachment of soldiers and a document identifying him as an agent of the Sovnarkom to the Russian Bank of Foreign Trade. He occupied the premises, seized their assets, and awaited the arrival of the representatives of the new ministry of finance.[3] This action was repeated several times, and in this simple, direct manner the new government of Baku enforced its will on the recalcitrant bankers who had defied the duma and the soviet up to this time. Another step taken was to levy a fifty-million-ruble tax on the owners of the second largest industry in the area, the fisheries.[4] To enforce the measures taken by the Sovnarkom, the Committee of Revolutionary Defense continued to

[3] *Dok.*, pp. 382–383. In an interview with Harrison Salisbury published in the *New York Times*, October 3, 1967, Mikoyan remembered his activities after the "March Days," arresting capitalists and seizing the assets of the banks. As Salisbury reports:

"I had heard that there were such things as safes, but I had never in my life seen one," Mr. Mikoyan said. "So I decided to get some practical experience in banking."

He got permission to "nationalize" one of the banks. He went to the bank with the fourteen-year-old son of Stepan G. Shaumyan, the local Bolshevik leader, and several Red Army soldiers. They walked into a big room filled with clerks, busy with their books. The soldiers carried their rifles at the ready.

"We shouted: 'Hands up! Everybody stand!' " Mr. Mikoyan said. "It was funny and very exciting. Then I asked: 'Where are the safes?' A deputy manager showed them to me. Everybody was still standing. I hadn't told them they could sit down. I said: 'Open this box.' The deputy said he couldn't do it—it took two keys, one which he had and one which the boss had."

Mr. Mikoyan did not know whether or not this was true.

"Since I wasn't up on the banking business," he said, "I had to believe him. I didn't want to blow up the safe. So I left a guard at the safe and went back to my newspaper (*Izvestiia*, of which he was an editor). Now do you think you could do that with a bank in Wall Street?"

[4] *Bakinskii rabochii*, no. 79, May 1, 1918; *Dok.*, pp. 387–388.

meet and did not hesitate to arrest officials who refused to comply with the directives of the commissars.[5] The Sovnarkom sought to alleviate the shortage of banknotes in the city by issuing their own money, which was to be honored throughout Baku Province and the Daghestan District (where Sturua had set up a separate Sovnarkom).[6] These first measures were moderate, though strictly enforced, but all knew that they were only the prelude to the more thorough economic restructuring which was promised with the nationalization of the oil industry.

The Council of People's Commissars met two or three times a week, usually at ten or eleven in the evening, after the daily work of the various commissariats had been completed, until two or three in the morning. The first order of business was most often the report by Fioletov on the amount of oil shipped to central Russia in the past few days.[7] These shipments were the vital link between Baku and Moscow, a lifeline to the infant Soviet republic. The Bolsheviks of Baku were prepared to make almost any sacrifice to keep open the flow of oil and oil products through Astrakhan. Sahak Ter-Gabrielian had been sent to that city at the mouth of the Volga, and there he directed the local revolutionary committee. From Astrakhan communications and oil flowed through Tsaritsyn, where Stalin maintained his headquarters.

Oil made Baku indispensable to Lenin, and irresistible to the Germans, Turks, and British, who from three directions were converging on the city. The Baku Sovnarkom was faced with a decline in oil production. The amount of oil drilled dropped from 370,000 tons in February 1918 to 290,000 in April. Far more serious was the drop in the amount refined: from 147,000 tons to 76,000 between

5 *Dok.*, p. 395.
6 *Ibid.*, pp. 399–400.
7 N. N. Kolesnikova, *Iz istorii bor'by za sovetskuiu vlast' v Baku (avgust 1917 g.—iiul' 1918 g.): Vospominaniia* (Baku, 1958), p. 81.

February and March.[8] Most importantly, the amount of oil exported from Baku had fallen drastically:

| | |
|---|---|
| January | 39,000 tons |
| February | 26,000 tons |
| March | 26,500 tons[9] |

With the firm establishment of soviet power and the placement of high priorities on the shipment of oil to central Russia, the figures showed a dramatic reversal:

| | |
|---|---|
| April | 94,000 tons |
| May | 182,000 tons |
| June | 464,000 tons |
| July | 492,000 tons[10] |

Since these latter figures far exceed the figures for the amount of oil drilled and refined in these months, it must be supposed that the stored supplies which had been reserved in Baku for a time when oil prices were more favorable were being depleted for shipment to Russia.[11]

[8] A. Dubner, *Bakinskii proletariat v gody revoliutsii* (*1917–1920 gg.*) (Baku, 1931), p. 63. In April the amount refined rose to 210,000 tons.

[9] *Ibid.*, p. 64.        [10] *Ibid.*

[11] In a telegram to Lenin and Stalin, dated July 1, Shaumian estimated the successes and failures of the Baku Commune in supplying oil to central Russia.

> The export of oil was increased as much as the means of transportation allowed. In that period, for May, from May 1 to June 1, new style, all together 16,609,332 poods of oil products were exported; in June, from June 1 to July 1, new style, 26,449,405 poods were exported. Only the export of benzine was reduced: in May 16,652 poods were exported, but for June, 12,216 poods; this is connected with the absence of ships for exporting. As for the general drilling of oil and the production of oil products for June detailed information will be delivered to you as soon as possible. The decline in drilling is collossal. For June altogether 17 million poods of oil products were obtained, for the same period in May (as a consequence of the change from old to new style only 19 days are considered) about 12 million poods. On the night of July 7 in Binagady 19 wells burned. The losses are very great. Their exact extent as a result of the fire has not yet been established. (Shaumian, II, p. 339.)

In view of the goal of the Baku Bolsheviks—to insure a steady flow of oil products to central Russia—the question of method became all-important. The oil industry was still completely in the hands of its prerevolutionary owners, still operated independently of government supervision. The labor contract, seven months after the preliminary agreement had been signed, had still not been finally edited and approved. The last stand of the bourgeoisie in Baku was being made by the oil industrialists, and the Bolsheviks were at their most cautious in reckoning with them for the simple reason that they feared above all the disruption of the production and flow of oil. Not only the industrialists, but the engineers too opposed limitations on the owners' prerogatives and opposed the introduction of workers' control into the industry.[12] Thus, the Baku soviet and its Sovnarkom were faced with the problems of falling production, dissatisfaction among workers, and a recalcitrant management, as they set out to impose their authority on the oil industry. The spectrum of solutions offered ranged from the simplest kind of workers' control to complete nationalization of industry.

Workers' control has been much misunderstood since that controversial slogan was adopted to describe the participation of the employees in the process of production control. Perhaps the word "inspection" or "check" might be substituted for the Russian *kontrol'* to convey the meaning intended. The slogan did not imply that the workers would control the factories in the sense of operating them completely. Rather it implied that, within the old framework of ownership and operation, the workers would act as supervisors to insure that the old managers and owners did not sabotage production by unnecessarily reducing output or raising costs.

In his pamphlet *The Menacing Catastrophe and How to Struggle Against It*, Lenin spelled out what he meant

[12] S. N. Belen'kii and A. Manvelov, *Revoliutsiia 1917 g. v Azerbaidzhane* (Baku, 1927), pp. 226, 229, 230–231.

by *kontrol'*. It was complementary to supervision, accounting, and regulation, but went further. *Kontrol'* was to be achieved by nationalizing banks and the largest industries (including the oil industry); by abolishing commercial secrets; through the compulsory syndicalization of industrialists, merchants, landlords, and other proprietors; and finally through compulsory unification of the population in consumer societies.[13] Lenin conceived of *kontrol'* as emanating from the workers themselves and, therefore, as democratic in nature. He contrasted workers' *kontrol'* with the bureaucratic control of the Kerensky government.

Oil was one of those key industries which had to be nationalized, Lenin wrote, if *kontrol'* was to be effective:

The nationalization of the oil industry is
possible *immediately* and is essential for a revolutionary-
democratic state, especially when it is living through
a great crisis, during which, no matter what, it is
necessary to conserve the people's labor and increase
the production of fuel. It is understandable that
here bureaucratic control will give nothing, and the
"oil kings" dealt as easily with the Kerenskys, the
Avksent'evs, and the Skobelevs, as they had with the
tsarist ministers. . . .
In order to do something serious, it is necessary
to move from bureaucracy, and to move in a
revolutionary manner, towards democracy, i.e., to
declare war on the oil kings and stockholders, to
decree the confiscation of their property and punishment
by imprisonment for interfering with the
nationalization of the oil business, for hiding
profits or accounts, for sabotage of production, for
not taking measures to raise production. It is necessary
to turn to the initiative of the workers and employees,
to call *them* immediately to conferences and

[13] V. I. Lenin, *Polnoe sobranie sochineniia* (5th ed.) (Moscow, 1962), XXXIV, p. 156.

congresses, to transfer to their hands such a share of
the profit on the condition of creating complete
control and increase of production.[14]

The oil industry was too large and too important to the
national economy to be allowed the degree of management
autonomy that smaller industries would enjoy as they were
being syndicalized.[15]

Once the Bolsheviks took power, Lenin assumed a more
moderate position on nationalization.[16] He adopted a plan
to use the old capitalists in the service of the Soviet state.
Despite Lenin's original enthusiasm for the nationalization of the oil industry, the Sovnarkom considered the
problem of oil in the context of a generally cautious economic policy. Rather than put immediate nationalization
into effect, they took intermediate steps that were designed
to prevent serious dislocations in the industry by allowing
time to train reliable personnel. On January 27, the
Sovnarkom in Moscow decided to create state oil enterprises on unused land as a first step to the nationalization
of the industry. The Supreme Council of People's Economy
(Sovnarkhoz) was ordered "to work out a plan of nationalization of the oil industry and present it in one week to

[14] *Ibid.*, pp. 169–170.

[15] Lenin explained that the consolidation of small industrial enterprises into syndicates would "not change by one iota the property relations, [would] not take one kopek from the property owner"
(*ibid.*, p. 177).

[16] Lenin's economic plans in the first half-year of Soviet rule
were based on "control and accounting" and did not call for the
complete nationalization of all industries that began in earnest in
the late spring of 1918. Nationalization was often used by the
Bolsheviks as a threat to industrialists who balked at the implementation of workers' control. Lenin's clearest statements on the need
for control and accounting rather than nationalization are contained in his polemics against Bukharin and the Left Communists,
in which he emphasized that the road to socialism lay through
state capitalism, i.e., through a state-regulated capitalist economy.
(For a Soviet account of Lenin's position, see V. P. Nasyrin, "O
nekotorykh voprosakh sotsialisticheskogo preobrazovaniia promyshlennosti v SSSR," *Voprosy istorii*, no. 5 [May 1956], pp. 90–99.)

the Sovnarkom."[17] A telegram was sent to Shaumian instructing him on the implementation of the Sovnarkom's plans:

> The Soviet of People's Commissars has published
> a decree on the construction of public oil enterprises.
> It had earlier been decided to nationalize the whole
> oil industry in the future. In publishing the decree,
> among other things, it was considered that in the
> organization of the enterprises cadres of employees
> (technicians, etc.) would be created in the process
> of the work from our people, who might, later on, direct
> the work of drilling and refining the oil in all the
> existing private enterprises after their nationalization
> in a case of sabotage by the technical personnel
> employed in these enterprises. . . .[18]

In other words, nationalization was a step to be avoided until sabotage forced the government to replace the old administration and technical apparatus with the loyal but less skilled Soviet cadres.

The central Sovnarkom discussed the oil industry again on February 15 and accepted a plan to nationalize the oil-fields. Again on March 1 the Sovnarkom agreed to projects dealing with oil's future.[19] Yet, strangely enough, nothing further was decided until late in June. In the interim local initiative in Baku made the matter more urgent than Moscow realized.

As early as August 1917, the conference of factory committees in Baku had advocated compulsory syndicalization of the oil industry, and in December two thousand Nobel workers called for nationalization of the oil-fields.[20] Frustration with the negotiations for a labor contract, both before and after the September strike, was frequently

[17] S. Sef, "Iz istorii bor'by za natsionalizatsiiu neftianoi promyshlennosti," *Istorik marksist*, nos. 18–19 (1930), pp. 30–31.
[18] *Ibid.*, p. 31.  [19] *Ibid.*  [20] *Ibid.*, pp. 32–33.

vented in a cry for nationalization or workers' control. In February 1918 a crisis arose when the industrialists refused to recognize the soviet's version of the labor contract. The IKS issued an ultimatum to the industrialists demanding that they accept the labor contract within two days or suffer the consequences.[21] The industrialists replied that before they could make a decision the entire condition of the oil industry must be discussed with the soviet.[22] Finding this answer inadequate, the soviet adopted the following resolution: "In order to save the whole industry, the oil fields are hereby transferred to the exclusive use of the Soviet republic. The executive committee is asked to take measures to work out technically this question, to implement workers' control, and to create a net of workers' organizations essential for the realization of nationalization."[23] A few days later the conference of factory committees also adopted a resolution for the establishment of workers' control and taking decisive steps toward the nationalization of the oil industry.[24] Baku, not Moscow, had initiated the move toward the nationalization of one of the largest industries in the republic. Such an action had to be coordinated with the central economic authority, the Sovnarkhoz.

Shortly after the "March Days" a commission of three men—Agapov, Sal'ko, and Dosser—arrived in Baku from the central Sovnarkhoz. Their mission was to promote the concept of *trestirovanie* (the consolidation of the separate oil companies into one trust which could then be centrally controlled) as the first step toward nationalization.[25] On April 19 Dosser reported to the soviet on the need for caution. He echoed Lenin's timetable: first organization of industry, then nationalization. The Socialist Revolution-

21 *Izvestiia*, no. 38 (260), March 2, 1918.
22 Sef, "Iz istorii bor'by . . . ," p. 34.
23 *Ibid.*, p. 35.
24 *Izvestiia*, no. 44 (266), March 9, 1918.
25 Sef, "Iz istorii bor'by . . . ," p. 37.

ary Topel'berg agreed with Dosser, but took issue with local Bolsheviks, saying, "I am very sorry that the arrival of Comrade Dosser did not coincide with that session of the Soviet in which we S.R.s expressed ourselves in the same spirit as Comrade Dosser does now. Shaumian then might have approached the question somewhat differently. We say now too—centralization and control are important, organize the industry, and later we will think about its nationalization."[26] Shaumian then rose to defend his party's position: "Topel'berg is wrong to think that we expressed ourselves differently earlier. We, both now and earlier, expressed ourselves for nationalization, and if we can be rebuked for something, it is only because we have done nothing to nationalize the oil industry. We have only demonstrated the necessity to create organs to prepare the way."[27] Then the Baku soviet, which a month earlier had declared the oil industry to belong to the Soviet republic, retreated to an acceptance of Dosser's modest plan of *trestirovanie*.

Early in May the oil industrialists rejected the plan of the central Sovnarkhoz to create a unified trust of the oil companies.[28] The "oil kings" would not agree to permit representatives of the government to sit on the board of directors of the industry. In view of the reduction in drilling and the inability of the industrialists to pay for shipment to the north, government intervention alone could secure the supply of oil products to central Russia.

The Baku Bolsheviks met to consider their response to the resistance of the oil industry and the caution of the central Soviet government. Shaumian told the May party conference that no authorization for nationalization had been received from Moscow and that the industry would have to be nationalized on local initiative. Some of Shau-

---

[26] *Ibid.*, p. 38; *Bakinskii rabochii*, no. 71 (187), April 21, 1918.
[27] *Ibid.*                        [28] Dubner, pp. 57–58.

mian's comrades balked at this point. Dzhaparidze revealed his doubts about nationalization, and Fioletov opposed it flatly. Shaumian proposed that a meeting be called of Bolshevik oil workers in Sabunchiny to obtain a sense of their views on nationalization. The workers proved to be enthusiastic supporters of nationalization, and Dzhaparidze later voted for the resolution to nationalize oil.[29]

On May 22 Shaumian took the first step by nationalizing the "bowels of the earth," i.e., all natural resources in Baku province.[30] In the process the Baku Sovnarkom raised the price of oil from 2r. 35k. to 2r. 50k., increased wages to the level of Petrograd workers, and issued the controversial labor contract as a state decree.[31] National-ization, rather than mere consolidation in a trust, was clearly the goal of the Sovnarkom. The industrialists themselves, by their rejection of the more moderate alter-native, had aided those Bolsheviks who were agitating for nothing less than nationalization. The only obstacle the Sovnarkom had to overcome was the resistance of cautious elements within the central government.

Lenin's government continued to involve itself in oil affairs throughout the period of the Baku Commune. On May 19 Lenin signed a decree which established a central oil committee (*Glavnyi neftianoi komitet* or Glavkoneft), which, like the other *glavki* being set up, was to super-vise the entire industry throughout the Soviet-controlled territory. The Glavkoneft was ordered to work out the practical measures by which private ownership of enter-prises could be turned into public ownership. The com-mittee hesitated to sanction nationalization and attempted to restrain Baku from precipitating a crisis in the industry.

[29] Anastas Mikoyan, "O dniakh bakinskoi kommuny (Iz vospo-minanii)," I, *Iunost'*, no. 11 (1967), pp. 74–75.

[30] *Izvestiia*, no. 98, May 26, 1918; *Dok.*, pp. 414–415.

[31] Shaumian's telegram to Stalin, May 22, 1918 (Shaumian, II, p. 245).

Glavkoneft's policy was consistent with Lenin's own preference for accounting as the means of state control rather than outright nationalization.

The Baku Sovnarkom was reluctant to take the decisive step of nationalizing the industry without the assurance that its action would be approved by the central Sovnarkom. But such assurance was not forthcoming, in part owing to difficulties in communication, in part owing to conflicts within the central government. On May 27 Shaumian telegraphed Lenin: "We received, after some delay, the telegram of Vysnarkhozneft [the Supreme Economic Council for Oil], No. 706, on the measures taken for the oil industry and today the telegram of the Sovnarkom, No. 3082, about the hundred million. We understand these decisions taken as nationalization. The absence of a governmental decree raises doubts. If there are no obstacles, telegraph us more definitely. I welcome a decision."[32] At about the same time Stalin telegraphed Shaumian that nationalization had indeed been authorized. He informed Baku that the oil commissariat had been liquidated and all functions had been transferred to the Glavkoneft attached to the Supreme Council of People's Economy. "In a word," Stalin wrote, "everything has gone your way." Without waiting for specific instructions from Moscow the Baku Sovnarkom issued its own decree nationalizing the oil industry on June 1. Shaumian defended his haste in these words in his letter to Moscow of the 7th: "We declared nationalization without waiting for instructions because there was danger that the oil industrialists, if they found out about your decision, would harm us unless the necessary measures were taken by us at once."[33]

The June 1 decree made it clear that the Baku Sovnarkom's action was taken in line with the earlier sanction by the government in Moscow and that the local

[32] Shaumian, II, p. 256.     [33] *Ibid.*, p. 292.

declaration of nationalization was meant to apply only until detailed instructions were received from the center.[34] The oil industry was placed under the supervision of the Baku Council of People's Economy (Sovnarkhoz) but all administrative and technical personnel were to remain in their positions. The factory committees and the trade unions were to subordinate all their activities in the field of production and labor to the Sovnarkhoz. Acts of sabotage or insubordination were to be dealt with by arrest and trial before the revolutionary tribunal. Workers' control was never introduced into Baku; rather, a command system, directed by the Sovnarkhoz and dedicated to creating labor discipline and raising productivity, was instituted along with nationalization.

Nationalization was not only greeted with inimical declarations from the Unions of Oil Industrialists; the workers and engineers too were disturbed by what they considered a rash act of the Bolshevik Sovnarkom. As Shaumian reported to Moscow, "The nationalization was not met with great enthusiasm in view of the food-supply crisis, in view of downright starvation. There was more enthusiasm among the sailors. Sabotage by the engineers is still not a reality. The Union of Engineers adopted a resolution disapproving of nationalization but calling on technical personnel to remain at their post."[35] The workers, especially those at the Nobel Plant, suspected that the Bolsheviks would not be able to pay their wages as well as the owners of the company had been.[36] In the midst of crisis, with a shortage of money in the city, the workers were not impressed by the Sovnarkom's appeal to save the Soviet revolution by increasing production and refining and shipment of oil products to central Russia.[37]

Two days after Baku read that the oil industry had been

---

[34] *Izvestiia*, no. 104, June 2, 1918; *Dok.*, p. 453.
[35] Shaumian, II, pp. 292–293.
[36] Dubner, p. 71.     [37] *Dok.*, pp. 457–460.

nationalized, the Supreme Council of People's Economy in Moscow sent a telegram to Shaumian which qualified their earlier decision on nationalization. The telegram arrived in Baku between June 12 and 14, and stated that, though nationalization had been approved by both the Sovnarkom and the Sovnarkhoz, the act of nationalization would be delayed until the central oil committee had presented its estimate.[38] Another week passed and Shaumian received a telegram from the Vysnarkhoztop (Supreme Economic Council for Fuel), signed by Solov'ev, which categorically stated that there had been no nationalization.[39] The industrialists had also received these telegrams and had made them public, thus causing confusion over the legality and permanence of nationalization. Shaumian, speaking to the soviet on June 22, discounted any thoughts that nationalization might be rescinded and urged the deputies to agitate among the workers against the views of the owners and engineers.[40] In the debate that followed Shaumian's speech, other Bolsheviks added to the arguments in favor of nationalization. Basin noted that not only the soviet but also the trade unions and the conferences of factory committees had approved nationalization, thus refuting the opposition of the Nobel and other skilled workers. Zevin, who had become people's commissar of labor in Baku, pointed out that nationalization had been dictated by local conditions as well as by responsibility to the center. Without nationalization, he maintained, "we would have committed political suicide. Some workers in Bibi-Eibat declared a strike because they had not received their wages, just at the time when the Sovnarkom was approving their wages."[41] The soviet voted to support Shaumian's position. Nationalization was to remain in effect.

The next day Shaumian sent a telegram to Lenin and

[38] Shaumian, II, p. 323.    [39] Ibid., p. 324.
[40] Ibid.
[41] Izvestiia, no. 123, June 27, 1918.

Stalin and a separate letter to Lenin explaining the confusion into which the central authorities had led Baku
by their conflicting communications concerning nationalization. "Such a policy," he wrote, "is incomprehensible to
us, extremely harmful; as I have already protested once
and I repeat once again, I protest strongly. After what has
been done and done very well, retreat is not possible. These
telegrams bring only disorganization. I ask for your personal intervention in order to prevent terrible consequences for the industry."[42] In his letter to Lenin Shaumian assured his comrade that Baku would not be foolish
or rash in dealing with this problem.

> You probably fear "left infantilism," but I can assure
> you that we have been very careful, and have handled
> and are handling the oil industry cautiously. I
> understand that this "nationalization," as is bound to
> happen, cost you a great deal in Russia; those arriving
> here tell of the pillage of the treasury which was
> accomplished under the flag of nationalization, but the
> atmosphere here is somewhat different, and we sit very
> firmly on the treasury-chest.[43]

[42] Shaumian, II, p. 326.
[43] *Ibid.*, p. 331. The division within the central government between those, like Stalin, who favored immediate nationalization
and those, like the group around the central oil committee, who
were more cautious, had made itself felt in Baku directly through
the agents sent from Moscow to revitalize the oil industry. Shaumian expressed his thoughts on this point to Lenin:

> One of those you sent to us—Comrade Sal'ko—is on his way
> to you. He will tell you in detail about the oil business. By the
> way, I ask you as a favor to regard him with trust. This whole
> fraternity which came here "in order to establish control over
> the oil industry" from the beginning twisted the line against
> nationalization, and we could not get along with them. Once
> we even thought, forgive me for my candidness, of putting them
> on a ship and returning them to Gukovskii. But [word
> undecipherable] a little, they were convinced of the necessity
> of nationalization as the only means of saving the oil industry
> from ruin and to secure the export of oil. (*Ibid.*)

Because of the difficulties in communication during the first months of the Civil War, Moscow was not fully informed of Baku's actions concerning nationalization. Once the *fait accompli* became known, immediate approval by Lenin was forthcoming. But before he found out about Shaumian's actions Lenin had notified Baku that nationalization was to be delayed:

> There has not yet been a decree on the nationalization of the oil industry. We propose to decree the nationalization of the oil industry toward the end of the sailing period. Until then organize a government monopoly on trade of oil products. Take all measures for the immediate export of oil products by way of the Volga. Inform the Glavkoneft daily on the situation of the oil industry.[44]

Plans were changed when on June 20 Lenin received a telegram from Dosser in Baku expressing concern that a reversal of nationalization would harm the industry in view of the attitude of the oil industrialists. That same evening the central Sovnarkom approved the decree on nationalization.[45]

Right up to the time when, late in June, he received notification of this, Shaumian had continued to protest and continued to refuse to rescind nationalization.[46] But meanwhile still another task had to be accomplished, namely, the nationalization of the Caspian Fleet. Baku had decreed its nationalization on June 5 as a necessary corollary to the decree on the oil industry. These combined actions insured that the whole process of producing and shipping oil would be in the hands of the soviet authorities.[47] But the oil committee in Moscow had telegraphed Baku that this latter decree was superfluous and that the fleet should

[44] *Dok.*, pp. 491–492.
[45] Sef, "Iz istorii bor'by . . . ," p. 57.
[46] *Dok.*, p. 500; Shaumian, II, p. 336.
[47] *Izvestiia*, no. 107, June 6, 1918; *Dok.*, pp. 464-468.

remain in the hands of its former owners under the general supervision of the oil committee.[48] Shaumian reacted immediately and telegraphed Lenin and Stalin requesting that the center not interfere "in our work."[49] In fact, once again Shaumian did not allow Moscow to interfere, and, on Stalin's suggestion, he continued with his plans as if no telegram had been sent.[50] Local initiative, not party discipline, took precedence when the orders from the center were contradictory, confusing, indecisive, or unclear. Although dependent on the center for physical survival, Baku risked asserting its limited autonomy when it could count on support (in Moscow) from at least one of the factions competing for influence.

While the Baku Sovnarkom itself consisted only of Left Socialist Revolutionaries and Bolsheviks, the Bolsheviks could not maintain their rule in Baku without at least the acquiescence of the Right socialist parties, the active support of the soldiers and workers (many of whom were sympathizers of the Socialist Revolutionaries and Dashnaks), and the cooperation of certain bourgeois elements, namely the owners and managers of the oil industry and the technical and academic intellectuals. The Bolsheviks in Baku were drawn into the same compromise as that into which Lenin led his comrades in Moscow—collaboration with the "bourgeois specialists." No other party in Russia would have found such an arrangement as discomfiting as did the Bolsheviks. Yet they were unwilling

[48] Suren Shaumian, *Bakinskaia kommuna* (Baku, 1927), pp. 23–24.

[49] Shaumian, II, p. 336.

[50] Stalin telegraphed Shaumian on June 8, 1918: "In the question of the nationalization of the Caspian Fleet you can act decisively without paying attention to the telegram [of the Glavkoneft]. You can be sure that the Sovnarkom will be with you." (Shaumian, *Stat'i i rechi* [Baku, 1924], pp. 224–225.) Stalin assured Shaumian that Lenin personally approved the nationalization of the Caspian fleet (*ibid.*).

to suffer the consequences of too rigid an ideological outlook. In Baku, Shaumian was prepared to work hand in
glove with the Dashnaks and the Armenian National
Council in the defense of the city, though with serious
reservations. He was prepared to employ the oil industrialists and their trained personnel, regardless of their personal feelings about soviet power, as long as they stopped
short of overt sabotage. And the same was true of the
commissariats of education and justice.

Nadezhda Nikolaevna Kolesnikova, the party's selection
for the post of people's commissar of education, took her
job fully expecting unyielding resistance from the academic establishment in Baku. The city's educational legacy
was not noteworthy. In all there were only two classical
schools (*gymnasii*), a technical school, a *real* school, and
a commercial school for men, as well as one state and
two private *gymnasii* for women and the closed St. Nina's
Institute. A network of elementary schools run by the city
duma, the churches, or the mosques operated within the
city proper, while in the industrial districts schools were
under the direction of the Council of the Congress of Oil
Industrialists.[51] Most of the teachers in the commercial and
industrial schools were Socialist Revolutionaries or Dashnaks; only a few were Bolsheviks. The instructors in the
church schools were for the most part monarchists. It was
over this mixed group of hostile intellectuals that Kolesnikova, a professional revolutionary, had to exert her influence. Her credentials engendered less than respect from
the teachers of Baku. Kolesnikova had completed a *gym-
nasiia* and pedagogical courses in Moscow, after which she
had spent four years teaching in an elementary school and
with adults in a Sunday school. Since 1905 she had worked
primarily in the revolutionary movement, with short stints
as a tutor in order to pay bills.[52] Shortly after taking
office Kolesnikova issued an appeal to the teachers to

[51] Kolensnikova, p. 186.     [52] *Ibid.*, p. 87.

cooperate with the new commissariat.[53] No reply from the teachers' organization was received. The people's commissar then held a meeting with the teachers, only to be greeted by catcalls, insults, and enough noise to keep her from speaking. One eye-witness reports, however, that she did manage to tell the assembled teachers, "Saboteurs! We broke you in Moscow! We will break you here too! Among you are many servants of autocracy, Russifiers, . . . but we will carry out a purge among you."[54] The teachers demanded that education be apolitical, but Kolesnikova required all teachers to agree to a formal recognition of soviet power. They had come to an impasse, but since the school year had come to a close no immediate effects were felt. Kolesnikova hoped that through the summer vacation the teachers would help in the reformation of the schools. Instead an exodus of educational personnel from Baku further embarrassed the commissar.[55]

On May 21, the soviet heard Kolesnikova's report on the activities of the commissariat of education. Shaumian joined in the defense of Kolesnikova's actions and warned the soviet that the teachers were "the most reactionary element in Baku."[56] Basin spoke of "sabotage by the intelligentsia in all walks of life."[57] To express its confidence in Kolesnikova, the soviet approved the commissar's plan for a council of education, on which would sit representatives of the soviet together with delegates elected by teachers, students, and the population of the industrial districts.

Kolesnikova's scheme for cooperation between the educators and the soviet through the council proved a dismal failure. The elections of the teachers' delegates were contested by a group of "teacher-internationalists" who sup-

---

[53] *Dok.*, pp. 396–397.

[54] *Biulleten' diktatury Tsentrokaspiia i prezidiuma vremennogo ispolnitel'nogo komiteta soveta*, no. 31, September 6, 1918. Hereafter this newspaper will be cited as *"Biulleten' diktatury."*

[55] Kolesnikova, p. 91.          [56] Shaumian, II, pp. 242–244.

[57] *Izvestiia*, no. 97, May 25, 1918.

ported the soviet's policies, but they did poorly, losing heavily to the anti-soviet teachers. Kolesnikova invalidated the elections, but in the second runoff not one "internationalist" was elected.[58] Parents' organizations protested against the inclusion of the students' representatives in the council, but Kolesnikova was firmly in favor of students' participation.[59] In this way she acquired some support among leftist students, many of whom had taken part in the students' strikes that had closed schools in February.[60] The wrath of the parents and teachers had fallen on Kolesnikova's head before the program for education had been worked out in detail by the people's commissariat. This hostility was not directed at any specific program, but rather against the intervention of the soviet government in the field of education, which the intelligentsia considered to be an autonomous realm independent of government. The Socialist Revolutionaries took a similar view: that education was not to be a class matter but should stand above class or outside of class.[61]

Kolesnikova's program entailed a fundamental dismantling of the tsarist educational structure and demanded loyalty to the new regime. Its major implication was that secondary education would be conducted in schools of mixed national composition to eliminate the national exclusiveness engendered by the old system. This point particularly antagonized the Dashnaks, who had consistently advocated the "nationalization" of schools in

[58] *Biulletin' diktatury*, no. 31, September 6, 1918.
[59] Kolesnikova, p. 95.
[60] The left wing of the student movement had been organized since January 1918 into the International Union of Worker Youth, an organization which operated in close cooperation with the Baku Committee of Bolsheviks. (G. A. Avetisian, *Komsomol Zakavkaz'ia v bor'be za pobedu i uprochenie sovetskoi vlasti [1917–1921 gg.]* [Erevan, 1964], pp. 107–119.)
[61] Ia. A. Ratgauzer, "Bakinskaia kommuna i narodnoe prosveshchenie," *Izvestiia vostochnogo fakul'teta azerbaidzhanskogo gosudarstvennogo universiteta imeni V.I. Lenina, Vostokovedenie*, II (Baku, 1928), pp. 116–117.

the sense of having teaching given in the national language of the pupil's parents. Kolesnikova also shared the feeling of much of the revolutionary intelligentsia that education in Russia should emphasize practical training for real life, rather than consist of the purely humanist studies that had characterized classical education.[62] While little information exists on Kolesnikova's educational philosophy, her commissariat's statement on art and theater suggests that she stressed the element of utility. The statement reads:

> The workers'-peasants' revolution frees art from the heavy chains fettering its development. However, freedom of art is misunderstood by many at this time. The theater, which should serve the people, is turned into a weapon of the social struggle against the people and the revolution. The cinemas, which can and should become factors of scientifically enlightening propaganda, are turned into commercial enterprises, which present amoral pictures of the degradation in human consciousness.[63]

But Kolesnikova's efforts in the arts were as ineffective as in the schools. One operetta star, a certain Amirago, agreed to work with her; the others pleaded that, like the school year, the theatrical season had ended.[64]

Little praise was given to the people's commissar for her energetic work in setting up preschool nurseries and parks, most of which operated as soup-kitchens when the city faced starvation, and in the creation of people's universities, adult schools primarily for workers, in which the history of Russian socialism, political science, and elementary physics were taught.[65] Her failure to achieve a working relationship with the teachers overshadowed those

[62] *Ibid.*, p. 119.          [63] *Dok.*, pp. 442–443.
[64] Kolesnikova, pp. 100-101.
[65] Ratgauzer, "Bakinskaia kommuna i narodnoe prosveshchenie," pp. 119–120.

few achievements of Kolesnikova's administration. In the last month of Bolshevik rule in Baku, the Left Socialist Revolutionaries criticized her work and refused to accept responsibility for the activities of the commissariat of people's education. The Bolsheviks in the Sovnarkom continued to support their appointee, though her three months in office had not brought them any visible benefits.[66]

The problem of having to recruit from the old professional intelligentsia also had to be faced by the commissariat of justice, headed by the veteran Bolshevik Artashes Karinian. Most of the lawyers, judges, and judicial officials in Baku were either members of the Kadet Party or sympathetic to it. Their respect for legal norms and limited government prerogatives had made them the opponents of the judicial innovations of the Baku soviet, notably of the formation of a revolutionary tribunal in January 1918. Yet Karinian hoped to attract the professionals to his staff, and invited the Kadet leader and well-known lawyer, Boris Baikov, to work in the commissariat. Baikov refused repeatedly, and Karinian was forced to fall back on loyal Bolshevik and Left Socialist-Revolutionary cadres.[67] As his chairman of the investigation commission Karinian appointed the Left Socialist-Revolutionary Ter-Organian, who in turn filled the commission with students, clerks, and a few jurists who consented to serve. Karinian, like Kolesnikova, had failed to attract the intellectuals to his side and, instead, operated with amateurs. During the three months of his administration, Karinian did not bring one case to trial.[68]

If practical results were lacking, projects and plans abounded. The essential features of the judicial reform of

---

[66] *Biulleten' diktatury*, no. 31, September 6, 1918.

[67] Boris Baikov, "Vospominaniia o revoliutsii v Zakavkaz'e (1917–1920 gg.)," *Arkhiv russkoi revoliutsii* (Berlin), IX (1923), p. 125.

[68] *Ibid.*

the Baku Commune were laid out in the decree of the Sovnarkom dated June 6, 1918.[69] Courts were to consist of one permanent judge and two lay assessors chosen by the soviets, and they were to operate under the judicial code of 1864 except where that code had been superseded by Soviet law. The revolutionary tribunal continued to operate, and a Baku branch of the Cheka, headed by Sahak Ter-Gabrielian, was organized to deal with the opponents of soviet power. Although opposition by "class enemies" and resistant intellectuals isolated the Bolshevik government from all but the lower classes, the Baku Bolsheviks were reluctant to resort to terror as an instrument to insure loyalty. Their military weakness vis-à-vis the Armenians did not permit the use of physical force against opposition parties.

The Baku Commune faced a most perplexing problem when it tried to apply both the lessons of the Paris Commune and pragmatic Leninism to the immediate difficulties which faced the city in the spring of 1918. The Marxist-Leninist interpretation of the Paris Commune consistently stressed the dangers of collaboration with the bourgeoisie, whether internally, as with the banks, or externally by tolerating Versailles. Yet Lenin himself, once he had taken power, abandoned the more romantic revolutionary stance of his Left Bolsheviks and came out for a pragmatic arrangement with the technical elite of Russia. Lenin wanted to use "bourgeois specialists" to keep his factories functioning and his army in the field. He sought to lead Russia through state capitalism to socialism, rather than take a straight road to certain disaster. He advocated, not nationalization, but workers' control. Factories were to remain in the hands of their former owners, but were to be watched over by the workers and state commissions. Lenin was prepared to move from a

[69] *Izvestiia*, no. 107, June 6, 1918; *Dok.*, pp. 473–475.

destructive period of revolution, in which the exploiters were expropriated, into a constructive period in which they were exploited to work for the Soviet state.

In Baku the proclamation of the Commune alienated not only the liberal and middle-class elements from the government but also most of the moderate socialists. The bloc of Bolsheviks and Left Socialist Revolutionaries was left to organize the economy, to establish a political authority, and to defend the city from counterrevolution with no more than its own resources. The policies of the Baku Sovnarkom did not encourage the anti-Bolshevik forces to reconcile themselves with the hated regime. Rather, nationalization, the reorganization of the courts and schools, and the factional composition of the Sovnarkom turned even passive and apolitical elements against the parties in power. Baku had lost the educated and propertied classes, a development the Mensheviks had always feared. And on a very narrow social base the Bolshevik government was attempting a far-reaching social revolution. The only chance for success was to gain time and to maintain the allegiance of the workers, the soldiers, and the few peasants who supported the new order.

# 9

## The Struggle for Baku

THE RUSSIAN CIVIL WAR was not fought in isolation from the rest of Europe. The great powers, locked in a life-and-death struggle since 1914, were intensely interested in the outcome of the contest for power in the east. Even the remote Apsheron Peninsula became an object of attention in the war councils in London, Paris, Berlin, and Constantinople. Caucasian oil was desired by both the Turks and the Germans, and even though they were allies they were divided on the question of the final disposition of Baku. Britain was most interested in denying that oil to the Central Powers, while Bolshevik Russia hoped to keep all foreign powers from Baku and preserve the city for "Sovdepiia."

Lenin warned Shaumian to be careful in dealing with foreign threats. In a message sent on February 14, the Bolshevik leader acknowledged that he was pleased at Shaumian's opposition to the separatist policies of the Zavkom, but he feared that over-aggressiveness in the face of Turkish imperialism would be disastrous:

Dear Comrade Shaumian!
    Thank you very much for the letter. We are in
raptures because of your firm and decisive policy.
Be able to combine with it the most cautious diplomacy
which the current, most difficult situation demands—
and we shall win.
    The difficulties are boundless. For the present only
the contradictions and conflicts and the struggle
between the imperialists are saving us. Be able to use

these conflicts: for the present it is necessary to learn diplomacy.[1]

Lenin had successfully dealt with the German threat to his revolution by signing the humiliating Treaty of Brest-Litovsk. In Baku the Soviet discussed the Brest negotiations, and, despite Menshevik and Right Socialist-Revolutionary opposition, decided to support the policy of the central Sovnarkom. The Left Socialist Revolutionaries did not at this time echo their comrades in Moscow and oppose the Brest treaty. They remained united with the Bolsheviks in their hostility to all foreign "imperialism."[2]

On March 2, Tiflis received a telegram from Karakhan at Brest-Litovsk bringing the shattering news that the Soviet delegation had agreed to cede Kars, Ardahan, and Batum to the Turks.[3] Article 4 of the Treaty read as follows:

[1] *Pis'ma*, p. 61.

[2] Within the Baku Bolshevik organization Dzhaparidze and others opposed the Brest Treaty, but they did not follow Bukharin's example and form a faction of Left Communists. In fact Dzhaparidze bowed to party discipline and spoke in support of the treaty in the soviet. (Mikoyan, p. 76.)

[3] After authorization by the Seim Chkhenkeli responded to Turkish pressure and accepted the terms of the Brest-Litovsk Treaty (April 10). So unpopular was this decision in Tiflis that it was reversed three days later when the Seim declared war on Turkey. The Moslem parties, Musavat and Islam in Russia (Ittihad), announced that they would not participate in a war against the Turks and warned that the unity of the Transcaucasian "democracy" would be threatened by an anti-Turkish policy. With Ardahan in Turkish hands and Kars and Batum under seige, the Seim a week later once again reversed its decision and reluctantly agreed to negotiations with Vehib Pasha. That same day (April 22) the Seim debated the question of independence for Transcaucasia. Only the Kadet Semenov and part of the S.R. faction opposed independence. (Of the faction's six members the three Georgians voted for independence while the two Armenians and the Russian voted against.) (Iu. F. Semenov, "Zakavkazskaia Respublika," *Vozrozhdenie*, 1 [Paris, 1949], p. 122.) The Dashnaks, Musavatists, and Mensheviks all voted for independence. On April 26, Chkhenkeli formed a government; the terms of Brest-Litovsk were finally accepted, and a dele-

Russia will do all that she must do to guarantee the most rapid evacuation of the provinces of Eastern Anatolia and their orderly return to Turkey.

The districts of Ardahan, Kars, and Batum likewise are to be immediately cleared of Russian forces. Russia will not interfere in the new organization of legal state and international relations of these districts and will leave the population of these districts to establish the new order in agreement with neighboring states, particularly with Turkey.[4]

The concessions to the Turks were very great, but the Bolsheviks had managed to preserve Baku for the Soviet Russian state.

During the Brest-Litovsk negotiations the Turkish government made repeated overtures to the Transcaucasian Commissariat to begin negotiations, but the Zavkom delicately sidestepped the invitations because it was not quite ready to act as an independent government. Although the Tiflis-based government was drifting toward separation from Russia, it nobly tried to resist Turkish pressure to hasten the process. But Turkish patience wore thin quickly, and on January 30 (February 12), 1918, the Turkish Army, under the command of Vehib Pasha, broke the Erzinjan Truce and advanced to the North. In a public statement Vehib justified the move as self-defense: Armenian units which had replaced the Russian forces were, he declared, "terrorizing" the local Moslems. While this immediate pretext for the advance has some basis in the facts, the overriding motivation was more closely con-

---

gation was sent to Batum to negotiate with the victorious Turks. (For detailed accounts of the Turkish–Transcaucasian discussions on the status of Transcaucasia, see Firuz Kazemzadeh, *The Struggle for Transcaucasia* [1917–1921] [New York, 1951], pp. 98–107; and *Dokumenty i materialy po vneshnei politike Zakavkaz'ia i Gruzii* [Tiflis, 1919], *passim*.)

[4] *Dokumenty vneshnei politiki SSSR*, I (Moscow, 1958), p. 121.

nected with the Pan-Turanian plans of the Young Turk leadership in Constantinople. An opportunity to link up with the Transcaucasian Moslems and take Baku was not to be missed.[5]

The Pan-Turkic aspirations of Enver Pasha, the leading figure in the ruling Turkish triumvirate, included the unification of all Moslems in Transcaucasia, the north Caucasus, the Volga basin, and even Transcaspia. A new Turkish Empire was to be built north of Anatolia to compensate for the losses of Arab lands. To prepare the Transcaucasian Moslems for the coming of the Turkish Army, Enver sent his younger brother, Nuri Pasha (1890–1949), to Azerbaijan early in 1918.[6] Nuri, who had already distinguished himself as a partisan leader in Libya, was an appropriate choice, for an organizer of Azerbaijani "self-defense" against the Armenians. Once local Azerbaijani irregular units had been formed, Nuri Pasha was named commander of the new "Army of Islam," which combined seven thousand Azeri irregulars with eight thousand Turkish regulars. It was this army which, after being reinforced, would capture Baku a half-year later.

In their spring offensive the Turks took the formerly Russian-occupied cities of Anatolia one by one: Erzerum fell on March 12, Batum on April 15, and Kars on April 27. By virtue of these victories the Turks became the dominant foreign force in Transcaucasia. Russia had only nominal suzerainty; Germany and Britain had only vague outlines of a policy toward Transcaucasia; but Turkey had a relatively well-equipped army and a potential base of support among the local Moslems.

[5] Ulrich Trumpener, *Germany and the Ottoman Empire, 1914–1918* (Princeton, 1968), p. 173. On February 14 Enver Pasha informed the Germans "that he meant to reach the Caspian Sea from where a 'connection' with Turkestan could be established."

[6] E. F. Ludshuveit, *Turtsiia v gody pervoi mirovoi voiny, 1914–1918 gg.* (*Voenno-politicheskii ocherk*) (Moscow, 1966), pp. 174–175.

THE STRUGGLE FOR BAKU

For Baku the "civil war" did not end with the "March Days." After defeating the anti-soviet Moslem forces within the city, the Red soldiers were forced to turn their attention to the imminent attack from the north Caucasian allies of the Baku Moslems. On April 8, troops of the Baku soviet engaged the forces of Imam Gotsinskii from Daghestan and the remnants of the Musavat units which had fought in Baku. For two days a battle raged in the area of Khurdalan, and only on April 10 did the Daghestani forces pull back to the railroad station Ialama to the north, separating from the Musavatists who retreated to the west in the direction of Elisavetpol.[7] The soviet troops continued their push westward, and between April 10 and 17 they fought the Moslems concentrated in Adzhikabul, where twenty thousand refugees had collected.[8] On April 20 the Baku soviet troops entered Adzhikabul, and the Moslems retreated to Kiurdamir.[9] The skirmishes and battles continued. Baku would see no peace while the soviet governed the city. The soviet, not content merely to attend to the immediate threats to its security, sent its troops to Lenkoran in the south, to Petrovsk in the north Caucasus, and to Shemakh west of Baku, to defeat the enemies of soviet power.

Baku had been involved in north Caucasian affairs since December 1917, and persuading the soviet to send a force to save Petrovsk from anti-Bolshevik forces was not difficult. The campaign was originally to have been launched from Astrakhan, but, owing to delays, detachments of Red Guards, commanded by M. G. Efremov and accompanied by Sukhartsev as political commissar, sailed aboard

[7] *Izvestiia*, no. 64 (286), April 11, 1918.

[8] *Bakinskii rabochii*, no. 62 (178), April 11, 1918; *ibid.*, no. 69 (185), April 19, 1918; *Dok.*, pp. 341–342.

[9] The area around Adzhikabul was the scene of much fighting. Although the town was lost a few days later, it was regained by soviet forces at the end of April. (*Bakinskii rabochii*, no. 71 [187], April 21, 1918; *Dok.*, pp. 364–365.)

the *Ardahan* north from Baku.[10] After a long bombardment from the sea, Petrovsk surrendered. Soviet power was
declared, and trains with flour soon left for Baku. Soviet
power, it had been demonstrated, could be exported by a
workers' army.[11]

The continuing military action, initiated by the "March
Days" and encouraged by harassment from without, bred
a peculiar mood of belligerence within Baku. On May 2,
the soviet resolved that the declaration of independence
by the Seim was an act of treason and promised that Baku
would "give decisive resistance to the treachery of the
Tiflis counterrevolutionaries."[12] Though the Baku Menshe-

[10] *Bakinskii rabochii*, no. 69 (185), April 19, 1918.

[11] *Dok.*, pp. 361–362. As part of its efforts to secure the towns
near Baku for the Soviet government, the Baku soviet sent G. F.
Sturua and G. A. Tagizade on the *Kars* to take Derbent. Sturua reported later:

> Derbent surrendered without a battle. A provisional Military-
> Revolutionary Committee of five has been created which is
> occupied with the organization of soviet power. The city has
> been placed under martial law. Our conditions have been accepted.
> All weapons are being surrendered to a special commission and
> to the Military-Revolutionary Committee. The population took
> it well. (*Bakinskii rabochii*, no. 74 [190], April 25, 1918.)

The Baku soviet consolidated its rule in the outlying areas by
appointing loyal Bolsheviks as commissars. For example: Baku
province, M. A. Azizbekov; Baku *uezd*, B. Efendiev; Daghestan,
V. I. Naneishvili; Kuba *uezd*, A. B. Iusifzade; Derbent *uezd*, K. M.
Agasiev; Dzevat and Lenkoran *uezd*, M. Israfilbekov (*ibid.*).

[12] *Bakinskii rabochii*, no. 81, May 5, 1918; *Dok.*, pp. 392–393.
Baku feared that Tiflis would launch an attack against the citadel
of soviet power in Transcaucasia, and, indeed, the Seim had discussed (on April 2) such an attack. In the wake of the "March
Days" N. Ramishvili told the Seim that the events in Baku were
the beginning of a campaign against Tiflis to establish Bolshevik
rule throughout Transcaucasia. Safikiurdskii, a delegate from the
Moslem socialist bloc, called for immediate measures for self-defense and the liquidation of Bolshevism. Resul Zade, then in Tiflis
and a member of the Seim, threatened a walkout by the Moslems if
decisive measures were not adopted. Further discussion was discouraged, however, once Ramishvili mysteriously hinted that measures were being taken by the Transcaucasian government. But Tiflis
did not, in fact, undertake any military action against Baku. The

viks equivocated, both the Right Socialist Revolutionaries
and the Dashnaks refused to recognize the Transcaucasian
Seim or the independence of the territory.[13] The soviet was
undecided as late as mid-May whether their policy toward
Tiflis would be defensive or offensive. All the same preparations for a military campaign were undertaken. On
May 23 the length of military service for Red Army men
was lengthened from two to six months.[14] Provocative
attacks against the forces of the Baku soviet had been
undertaken from Elisavetpol on May 21, and Shaumian
again telegraphed Stalin for supplies.[15] Korganov complained to Moscow that the shortage of weapons pre-
cluded efficient organization of a Red Army in Baku.[16]
Half of his soldiers were unarmed, and qualified commanders were lacking. Firm support from the center was
essential for a successful military campaign, and Korganov
and Shaumian reiterated their requests for aid through
May, June and July.

On May 24 Shaumian informed the Sovnarkom in Moscow about his military plans.

We are preparing to move on Elisavetpol in the near
future. We intercepted telegraphic conversations from
Elisavetpol about preparing an attack on Baku from
there with regular forces (according to the information,
they have about six thousand already in Elisavetpol, led

Moslem National Council in Tiflis did send a corps against Baku
without the sanction of the Seim, and Semenov writes that the
Georgian Mensheviks sympathized with this separate action by the
Moslems (Semenov, p. 136). Nevertheless, Zhordaniia reassured
Baku in a telegram that no revolutionary organization and no
governmental agency was participating in the attack on Baku
(*Bakinskii rabochii*, no. 63 [179], April 12, 1918).

[13] *Ashkhatanki droshak*, no. 16, May 19, 1918; *Arev*, no. 102,
June 1, 1918.
[14] *Izvestiia*, no. 97, May 25, 1918; *Dok.*, p. 422.
[15] *Dok.*, pp. 413–414; *Pis'ma*, p. 168.
[16] *Dok.*, pp. 415–420.

by the Georgian prince, Magalov). . . . If this will be
only Elisavetpol forces, they will be easy to beat here
and the road to Elisavetpol will be cleared and, perhaps,
even as far as Tiflis. If Turkish forces from Batum (and
from the south) follow behind them, it will be essential
for us in any case to occupy the Evlakh bridge and a
defensive line along the Kura. We must hurry to
Elisavetpol in order to stir up an uprising of the
Armenians there and further on. This will influence the
Georgian peasantry, and the Seim will be overthrown.

If this uprising does not take place and the Turks
manage to lay hold of Georgia and Tiflis, then we will
be completely isolated and will be forced to defend only
the Apsheron Peninsula. We cannot start the move on
Elisavetpol yet because we are not ready.[17]

At the joint session of the Baku soviet and the congress
of peasant soviets on May 29, Shaumian delivered a long
analysis of the latest developments in Transcaucasia,
cheering the demise of the Seim but condemning the
creation of the independent republics.[18] The Dashnak
Zarafian tried to defend the actions of the Tiflis Dashnaks
as efforts to prevent national wars, but ended up shaking
his head in dismay at what they had done. The Right

[17] *Pis'ma*, pp. 73–76; *Dok.*, pp. 423–425.
[18] The Transcaucasian Federation was dissolved on the initiative
of the Georgian Mensheviks, who had become convinced that the
Azerbaijanis felt greater loyalty to the Ottoman Empire than to the
Transcaucasian Republic. The Georgians feared at the same time
that continued ties with the Armenians would involve the Georgians in the bloody fighting between the Armenians and the Turks.
On May 26, in Tiflis, a declaration of independence was read. Two
days later the Armenian leadership in Tiflis declared the birth of an
Armenian Republic and began the difficult journey to its new
capital, Erevan. The Azerbaijanis set up their government in Elisavetpol (Ganja, now Kirovabad) temporarily, hoping that they soon
would be able to "liberate" Baku. Thus, as June began, four different "governments" operated in Transcaucasia: the Georgian Republic, the Armenian Republic, the Azerbaijani Republic, and the
Baku Commune. (Kazemzadeh, pp. 118–127.)

Socialist Revolutionaries, who had consistently attacked movements toward national autonomy and separation from Russia, moved close to the Bolsheviks in advocating an aggressive retaliation against the Georgian Mensheviks. The Socialist-Revolutionary leader Umanskii said, "When they point out our mistakes, when the Mensheviks say that an agreement is needed within the democracy, that the Civil War must be ended—we say, that if in individual cases we have (tactical) differences with our comrades, the Bolsheviks, in the conditions of Transcaucasian reality only one road is left for the S.R.s, together with the Bolsheviks, who are the only true revolutionaries, marching on to Tiflis and further to Batum. [Applause]"[19] The soviet unanimously adopted Shaumian's resolution rejecting all attempts at peace "with this 'heap' of usurpers."[20] The road to war lay open. As the Bolshevik Amirian reminded his comrades, the Commune would not be safe until "Versailles" had been rendered harmless.[21] The historical analogy was to be played out.

Early in June, after just over a month in power, the chairman of the Baku Sovnarkom spoke to his constituents about the Paris Commune. In the current revolution, said Shaumian, the ideals of the Communards could be realized. He reminded his audience of Lenin's words:

In Lenin's first words to the workers who had gathered to greet their arriving leader, he said:
"Russia must be turned into a republic of Soviets, into a republic of communes."
This slogan was at that time little understood, either by the workers, or by people closely associated with Lenin.[22]

[19] *Izvestiia*, n. 105, June 4, 1918.
[20] *Bakinskii rabochii*, no. 100, May 31, 1918; *Dok.*, pp. 446–447.
[21] *Bakinskii rabochii*, no. 104, June 5, 1918.
[22] *Ibid.*, no. 103, June 4, 1918; *ibid.*, no. 104, June 5, 1918; Shaumian, II, pp. 283–290.

As for Baku, Shaumian explained that the past hesitations of the soviet had only delayed the construction of a communist society. Now that full political power was in the hands of the soviet, "we must immediately set out to organize the communist order."[23] With one eye on Paris and the other on Baku, Shaumian reviewed the three mistakes that the makers of the first proletarian revolution had committed:

(1) Isolation of the city from the provinces;
(2) failure to arrest the internal enemies of the regime:
(3) hesitation to seize Versailles, seat of the external counterrevolution.

During the whole time of the Commune in Paris a spirit of conciliation reigned, and in the moment of military struggle the leaders of the revolution concerned themselves with petty questions of a socio-economic character.[24]

The speech on the Commune was made on the same day that the soviet nationalized the oil industry, an act which Shaumian hailed as "the proclamation of the labor commune in Baku."[25] The tasks of the commune were set down by its chairman:

First. The complete change of workers' psychology in line with the revolution in the economic structure of society. A socialist form of thinking, feeling, and psychology should correspond to the new socialist system. A social and public manner should replace the petty property-minded attitude toward environment.

The second task at hand is the raising of labor productivity. With this task is tied the question of labor discipline.[26]

[23] Ibid.
[25] Ibid.
[24] Shaumian, II, p. 285.
[26] Ibid., pp. 289–290.

Shaumian's timetable regarded the seizure of political power as the first step, the economic revolution as a consequence of the seizure of power, and finally the reconstruction of social and psychological attitudes as the result of the new political and economic order. Baku by June 1918 had succeeded in establishing a new political and economic order; the changes in attitude would take time. The question that faced the Bolshevik government was whether or not events in the rest of Transcaucasia would grant them the necessary time. Shaumian ended his speech with a call for a revolutionary war on two fronts simultaneously—the economic and the military. Baku was to be "the liberator of all the laboring people of Transcaucasia."[27]

Baku began its military campaign against Elisavetpol on June 10, starting out from Adzhikabul, the westernmost position held by the Red Army.[28] Despite Dashnak urgings, the advance had been delayed until supplies from the north Caucasus had arrived.[29] Morale was high among the soldiers and in the city. Dashnaks, Socialist Revolutionaries, and Bolsheviks alike stood firmly behind the military advance. Only the Mensheviks wavered, fearing that the attack was not directed only against the Moslem counterrevolution but against the Mensheviks of Georgia.[30] Shaumian explained to the soviet on the eve of the attack that "We ought to meet the enemy not there where they would like but there where it is more advantageous for us. The tactic of attack is considered better and more reliable. It is true that it is dangerous and requires responsibility from the people in command, but persons in power do not fear responsibility and criticism.[31] He fully expected

[27] *Ibid.*, p. 290.
[28] Telegram from Shaumian to Lenin, June 14, 1918 (*Dok.*, pp. 508–508).
[29] *Izvestiia*, no. 112, June 12, 1918.
[30] *Ibid.*
[31] *Ibid.*, no. 111, June 11, 1918; Shaumian, II, p. 298.

the Georgian and Armenian peasantry to rise in support of
the Baku army, and the armed forces of Georgia and in
Elisavetpol Province to join the crusade for soviet power.[32]
Calculating that the Turks had only eighteen to twenty
thousand soldiers in Transcaucasia, Shaumian estimated
that they could afford to send only insignificant numbers
against Baku. The adventure was on, enthusiasm rose, and
the Baku Commune took its final gamble to capture
"Versailles," the citadel of counterrevolution.

The military arm of the Baku soviet, the Caucasian Red
Army, consisted of twenty thousand men, of whom 60 to
70 percent were Armenians. The chief of staff was the
Dashnak Z. Avetisov, formerly a colonel in the tsarist
army. Most of his officers were also Dashnaks, but the
political leadership in the army was in the hands of
elected commissars, among whom served Anastas Mikoyan. Soldiers' committees had only supply functions,
and conflicts between the committees and the commanders sometimes led to arrests of rebellious soldiers. On the
commanding staff, B. P. Sheboldaev wrote to Trotsky,
"The commanders are bad and their support of soviet
power might last only as long as the Dashnaks have a
'Russian orientation,' since the vast majority of the Armenian officers are Dashnaks. It is possible that there will
be a switch in orientation to an English one, and how the
army will react to this then it is difficult to say for certain,
but, keeping in mind that 60–70 percent of the army is
Armenian, anything could happen."[33] Sheboldaev requested purely Russian units to add to the army to increase its "international" character. He was very confident
that Baku could be defended from the Turks and even the
Germans if proper support was provided from the center.
Baku, however, could not be expected to add many more

[32] *Ibid.*
[33] *Dok.*, p. 525. Sheboldaev later worked as party chief in Rostov-on-Don and died in the purges in 1939.

to its contribution of twenty thousand fighting men.[34] Baku's military deficiency up to this time had always been arms, but in June 1918 arms were abundant and men in short supply.[35]

At first the fighting went well for the Red Army. The enemy forces were made up of irregular Georgian units, pro-Musavat Azerbaijanis, and Daghestanis.[36] Against such antagonists the Red Army had little to fear, but Shaumian expected German and Turkish intervention.[37] In a letter to Lenin, Shaumian regretted that Baku had not taken this action earlier, immediately after the "March Days," when the penetration of the Germans and the

[34] *Ibid.*

[35] *Izvestiia*, no. 127, July 2, 1918. Until the end of June recruitment into the Red Army had been on a voluntary basis, but with the first news of setbacks at the front the Bolsheviks shifted from their earlier reliance on voluntary recruitment to conscription. The central Soviet government had authorized a general mobilization on June 12, and the Baku Sovnarkom approved it on the 24th. Five days later the soviet voted unanimously to support mobilization. A Menshevik deputy, Belen'kii, was particularly gleeful at the adjustment the Bolsheviks had made toward the draft. He told the soviet:

> I want to greet the circle which the Bolsheviks have completed here. In October they began by dispersing the mobilized army (which now they want to mobilize again), since then they considered the army organized on bourgeois principles. But time and life take their own. They were convinced that the new army, which they have had until recently, could not protect the country, all over Russia as well as in Baku, and they have had to embark on a new (it's also an old) way of organizing the general defense, i.e., on that which was earlier called mobilization of the army.
> ... The Mensheviks consider it their duty to announce that they will support this mobilization and defense of the city of Baku, but our support of the defense does not in any way signify support of the existing government. (Shouts and noise!) (*Izvestiia*, no. 128, July 3, 1918.)

The mobilization which began on July 3 called up all men living permanently or temporarily in Baku from the ages of twenty-one to twenty-five (*ibid.*, no. 126, June 30, 1918).

[36] *Dok.*, pp. 513–514.     [37] Shaumian, II, p. 327.

Turks had not been so deep. Responding to Lenin's request that Baku wait out the current international complexities, Shaumian reported that local conditions (heat, swamps, malaria) did not permit his army to stand and mark time. He conceded, however, that "we have not decided to march directly to Tiflis (in our plans). But lately conversations about this have been going on among us."[38] The Red Army moved westward, and the foremost units reached the Kura River.

The tide turned decisively in the four-day battle (June 27–30) outside the town of Geokchai. Red Army men, fainting from the heat and lack of water, fell back before the enemy cavalry charging the left flank. Regular Turkish troops had entered the battle in full force.[39] The situation was desperate. Shaumian left for the front. Baku was now at war, not only with the internal counterrevolution, but with a foreign power. And in that position the Baku Bolsheviks were wooed as potential allies by the British army to the south, in Persia.

British policy in Transcaucasia has been the subject of an intense debate between Western and Soviet scholars, memoirists, and diplomats. The debate centers on the intentions of the British in Baku and on murky aspects of their activities which have never been adequately illuminated. Did the British limit their aims in the intervention to purely military considerations, namely the prevention of a German or Turkish advance to the east, or were they primarily or in part motivated by desires to overthrow Bolshevik power and provide the peoples of Transcaucasia with alternatives? Or, to go further, were the British simply old-fashioned imperialists who could not afford to let a prize like oil-rich Baku slip from their grasp? Soviet writers have contended that while the

[38] *Ibid.*, p. 328.
[39] *Izvestiia*, no. 127, July 2, 1918.

British opposed the expansion of German and Turkish power in eastern Transcaucasia, they were at the same time dedicated to the overthrow of the Bolshevik government in Baku and its replacement by a moderate socialist administration, and contemplated a long occupation of the oil region. Their contentions are based on the Bolshevik outlook at the time of the intervention, as well as on a general interpretation of British and, indeed, Allied policies in Russia.[40]

The Western version holds that the British force under General Dunsterville had no purpose beyond keeping Baku for the Allied cause and the east from falling into Turkish or German hands. The intervention is seen from the West as an event in the First World War and only incidentally as part of the Russian Civil War. Old soldiers, retired diplomats, and professional historians have on occasion interpreted the action in the total context of Anglo-Russian competition for strategic advantage in relation to the British empire in India. One historian has gone so far as to entitle his chapter on the intervention in Transcaucasia and Transcaspia "The Defense of India."[41] Other writers take issue with interpreting the action as anything more than a limited military move. C. H. Ellis, who served under Major-General W. Malleson in Meshed, Turkestan, contends:

[40] See, for example, E. Burdzhalov, *Dvadtsat' shest' bakinskikh komissarov* (Moscow, 1938), *passim*, and A. B. Kadishev, *Interventsiia i grazhdanskaia voina v Zakavkaz'e* (Moscow, 1960), p. 140. A rather sophisticated analysis by V. A. Gurko-Kriazhin postulates that the danger of a Turko-German advance into Persia, Central Asia, or India had completely disappeared by 1918, and that the British had rightly calculated this. The real reason for Britain's intervention, he argues, was to destroy the anti-British alliance between the Bolsheviks and revolutionaries, like Kuchik-khan, in Persia. ("Angliiskaia interventsiia v 1918–19 gg. v Zakaspii i Zakavkaz'e," *Istorik marksist*, II [1926], pp. 115–139.)

[41] Richard Ullman, *Anglo-Soviet Relations, 1917–1921: Intervention and the War* (Princeton, 1961).

These operations, primarily undertaken against Turko-German arms as part of a hastily improvised plan to block an enemy advance through the Caucasus towards India and Afghanistan, brought British troops into conflict with Soviet Russian naval and military forces on the Caspian and in Transcaspia. They were, however, not planned as anti-Bolshevik moves, although their commanders took advantage of the opportunities presented by the existence of anti-Bolshevik and nationalist regimes in the Caucasus and in Transcaspia to pursue their military objectives. Nor did they arise from the traditional conflict of interests in Asia between Great Britain and Russia—the "Great Game" of diplomatic moves and counter-moves that had exercised the minds of the political and military leaders of both countries for the best part of a century. As military operations, they were tactical moves, undertaken with the minimum of troops, to cope with an emergency brought about by the Russian collapse and an enemy advance eastwards in which involvement with the revolutionary and counterrevolutionary forces in Russian territory could hardly be avoided.[42]

The formation of British policy toward the Soviet government was hesitant in all aspects but one, its subordination to Allied military interests. The Bolshevik government, by its opposition to the war, its unilateral *Decree on Peace*, and its signature of an armistice with the Germans, had broken the alliance which had bound Britain, France, Italy, and the United States with Russia in common battle against the Germans and Turks. Not unnaturally within the British government and among British agents in Russia there were those who favored the support of anti-Bolshevik groups and, thus, were willing to intervene in the internal affairs of Russia. British contacts with the

[42] C. H. Ellis, *The British "Intervention" in Transcaspia, 1918–1919* (Berkeley, 1963), pp. 12–13.

counterrevolution date back to December 3, 1917 (November 20), when the British war cabinet decided to support the Cossack Kaledin with all the money he might need.[43] At that same meeting the war cabinet also pledged itself to meet any reasonable demands for money made by the Russian Caucasian Army and the Cossack division operating in Persia.[44] Although these payments were motivated by an interest in keeping the Eastern and Caucasian Fronts intact, they were viewed by the Bolsheviks as deliberate intrusions into the internal affairs of Russia and, therefore, as a challenge to the authority of the Bolshevik government. The effect of the Allied support of the anti-Bolsheviks was to threaten the very existence of the Soviet government. Likewise, the personal animosity of British officialdom to the Bolsheviks fostered the impression that Britain's intentions were not limited to the defense of her vital interests from German-Turkish advances.

By the Anglo-French agreement of December 23 (10), the British were assigned "the Cossack territories, the territory of the Caucasus, Armenia, Georgia, Kurdistan" as "zones of influence."[45] The next day General Dunsterville, then stationed on the Northwest Frontier in India, received secret orders to proceed to Delhi. Within a month this professional soldier, the hero of Kipling's novel *Stalky and Co.*, had arrived in Baghdad and fitted out a mission of two hundred officers, two hundred noncommissioned officers, some Russian officers, and forty-one Model-T Fords. His purpose was, in his own words, "to prevent German and Turkish penetration" in the southern Caucasus, Baku, and the Caspian Sea.[46] To accomplish this purpose Dunsterville was to assist the Transcaucasian government in forming loyal military forces which could shore up the

[43] Ullman, p. 46.    [44] *Ibid.*, p. 51.    [45] *Ibid.*, pp. 53–56.
[46] L. C. Dunsterville, *The Adventures of Dunsterforce* (London, 1920), pp. 1–2, 9–11, 16.

collapsing Caucasian Front.[47] After a difficult march across Mesopotamia, Dunsterville arrived with his men and automobiles in Enzeli at the southern end of the Caspian Sea in February. The small port-town was loosely governed by a revolutionary committee made up of Bolsheviks and sympathizers of the Persian nationalist "Gilani" movement, led by Mirza Kuchik-khan, who were in close contact with Shaumian in Baku. Cheliapin, chairman of the Enzeli committee, refused to allow Dunsterville to proceed to the Caucasus unless he officially recognized the Bolshevik government. Dunsterville declined to comply, and withdrew southward to Hamadan, where he remained until June.[48]

While Dunsterville sat in Hamadan the political allegiances in Transcaucasia shifted, causing the British command to reformulate its policy. The Tiflis government with which Britain had hoped to oppose the Turks entered into negotiations with the advancing Ottoman army. The Bolsheviks, who had already signed a peace with the Germans, were soon preparing to prevent the Germans, Turks, and local Moslems from taking Baku. Ironically, Britain and the Baku Bolsheviks found themselves to be on the same side, opposing the expansion of the Central Powers in Transcaucasia. Yet agreement with the local Bolsheviks was difficult for the British to reach, both because of suspicions on the part of the higher command and because of resistance from the soviet government.

Dunsterville attempted both to open channels to the Bolsheviks and to establish contacts with anti-Bolshevik forces in Baku. The British agent, MacDonell, sent Dunsterville information from "several Russian officers of guaranteed integrity and proven ability, who had fled from the clutches of the Bolsheviks of Baku."[49] Shortly

[47] Brig.-Gen. F. J. Moberly (comp.), *The Campaign in Mesopotamia, 1914–1918*, IV (London, 1927), p. 105.
[48] Dunsterville, pp. 36, 47–49, 50.
[49] *Ibid.*, pp. 77, 126.

afterwards the general received an Armenian doctor from
Baku who brought suggestions from the Armenian National Council "with regards to possibilities of our helping
to put things straight in that part of the world."[50] From
such sources, official and informal, Dunsterville concluded that there was "a growing feeling on the part of
the people" of Baku against the Bolsheviks, that "their influence was distinctly on the wane."[51] Britain's hope was
either for an alliance with the local Bolsheviks or, in the
event that such an alliance was rejected, for a Right
socialist *coup d'état.*

General Dunsterville did not confine his personal views
about the Bolsheviks to criticism of their peace policy.
Rather he sensed that a new force of great evil had
emerged which could threaten Britain in the future. On
May 5, he wrote to his government from Hamadan:
"Bolshevism is far from being firmly rooted in the Caucasus, but its malevolent tendencies have permeated the
blood of all the races in this part of the world: the present ultra-democratic movement in Persia is really the same
spirit as Bolshevism. The name is new, but the spirit is
the old spirit of revolution, the spirit of men gone mad."[52]
Dunsterville repeatedly reveals in his memoirs an instinc-
tive hostility to revolution and revolutionaries, particularly to the Bolsheviks.

Dunsterville's superiors reacted to each new piece of
intelligence about the Turkish advance and the political
situation in Transcaucasia with a telegram to the British
armies in Persia, modifying a previous order or changing
their minds about their plans for the future. After being
rebuffed by the Enzeli Bolsheviks, Dunsterville had suggested that his force occupy Enzeli, but orders arrived
that for the time being Dunsterville was to remain in
position and not attempt a move into Transcaucasia.[53]

[50] *Ibid.,* p. 115.  [51] *Ibid.*  [52] *Ibid.,* p. 119.
[53] Moberly, pp. 113–114.

Abandoning plans to move to Tiflis, Dunsterville concentrated on the project for gaining control of the Caspian, that is, occupying Enzeli and Baku.[54] Colonel Lazar Bicherakhov, commander of a Cossack unit in Persia, expressed his willingness to cooperate with the British in such an enterprise, but on May 27 the War Office again ordered Dunsterville and Bicherakhov to remain in Persia —not to proceed past Enzeli, but work on gaining control of the fleet.[55] The defense of Persia was not to be sacrificed to the Russian adventure.

Only on June 6 did the Chief of the Imperial General Staff consent to send an armed force to Baku, though not until reinforcements had arrived to consolidate the British position on the Kazvin-Enzeli road against the harassment of Kuchik-khan's bands.[56] The Persian danger was quickly dealt with by Colonel Bicherakhov, whose loyal troops cleared the way for Dunsterville. The Cossack colonel not only brought Kuchik-khan to his knees but forced the Enzeli Bolsheviks to deal with the British. Dunsterville arrived in Enzeli on June 27, the day before the War Office sent the following telegram, expressing its bewilderment at British actions in northwest Persia and outlining His Majesty's Government's policy vis-à-vis Baku:

> Regarding Enzeli and Baku, we are still in the dark and feel that Dunsterville is not keeping you fully advised with information on these places, for surely at Resht he must be able to communicate with Bicharakoff and get details regarding situation at Baku and Caspian shipping. Bearing in mind that a permanent occupation of Baku is not in question, you should call on Dunsterville for a full appreciation on these points. If we can get complete control of Caspian shipping, destroy the Baku pumping plant, pipe line and oil

[54] *Ibid.*, p. 172.
[55] *Ibid.*, p. 173; Ullman, p. 307.
[56] Moberly, p. 179.

reservoirs, we shall have attained our present object. Dunsterville should be asked exactly what he requires in troops for this definite purpose, knowing as he presumably does your transport problems and the present capacity of the Hamadan–Resht road. We are unable to advise the War Cabinet regarding the despatch of troops to Baku until we receive such considered opinion from you and Dunsterville.[57]

Now within striking distance of Baku, Dunsterville reported to his superiors that he and Bicherakhov agreed that a successful defense of Baku against the Turks was possible.[58]

His personal animosity toward Bolshevism notwithstanding, General Dunsterville adopted a pragmatic posture toward the Enzeli and Baku Bolsheviks and was willing to work in close contact with them to achieve his military ends. Cooperation with the Bolsheviks was only partly possible, however, for two reasons: (1) British and Bolshevik aims diverged and the Bolsheviks were not authorized to fight together with the British, and (2) the British government was suspicious of Dunsterville's temporary accommodation with the Bolsheviks and his arrangement with Bicherakhov, who was independently negotiating with Shaumian. In Enzeli Dunsterville arranged with the Bolshevik Cheliapin and Bicherakhov's liaison officer, Al'khavi, to sell Fords to the Baku soviet in exchange for badly needed fuel. Altogether Dunsterville purchased fifty thousand pounds of gasoline but delivered only ten Fords before the end of July and the fall of the Bolsheviks in Baku.[59]

Dunsterville's tactic was to delay a threatening move in Enzeli or toward Baku until the political atmosphere in the latter city had improved for the British. He expected the Socialist Revolutionaries, "our friends," to bring off a

[57] *Ibid.*, p. 187.
[58] *Ibid.*, p. 188.     [59] Dunsterville, p. 170.

*coup d'état*, throw out the Bolsheviks, and establish a government which would invite British assistance.[60] On July 13 he wrote, "I have had several talks with the S.R.s, whose programme is far more suitable for our purposes and is constructive instead of being, like that of the S.V.s [*Sovetskaia Vlast'*, i.e., the Bolsheviks], purely destructive. They want our aid, especially financially."[61] In the same letter he explained that Bicherakhov's turn toward Bolshevism was merely a tactical maneuver, "the only way to get a footing, and once he is established it will be a case of the tail wagging the dog."[62]

Britain and Turkey were not the only foreign powers that were willing to expend money and military might to secure a foothold in Transcaucasia. Since the beginning of the war the Germans had devoted considerable energy to promoting revolution among the Georgians, and had developed, as part of their overall war aims, a notion that an independent Georgia would be strategically and economically useful to the German Empire.[63] Opportunities arose in January 1918 when Transcaucasia severed its legal tie to Russia, and Germany entered Transcaucasian politics just as her Turkish allies began their military advance to the north. The situation was delicate. Germany could not afford to offend Soviet Russia, with whom she was negotiating at Brest-Litovsk, nor did she want to alienate her

[60] Dunsterville, p. 182.     [61] *Ibid.*, p. 186.

[62] *Ibid.* The War Office accepted none of Dunsterville's explanations and, fearing that time was being lost against the advancing Army of Islam, ordered that Enzeli be occupied at once and Bolshevik influence there eliminated (Moberly, p. 201). Dunsterville responded: on August 4, the three-man Bolshevik committee in Enzeli, by this time largely impotent, was arrested by the British (Dunsterville, pp. 201–210). But by August Bolshevism was no longer a power to be feared by the British in Persia, for the Bolshevik government in Baku had fallen at the end of July.

[63] For an account of Germany's policy toward Transcaucasia, see Fritz Fischer, *Germany's Aims in the First World War* (New York, 1967), pp. 134–136, 550–562.

ally, Turkey, by interfering in a settlement of a "border dispute." But Germany was opposed to Turkish hegemony over Transcaucasia, which would block her direct access to Persia and central Asia.[64] In the spring of 1918, therefore, the Germans revived their contacts with the Georgians and worked to create a pro-German Georgian state or, at least, a Transcaucasian federation led by the Georgians.

The Georgian Mensheviks, who a few weeks earlier had condemned Bolshevik concessions to the Germans at Brest-Litovsk, now saw German penetration into Transcaucasia as a useful guard against the predatory designs of the Turks.[65] German representatives were present at the Batum Conference which led to the declaration of the independent Transcaucasian Federation in April. But whereas it was largely Turkish pressure which brought about Transcaucasian independence, promises of German support were instrumental in precipitating Georgia's withdrawal from the federation and the creation of an independent national republic in May.

One of the most influential voices in the formation of German policy toward Transcaucasia, General Ludendorff, made a clear distinction between Germany's interests in Georgia, where a friendly power was to be created, and in Baku. In a note to the state secretary, dated June 9, 1918, Ludendorff wrote:

> In Georgia, as in Finland, we have the opportunity of strengthening our fighting forces; we must organize a Georgian army. It is therefore necessary to recognize and protect the Georgian state. An ethical point should be taken into consideration in this case; Georgia is a Christian state whose hopes we have been raising for a long time. Germany's recognition and protection will at the same time give Georgia security against the greedy

[64] *Ibid.*, p. 551.
[65] Zourab Avalishvili, *The Independence of Georgia in International Politics, 1918–1921* (London, n.d.), pp. 37–38.

Turks. Otherwise, the difficulties there will never be over. I beg you to examine M. Chenkeli's full powers while he is with you and to carry out the policy I have suggested to ensure that Georgia, like Finland, should support our war effort. . . . If Georgia is our advanced base, it is to be hoped that the Caucasian territory will gradually be pacified and that we should be able to draw from there the raw materials we so urgently need.[66]

As for Baku, Ludendorff had no suggestions as to its final disposition, only that it must be kept out of Turkish hands and its oil secured for Germany:

I should like to stress that Turkey must be taken into account and that we must, to a certain degree, regard its wishes. The railroad line from Batum through Tiflis to Djulfa is extremely important to their operations. We should not forgo running the Tiflis–Baku line under German control. There the Turks will have to give way to us. Also, Baku should not be ceded to the Turks. . . . The guiding principle should be that Turkey not hinder the development of the Georgian Army and the provision of raw materials from the Caucasus. It would be an act of hostility toward us if the Turks were to occupy the Tiflis–Baku line and Baku itself, an occupation which might lead to the destruction of the local oil industry.[67]

Germany was as anxious to gain control of Baku's oil as Britain was to keep it out of the enemy's hands. From late May Germany was committed to protecting Georgia from the Turkish threat and to securing for it some kind of recognition from the Soviet government.[68] Moscow was

[66] Z. A. B. Zeman (ed.), *Germany and the Revolution in Russia, 1915–1918* (London, 1958), pp. 134–136.

[67] *Ibid.*

[68] Even before Georgia separated itself from the Transcaucasian Federation, the German Ambassador in Moscow, Count Mirbach, had made overtures to the commissariat of foreign affairs suggest-

willing to open negotiations with the Georgians, though it would not commit itself to promises of recognition.

Once the war between Baku and the Azerbaijani-Turkish forces began in June, German and Soviet interests in Transcaucasia coalesced. Both powers wanted to keep the Turks out of Baku. The Soviets were now prepared to make a further concession to the Germans on the Georgian question if Baku was kept for the Bolsheviks. On July 1, Stalin telegraphed Chicherin, expressing doubts about German sincerity: "The Baku region is really threatened. The Turkish forces, headed by German officers, are carrying on real war with the Baku units. One can think that the so-called agreement with the Germans is a screen for the attack on Baku. Needless to say, the whole bourgeoisie is for the Turks."[69] Although Stalin's information about

---

ing recognition of Transcaucasian independence. Chicherin's answer to Mirbach was contained in the following note:

> The People's Commissariat considers it its duty to point out that in many places in Transcaucasia the power of the so-called Transcaucasian Government is rejected completely, and in Transcaucasia generally the broad popular masses have spoken out against it; in Tiflis and Kutais provinces the population protested against the separation from Russia; in Sukhumi, Poti, Kutais, Gori, Tiflis, Dushet, and other Georgian cities and places at huge meetings resolutions were passed branding the Seim as usurpers and actually demanding a referendum. ... Armenian cities and villages with still greater persistence demand a referendum, insisting on withdrawal of their delegates from the Seim. Many Georgian and Armenian delegates have left the usurpers; in the same sense, Lenkoran, Aliat, Derbent, Petrovsk, Adzhikabul, Kiurdamir, and all, generally Eastern Transcaucasia up to Elisavetpol has expressed itself. (*Dokumenty i materialy po vneshnei politike Zakavkaz'ia* . . . , pp. 291–292.)

The Soviet government, however, was willing to negotiate with the Germans and the Georgians about the question of independence. Shaumian, in fact, was informed by telegram from Moscow that negotiations between the Soviet government and the Georgians were to be held either in Vladikavkaz or Baku. (TsGAOR, f. 1318, op. 1, d. 33, 1. 414; Shaumian, II, p. 271.) These negotiations were never held.

[69] Suren Shaumian, *Bakinskaia kommuna* (Baku, 1927), p. 38.

German officers at the head of the Turkish troops was incorrect, his doubts were understandable in the light of the German failures to hold back the Turks. The Soviet ambassador in Berlin, Ioffe, had been promised by the Germans that they would intervene with the Turks, but no concrete effect could be discerned. Lenin, nevertheless, wanted Shaumian to know about the Soviet government's attempts to mediate through the Germans, and telegraphed Stalin: "As for Baku, the most important thing is that you keep in constant touch with Shaumian and that Shaumian know of the proposal of the Germans made to our ambassador, Ioffe, in Berlin, concerning the Germans agreeing to stop the attack of the Turks on Baku if we would guarantee the Germans a part of the oil. Of course, we agreed."[70] The next day, July 8, Stalin telegraphed Shaumian, explaining Soviet policy in Transcaucasia:

> Our general policy in the question of Transcaucasia consists of forcing the Germans to recognize officially that the Georgian, Armenian, and Azerbaijani questions are internal questions for Russia, in the resolution of which the Germans should not participate. For exactly this reason, we will not recognize the independence of Georgia which is recognized by Germany.
>
> It is possible that we will have to give in to the Germans in the question of Georgia, but we will make such a concession in the end only under the condition that the Germans recognize that Germany must not interfere in the affairs of Armenia and Azerbaijan.
>
> The Germans, having agreed to leave Baku to us, ask us to share a certain amount of oil in reciprocation. We, of course, can satisfy this "request."[71]

[70] V. I. Lenin, *Polnoe sobranie sochineniia* (5th ed.), L, p. 114.
[71] Published in Shaumian, *Stat'i i rechi, 1902–1918 gg.* (Baku, 1924), pp. 224–225.

The Baku soviet several weeks earlier had taken a more militantly anti-German position than the central government. Shaumian's resolution, accepted by the Soviet, had stated: "Neither in victory nor in defeat will we give the German plunderers one drop of oil produced by our labor." The implicit contradiction between the positions of the Baku soviet and the central government on policy toward the Germans never became explicit. Neither the Soviets nor the Germans were able to retain control of the Baku oil fields.

Moscow and Baku were in complete harmony in June 1918 in their plans to make concessions to the Georgians. Baku carried on its own diplomacy with the Georgian government in Tiflis through the local Bolsheviks. On June 25, Tiflis Bolsheviks appeared before Zhordaniia with a letter, dated June 6, from Shaumian, proposing that the Georgians aid Baku in the common struggle against the Turks.[72] In exchange for the aid, Shaumian was prepared to promise autonomy for Georgia in the future Soviet Transcaucasia. Shaumian wanted only the assurance that Georgia would not permit Turkish units to cross Georgian territory or use its railroads. Zhordaniia assured the Bolsheviks that no Turkish forces had crossed Georgia and that none would be permitted to use the Georgian Military Highway to the north Caucasus.[73] There the matter stood.

Neither Georgia nor its German allies had sufficient military might in the area to stop the movement of the

[72] The Tiflis Bolsheviks were not united in their support of Shaumian's negotiations with the Tiflis government. On July 8, Nazaretian and Makharadze wrote to Shaumian: "We were very disturbed by your proposal to negotiate with Zhordaniia at the moment of an uprising and an actual, formal war with the Transcaucasian government. But we found out about this late and only after the fact of the negotiations of Danush [T. Shaverdov] and Budu [Mdivani] with Zhordaniia." (Suren Shaumian, p. 98.)

[73] *Biulleten' diktatury*, no. 7, August 8, 1918.

Turks across nominally Georgian territory, and to the Bolsheviks of Baku the movement appeared to be accomplished with the approval of the Georgian government. At no time did the Georgians seek to preserve Bolshevik power in Baku or to assist the defenders of the city against the Turks and Azerbaijanis. Rather they seemed to rely on the predominance of Germany in Europe at that time to bring pressure to bear for a settlement of the Baku question in Georgia's favor. On June 24 Chkhenkeli sent a telegram from Berlin to Tiflis in which he claimed that the German government had decided to include Baku in the Georgian Republic, to cooperate with the Georgians in exploiting the natural resources of the region, and to compensate Georgia for what Germany had obtained.[74] Germany was indifferent to who held Baku formally as long as an economic agreement favorable to Berlin could be concluded.

German–Soviet cooperation seemed about to be realized in the early summer of 1918. In order not to provoke the Germans unnecessarily Stalin asked Shaumian to keep the Red Army from advancing further than Elisavetpol should they reach it, i.e., not to move into the territory of the Georgian Republic.[75] And the Germans, for their part, did make repeated requests to the Ottoman Porte that the Turks' advance against Baku be brought to a halt.[76] The Turks chose to ignore the wishes of their ally.

[74] TsGAOR, f. 393, op. 4, d. 39, 1918–1919, I. 130–131.
[75] Published in Shaumian, *Stat'i i rechi* (Baku, 1924), pp. 224–225.
[76] Suren Shaumian, pp. 38–39. Only after August 17, when Enver Pasha demonstrated to the Germans that additional British forces had joined in the defense of Baku, did Ludendorff change his mind and agree to German-Turkish cooperation to secure the city. Ludendorff tried to convince Moscow of the necessity of the operation. (Trumpener, p. 189.) On September 10, 1918, Ludendorff ordered General Kress in Tiflis to advance on Baku as soon as possible. But the order came too late, for five days later Baku fell to the Turks. (*Ibid.*, p. 195.)

Turkish war aims in Transcaucasia went far beyond the gains of the Brest-Litovsk Treaty. Kars, Ardahan, and Batum had been granted to the Ottomans at the peace conference, but not Baku. While the Turks agreed under German pressure to desist from deep penetration into Georgia, they were not ready to give up the tempting prize of Baku, even though the Soviet government argued, through the Germans, that capture of the city would be a violation of the Brest-Litovsk agreement. By the end of May Turkish troops arrived in Elisavetpol in preparation for the dash to Baku. On June 4 the Ottomans signed treaties with the newly independent republics of Georgia and Armenia, pledging to respect their sovereign rights, but not with Azerbaijan, with whom the question of sovereignty over Baku had yet to be settled. The Moslem National Council moved from Tiflis to Elisavetpol on the request of the Turkish Commander-in-Chief, Nuri Pasha, and by agreement with the Turks dissolved itself and elected a government for the Azerbaijani republic, headed by Fataly Khan-Khoiskii.[77] The dispersal of the National Council and its replacement by a more conservative government has been seen as an effort on the part of the Turks to reduce the influence of the Musavat, which had a majority on the Council, and to create an administration made up of more pliable, pro-Turkish elements.[78]

Only on July 14 did the Turkish military command conclude a treaty with the government of Azerbaijan, but

[77] A. M. Raevskii, *Musavatskoe pravitel'stvo na versal'skoi konferentsii. Doneseniia predsedatelia azerbaidzhanskoi musavatskoi delegatsii* (Baku, 1930), pp. 3–4. When the National Council and its government moved to Elisavetpol on June 16, they met with considerable opposition from the more conservative local nobility and the bourgeois who had fled from Baku. Nuri Pasha refused to aid the Council and told them he was neutral in such political matters. The Council understood this as a vote of no confidence and on the following day dissolved itself. (*Azerbaidzhan*, no. 110, May 28, 1919.)

[78] Raevskii, *Musavatskoe pravitel'stvo* . . . , pp. 3–4.

even this treaty did not imply *de jure* recognition. It merely specified that all railroads in Azerbaijan were to be controlled by the Turks for a period of five years. Not until the end of the war was Ali Mardan-bek Topchibashev, Azerbaijan's representative in Constantinople, received officially by the sultan and his country recognized as an independent state.[79] In other words, as long as Turkish military presence in eastern Transcaucasia gave the Ottoman Empire a dominant position there, the Porte subordinated Azerbaijani national interests to the interests of the Turkish Empire.

Inside Baku a crucial debate on the question of allies took place, first within the Sovnarkom, then in the soviet, and finally and most decisively in the populace itself. Shaumian wished to rely exclusively on aid from the central Soviet government, but was willing to make a temporary alliance with an ideological enemy, the Cossack colonel, Lazar Bicherakhov. Early in May Shaumian established contact with Bicherakhov and telegraphed Moscow about the possibility of inviting him to participate in the defense of Baku.[80] At the same time Shaumian was reluctant to allow a British force to come to Baku. In a meeting with the British vice-consul, MacDonell, Shaumian asked ironically, "Is your General Dunsterville coming to Baku to turn us out?" As MacDonell tells it,

I assured him the General as a soldier had no political axe to grind, but was merely concerned in helping those who wished to keep the Turk out of the Caucasus.

"And you believe that an English General and a Bolshevik Commissar would make good partners. No!" he continued. "We will organize our own forces to fight the Turk. If the Turk wins, then I shall lose, but if your English General and I form a partnership it is impossible

---

[79] *Ibid.*, p. 3.     [80] Shaumian, II, p. 224.

that both can gain, for Communism and Capitalism can never share the spoils."[81]

A little while later Shaumian had second thoughts on the matter and informed MacDonell that, in the event of his accepting British aid, the entire force must be placed under the control of the Military-Revolutionary Committee, which would have full powers to establish courts martial and to pay and to dismiss officers. At the same time Dzhaparidze was arguing that British aid should be accepted unconditionally, and the two Bolsheviks discussed the morality of "selling the revolution to a band of bourgeois capitalists."[82] In fact, even if Shaumian temporarily equivocated on inviting the British (we have only Mac-Donell's word that Shaumian considered such an invitation), on June 5, after receiving instructions from Moscow, the Bolshevik leader informed the vice-consul that the Soviet government could not permit British troops in Baku. But even as Shaumian's resistance to British overtures stiffened, his feelers to Bicherakhov were being extended.

On June 7 Shaumian wrote a letter to the central Sovnarkom in which he expressed his doubts concerning Bicherakhov:

This question somewhat puzzles me. You know already about our negotiations with him. In his last letter he put down the condition to us that the British mission be permitted in Baku. After I received your decision I immediately sent him our conditions. Among others was the condition that his detachment be made up exclusively of citizens of the Russian republic. The main thing is not that a certain number of Englishmen will be with him but what he himself with his

[81] Ranald MacDonell, "*And Nothing Long*" (London, 1938), pp. 210–211.
[82] *Ibid.*

detachment represents. All those whom I authorized to negotiate with him and persons who have known him for many years or who are acquainted with him—all assure us of his probity and that we should accept his services without hesitation.[83]

From Enzeli Shaumian received word that Bicherakhov was turning from his British orientation toward sympathy with soviet power. The sincerity of Bicherakhov's shift to the left remained in doubt. Nevertheless, the worst fears of the soviet government in Baku were allayed, and Shaumian quietly received Bicherakhov for discussions. Shortly after their secret meeting Shaumian wrote to Lenin:

A few days ago, after his detachment arrived in Enzeli, he came here. We had conversations, cleared up all disputed or seemingly disputed and doubtful points, and became calm. We already do not fear that he might become a weapon in the hands of the English and Dashnaks, and he does not fear us, is not afraid that we will disarm his detachment, fire at them from the sea with the help of our fleet, etc. He wants to bring with him English armored cars with English operators and English airplanes, but we have been told to expect armored cars and airplanes from you and persuaded him to decline such things from the English. This question was decided but not finally. . . . After clarifying the question with Bicherakhov, the English do not worry us so much any more.[84]

The dangers for the soviet government in Baku of depending on Bicherakhov were great, and Shaumian was aware of them. Yet at the soviet session of June 15, he assured the deputies that after two months' consideration of Bicherakhov, "we have received the impression that

[83] Shaumian, II, pp. 291–292.     [84] *Ibid.*, pp. 328–329.

Bicherakhov makes his declarations honestly and sincerely."[85] Five days later, Lazar Bicherakhov's brother, Georgii, began a rebellion in Mozdok in the north Caucasus, which succeeded in cutting the line between Baku and the Bolshevik government in Terek.[86] Shaumian realized that the two Bicherakhov brothers might wish to join hands in an anti-Bolshevik alliance, but even this consideration did not prevent him from giving his final approval to the invitation of Bicherakhov. In the first few days of July, Lazar Bicherakhov sailed with his twelve hundred men, a few British officers, and four armored cars to Aliat, thirty-five miles southwest of Baku.[87]

When Bicherakhov arrived at the front on July 6, Shaumian and Korganov were there to greet him. The situation was not as good as Bicherakhov had hoped, since the Turks had already crossed the Kura. Discipline had broken down in the ranks. Soldiers refused to stay in the trenches, voted against their commander, elected their own leaders. Dysentery was widespread, though it affected both the Red Army and the Army of Islam.[88] Nevertheless, Bicherakhov was confident as he assumed command:

> The enemy is near us, but his strength is little, and
> his impudence and insolence great. Our army is still
> young; it is not yet used to those deprivations and
> adversities which war entails.[89]

His confidence was short-lived. From July 8 to 10 the Red Army fought the desperate battle of Kiurdamir, at the end of which it was forced to fall back, evacuate the town of Kiurdamir which had been its commanders' head-

[85] *Izvestiia*, no. 117, June 19, 1918.
[86] Sef, *Kak bol'sheviki prishli k vlasti v 1917–1918 gg. v bakinskom raione* (Baku, 1927), p. 51.
[87] Moberly, p. 190.
[88] Suren Shaumian, p. 35; W. E. D. Allen and P. Muratoff, *Caucasian Battlefields. A History of the Wars on the Turco-Caucasian Border, 1828–1921* (Cambridge, 1953), p. 489.
[89] *Izvestiia*, no. 133, July 9, 1918.

quarters, and retreat to Kerar station. The roads were filled with Armenian refugees fleeing before the Turks to seek safety in Baku.[90] Shaumian pleaded with Moscow for help.

> The situation at the front has worsened. By themselves our forces are insufficient. Solid help from Russia is essential. I have telegraphed to Astrakhan and to Tsaritsyn to Stalin. Give orders. The situation is too confused. So-called orientations are quickly changing. The English are moving toward Enzeli.[91]

What had begun at the end of March as an internal power struggle within the city had, by July, become an international contest for control of Baku. No longer was the battle being fought between Moslems, Armenians, Bolsheviks, and Socialist Revolutionaries. By the summer of 1918 Baku had become a theater in the World War, an objective coveted by the Ottoman Empire, Germany, Great Britain, and Soviet Russia. The outcome of that struggle depended on how those powers deployed their limited resources in this area. But before the final skirmishes were fought, the soviet government in Baku was to pay a heavy price for initiating the war.

[90] Allen and Muratoff, p. 448–489.
[91] Shaumian, II, p. 340.

# 10

# The Fall of the Commune

THE BAKU COMMUNE lasted only ninety-seven days. In that time the Sovnarkom of Bolsheviks and Left Socialist Revolutionaries attempted to carry out an extensive program of institutional and economic reform. The middle classes, which had maintained financial and organizational influence in the first year of the revolution, were eliminated from any effective exercise of power. Government was completely in the hands of a narrow group of professional revolutionaries who ruled in the name of the workers, peasants, and soldiers of Transcaucasia. The stability of this "maximalist" government depended on its ability to keep its constituents loyal so as to prevent the rival Right socialist parties from creating a viable opposition. But the Commune's energetic military advance could do nothing to alleviate the grave problems, the continuous crisis which had faced Baku since the outbreak of the revolution. And with the first defeats of the Red Army the attention of the masses was once again turned to the sources of their unending discontent and their physical misery.

The most evident failure of the Bolsheviks and their allies had been in their efforts to mobilize support among the Azerbaijani peasantry. In January 1918, Moslem peasants had ravaged a series of noble estates, burned manor houses, and killed the families of the beks. To some Bolsheviks this spontaneous violence seemed to be evidence of class warfare in the villages.[1] But the movement was

[1] The volatility of the Azerbaijani peasantry in the last weeks of 1917 and the first of the new year was a delayed reaction to the

isolated and did not loosen the traditional ties which bound the peasantry to the clergy and nobility. The revolution remained distant to most of the villagers, with the notable exception of those in Baku *uezd*, Lenkoran, and Elisavetpol.

The Baku soviet was most immediately threatened by the anti-Bolshevik Moslems of eastern Transcaucasia and the north Caucasus, who in time would attempt to conquer the city. To counter such a move, the Bolsheviks had to gain support in the villages and small towns near Baku. Dzhaparidze, long an advocate of accommodation with the Moslem peasants, told the soviet,

> We know that if we do not attract the peasants to our side, then our position will become untenable because it is impossible to live forever surrounded by enemies....
>
> Our whole policy in the past came down to winning the time necessary for organizing the peasants....
>
> Our task now is to tear away the peasant masses from their class opponents and lead them into battle against the counterrevolutionaries in the name of the triumphant revolution.[2]

---

revolution that had already affected the urban population. In January peasants boldly attacked their former lords, killing their families and burning the manor houses. Shaumian greeted this spontaneous outburst as "the agrarian movement" of the local Moslems, though he advised them that seizure of the land was adequate, killing unnecessary. The Bolsheviks saw the village class-struggle as an alternative to the national warfare between Moslems and Armenians. Mikoyan told a gathering on January 21, "Only a healthy international struggle in the village will save us from national warfare and the counterrevolution of the landowners" (*Dok.*, p. 264). Bolsheviks called for a widening and deepening of the revolution in the village, but their inexperience in dealing with the peasants could not be overcome in the short period of their hegemony in Baku. No authority from Baku was recognized in most villages. Political power was in the hands of local Moslem military bands.

[2] *Izvestiia*, no. 63 (285), April 10, 1918.

Azizbekov was sent on a trip around Baku province to propagate the idea of soviet power. He was remarkably successful in having the villagers pass resolutions supporting the Baku soviet. At the end of May a congress of peasant soviets was held in Baku *uezd*, and twenty-six villages sent deputies.[3]

The peasants who gathered in Baku for the congress were not representative of their neighbors in the rest of eastern Transcaucasia. As Shaumian explained in his analysis of the congress, the seventy-seven delegates were not agricultural workers but came from the industrial districts of Baku *uezd*. Baku *uezd*, moreover, contained none of the Azerbaijani nobles' large landholdings.[4] Notwithstanding these serious qualifications, the congress was characterized by the local Bolsheviks and Hummetists as roughly representative of a new, pro-soviet mood within the Moslem peasantry. Efendiev reminded the delegates that not one Musavatist had been elected to the congress.[5] An executive committee for Baku *uezd* was elected with Narimanov as its chairman, and the committee immediately merged with the IKS of the Baku soviet, thus symbolically uniting the representatives of the workers and the peasants.

With a minimum of peasant organization established, the Baku commissar of agriculture, M. G. Vezirov (most of whose department's activity had until then centered on securing foodstuffs for the hungry population of Baku) sought in mid-June to solidify the support won for soviet power by taking the initiative in promulgating land reform. The decree could not be enforced, for Baku's authority was limited to the immediate area of eastern Transcaucasia and Daghestan. Nevertheless all land throughout Transcaucasia was declared socialized. While

[3] *Ibid.*, no. 99, May 28, 1918.
[4] Shaumian, *Stat'i i rechi, 1917–1918 gg.* (Baku, 1929), p. 302.
[5] *Bakinskii rabochii*, no. 99, May 30, 1918.

its effects were only agitational, the decree of June 18 did outline a program with potentially far-reaching repercussions. Basing itself on the February 19 decree of the central Sovnarkom, Baku's decree alienated all land from private ownership and ordered that soviet land committees transfer the land into the hands of the working peasantry.[6] These land committees did not yet exist in most of Transcaucasia, and therefore still had to be created. The equal distribution of land did not take place.

Time was running out for the Baku Commune, and its attempts to attract the Moslem peasantry to the side of soviet power had been successful only in those areas close to Baku or occupied by soviet military units. Unlike those of central Russia, the Azerbaijani peasants had not seized land on a wide scale, and the land reform proclaimed by the Baku Sovnarkom was gratuitous and meaningless. The Leninist *smychka* (union) of peasants and workers was never realized in Baku province, and the Commune was seriously weakened, first, by its failure to attract the poor peasantry, and, finally, by the defection from the Bolsheviks of their constituents, the workers.

The Bolsheviks in Baku never managed to consolidate their influence over the whole working class. The more skilled, literate, and urbanized workers remained loyal to the Mensheviks and the Right Socialist Revolutionaries. Even so, as long as the Bolsheviks appeared to be the most energetic spokesmen for the labor contract, higher wages, and the eight-hour day, all workers followed their lead. And when the city was in danger from the Moslem rebellion the Russian and Armenian workers also subordinated themselves to Bolshevik direction. The Bolsheviks stood at the head of a *de facto* "defensist" alliance. But with the establishment of the Commune and the failure of the military campaign against Elisavetpol, the old stratifications and loyaties of the Baku proletariat reappeared.

[6] *Izvestiia*, no. 116, June 18, 1918; *Dok.*, pp. 492–498.

Discontent was directed against the party in power. Grievances were articulated, not by Bolsheviks, but by the opposition parties, by the Right socialists.[7]

The disaffection of the workers toward the Bolsheviks began over the perennial problem of feeding the people of Baku. Before the Baku Sovnarkom could secure the sources of food and work out means of transporting supplies to the city, the food shortage grew worse. The tremendous physical and psychological pressure drove people from the city. Hundreds took any opportunity to flee to Astrakhan—so many that the authorities there threatened to turn back additional refugees. The Baku soviet limited the right to leave the city in an attempt to prevent the rapid loss of workers' hands, but this provoked the workers to protests. The Menshevik leaders took advantage of the discontent to hold meetings at which they denounced current policies of their Bolshevik rivals.[8] In the first two weeks of May the railroad workers joined with other workers in Black City, White City, and the Nobel Company to protest the small grain-ration and the restrictions on movement from Baku. Over six thousand Nobel workers adopted a resolution calling for free departure from Baku if grain was not delivered to the city in a week.[9] They also

[7] One Soviet writer points out that the Bolsheviks had neglected to build up their primary party cells, and that during the period of the Commune there were no immediate links between the party and the workers. Many Bolsheviks worked independently of the Baku Committee in their sporadic agitational efforts. With the Bolsheviks in power, the best cadres were removed from party to governmental work. As he puts it, "Party work was in the background; in the foreground was work in the state apparatus. The politically won masses moved away from us as a result of the absence of work for the party itself. The politburo ceased to exist, and this circumstance played a great role in the weakening of our organization's power." (Sarkis, "Beglye zametki o partiinoi rabote v period bakinskoi kommuny," *Iz proshlogo* [1924], p. 80.)

[8] Shaumian, II, pp. 221–223.

[9] *Izvestiia*, no. 87, May 12, 1918. Shaumian informed Lenin in a letter of the double danger to continued Bolshevik support: "In Baku the food question has made things very difficult for us. The

resolved that the Baku soviet should be reelected, Shaumian replaced, and all socialist parties allowed to participate in the government of the city.

The agitation by the Mensheviks troubled Shaumian precisely because workers responded to it. At the conference of factory committees in mid-May, Shaumian complained that the workers were too narrow in their outlook and interests:

> Unfortunately, the old psychology has eaten its way in, and the workers defend their personal interests. Against whom? Against the general mass. The defense of personal interests often does not help the revolution; on the contrary, it sometimes contradicts its general goals.

> As a representative of soviet power, I say, personal interests should be subordinated to general ones. And conscious workers ought to unite in the name of the common good. Now there is a different kind of power, our power of the workers. Soviet power is a power not of individual people. It is too little only to elect your representatives and let them manage things. Each worker ought to participate in this work, each ought to feel that he is not only a legislator but also an executive. Soviet power is mass power. Only with general participation will the Soviet work for the good of the worker, will the revolution move forward.[10]

Shaumian rejected Menshevik complaints that the Bolshevik government had repressed opposition by closing the newspaper *Nashe slovo* and intimidating the Right socialists in the Bolshevik press. Not enough had been done, answered Shaumian; in Tiflis Mensheviks had closed all

---

workers are starving. Because of the hunger and the fear of the Turks there is great discontent in the masses." (Shaumian, II, p. 225.)

[10] *Ibid.*, pp. 232–233.

Bolshevik papers, broken up a mass meeting (on February 23 in Alexander Garden) with gunfire, and arrested leading Bolsheviks. Shaumian suggested, as did the leftists within the Bolshevik party, that his government was guilty only of being too permissive. The example of the Paris Commune, which had been so reasonable in its tolerance of internal opposition, stood as a warning to the Baku Bolsheviks.[11]

On May 15 the conference of factory committees heard the report of Dzhaparidze on the measures taken by the new food-supply directory to improve conditions. Dzhaparidze explained that, once Baku had broken with Tiflis, it had lost the use of the Transcaucasian purchasing apparatus in the north Caucasus and had had to replace that system with one of its own. Such an apparatus had been created, thanks to the assistance of pro-Soviet forces in the north, and the principal problem at the moment was not securing supplies but transporting them through enemy territory to Baku. Besides the railroad from Petrovsk, which was still harassed by roaming bands, two other routes existed: the Tsaritsyn–Astrakhan route and the one through Shendrikov Pier. The first route was obstructed by a lack of fuel for trains and a shortage of locomotives, while the second required the building of a small railroad line from Kizliar in the north Caucasian steppe to Shendrikov Pier at the coast. Dzhaparidze was confident that these transport problems would soon be resolved, and added that efforts were also being made to bring rice from Persia and grain from Lenkoran and Dzhevat *uezdi*. He cautioned the conference, however, that a great danger faced the revolution if local needs were allowed to take

[11] Nevertheless, the Bolsheviks did nothing more than close the Armenian S.R. newspaper, *Ashkhatanki droshak*, in May, and the Russian organ of the Dashnaks, *Vpered*, three days before the Commune fell at the end of July. The Baku Bolsheviks never resorted to the use of terror. (*Biulleten' diktatury*, no. 4, August 5, 1918; *Znamiia truda*, no. 55, May 29, 1918.)

precedence over national needs in the matter of exchanges in oil:

> The industrial center of Russia needs fuel, and we cannot bypass the all-Russian organs of power and take upon ourselves the distribution of our oil, for if they will give us grain in exchange for oil and kerosene, and if we were led only by our Baku interests, then one fine day not the grain-growing provinces but the main, industrial centers, such as Moscow and Petrograd, would be left without fuel. We, consequently, must coordinate our activities in the question of fuel distribution with the Central Council of People's Economy; but you comrades know how difficult communications are at this time.[12]

Then the conference ended its meeting with resolutions to form workers' detachments that would go to the north to build the railroad to Kizliar, and also to Lenkoran, to aid in delivering the harvest.[13]

The results of Dzhaparidze's energetic measures to end the food crisis were felt immediately. In late May and June imports into Baku improved.[14] In June the price of meat, potatoes, and bread fell for the first time in a year.[15] Simultaneously real wages experienced a slight rise, and the situation of the workers was consequently improved. The relief was felt by all classes, as this reminiscence by the British agent, Ranald MacDonell, illustrates: "The food situation had now become less acute, in fact we were almost feeding well; Shaumian had certainly done good service to the town in organizing the food supplies. I remember the first white loaf that appeared in the hotel; it was brought round on a plate for us to smell and handle."[16]

[12] *Izvestiia*, no. 91, May 17, 1918; Dzhaparidze, pp. 232–233.
[13] *Ibid.*, pp. 235–236.
[14] A. Dubner, *Bakinskii proletariat v gody revoliutsii* (1917–1920 gg.) (Baku, 1931), p. 82.
[15] *Ibid.*, p. 87.
[16] R. MacDonell, "And Nothing Long" (London, 1938), p. 229.

But the euphoria was short-lived. In July imports of grain fell to one-third of what they had been in June.[17] In the second half of July the work of the requisitioning department brought in nothing but six kilos of tobacco, eighty-three packs of cigarettes, and twenty-three kilos of tea.[18] The promise of the Lenkoran harvest had never been fulfilled because of local opposition to Baku on the part of Molokan villagers.[19] The railroad from Kizliar to the coast was not completed by the time the Baku Commune fell. Food prices again soared, and real wages plummeted.

The temporary improvement in supplies did not alleviate the discontent or frustration of the workers. The conference of factory committees of the five oil-field districts met on June 5 and openly challenged the monopoly on purchasing established by the soviet by authorizing purchases by groups of workers.[20] Their representative, Slepchenko, went to the next session of the soviet to defend group purchases. He told the deputies, "When the workers travel around the city and see that the cake-shops are full, when bread sells for ten rubles a pound and they receive four rubles, this is the most evil of agitators. I myself spent a thousand rubles which I had accumulated over twenty years. Here is the most evil agitator and the counterrevolutionary. Give the worker the possibility to eat and soviet power will be strengthened."[21] But instead of acting on Slepchenko's suggestion to permit group purchases, the soviet and the Sovnarkom prohibited all but governmental purchases, even restricting independent acquisitions by the cooperatives.[22]

On the day after the soviet rejected group purchases, the full conference of factory committees repudiated the soviet leadership and passed a resolution in favor of group pur-

---

[17] Dubner, p. 82.    [18] Ibid.    [19] Ibid., p. 84.
[20] Izvestiia, no. 113, June 13, 1918.
[21] Ibid.
[22] Kavkazskaia kooperatsiia, no. 2, July 22, 1918.

chases.[23] Dzhaparidze explained to the conference that the food shortage was no longer caused by the unwillingness of the peasants to sell their product but rather was the result of the disruption in transportation. The Provisional Government's failure to fix prices on manufactured goods had priced them out of the reach of the peasants, who for their part were forced to sell grain at low fixed prices. The Soviet government, however, had fixed the prices for manufactured goods, such as nails and farming implements, and the peasants had begun to sell. The Baku food-supply organ had managed to buy eight hundred thousand poods of grain recently, but could not find a way to deliver it to Baku.[24] For this reason, and also because of the prohibitions placed by the central Soviet government on group purchases, Dzhaparidze argued that group purchases should not be authorized. His arguments went unheeded.

The question of the group purchases soon mushroomed into a political question which threatened the authority of the Baku soviet. On June 15 Slepchenko insisted at a soviet session that the people's commissar of food-supply aid in the group purchases. Zevin argued against Slepchenko, pointing out that such a system would favor the "fortunate" workers and hurt the majority of the proletariat—especially the Moslems, who had suffered the most from the food shortages since they were the poorest.[25] Speaking as a representative of the conference of factory committees, Slepchenko irreverently compared the soviet to the House of Lords, distant from the masses, arguing in a vacuum. Shaumian angrily attacked the factory committees, the very bodies in which a year before Bolsheviks had predominated: "In the Soviet you see the true po-

[23] *Izvestiia*, no. 113, June 13, 1918.

[24] *Bakinskii rabochii*, no. 112, June 13, 1918; P. A. Dzhaparidze, *Izbrannye stat'i, rechi i pis'ma, 1905–1918 gg.* (Moscow, 1958), pp. 251–252.

[25] *Izvestiia*, no. 118, June 20, 1918; *Bakinskii rabochii*, no. 117, June 20, 1918.

litical representative of the Baku proletariat. The conference also has in its membership representatives of the workers, but the factory committees are not political organizations. They often change and reflect the momentary mood of the masses. Under the pressure of hunger it is easy to confuse them."[26] The soviet accepted the Zevin–Shaumian resolution against group purchases, thus risking a complete break between the two organs which together had raised the Bolsheviks to primary influence in Baku.[27]

A few days later Dzhaparidze replaced Tsypul'skii as commissar of food-supply and immediately put his program into high gear.[28] The IKS formed a soviet battalion to aid in harvesting and, incidentally, in restoring order.[29] A weekly journal of the food-supply commissariat, *Ekonomika*, appeared. With dictatorial powers granted by the soviet, Dzhaparidze set about reforming the entire supply apparatus. True to his "conciliatory" nature he promised to invite all able persons to work with him, "even an Octobrist."[30] The cooperatives, which after the "March Days" had become organs of distribution, were once again consulted.[31] All these measures, while not notably effective, at least provided the population with a feeling that the energy of the Bolsheviks was being applied to the most serious internal problem of the city.

Dzhaparidze's first setback came on June 23, when the conference of factory committees refused to reverse its position.[32] Undaunted, he drew up a compromise plan, by which group purchases would be permitted but only under

26 *Ibid.*          27 *Ibid.*

28 Tsybul'skii was named commissar of social welfare (*Izvestiia*, no. 118, June 20, 1918).

29 *Ibid.*, no. 119, June 21, 1918.

30 *Ibid.*, no. 124, June 28, 1918.

31 *Kavkazskaia kooperatsiia*, no. 1, July 14, 1918. Dzhaparidze gave the cooperatives two seats on the business council in his commissariat.

32 *Izvestiia*, no. 125, June 29, 1918; *Bakinskii rabochii*, no. 122, June 27, 1918.

the auspices of a district organization which would purchase for the whole population of a specific district. He
presented the project on July 4. Slepchenko opposed
Dzhaparidze's compromise and advocated complete independence for the workers. The conference gratified the
new commissar of food-supply by voting for his plan. The
resistance of the workers to the government monopoly had
been overcome by Dzhaparidze's proposal for worker–
commissariat cooperation.[33]

The victory of Dzhaparidze could not change the fact
that the physical condition of the population of Baku was
steadily worsening at the end of June and through July.
The principal diet of the people was, of necessity, fish and
caviar. Bread was mixed with nuts, and water was distributed by ration cards. Typhus and cholera made the
citizens' plight unbearable.[34] Demoralization set in; dema-
gogy flourished; easy solutions were sought.

In June a complicated network of right-wing conspira-
cies against the Bolshevik government developed in Baku.
They centered around the Naval Aviation School, were
connected to the sailors' union, Tsentrokaspii, and were
financed by the British vice-consul, MacDonell. The men
involved in these plots had little mass backing and were
supported by no political party of significance. Yet they
hoped to take advantage of the desperate situation to seize
power, oust the Bolsheviks, and invite the British to come
to the aid of the city. MacDonell, who had close personal
relations with Shaumian, was wary of these plots but went
along with them:

> From the beginning [he wrote] I never had any faith
> or trust in these counter-revolutionary intrigues. I felt
> sure that our best chance of obtaining a footing for

[33] *Izvestiia*, no. 131, July 6, 1918; *Bakinskii rabochii*, no. 130,
July 6, 1918; Dzhaparidze, pp. 261–264.
[34] TsGAOR, f. 1318, op. 1, 619, 1. 17–24; *Nash golos*, no. 12,
April 21, 1918.

Dunsterville was to persuade the Bolshevik government, through the Armenians, to accept his help, and that the same persuasive methods should be used with the Fleet. There was absolutely no cohesion among the counter-revolutionary forces; every Tsarist captain had gazetted himself colonel or general, and the whole thing was rather like a comic opera.[35]

The plots took on more definite form with the arrival of Captain Reginald Teague Jones in Baku. MacDonell recalls:

> My first intimation of what our policy really was came with the arrival of Captain Teague Jones, Intelligence Officer attached to General Malleson, who commanded a small force near Meshed in Persia. Teague Jones told me that the new policy of the British and French Governments was to support the anti-Bolshevik forces which were rallying at various points on the outposts of the Russian Empire. It mattered little whether they were Tsarist or Social Revolutionary as long as they were prepared to oust the Bolsheviks. Great things were expected in the south from the anti-Bolshevik forces.[36]

Teague Jones believed that an anti-Bolshevik coup could be arranged with the help of the Caspian Fleet, which since the "March Days" had reverted to its earlier Socialist-Revolutionary orientation. He also hoped to interest the Armenians and the remnants of the Aviation School in the "show-down."[37] Using the two million rubles hidden in his apartment, MacDonell supplied the old officers, Russian priests, and aviation cadets with funds with which to lubricate the machinery of counterrevolution.[38] Besides the plots for evicting the Bolsheviks, the British vice-consul was authorized to associate himself with

[35] MacDonell, p. 222.   [36] *Ibid.*, p. 223.
[37] *Ibid.*, p. 224.   [38] *Ibid.*, pp. 225–229.

schemes for destroying the oil-fields in order to prevent their capture and use by the Germans or Turks.[39]

While secret meetings were being held and cryptic notes passed around, one conspiracy against the Bolsheviks erupted, fizzled, and led to investigations by the soviet government. At the soviet session of June 15, Shaumian gave a detailed report of how two sailors, Socialist Revolutionaries by choice, had planned to arrest him and invite the English to Baku. Shaumian exonerated the Socialist Revolutionary Party from complicity in the plot, but he implicated the Union of Front-Line Soldiers, the former tsarist bureaucrat Dzhunkovskii, and the English.[40] MacDonell was brought before the revolutionary tribunal, on which Shaumian and Dzhaparidze sat, but denied knowing anything about the conspiracy.[41] The Union of Front-Line Soldiers was dissolved and its members arrested, and Dzhunkovskii disappeared from Baku.[42] The British intrigue within Baku seemed to have failed, but agitation and the not too distant presence of Dunsterville were to have their effect.

By mid-July, with the Turks rapidly approaching the city, tensions had increased within Baku. On the 15th Shaumian authorized the Cheka to take charge of all military units within the city, except those intended for the front, and to use them to keep order. All soviet organs were to fulfill the orders of the Cheka.[43] The next day, as the city prepared for a state of siege, the soviet met to discuss the question of inviting the British to aid in the defense of Baku. The Right Socialist Revolutionary Velunts, who had been at the front, reported to the deputies that the army was tired, demoralized, disorganized. Specula-

[39] *Ibid.*, p. 232.
[40] *Izvestiia*, no. 116, June 18, 1918; *ibid.*, no. 117, June 19, 1918; *ibid.*, no. 118, June 20, 1918.
[41] MacDonell, pp. 244–248.
[42] *Izvestiia*, no. 122, June 26, 1918.
[43] *Ibid.*, no. 145, July 24, 1918.

tion in supplies and desertion were common. He called for inviting the English to Baku and for broadening the soviet government to include the Right socialist parties. Velunts made the point that English interests and soviet interests coincided. Both wanted to keep the Turks out of Baku, and if the Bolsheviks could deal with the Germans they surely could deal with the English. Shaumian shouted from his seat: "You should be put in prison!"[44] The Right Socialist Revolutionary was followed by a representative of the sailors and by Melik-Eolchian of the Dashnaks, who also spoke in favor of inviting the English.[45] Aiollo used the opportunity to point out that the Bolsheviks "are moving farther and farther toward autocracy; they isolate themselves from all the remaining political parties."[46] Even the Left Socialist Revolutionaries attacked the Bolsheviks for their ties with the Germans, though Vezirov assured the deputies that

> We are speaking out not against soviet power, but against the Bolsheviks, against that party which is in agreement with German imperialism.[47]

[44] Ibid., no. 150, July 30, 1918.
[45] Ibid., no. 151, July 31, 1918.
[46] Biulleten' diktatury, no. 1, August 2, 1918.
[47] Izvestiia, no. 145, July 24, 1918. The Left S.R.s opposed the Brest-Litovsk Treaty and Soviet–German cooperation, and on July 6 a Left S.R. terrorist in Moscow killed the German ambassador, Count Mirbach, beginning a short-lived insurrection by the former allies of the Bolsheviks. Word of the insurrection first reached Baku in Stalin's telegram of July 8, in which he instructed Shaumian to take measures to prevent excesses by the Left S.R.s, "those pitiful provokers of a war with Germany" (Shaumian, Stat'i i rechi [Baku, 1924], pp. 224–225). The Baku Left S.R.s made no attempt to imitate their Moscow comrades, nor did they condemn the uprising. Most importantly, they chose not to break their alliance with the Bolsheviks. The party wavered, however, in mid-July on the question of inviting the British to Baku. Both the Left S.R. newspaper, Nashe znamiia, and the spokesman for the party in the soviet session of July 16 came out for inviting Dunsterville. (Izvestiia, no. 145, July 24, 1918). But at the July 20 conference of the Baku Left S.R.s the party adopted resolutions condemning agreements with

When Shaumian rose to speak, he faced an audience which had been exposed to considerable argumentation in favor of inviting the British. In a long speech he tried to convince the deputies that Baku had enough force to repel the Turks, that the English would help little, and that the dangers of inviting the English, namely that their occupation could become permanent, far outweighed the imagined advantages. Shaumian graphically drew the issue as a choice between commitment to a united Soviet Russia and separation from Russia under the tutelage of Great Britain.[48] The four hundred deputies, among whom were representatives of ship committees, the military, and local soviets, voted by a small margin to adopt the Bolshevik resolution against the invitation. But the decision was not considered final. A commission was sent to the front to investigate conditions there, and Shaumian was requested to find out the central government's opinion on the matter of the invitation.[49] The final confrontation came at a session of the soviet nine days later.

In the period that separated the two sessions, the Bolsheviks and Left Socialist Revolutionaries solidified their shaky alliance and took their appeals against the British to the people of Baku. The Caspian Military Fleet adopted a resolution against the English on June 17, but smaller meetings of sailors came out in favor of the invitation.[50] While the fleet was not united, most sailors had returned to the Right Socialist-Revolutionary orientation and were pro-British. The Bolsheviks organized meetings of workers

---

any imperialist power, be it England, Turkey, or Germany, and recognizing only one orientation, Soviet Russian (*ibid.*). In Baku, because the soviet was at war with one of the Central Powers, the distinction between the Bolshevik and Left S.R. lines toward Germany lost all meaning.

[48] *Ibid.*, no. 143, July 21, 1918.

[49] *Biulleten' diktatury*, no. 2, August 3, 1918.

[50] *Bakinskii rabochii*, no. 140, July 19, 1918; *Dok.*, p. 561; Shaumian, *Stat'i i rechi* (Baku, 1929), pp. 280–281.

to rally anti-British feelings, and to their surprise they found the tide of opinion turning rapidly against them. In a letter to Moscow, a member of the Baku Committee of Bolsheviks reported on the workers' mood: "A petty fear for their own skins seized the workers, and almost all of them, except the members of the leftist parties, unanimously demanded the invitation of the English. The best expression of the real mood of the workers (and of the common people) was the result of a series of meetings (more than ten) which were organized by our party on July 25 at which we received not more than a few tens of votes out of the vast number cast."[51] The Bolsheviks had no alternative but to bow to the overwhelming desire of their constituents to invite the British or face defeat in the soviet. Their courses of action were limited, however, by the official position of the central Soviet government.

Shaumian received a telegram from Stalin, dated July 21, which stated categorically the policy of the Soviet government toward cooperation with the English:

> According to the latest information, the populist factions in the Baku Soviet are trying to get the English Varangians' mission allegedly to help against the Turkish plunderers. Keeping in mind the experience of such help from the Anglo-French in Murmansk and in the Far East, one can with certainty say that the Populist factions, without knowing it themselves, are preparing the soil for the occupation of Baku and its districts. Likewise, it is certain that the attempt of the Populist parties is deciding amateurishly a question of international politics at the same time as the Fifth All-Russian Congress of Soviets definitively has expressed itself for an independent policy for the Russian Soviet Republic, independent of the Germans as

[51] M. Lifshits and P. Chagin (eds.), *Pamiati 26. Materialy k istorii bakinskoi kommuny* (Baku, 1922), pp. 188–189.

well as of the English. The policy of the Populist parties is a crude violation of the organized will of Russia to please a bunch of Anglo-French imperialists.

In the name of the All-Russian TsIK and the Council of People's Commissars, I demand from the whole Baku Soviet, from the army and the fleet, full subordination to the will of the workers and peasants of all Russia. In carrying out the decisions of the Fifth Congress of Soviets, I demand from the Baku Sovnarkom the unconditional realization of an independent international policy and a determined struggle with agents of foreign capital, right up to the arrest of members of the appropriate commissions.[52]

Lenin also sent a short note to Shaumian in which he stated his full support of Stalin's telegram.[53] Shaumian had no choice but to obey the central government's unambiguous directives. By doing so he alienated his government from the newly formed popular mood.

At 2:50 in the afternoon of July 25, 459 soviet deputies, members of Tsentrokaspii and of ship committees, and the Military-Revolutionary Committee met in joint session.[54] Shaumian asked that the question of inviting the English be removed from the agenda, since it constituted a matter of foreign policy on which the central government had already made its position clear. But the Right socialists won the vote on the agenda. Shaumian issued an official protest and repeated Stalin's warning that foreign policy could not be decided "amateurishly" (*kustarnym obrazom*). From his seat a deputy shouted: "Why, then, did you start a war 'amateurishly'?" Shaumian replied that the war had been

[52] *Dok.*, pp. 574–575.

[53] *Ibid.*, p. 579; Lenin, *Polnoe sobranie sochineniia* (5th ed.), L, p. 125.

[54] The complete stenographic record of the July 25 session of the Baku soviet can be found in *Biulleten' diktatury*, no. 2–5, August 3–6, 1918, and in Shaumian, *Stat'i i rechi* (Baku, 1929), pp. 255–291.

begun with the sanction of the central government, and went on to define the prerogatives of local soviets in foreign policy: "An allusion was made here that this question can be decided by the local soviet because we have our own commissar for foreign affairs. We have a *commissar for external* affairs [*vneshnei del*], that is, for those affairs which have to do with relations with other parts of federal Russia. As for foreign affairs, just as in any federative country, this is the right of the central federal power."[55] Nonetheless, Shaumian continued, the Baku soviet decided to assume the prerogatives of a sovereign state and conduct its own foreign policy. Although they had never recognized the central Soviet government, by this act the Right socialists in Baku took their first step in separating the city from central Russia. By this act they started down the same road already traveled by their party comrades in Tiflis.

The Dashnak Ter-Oganian argued that a rejection of the English would in itself cause the loss of Baku for Russia. His comrade, Mirakian, blamed the dogmatism and narrow party politics of the Bolsheviks for the defeats suffered by the Red Army. He saw the Bolsheviks flawed by their party pride: "The Council of People's Commissars in sending people to the front thought that our army would have the same success outside Baku *uezd* that it had had on the internal front. This confidence was so great that the representative of the central government in his speech to the troops said: we are going to fight, not only Turkish imperialism, but also the Dashnaks. Confidence about victory was so great that they counted on going on to Tiflis."[56] The leader of the Dashnak faction in the soviet, Melik-Eolchian, took a position a little to the left of the other Dashnak speakers. Also committed to the invitation of the British, Melik-Eolchian saw in that prospect the means to save soviet power in Baku and the Bolshevik government.

[55] *Ibid.*        [56] *Ibid.*

Therefore, speaking for the faction, he stated that the Dashnaktsutiun was for the Right Socialist Revolutionaries' resolution to invite the English but against their resolution on the composition of the local government. The Dashnaktsutiun was much less willing than the Right Socialist Revolutionaries were to break with the central Russian government.

Throughout the long session deputies continued to arrive in the soviet chamber. Finally, late in the evening, the question was put to a vote. The Right Socialist Revolutionaries' resolution to invite the English received 259 votes; the resolution of the Bolsheviks, Left Socialist Revolutionaries and Left Dashnaks, proposed by Shaumian, received 236 votes.[57]

Shaumian protested energetically against the decision of the soviet: "You have not yet found England, but you have lost the central Russian government. You have not yet found England, but you have lost us. (Noisy applause from the Left.) . . . I declare as the representative of the government that I take no responsibility for further policies. In the name of our party I declare that we will not take responsibility for this treason on ourselves."[58]

The session of the soviet did not end with the vote to invite the British. After a one-and-a-half-hour recess, the soviet continued its meeting, turning to the question of the nature of the current government in Baku. In his official protest in the name of the three leftist parties, Shaumian stated that "A government is a technical organ, which can work only when it is homogeneous. We speak of a homogeneous government especially in such critical minutes. Having a homogeneous government as a technical apparatus, we call all parties to work in the name of defending the front and uniting the proletariat. Those who speak of the factional policy of the Bolsheviks are shamelessly slandering. We will not participate in any kind of coalition

[57] *Ibid.*          [58] *Ibid.*

government."[59] Shaumian pointed out that in voting for the Right Socialist Revolutionaries' resolution the Dashnaks and the sailors had both reversed their earlier positions supporting the central Soviet government.[60] The Dashnak Arakelian denied this: "The only parties with a Russian orientation have been the Dashnaktsutiun and the Bolshevik party. We never wanted to break the tie with the center. We recognized the power of the soviets both in the center and in localities. We knew that after the revolution the only organ of power should be soviets in the provinces."[61] Arakelian took pains to point out that the invitation to the English would have been the lesser of two evils, the worse being the occupation of Baku by the Turks. He ended by asking the Bolshevik government to stay in power. Velunts, the Right Socialist Revolutionary, was less generous to the Bolsheviks than the Dashnak speaker. He claimed that if real help had come from Russia the invitation to the English would have been superfluous, but that Russian help could not be expected because civil war was being waged throughout Russia. He told the soviet, "We did not break with Russia, but we did break our ties with the Bolsheviks with whom all of Russia has broken ties."[62] The Mensheviks simply took pride in the fact that they had never recognized soviet power, and Aiollo attacked Shaumian for not recognizing the will of the soviet.

Dzhaparidze told the deputies that the Bolsheviks did not intend to walk out of the soviet, as the Right socialists had done when they had been defeated in November 1917. Shaumian seconded Dzhaparidze's declaration, but told the Right, "We will work, but we will fight against the Ger-

---

[59] *Ibid.*

[60] Mikoyan states that "this turn of events was predetermined by the shift of the group of sailors—some deceived, others bribed by the English—to the side of the Rightist Parties" (Anastas Mikoyan, "O dniakh bakinskoi kommuny [Iz vospominanii]," II, *Iunost'*, no. 12 [1967], p. 57).

[61] *Ibid.*     [62] *Ibid.*

mans and against that treacherous policy for which you stand."[63] In any case, the Sovnarkom had abdicated its powers, though the Right socialists asked the commissars to remain at their posts through the current emergency. Only after the IKS, the Baku Committee of Bolsheviks, and a city-wide Bolshevik conference had also requested that the Sovnarkom continue to serve did the commissars begin again officially to carry out their duties.

Shaumian immediately telegraphed Lenin about the defeat of the Bolsheviks and the acceptance of the Right Socialist Revolutionaries' resolution. He described the consequences for Baku:

> After the acceptance of the resolution, the atmosphere in the city was extremely tense; it smelled of civil war. The English help is being widely doubted, but the resolution for their invitation has finally demoralized the army and disorganized the rear, increasing the danger of the city's capitulating. In order to save Baku for Russia, it is essential to have immediate help by troops from Russia. I urgently request all measures to be taken for the immediate transfer of regular military units.[64]

The "smell of civil war" arose from the activities of a hundred soldiers of Bicherakhov's detachment who had come to Baku without authorization and for two days demonstrated in the streets in support of the English. The executive committee of the soviet ordered the units out of the city and empowered the Cheka to take measures against persons carrying on counterrevolutionary agitation.[65] Meanwhile the Bolsheviks organized meetings of workers to gather support for an anti-British policy; but it soon became apparent that the meetings were unpopular, and they were canceled.[66] Meetings among the military

---

[63] *Ibid.*      [64] Shaumian, II, pp. 368–369.
[65] *Izvestiia*, no. 149, July 28, 1918; *Dok.*, pp. 599–600.
[66] Suren Shaumian, *Bakinskaia kommuna* (Baku, 1927), p. 51.

were even less successful. Of all the units, only the battalion on the armored train opposed the invitation of the English.[67] Another attempt to mobilize the young men of the city for the front failed even worse than the earlier draft.[68]

In a speech in Moscow Lenin praised the actions taken by Shaumian and the Baku Bolsheviks in rejecting any collaboration with the English. He stated simply that "it is impossible to invite them without turning an independent socialist power, even though it is located in a cut-off territory, into a slave of the imperialist war."[69] That same day, July 29, he sent a telegram to Shaumian: "Any action by the Dashnaks against the decisions of the Fifth Congress of Soviets and the central Soviet government will be looked upon as an uprising and as treason. As for the sending of troops we are taking measures, but we cannot promise for certain."[70] Lenin wired Astrakhan for information on the situation in Baku. He asked if the Baku Sovnarkom had already resigned from power and, if not, how much time the power of the Bolsheviks could be extended there. With a shortage of troops in the center, Lenin was unable to promise anything more than moral support for Baku.[71]

In the field the soldiers were affected by the pro-British agitation of their Dashnak officers. The bureau of the press of the Sovnarkom reported:

In the army the commanding staff carries on agitation for calling the English. Individual units pass resolutions on the need for such a call. Today a telegram was received by Shaumian from the temporary commander of the army, Avetisov, [which] sharply dealt with his attitude toward the English; the number of deserters is

[67] *Ibid.*, p. 52; *Izvestiia*, no. 151, July 31, 1918.
[68] *Biulleten' diktatury*, no. 1, August 2, 1918.
[69] Lenin, XXXVII, pp. 4–7.
[70] *Ibid.*, L, p. 129.     [71] *Ibid.*

great; an energetic struggle is being waged with them in the rear. In this way, it is clear that there is a single policy of the Anglophiles in the rear and at the front. Combined with the great deficiency of supplies for the army and the treacherous behavior of part of the commanding staff, [the Anglophilia] has resulted in the current retreat.[72]

Particularly noxious was the behavior of the Dashnak leader, Amazasp, who, independently of his political commissar, Mikoyan, ordered the armored train to pull back. His infantry followed behind.[73] A general retreat followed.[74] Shaumian continued his barrage of telegrams to Moscow, imploring them to send help:

I request that you send the command staff of the division promised by the operations department. Besides this, troops are essential. The main contingent of our forces are Armenian units, which bravely fought in the beginning but which are now demoralized, thanks to the cowardice of part of the command staff and the English agitation. Fresh forces from Russia are essential, as well as a politically reliable command staff. I ask you earnestly to hurry.[75]

Aid came, but too little and too late. Astrakhan sent a cavalry contingent of 170 men.[76] The only significant assistance from central Russia arrived in Baku on July 19. Commanded by twenty-six-year-old "Grisha" Petrov, a detachment of 780 experienced and politically reliable men came to stabilize the front.[77] But before Petrov's soldiers could move to the front, the front moved toward them. In the evening of July 16, Bicherakhov had retreated to

[72] Dok., p. 579; Lenin, L, p. 125.
[73] Izvestiia, no. 144, July 23, 1918.
[74] Dok., p. 582.     [75] Ibid.
[76] Izvestiia, no. 146, July 25, 1918; Dok., p. 583.
[77] A. Checheneva, Polpred revoliutsiia (Moscow, 1965), passim. This short work is a biography of Georgii Konstantinovich Petrov.

Kerar. To the north, the Red Army's right flank fell back four days later from Shemakh to Marasy. Bicherakhov ordered the retreat continued to the outskirts of Baku. By July 30 the army was holding Baladzhary, the last railroad station before Baku, and a line extending south to the station at Bibi-Eibat; this new front was at its closest point within four miles of the center of Baku.[78] Defense seemed impossible as various Dashnak commanders withdrew their units. Desertion was commonplace, and the Armenian National Council refused to send its fresh troops from the city to the front. On July 30 a staggering blow befell the defenders when Bicherakhov suddenly withdrew his troops from the front and retreated to the north Caucasus. Then the Turks attacked. Weakened and discouraged, the Baku soldiers were badly battered by the Turkish troops—but held their positions. Petrov, now commander-in-chief, went to Baku to discuss the military situation with the political leaders, and a conference of military specialists and leaders of political parties decided to maintain the resistance rather than sue for negotiations. In the evening, rumors that Bicherakhov's forces were firing on the enemy from the rear with artillery cheered the soldiers and stopped the desertions which had depleted their ranks. Soon the enemy attack collapsed.[79]

But by July 30 the mood in the city was one of despair. Only four hundred soldiers remained on a front that stretched thirty-two versts, and air reconnaissance revealed that large Turkish forces were moving toward these last defenses.[80] A conference of Armenian leaders, called by the Dashnaktsutiun, decided that surrender was the most prudent policy. The matter was broached with the Bolsheviks, but Shaumian rejected the Dashnaks' offer of three thousand troops to hold off the Turks during negotia-

[78] Gen. G. Korganoff, *La participation des arméniens à la guerre mondiale sur le front du Caucase (1914–1918)* (Paris, 1927), pp. 195–196.
[79] *Ibid.*          [80] *Dok.*, p. 617.

tions for peace.[81] The Bolsheviks, although convinced that further resistance was useless, were unwilling to participate in the surrender of the city. Their only alternative was to relinquish their formal powers to permit the Dashnaks to negotiate with the Turks. The Military-Revolutionary Committee relocated its headquarters to a steamship in the port as the Bolshevik loyalists loaded supplies on board.[82] Shaumian feared that the soviet would be dispersed and pogroms against the Bolsheviks begun.[83]

The Baku soviet met under Dzhaparidze's gavel for a half-hour on July 31. The chairman reported that Avetisov, recently replaced as commander of the army, had repeatedly demanded that negotiations be started with the Turks, and had been supported in his demands by the Dashnaktsutiun and the Armenian National Council.[84] Shaumian read a proclamation from Shefket Pasha, commander of the Turkish forces, calling for surrender and promising freedom and safety. Shaumian took the opportunity to abdicate his authority:

> In the name of the Council of People's Commissars,
> I declare that we decline all responsibility and, of course,
> as a government we cease to exist. Those elements which
> want to begin peace negotiations have had their hands
> untied and they can act.[85]

[81] *Ibid.*

[82] N. N. Kolesnikova, *Iz istorii bor'by za sovetskuiu vlast' v Baku (avgust 1917 g.—iiul' 1918 g.): Vospominaniia* (Baku, 1958), p. 111; *Biulleten' diktatury*, no. 1, August 2, 1918.

[83] Kolesnikova, p. 111. The Sovnarkom was not so disoriented in its last days in power as to allow misuse of public authority. The only two people shot by the Cheka during the Baku Commune were executed on July 30, one day before the Commune fell. At five in the morning Aleksandr Kireev, Left S.R. commissar of finance, and Sergei Pokrovskii, commissar of the steamship *Meve*, were executed for embezzlement of public funds (*Izvestiia*, no. 151, July 31, 1918).

[84] *Biulleten' diktatury*, no. 6, August 7, 1918.

[85] *Ibid.*

Shaumian by his retirement had freed the Right socialists to launch their own negotiations with the Turks; but the Right was neither united in its approach toward the crisis nor pleased with the Bolshevik abdication. Melik-Eolchian stated the Dashnak position: "I think that the people who have brought us to such a position ought to say: 'No! Until the last drop of blood we will defend ourselves and remain at our posts in order to win victory or die.' "[86] Melik-Eolchian did not accept the opinion of the Dashnak commanders and those members of the Armenian National Council who had in desperation called for surrender. The Mensheviks too were unwilling to surrender the city: Aiollo asked Petrov if the city could be held, and was told that it could be, despite the unwillingness of the workers to fight. Aiollo proposed that an interparty conference be held to organize the defense of the city. The motion was passed unanimously; but Dzhaparidze, convinced that defense was impossible, declared "the last session of our Soviet closed."[87]

The Bolsheviks' dilemma on July 31 was the product of two factors: the incomplete intelligence which convinced them that the city would fall within hours, and their loyalty to the position of the central government which permitted neither acceptance of British aid nor a negotiated settlement with the Turks. With no effective choice in Baku, Shaumian decided that, rather than attempt an armed seizure of power and reverse the soviet's position, the Bolsheviks should leave the city as soon as possible. As he wrote to Moscow:

> The Council of People's Commissars preferred not to open a civil war at the moment of the enemy's invasion of the city, but resorted to the parliamentary device of abdicating power in order that those who might make

[86] *Ibid.*        [87] *Ibid.*

peace with the Turks or invite the English to Baku would take the responsibility for what followed on themselves.

We could not be among those who placed themselves at the mercy of the Turkish pashas, who saved their skins by allowing the Bolsheviks and the Russian troops to be torn to pieces by Turkish bands, nor among those who, despite hypocritical phrases about patriotism, are ready to surrender Baku to the English. We have decided to save the revolutionary troops we have which are loyal to the Russian Soviet government, in expectation of the troops coming from Astrakhan, together with which we will declare war on two fronts, on Turkish and English imperialism, to defend Baku for a revolutionary Soviet Russia.[88]

Effective resistance to the Turks was impossible in the face of the disunity of command. Some Dashnak commanders, like Avetisov, were anxious to surrender, but the political commissars, like Mikoyan, were prepared to shoot the commanders rather than permit this. In the city the Armenian National Council was calling for surrender and, as if to underline its position, withholding its reserve troops from the front. The Sovnarkom was already set on abandoning the city, while the soviet impatiently awaited the arrival of British troops.

Throughout July 31 Shaumian was in touch with Avetisov at the front. The Dashnak commander repeatedly requested that a white flag be raised; Shaumian refused to sanction an armistice and told Avetisov to take the responsibility on himself. But Avetisov declined to surrender without a written order, even after Giulkhandarian, chairman of the Armenian National Council, told him by telephone to proceed to negotiations. With the front deserted disaster seemed near. Intelligence reports indicated

[88] *Dok.*, p. 619.

that the city would fall in a few hours. Petrov returned from the front and informed Shaumian that his detachment had suffered heavy losses and was retreating into the city. The Bolshevik commissars decided that further delay would cut off their chances for an orderly withdrawal to Soviet Russia. Uppermost in their calculations was the preservation of Bolshevik personnel for a possible return to Baku in the near future. The Bolsheviks and Petrov's men boarded a ship and steamed out of the harbor. The decision to leave was made during a general panic in the city, and its haste shocked Mikoyan, who returned from the front only to find that his comrades had left him behind.[89]

But a miraculous turn of fortune delayed the fall of the city. According to Avetisov's own report, the news that the Bolsheviks had left the government and that the English were on their way cheered the front-line soldiers and encouraged reinforcements to move up to the front. Early in the evening, the Twentieth Battalion—made up of nine hundred men, most of them hardened fighters—began an advance against the Turks, thus delaying the capitulation of the city for a month and a half.[90]

The Baku commissars and Red Army soldiers who had attempted to leave the city by ship were stopped by the warship *Ardahan* and ordered to return to port. The commissars returned to Baku but remained together in the ship, guarded by the Red Guards and Petrov's detachment. Escape was impossible, but equally impossible for the Bolsheviks was participation in the new political order in Baku. For several weeks the old government of Baku, keeping itself intact in the port, posed a threat to the new Right-socialist government in the city. A new kind of *dvoevlastie* appeared in Baku.

[89] Mikoyan, II, p. 62.
[90] *Biulleten' diktatury*, no. 9, August 10, 1918.

Soviet historians of the 1920s and 1930s were almost unanimous in attacking the Baku Bolsheviks from the left, criticizing them for their lack of resolution in failing to establish a firm dictatorship and to eliminate the opposition parties within the city. Sarkis, a young participant in the events in Baku, writes that "the basic mistake of the Baku Communards was that they shifted from an uncompleted civil war to the parliamentary method of 'struggle,' *from criticism by rifles to criticism of the pen.*"[91] A later writer scornfully notes, "The sessions of the Soviet were very often reminiscent of a bourgeois parliament."[92] The Baku Bolsheviks, it can justly be pointed out, were unwilling to use terror against their opposition. During the whole period of the Commune not one member of the anti-Bolshevik parties was arrested, let alone executed. The local Cheka was kept relatively inactive. Shaumian's strategy was to rely on the military and organizational forces of the other parties without surrendering any political power. He understood that the Bolsheviks could not control the local government and defend the city without Dashnak troops and the acquiescence of the Socialist Revolutionaries. Yet he refused to form a real coalition with the Right socialists, largely because these parties rejected recognition of the central Soviet government. Shaumian thus placed himself in the paradoxical position of antagonizing needed allies. Only their firm allegiance to the Bolsheviks in a working-class bloc could prevent the Right socialists from seizing an opportunity to make their weight felt. That opportunity arose in mid-July when the workers deserted the Bolsheviks over the issue of the British intervention.

The criticism of Bolshevik strategy from the left made by Soviet historians neglects to consider certain realities in

91 Lifshits and Chagin, p. 42.

92 V. E. Bibineishvili, *Akhcha-Kuimskaia tragediia. Vozhdi bakinskoi kommuny* (Tiflis, 1931), p. 55.

Baku. The possibility of setting up a Bolshevik dictatorship and suppressing the Right socialist parties never really existed, even after the "March Days." There was no way to defend the city from outside enemies except by employing Armenian troops loyal to the Dashnaktsutiun, and the workers of Baku were never so solidly pro-Bolshevik that they would have permitted the other "democratic" parties to be willfully destroyed. Baku workers had, consistently since March 1917, been primarily interested in unity among the "democratic" parties, rather than in partisan politics. The Azerbaijani peasantry remained inert throughout the revolution, except for the sporadic outbursts in January and February 1918. After the "March Days" the peasants, with the exception of those closest to Baku, were saturated with Musavatist and nationalist propaganda about the Armenian–Bolshevik alliance in Baku. When the Red Army moved out from Baku toward Elisavetpol, they marched through the villages of Azerbaijani peasants who were seldom friendly and were awaiting their Moslem brothers, the Turks. In the minds of the Moslems the Baku soviet after the "March Days" was identified with the Armenians and therefore completely unacceptable.

Given the precarious political balance within the city and the hostile peasantry without, the decision by the Sovnarkom to launch a military campaign can only be considered ill-advised. The Bolsheviks attempted in a four-month period to institute a socialist economy and to wage a war without ever securing their power-base within the city and countryside. It was from the failure of the military effort that the other difficulties faced by Shaumian derived. Workers' discontent grew as the food-supply again fell to starvation level. Once the regular Turkish forces joined the Azerbaijani nationalists against the Red Army a paralyzing fear gripped the population of the city, a fear which drove them to grasp at the straw offered by the British. The Bolsheviks were correct in their warning to the soviet that the small English force in Persia could not and would not give sufficient aid to Baku, but by mid-July the situation had deteriorated to the point where the workers and their representatives in the soviets were no longer willing to wait for help from central Russia.

Marx's advice, however appropriate it may have been for Paris in 1871, proved the undoing of the Baku Commune. The Bolsheviks did manage to break the hold of the bourgeoisie on the economy and to seize state power. But the campaign against "Versailles" was lost, and in its wake the workers became generally demoralized. And their disaffection led not only to the defeat of the Bolsheviks, but ultimately to the defeat of all socialists, of the city itself. The final triumph belonged to the nationalists.

# 11

## The Dictatorship of Tsentrokaspii:
## Right Socialists in Power

THE FAILURE of the Turkish army to take Baku on July 31 resulted in a most peculiar political situation. The former government of people's commissars was huddled in the port and on Petrovsk Square, hoping to leave the city, while the Right socialists, having rededicated themselves to the defense of Baku, organized a new government. On August 1, an interparty conference attended by the leaders of the Right Socialist Revolutionaries, the Right Dashnaks, and the Mensheviks expanded the old executive committee of the soviet and elected a smaller presidium to work together with the sailors' union, Tsentrokaspii. Aiollo, Umanskii, and Melik-Eolchian entered the presidium, which then joined with five members of Tsentrokaspii (Pechenkin, Tiushkov, Bushev, Lemlin, and Ermakov) and additional members of the executive committee (Arakelian, Velunts, and Sadovskii) to create the Dictatorship of the Tsentrokaspii and the Presidium of the Temporary Executive Committee.[1] On the following day the first issue of the government's official newspaper appeared with a statement of purpose by the new leadership:

> In the most difficult moment when the enemy of the Russian revolution appeared at the gates of the city of Baku, the Baku Council of People's Commissars gave up its powers. Saturated with a narrow party policy, this government, during its short existence, brought matters

[1] *Biulleten' diktatury*, no. 1, August 2, 1918.

to the point where neither on the external nor on the internal fronts were the moral and material conditions created which would have guaranteed to the Baku proletariat and the Red Army the possibility to wage a struggle for the preservation of Baku for revolutionary Russia. . . .

In the critical minutes three parties—the Socialist Revolutionaries, the Social Democrats–Mensheviks, and the Dashnaktsutiun—stayed at their revolutionary posts in the face of the danger advancing on our city, not abandoning their position until the last possibility of defending against the German–Turkish hordes [had been exhausted].[2]

The Dictatorship set about the defense with great energy. A new mobilization was decreed; Bicherakhov, though his maneuvers were suspect, was nevertheless appointed commander-in-chief of the Baku army; and the invitation was sent to Dunsterville in Enzeli. On August 3 the Armenian National Council received a message from the Turkish commander promising safety for Armenians if the city were surrendered immediately. The Council and the Dashnaktsutiun, however, were no longer interested in surrender as they had been three days before.[3] On the 4th, the first British detachment landed in Baku, forty-four officers and men commanded by Colonel Stokes. Even though the small size of the force disappointed the Baku authorities, the arrival of the British inspired the soldiers at the front.[4] On the morning of the 5th the Turks made a determined effort to break through to the city; they reached Bibi-Eibat, and the city seemed about to fall. But Shaumian ordered Petrov to use his artillery against the Turks,

[2] *Ibid.*

[3] *Ibid.*, no. 7, August 8, 1918.

[4] Brig.-Gen. F. J. Moberly (comp.), *The Campaign in Mesopotamia, 1914–1918*, IV (London, 1927), p. 204.

and by noon the battle was over, the city safe for a while.[5] The Armenian soldiers, aided by the meager British detachment and Bolshevik artillery, had managed to push the Turks back beyond the positions they had held before the attack.

Stokes reported to Dunsterville that the situation in Baku was not hopeless and that with the help of Bicherakhov the city might be successfully defended.[6] Although the eight thousand troops in the local army were under five different political organizations, central control and coordination was possible. Difficulties had arisen, he went on, over the arrangements to destroy the oil fields, owing to opposition from the Azerbaijani workers and from some Russians who were unwilling to destroy the source of their livelihood.[7]

To guarantee their maneuverability, British troops seized three ships in the Caspian—the *President Kruger*, the *Kursk*, and the *Argo*—ostensibly for the purpose of transporting their men to Baku. Tsentrokaspii attempted to persuade General Dunsterville to give up control of the ships, but the British politely refused and kept their guards on board.[8] Friction between the government and its allies was already evident.

The British command (and MacDonell earlier) had maintained that the British presence in Baku would not in any way affect the political situation and that the British army would refrain from interfering in local politics. But in fact, the British had become involved in the intricate political situation in Baku even before they landed. Once in the city the British could not help but promote their allies and work to undermine their enemies. On Au-

[5] *Biulleten' diktatury*, no. 4, August 5, 1918; Suren Shaumian, *Bakinskaia kommuna* (Baku, 1927), p. 55.

[6] Moberly, pp. 204–205.       [7] *Ibid.*, p. 205.

[8] *Ibid.*

gust 7, Colonel Keyworth in Baku telegraphed Dunsterville that the Dictatorship was in a precarious situation
and might come into conflict with the Bolsheviks at any
moment. Dunsterville thereupon authorized the colonel
to support, if necessary with force, the Dictatorship against
the Bolsheviks.[9]

The British commanders in Baku, Colonels Keyworth
and Stokes, warned their superiors in Persia that only
British troops were reliable and that to hold the front a
British division was required.[10] Both the War Office and
General Cobbe, the new commander in Mesopotamia, were
reluctant to sacrifice new troops to what seemed to be a
losing cause.[11] Cobbe reminded Dunsterville that his main
object was to deny oil to the enemy and to seize as much
shipping as possible in order to insure the evacuation of
British troops should that become necessary.[12] At this same
time the British were penetrating the Transcaspian region
as well as Transcaucasia in an effort to prevent the cities
of Turkestan from falling to the Bolsheviks. On August 14,
the War Office telegraphed to India and Mesopotamia its
principle objectives in the Caspian area: control of shipping, the occupation of Baku as long as there was a hope
of holding it, and the permanent occupation of Krasnovodsk.[13] The War Office also authorized Dunsterville to
eliminate any remaining Bolshevik influence at Baku, as-
suring him that he could rely on the full support of the
War Office in carrying out these instructions.[14] This all
meant that the British in the area were using minimal resources for an extensive effort to stop the Turks, destroy
the oil fields in Baku, control the Caspian, and, incidentally, destroy Bolshevik influence. With these purposes in
mind, General Dunsterville arrived in Baku on August 17.[15]

[9] *Ibid.*, pp. 205–206.
[10] *Ibid.*, p. 210.   [11] *Ibid.*   [12] *Ibid.*, p. 211.
[13] *Ibid.*, p. 212.   [14] *Ibid.*, p. 213.   [15] *Ibid.*, p. 216.

The Bolshevik position in Baku deteriorated catastroph-
ically in the first half of August, both physically and
morally. On August 3, Shaumian and Ter-Gabrielian attempted a second escape from the city but were captured
by the sailors. Only after Petrov threatened to shell the
city did the sailors release the Bolshevik leaders.[16] A Bolshevik conference was called to decide on the party's
strategy in its new, exposed position. After much debate
the Bolsheviks resolved not to evacuate to Astrakhan but
to exploit the changing mood of the Baku population and
to seize power while most Right-socialist troops were at
the front.[17] This victory of the Bolshevik left wing was
short-lived, for shortly after the conference the British
landed in Baku. To launch a civil war in the city against
British troops was considered too risky. A second Bolshevik
conference was held on August 10. Shaumian proposed the
following resolution: "Taking into account the fact of the
change of government and the arrival of the English, after
which the war ceased being revolutionary and took on the
character of an imperialist one, the evacuation of Soviet
troops from Baku is required." A second resolution by the
leftists was also introduced: "Considering the first retirement and abdication of power to have been a mistake, [the
party] should remain, mobilize forces, utilize the changing
attitude in the working masses, and wait for the arrival of
the two to three thousand battle-ready troops from Petrovsk
to begin a civil war, to take power, and with the forces of
the Baku proletariat to organize the defense."[18] By a vote

[16] Ia. A. Ratgauzer, *Arest' i gibel' komissarov bakinskoi kommuny*
(Baku, 1928), pp. 19–20.

[17] Anastas Mikoyan, "O dniakh bakinskoi kommuny (Iz vospominanii)," III, *Iunost'*, no. 1 (1968), p. 62. The conference was held
on August 2 or 3.

[18] Quoted in the letter of a member of the Baku Committee, published later in M. Lifshits and P. Chagin (eds.), *Pamiati 26.
Materialy k istorii bakinskoi kommuny* (Baku, 1922), p. 189.

of 22–8 the first resolution—to leave Baku—was adopted by the conference.[19] Shaumian's strategy was based on a pessimistic reading of the possibility of reestablishing Bolshevik authority in Baku. He felt that he and his men could be of more use to the revolution in Soviet-held territory in the north, where they could aid the beleaguered forces on the Volga. In any case the evacuation was to be temporary. With fresh troops from Petrovsk and Astrakhan Baku could be retaken.[20]

Preparations were made for a new evacuation. A bureau of Bolsheviks, Left Socialist Revolutionaries, and Left Dashnaks was created to remain behind in the city and coordinate party affairs until the leadership's return. Negotiations were opened with the Dictatorship for the grant of an unencumbered exit from Baku. The Dictatorship invited Petrov to fight alongside the defenders of Baku against the Turks, but the Left Socialist-Revolutionary commander refused to participate in the fighting as long as the English were in Baku.[21] On August 12 the representatives of the Caspian Fleet decided that Petrov's detachment would be permitted to leave Baku if it surrendered its weapons.[22] Petrov agreed in writing to the surrender of weapons, but Shaumian and other Bolsheviks opposed giving up everything and held out for ten armored cars, ten artillery pieces, and ammunition—with the effect that, when the Bolsheviks and Petrov's men sailed out of Baku on August 14, only two barges with cannon were left behind.[23] A flotilla of fifteen ships carrying the Sovnarkom, the soviet troops, and the leading Bolsheviks, Left Socialist Revolutionaries, and Left Dashnaks left the port, only to be forced by a storm in the

[19] *Ibid.* Mikoyan voted for the second resolution (Mikoyan, III, p. 63).
[20] Lifshits and Chagin, p. 190.
[21] *Biulleten' diktatury*, no. 13, August 15, 1918.
[22] *Ibid.*, no. 12, August 14, 1918.
[23] Lifshits and Chagin, p. 190.

Caspian to stop at Zhil Island not far from shore. The next morning three warships from the Dictatorship arrived and demanded that the flotilla return to Baku. The warships opened fire on the flotilla until it surrendered. The commissars tried to escape on a small ship, but they were sighted and arrested.[24] They were imprisoned in Baku, while the soldiers were permitted to leave Baku for Astrakhan. The leadership of the Bolsheviks and Left Socialist Revolutionaries was now isolated from its protectors and at the mercy of the Dictatorship and its British allies.[25]

The arrest of the leadership ended the *dvoevlastie* which had existed in Baku since the end of July, with some of the armed troops and part of the fleet obeying the Dictatorship and others carrying out the orders of Petrov and Shaumian. Even with the Bolsheviks discredited and under suspicion, the *Kars* and the *Uzbek*, two ships in the Caspian Fleet, declared themselves for the Bolsheviks. For the Dictatorship Shaumian was a serious internal threat and the personification of an alternative policy. His case was turned over to the Cheka, now operated by the Right socialists.[26]

The underground party organization quickly launched operations to free its imprisoned leaders. With little popular support and no armed force, the Left socialists decided that the only tactic left to them was "personal terror," the threat of assassination. Mikoyan led a delegation to Sadovskii, one of the most influential Mensheviks in

[24] Suren Shaumian, pp. 58–60.
[25] The isolation of the Baku Bolsheviks from central Russia can be gauged by the tone of Lenin's frantic telegram to the chairman of the Astrakhan soviet: "The situation in Baku is still not clear to me. Who is in power? Where is Shaumian? Ask Stalin and act after considering all the circumstances; you know that I trust Shaumian completely. From here it is impossible to look into the situation and there is no chance to help at this moment." (*Dok.*, p. 621.)
[26] *Biulleten' diktatury*, no. 21, August 24, 1918.

the Dictatorship, and delivered an ultimatum: either the commissars were released or the leftists would initiate a series of political assassinations of members of the Dictatorship.[27] The threat impressed Sadovskii. At least no immediate reprisals were taken against Shaumian.

On August 18 the conference of factory committees met for the first time since the fall of the Baku Commune.[28] Sadovskii defended the new order as a temporary solution pending the reconvening of the Baku soviet. He invited the leftist parties to join the new government on the condition that they participate in the defense of the city. Sadovskii condemned the actions of Petrov, who, he claimed, had agreed to surrender his weapons and then tried to escape without giving them up. And Shaumian, he said, the sailors would have killed "like a dog" had not the crew of the *Geok-Tepe* handed him over directly to be tried. Mikoyan, now the chief spokesman for the Bolsheviks since the older men were in prison, denied that Petrov and Shaumian had attempted to sneak out of Baku. Preparations had been open and visible to all.[29] The conference, however, was defensist in mood and decidedly anti-Bolshevik, and it adopted (by 131 votes to 16) a Socialist-Revolutionary resolution which called the former commissars traitors and enemies of the people.[30] The Bolshevik and Left Socialist-Revolutionary commissars were indicted and scheduled to be tried.

[27] Mikoyan, III, p. 65.

[28] *Biulleten' diktatury*, no. 19, August 22, 1918. Mikoyan reports that there were few real workers at the conference for two reasons: "the best part of the Baku proletariat (above all communists) were at that time in the ranks of the Red Army (they had been disarmed by the Tsentrokaspii and sent to Astrakhan)," and "the organizers of the Conference attempted to bring their supporters to the Conference who in no way represented the interests of the workers" (Mikoyan, III, p. 66). In fact the conference did represent the existing workers in Baku, for the proletariat of which Mikoyan speaks and whose support the Bolsheviks had enjoyed had long since disintegrated.

[29] *Ibid.*, no. 21, August 24, 1918.

[30] *Ibid.*, no. 23, August 27, 1918.

Even as the fighting with the Turks continued, the revolutionary forms of self-government were observed, and on August 28 elections were held for a new Baku soviet. There was no campaigning and little enthusiasm for the elections—less than eleven thousand voted—but the Dictatorship needed the legal sanction for its government.[31] The totals were disappointing to all parties, but particularly to the leftists:

| | |
|---|---|
| Right Socialist Revolutionaries | 3,419 |
| Dashnaktsutiun | 2,734 |
| Mensheviks | 2,295 |
| Bolsheviks | 934 |
| Left Socialist Revolutionaries | 533 |
| Water Transport Workers | 446 |
| Auto Transport Workers | 194 |
| Left Dashnaks | 164 |
| 26th Battalion | 109 |
| Nobel workers (Black City) | 76 |
| Hnchaks | 14 |
| Shubanin district group | 3 |
| Total | 10,921[32] |

Shaumian and the other imprisoned commissars were among those elected to the soviet. The Bolsheviks, on the

[31] Mikoyan complains that during the brief campaign the Bolsheviks were not permitted to use the legal press to publish their statements and list of candidates, nor to campaign among the soldiers (Mikoyan, III, p. 69).

[32] *Biulleten' diktatury*, no. 25, August 30, 1918. The soviet was relatively confident that Baku could be successfully defended and, therefore, set about constituting a governmental authority. On September 7, the new soviet elected the S.R. Sahakian its chairman and voted to continue the Dictatorship until a new government could be elected (*ibid.*, no. 34, September 9, 1918). On September 10, a presidium of the soviet was elected. The Bolsheviks and Left Dashnaks refused to participate in the new presidium, but the Left S.R.s agreed to work within it (*ibid.*, no. 38, September 14, 1918). Two days later a new government, the Council of Popular Direction, composed largely of Right S.R.s, was formed. The Mensheviks declined to participate. (Lifshits and Chagin, p. 171.) Two days later the city fell to the Turks.

basis of just over nine hundred votes, received twenty-eight seats, but the faction was unable to persuade the Right socialist majority to release the imprisoned deputies.[33]

The fall of Baku had been delayed more by the disorganization and inertia in the Turkish forces than by determined resistance from the defenders. But the British presence was an important factor in Turkish calculations for launching a final attack against the city. Late in August the Turks launched their first attack in three weeks. Disturbed at the desertion among Armenian troops, Dunsterville announced on September 1 that he intended to evacuate his men. The Dictatorship was shocked and in a letter to the General expressed its distress:

> After the overthrow of the Bolshevik power in Baku, the representatives of Lenin's government were willing to recognize a coalition government in Baku, to supply soldiers, ammunition and *materiel*, etc., and to afford us active assistance in the defense of Baku on one condition, viz., *the withdrawal of British troops from Baku and its districts*. We were unable to accept these conditions. . . .
>
> You have not rendered the aid which we were entitled to expect of you. . . .
>
> Moreover, having in view the terms as offered to us by Lenin's government, we assert that your forces have not only failed to augment but have actually reduced the defensive strength of Baku, on which we might have relied had we accepted the terms of the Bolshevik party.[34]

[33] On September 11 the trial began. The Bolsheviks were charged with incompetence in organizing the army and the rear. Shaumian refused to testify, calling the trial a comedy. (Suren Shaumian, p. 62; Ratgauzer, *Arest' i gibel'* . . . , p. 29.) The trial was never completed, though one may guess what the verdict would have been. The commissars were still in prison when the city fell to the Turks.

[34] L. C. Dunsterville, *The Adventures of Dunsterforce* (London, 1920), pp. 283–285.

The alliance of the Right socialists and the British Army had always been characterized by suspicion and mutual accusations, perhaps inevitably in the worsening military situation. But by September each party in the alliance was seriously considering undermining, if not destroying, the other. The Dictatorship warned Dunsterville that the fleet would fire on his ships if they should attempt to evacuate the troops from Baku. And Dunsterville writes, "It had sometimes appeared to me that the only solution of the difficulty would be forcibly to remove the Dictators and set up an allied government, with full powers of civil and military administration in my own hands."[35] Altogether the British had supplied Baku with not more than one thousand soldiers. They had failed to rally local forces more than temporarily, and they had lost their most effective ally, Bicherakhov. The Right socialists' gamble had not paid off. As Shaumian had warned, Baku had lost the Bolsheviks, lost, indeed, Russia, but had not really found the British.

The Turkish attack at the end of August and the beginning of September failed to break through the last defenses of the city. But demoralization was complete. The Dictatorship attempted negotiations with the Turks through Tiflis, the Georgian Mensheviks, and the Tiflis Armenian National Council.[36] But the efforts came to naught.[37] On the morning of September 14, the Turks launched their final attack against Baku. By mid-afternoon the British had concluded that further resistance was useless and evacuation should be commenced. By ten at night all the men were on board ships, and, despite the orders of Sadovskii and Lemlin to remain in the city, General Dunsterville and his ships left Baku, made their way through

[35] *Ibid.*, p. 294.
[36] *Dokumenty i materialy po vneshnei politike Zakavkaz'ia i Gruzii* (Tiflis, 1919), pp. 440–441.
[37] *Ibid.*, p. 443.

the fire of the Caspian Feet, and sailed back to Enzeli.[38]

On the eve of the fall of Baku, the local Bolsheviks became alarmed at the danger faced by their imprisoned leaders. Mikoyan requested that the Dictatorship release the commissars or transfer them to a safe port, either Enzeli or Krasnovodsk. His repeated entreaties were denied.[39] Shaumian's son, Suren, gathered a small band of armed men and set out to take the prison by storm, but they were arrested *en route* by sailors who suspected them of being Turkish spies.[40] As these would-be liberators were cleared and freed, Mikoyan persuaded the Socialist Revolutionary Velunts to evacuate the commissars under an armed guard.[41] The Dictatorship had abandoned the city and the imprisoned commissars to the mercy of the Turks, and only Mikoyan's persistence saved the Bolshevik leaders. In the chaotic night of September 14–15, with thousands fleeing the city under Turkish fire, Mikoyan led the commissars through the city toward the port and a waiting ship. On the way the armed guard provided by the prison panicked and fled when a Turkish shell exploded nearby. The commissars were for the moment free, though still in danger of being left behind in Baku. At this critical moment the Bolsheviks met Tatevos Amirian, a Dashnak commander and the brother of Arsen Amirian, former editor of *Bakinskii rabochii*. The Dashnak offered the commissars berths on the *Turkmen*, the ship on which he was evacuating his troops. The commissars accepted the generous offer, and thus, after three vain attempts, finally escaped the doomed city.

By the morning of September 15 the city was in the hands of the Moslems. The Turkish commander kept most of his regular army outside the city as irregulars, local

[38] Dunsterville, p. 308–311; Moberly, pp. 246–247.

[39] A. S. Bukshpan (comp.), *Poslednie dni komissarov bakinskoi kommuny po materialam sudebnykh protsessov* (Baku, 1928), p. 57.

[40] *Ibid.*, p. 58; Mikoyan, III, p. 73–74.

[41] Bukshpan, pp. 59–60; Mikoyan, III, p. 73.

Moslems, and a part of his army pillaged and burned within. The "March Days" were avenged many times over. Almost the entire population of Armenikend, the Armenian suburb of Baku, was massacred. Even hospitals were not spared in the search for Christian victims. Estimates of the number killed range from nine to thirty thousand.[42] The Bolsheviks had fled; the Armenians were massacred or turned into refugees. The Moslems, for the first time since 1806, were again in control of Baku.

Nuri Pasha and the remainder of the Ottoman Army entered Baku on September 16 and celebrated their victory with a parade. The city had been taken by the Turks but in the name of the Azerbaijani Republic. Nuri Pasha invited its Prime Minister, Fataly Khan-Khoiskii, to move his government from Elisavetpol to Baku, and within a few days Baku became the working center of independent Azerbaijan. The republic functioned under Turkish and, from November, under British occupation, but never achieved real security from the Soviet giant in the north. On April 27, 1920, after less than two years of existence, the Republic of Azerbaijan handed its power over to the Bolsheviks. Soviet power returned to Baku, backed by the bayonets of the Red Army.

The Bolshevik leaders of Baku had succeeded on the evening of September 14 to escape from the advancing Turks, but before two days had run out they found that they had moved from the proverbial frying-pan into the fire. Shaumian expected the *Turkmen* to carry his men and their families to Petrovsk or to Astrakhan in the North. Instead, because of prevailing winds from the

[42] The most detailed study of the massacres of Armenians in Baku in September 1918 was written by B. Ishkhanian, *Bagvi mets sarsapnere anketayin usumnasirutyun septemberyan antskeri 1918 t.* (Tiflis, 1920). A Russian edition of this work was published under the title *Velikie uzhasy v gorode Baku. Anketnoe issledovanie sentiabrskikh sobytii 1918 g.* (Tiflis, 1920).

north and the crew's refusal to sail to Bolshevik Astrakhan, the ship's captain steamed toward Krasnovodsk, directly east from Baku. There the commissars were discovered by local authorities and thrown into prison. Their fate was now in the hands of the Socialist-Revolutionary governor of Krasnovodsk, Kun, a Caucasian Cossack officer, known for his cruelty. Kun had subordinated himself to the executive committee in Ashkhabad, largely made up of Socialist Revolutionaries and nonparty anti-Bolsheviks. The Ashkhabad Committee headed by F. Funtikov, a Socialist-Revolutionary worker, was in turn closely associated with the British military mission of General Malleson. This chain of command from Kun through Funtikov to Malleson was irregular and plagued by conflicting interests, so that officials in Krasnovodsk acted sometimes independently of Ashkhabad which in turn was sometimes unresponsive to the British headquarters in Meshed. But somewhere along this chain the decision was made and the order carried out to execute twenty-six of the captured Baku commissars.

On September 17 the British intelligence officer, Battine, telegraphed Malleson from Krasnovodsk that among the arrivals from Baku were the arrested Bolshevik commissars. Malleson immediately informed his commander-in-chief in India: "I am asking Ashkhabad Government to give me Bolshevik leaders names for despatch to India as at present times their presence in Trans-Caspia is most dangerous as probably at least half the Russians are ready to turn their coat once more at slightest sign of enemy success."[43] On the 18th, Dokhov, the Ashkhabad Committee's liaison official in Meshed, informed Malleson of the arrival of the Baku commissars in Krasnovodsk, told the general of the Committee's alarm that the opposition might take this opportunity to stage a revolt against his

[43] Public Record Office (London), Box WO 106/60.

government, and asked for the British command's position on this matter.[44] General Malleson replied that the commissars should not be permitted to proceed along the railway to Ashkhabad. This railroad had been the scene of a series of revolts and counter-revolts, both pro- and anti-Bolshevik. The general requested that the Committee hand the commissars over to the British authorities for immediate transportation to India. Dokhov agreed to relay Malleson's suggestion to his government "if it is not already too late,"—meaning, presumably, if the Committee had not already decided the fate of the commissars.[45]

That same evening the Ashkhabad Committee met to discuss what to do with the commissars. Captain Reginald Teague Jones, as an intelligence officer attached to the Committee, was invited to the meeting. He reports:

> There were present the President, Funtikov; the Deputy-President, Kurilef; the Foreign Minister, Zimin; and one or two others whom I cannot remember.
>
> The committee having assembled, the President (who was in a semi-intoxicated condition) made a statement to the effect that they had been informed from Meshed that General Malleson had declined to take over the prisoners, or, at any rate, had expressed his disinclination to do so, and had told the Ashkhabad representative that their Government must make its own arrangements.
>
> It was then argued that the local prison was full, that Krasnovodsk had refused to keep the prisoners for the same reason, and that therefore there was no alternative but to shoot them.
>
> This suggestion was opposed by Zimin, but was supported by Funtikof and Kurilef. The arguments

[44] C. H. Ellis, *The British "Intervention" in Transcaspia, 1918–1919* (Berkeley, 1963), p. 59. Ellis was stationed in Meshed with Malleson's mission at this time.
[45] *Ibid.*, p. 60.

continued endlessly, and finally I left the meeting before anything had really been definitely decided.[46]

It should be noted that Teague Jones, according to his own account, took no part in the discussions of the Committee. Rather he sat silent and apparently failed to mention that he had himself received word earlier that same day from Malleson confirming his willingness to transport the commissars to India.[47] Teague Jones's passivity was most uncharacteristic of this energetic and experienced conspirator. Just a few days before, in a letter to a colleague, Captain Teague Jones had expressed his personal feelings about the Ashkhabad Committee and his own influence over it:

> I am lying up in Ashkhabad for the time being and
> am representing Genl. Malleson who remains in Meshed.
> We have a wretchedly weak executive committee whom
> we have to keep galvanizing into action the whole
> time.—The work is nothing like so interesting as it was
> in Baku.—We had a great scare here yesterday when we
> heard that Baku had fallen. The impression we got here
> was that the town had fallen and that Dunsterville had
> had no time to get away, and that an enemy attack was
> to be expected in Krasnovodsk. I sat up drawing up a
> "defense of the realm scheme." It was put before the
> committee and passed in the early hours of the morning
> and is said to be going to be put into practice. What
> we can do when people really get frightened![48]

Thus the decision to shoot the commissars was made by the Ashkhabad Committee without, if Teague Jones's

[46] Letter of Major Teague Jones to the under-secretary of state, Foreign Office, November 12, 1922; published in Cmd. 1846 (Russia No. 1 [1923]), pp. 8–9.

[47] *Ibid.*, p. 8.

[48] Letter from Teague Jones to an unknown colonel, Public Record Office (London), Box WO 95/5043, Dunsterforce "G" Section, Base W–182, Part II, Krasnovodsk Mission.

account is to be believed, active interference from the British agent in the city. While the more exaggerated claims by Soviet historians of British responsibility in the death of the Twenty-six cannot be substantiated, there is enough evidence to conclude that the British agents in Transcaspia could have prevented the execution if they had been interested in doing so. This they simply were not, and British protests were filed only after the fact.[49]

Teague Jones was told of the decision to shoot the commissars on the 19th, that is, on the eve of the execution. He wired the information to General Malleson, who in turn called in Dokhov and expressed his horror at their decision. Dokhov told the general that he had already received confirmation that the executions had taken place. Malleson washed his hands of the matter with the remark "all alike—Red or White."[50]

In the Krasnovodsk house of detention Shaumian and most of his comrades were optimistic about their fate. They seemed unaware of the viciousness with which the Civil War was being fought throughout Russia. In Baku the Bolsheviks had never arrested fellow-revolutionaries even of the opposition parties. Now they were the prisoners of the Socialist Revolutionaries and were to pay for the actions of their comrades in other parts of Soviet Russia. On September 18, 1918, the Socialist-Revolutionary newspaper *Golos Srednei Azii* ("Voice of Central Asia") published an ominous announcement:

> Yesterday the Baku Bolshevik Commissars were
> arrested, among them the Caucasian Lenin—Stepan

[49] The most damning evidence against the British is an affidavit, dated March 2, 1919, by Funtikov in which he states that Teague Jones "told me personally before the execution of the Commissars that execution was imperative, and after the execution he expressed satisfaction that the execution had been carried out in accordance with the views of the English mission" (V. A. Chaikin, *K istorii rossiiskoi revoliutsii*, I: Kazn' 26 bakinskikh komissarov [Moscow, 1922], p. 55).

[50] Ellis, p. 61.

Shaumian. . . . We will not stop at quartering and the most torturous torments. Thus we will be revenged for the hundreds and thousands of our comrades languishing in Bolshevik torture-chambers in Russia . . .[51]

At one in the morning on September 20, the prisoners were suddenly awakened. Twenty-six men were isolated from the rest and told to prepare for transfer to Ashkhabad. Mikoyan, who was to be left behind, requested to be allowed to accompany Shaumian, but his request was denied. The "twenty-seventh commissar" relates the last conversation he had with Shaumian:

> Then Shaumian, taking me aside, said: "This is nothing, that they refused your request. They will free you—you together with Surik and Lev (Shaumian's sons) attempt to get through to Astrakhan, from there to Moscow, you will meet with Lenin, tell him everything that happened here to us. Make a proposal in my name— to arrest a few well-known Right S.R.s and Mensheviks (if they have not already been arrested), declare them hostages, and propose to the Transcaspian government an exchange for us."[52]

From Krasnovodsk the Twenty-six Commissars were taken by train 207 versts to the east. At a desolate spot in the desert they were made to disembark. Within forty minutes the Twenty-six were dead—some shot, others mutilated by swords. The bodies were quickly and crudely buried.[53] There they lay until 1920, when they were re-

[51] Suren Shaumian, "Es-ery v roli palachei," *Pamiati 26. Materialy k istorii bakinskoi kommuny 1918 g.* (Baku, 1922), ed. M. Lifshits and P. Chagin, p. 17.

[52] Mikoyan, IV, p. 87.

[53] *K protsessu F. Funtikova* (Baku, 1926), pp. 63–64. The Twenty-six Baku Commissars were Stepan Shaumian (Bolshevik), Prokofiia Dzhaparidze (B.), Meshadi Azizbekov (B.), Ivan Fioletov (B.), Mir-Hasan Vezirov (Left S.R.), Grigorii Korganov (B.), Pavel Zevin (B.), Grigorii Petrov (Left S.R.), Vladimir Polukhin (B.), Arsen Amirian (B.), Suren Osepian (B.), Ivan Malygin (B.), Bagdasar

turned to Soviet Baku and buried in Freedom Square. Today the Square is a shrine to the memory of the leaders of the Baku Commune. An eternal flame burns above their common grave. In the Soviet Union the Twenty-six Commissars are legendary figures remembered for their spectacular rise to power and their all too brief attempt to bring socialism to one city.

---

Avakian (B.), Meer Basin (B.), Mark Koganov (B.), Fedor Solntsev (B.), Aram Kostandian (B.), Anatolii Bogdanov (B.), Solomon Bogdanov (B.), Armenak Borian (B.), Eizhen Berg (B.), Ivan Gabyshev (B.), Ivan Nikolaishvili (B.), Iraklii Metaksa (B.), Tatevos Amirian (Dashnak), and Isai Mishne (nonparty).

# 12

## Conclusion

THE HISTORY OF BOLSHEVISM in Baku belies the hoary myths which have clung to Lenin's party since the revolution. The picture of a highly disciplined, conspiratorial party seizing power by force and then imposing its will on a reluctant population by terror bears little resemblance to what actually happened on the Apsheron Peninsula. In Baku the Bolsheviks' actions were neither bloodthirsty nor particularly surreptitious. More moderate than their Petrograd comrades, they had deep roots in the city, long training in the economic struggle, and a sensitivity to the dangers of interethnic warfare. While in power they refrained from using terror. The leadership of Shaumian and Dzhaparidze was forced to operate within a context in which they did not hold a monopoly on military force and in which the "economism," "defensism," and nationalism of the population weakened their hold on the local soviet. Despite these inhibitions the Bolsheviks managed in six months to rise from their wartime isolation to primacy in the soviet. Before six more months had passed the Bolsheviks formed a soviet government. These extraordinary successes were only equaled by the party's rapid fall. Ultimately the unity of the Baku working class was destroyed by nationalism, while "economism" and "defensism" turned significant sectors away from the Bolsheviks.

In the prerevolutionary years the Baku Bolsheviks learned to work with workers who were almost exclusively interested in economic issues. Even in 1905 Baku workers could not be persuaded to engage in political activities.

After losing the initiative to the Shendrikov brothers in 1904–1905, the Bolsheviks rebuilt their base in the legal trade unions and among the Moslem and unskilled workers of the outlying districts and by openly agitating for a conference with the oil industry. To an extraordinary degree the Bolsheviks abandoned their earlier hostility to the economic struggle and participated with the workers in their mass organizations. Unlike the Menshevik-Liquidators, however, the Bolsheviks never abandoned their underground organization, though it tended to atrophy in the years of "reaction" from 1908 to 1912. Bolshevik success in the years immediately before the war again came from their leadership of essentially economic strikes, although the great strike of 1914 can be considered a political event because of its very scope and duration. Through the years of war and revolution the Bolsheviks enjoyed their greatest popularity while they were leading the workers in labor negotiations or strikes; they suffered their greatest defeat once they took power and left the leadership of the economic struggle to the Mensheviks and Right Socialist Revolutionaries.

In Baku the equivalent of the Provisional Government was formed even before the local soviet met. The Executive Committee of Public Organizations (IKOO) hoped to represent all of society, including the workers, and thus in its origins embodied the idea of coalition. The workers, however, soon formed their own class organs, the soviets and the factory committees, which in turn expressed labor's suspicion of the IKOO. Even more suspect was the old city duma, considered the representative of the *tsentsovoe obshchestvo*. On the first major issue in the revolution, the incorporation of the oil-field districts into the city, the duma opposed, but the IKOO supported, the workers' soviet. In fact, the IKOO had already become little more than a façade for the soviet—a convenience when it supported the soviet, an irrelevance in the rare moments when it hesitated to go along with it. Political power in Baku was polarized between the soviet and the city duma, but a stalemate developed when the soviet refused to take power and the duma delayed its democratic reelection until well into October.

Through 1917–1918 the Russian and Armenian workers of Baku supported the war effort, acquiesced in the alliance with the bourgeoisie and the liberals, and were concerned about safeguarding the freedoms won in February and consolidating their economic position through the labor contract. The fact that the contract could not be won through negotiations but only after a shutdown of the industry convinced many workers that a basic conflict of interests divided them from the propertied classes and that they had little to gain from a coalition with the bourgeoisie. They then listened more sympathetically to the Bolsheviks, who had led them in the September strike.

At the same time as the urban workers were becoming radicalized in the economic struggle, the oil-field workers and the Moslems were feeling the pinch in a much more direct way. Hunger stalked the grimy huts of the poorest workers, most of whom were Moslems with no access to political levers in Baku. In massive demonstrations and through the activities of the Musavat and Hummet the Moslems manifested their discontent with the moderate socialist leadership of the soviet. At this point Moslem activism aided the extreme Left in its campaign against the Right socialist soviet, but it also foreboded the future disintegration of the Baku proletariat into its national components.

The political response of the local parties to the gradual radicalization of the workers and soldiers was, with the exception of the Bolsheviks, based on misconceptions of the nature of revolution and of the imperatives of power in a revolutionary situation. The Kadets limited their political activity to legal channels, i.e., to the press, the city duma, the IKOO, Tsentrodom, etc. For the liberals the soviets were illegitimate bodies, beyond the political pale. Besides their limited tactical imagination the Kadets suffered from a political program which found little response among the new players on the political stage. As liberals they held out for limited representation and were prepared to disenfranchise the uneducated workers of the industrial districts. Their constituency was limited to the city proper, to men who all too readily were identifiable as the remnants of the *tsentsovoe obshchestvo*. Although the membership of the Party of People's Freedom consisted largely of professional men and intellectuals, their political program and outlook was eminently "bourgeois." Their ideal was the middle-class democracies of Western Europe. Within weeks of the February Revolution, the Kadets, the only alternative to the socialist parties, had become isolated in Baku. Within ten months the bourgeoisie too had lost all semblance of power and influence.[1]

Power was in the streets, in mass meetings on Freedom Square, in the factory committees, as well as in the meetings of the soviets. With the liberals eliminated the struggle was restricted to the socialists and nationalist parties. The nationalists, however, could not hope to emerge victorious without some *modus vivendi* with the socialists. Both the Musavat and the Dashnaktsutiun attempted alliances with the "internationalist" parties, but with only partial success. From February 1917 until the "March Days" the Dashnaks were closely associated with the moderate socialist bloc, with those socialists who were committed to the war effort. By early 1918, faced with the double danger of the Turkish advance and internal disorder, the Dashnaks gravitated toward the local represen-

---

[1] For discussion of the Kadets on the national level see Thomas Riha, "1917—A Year of Illusions," *Soviet Studies*, XIX, 1 (July 1967), pp. 115–121; and William G. Rosenberg, "Russian Liberals and the Bolshevik Coup," *The Journal of Modern History*, XL, 3 (September 1968), pp. 328–347.

tatives of Soviet power. This marriage of convenience was a matter of self-preservation. The dilemma of the Armenians was acute. To avoid extermination at the hands of ancient enemies, they were willing to ally with any force great enough to preserve their nation. In Georgia it was the Mensheviks; in Baku it was the Bolsheviks and later the English.

The Musavatists also were forced to rely on other political parties in order to survive in Baku politics. Until the Shamkhor events in January 1918 the Musavat maintained a tacit, uncomfortable liaison with the Bolsheviks. Like the Bolsheviks the Musavat wanted an immediate end to the war. But under the pressure of the Moslem risings in Transcaucasia and the north Caucasus, the flimsy alliance fell apart. The Musavat and other Moslem parties joined in the desperate rebellion against soviet power in Baku and were momentarily defeated. Without support in the city proper and faced by armed Armenians and Bolshevik supporters, the Musavat retreated to the west, to Elisavetpol, to await their Turkish brothers who would reinstate them in the capital of Azerbaijan.

The real contest for power was between the Left socialists—the Bolsheviks, Left Socialist Revolutionaries, and Left Dashnaks—and the Right socialists—the Mensheviks and Right Socialist Revolutionaries. The Right socialists dominated the soviet immediately after the February Revolution and reflected the moderate, defensist mood of the urban workers, but their reluctance to assert themselves against the capitalists made them ineffective contestants against the Bolsheviks. As the negotiations for the labor contract stagnated and the food shortage worsened, workers began to drift left toward the Bolsheviks. As the war effort floundered, soldiers too began to respond to the Left. In time more and more poorer workers in the outlying districts made themselves felt in the city proper, through additional elections to the soviets and, more importantly, through the conferences of factory committees. The chief beneficiaries of labor discontent were the Bolsheviks, the party which had energetically led the September strike and which alone was opposed to coalition with the bourgeoisie. October marked the zenith of Bolshevik influence over the working class and the high-water mark of proletarian cohesion. In the wake of the successful September strike the Bolsheviks maneuvered the merger of the conference of factory committees with the soviet, dislodged the moderate socialist leadership, and passed a resolution declaring soviet power in Baku. Besides workers' support the Bolsheviks enjoyed the sympathy of the Baku garrison. All the requirements for an armed seizure of power seemed at hand. Yet the local Bolsheviks hesitated to emulate their comrades in Petrograd. There was no Lenin in Baku who combined a resolute will to power with the necessary influence within the party, no one to argue that: "To wait is a crime against the revolution." The Shaumian–Dzhaparidze strategy of "peaceful transition" was substituted for an armed insurrection, and "October" was delayed. Although the moribund IKOO was easily dispersed in November, the city duma, reelected and revitalized, remained to plague the supporters of soviet power. In the coming months the united working class disintegrated into feuding nationalities. The Baku garrison disappeared. With the armistice declared by the Soviet government, the soldiers began drifting back to Russia. By December 1917 the Bolsheviks had lost their military support. Yet at the same time the Bolsheviks, now in control of the Russian government, had become "defensists," willing to protect the country against "imperialist" incursions. Before long the Socialist Revolutionaries and Dashnaks rallied behind the soviet leadership.

For the next three months the soviet was the only effective governing force in Baku and was recognized as such by most of the political parties. In January the Red

Guards were formed, thus giving the soviet a military force of its own. Still the city duma was tolerated, and the Moslem and Armenian National Councils controlled significant segments of the population. The strategy of "peaceful transition" had reached its limit. An insurrection would be necessary after all. Initiated by the Moslems, the "March Days" were simultaneously a soviet–Moslem struggle for power and an interethnic bloodletting. The short-term victors were the Armenians and the Bolsheviks. The soviet was now the supreme power in the city, but in large part its power rested on the bayonets of the Dashnak troops.

Ultimately nationalism and self-interest proved the undoing of the Bolsheviks in Baku. A viable Bolshevik government in Baku could not exist without a united working class. Stratified by skills and wage-levels, and divided by nationality, Baku workers had seldom come together for more than a short time and then only on immediate economic issues. Yet in the September strike of 1917 the Bolsheviks had managed to achieve an extraordinary degree of cohesion among the workers. The victory was astounding to an old labor leader like Dzhaparidze. Within a few months the superficial unity had broken down. The spectre of interethnic warfare arose, and the ranks of the national parties swelled. The tacit Bolshevik–Musavat alliance fell apart, and many Moslems began to suspect the Bolsheviks of being pro-Armenian. When it came, the armed victory of the Bolshevik–Dashnak forces in the "March Days" was a hollow one indeed. Thousands of Moslems left the city to join the counterrevolution, and the Bolsheviks became dependent on the Armenians for support.

A second wave of disaffection of workers toward the Bolsheviks took place during the Commune. The vertical stratification by wage-levels and skills reasserted itself.

Many urban workers began agitating for private food-purchases (group purchases), a measure which would have benefited only those with money. The Bolsheviks opposed any challenge to the soviet monopoly on food-purchases, but the factory committees came out for the group purchases. Fear and hunger led this time to the disaffection, which, although temporary, gnawed at the remaining loyalties to the Bolshevik party.

A third wave of workers' disaffection proved to be the final one. The Bolsheviks undertook a task too difficult for their meager resources—the sovietization of all of Transcaucasia. By launching a war against Elisavetpol and Tiflis, Shaumian precipitated the final defeat of the Commune. Overwhelmed by Turkish regulars, the Red Army fell back to the hills surrounding Baku. In panic the workers of Baku turned for the last time from the Bolsheviks and voted in the soviet and in street meetings to invite the British.

Shaumian had attempted to deal a death-blow to the counterrevolution in the rest of Transcaucasia while simultaneously undertaking a maximalist social reformation within the city of Baku. These tremendous endeavors were attempted without the full participation in the government of the Right socialist parties, for, although dependent on Dashnak troops and at least the acquiescence of the Mensheviks and Socialist Revolutionaries Shaumian refused to admit representatives of these parties into the Sovnarkom as long as they did not recognize the central Soviet government. On the other hand the parties continued to enjoy full freedom in the soviet and, apart from having two newspapers closed down, were untouched by the Bolshevik government. The Cheka made no arrests. In fact, under the conditions of a civil war, the Baku Commune was a remarkably democratic, effectively representative government. No dictatorship of one party was

( 351 )

established. When the Bolsheviks lost the confidence of the soviet, they retired from government in parliamentary fashion.

The Bolsheviks of Baku lost power when they lost the workers. They lost the workers because they could no longer respond to the workers' demands. The Bolsheviks were unable to summon the British because the central Soviet government, to whom they owed their first loyalty, would not permit the invitation. The safest course therefore seemed to be retirement and evacuation. But with the city under bombardment the flight of the commissars appeared treasonous to the Right socialist Dictatorship. Shaumian and his comrades were arrested, tried, and imprisoned. The fate of the Twenty-six Commissars is ironic indeed. Moderate, democratic, unwilling to use the instruments of terror, Shaumian, Dzhaparidze, and the others fell into the hands of their opponents in the Civil War who did not hesitate to cut them down. The ferocity of the Civil War was already apparent by the late summer of 1918. The hope that a democratic republic of soviets would emerge after October was buried in the course of that war.

# Appendix:
# The Marxist Image of
# the Commune

THE IMPORTANCE of the Paris revolution of 1871 for Marxist socialists is well known, but less fully appreciated is the powerful influence of the Marxist image of the Commune during the Russian Revolution. Socialists of various stripes used the "lessons" of the Commune to defend a favorite point in their program or defeat a tactical maneuver of their opponents. The best-known use of the Commune was in Lenin's *State and Revolution*, perhaps his most maligned work. For his apparently "anarchistic" and "utopian" enthusiasms in this pamphlet Lenin has been accused of everything from political naïveté to simple deception. Yet both before and after *State and Revolution* the Commune as the concrete embodiment of socialism was revered and occasionally imitated by Russian socialists. Heroic defenders of beleaguered cities were often dubbed "communard." In 1919, as the White Army closed in on Petrograd, the city was referred to as the "Petrograd Commune." Paris was a source of inspiration and instruction—not directly, but through the writings of Marx and Lenin.

Marx's position on the Commune as stated in *The Civil War in France* modified his earlier writings on the tactics of the proletariat in the revolution. Starting with the *Communist Manifesto*, Marx had argued that the workers must seize the state and use its great power to destroy the bourgeois order and build the new society. "The first step in the revolution by the working class is to raise the proletariat to the position of ruling class, to win the battle of democracy. The proletariat will use its political supremacy to wrest, by degrees, all capital from the bourgeoisie, to centralize all instruments of production in the hands of the State, i.e., of the proletariat organized as a ruling class; and to increase the total productive forces as rapidly as possible."[1] Despite his statist approach to socialism in the past, Marx enthusiastically greeted the Paris Commune as a genuine working-class manifestation, and, in the face of opposition from members of the International, he had his addresses on the Commune published.[2]

In his discussion of the Commune Marx attacked the popular notion that the Communards were bloodthirsty vandals set on destroying French civilization. He emphasized that they had been reluctant to use violence against their enemies until Versailles had unleashed its full fury on the capital. Though he did not explicitly argue in his address to the International that the Communards were mistaken in not resorting to terror, Marx was more candid

[1] Karl Marx and Friedrich Engels, *Basic Writings on Politics and Philosophy*, ed. Lewis S. Feuer (New York, 1959), pp. 27–28.

[2] George Lichtheim, in his excellent analysis, *Marxism: An Historical and Critical Study* (New York, 1961), writes that Marx's 1871 view of the Commune was a throwback to an earlier Jacobin-romantic period in his writings when he favored revolutionary action over the painstaking work of creating a democratic mass labor movement. Later in life Marx abandoned this "utopian" view of the Commune. He wrote in 1881: "Apart from the fact that this was merely the rising of a city under exceptional conditions, the majority of the Commune was in no way socialist nor could it be. With a modicum of common sense, however, it could have reached a compromise with Versailles useful to the whole people—the only thing that could be attained at the time. The appropriation of the Bank of France alone would have been enough to put a rapid end to the rodomontades of the Versailles crowd." (Lichtheim, p. 121.) Despite Marx's second thoughts on the Commune, it was the views expressed in *The Civil War in France* which found their way into *State and Revolution* and the Bolshevik view of the proletarian revolution.

in the well-known letter to Dr. Kugelmann (April 12, 1871) in which he listed the glaring mistakes of the Parisians:

> If you look at the last chapter of my *Eighteenth Brumaire* you will find that I say that the next attempt of the French revolution will be no longer, as before, to transfer the bureaucratic-military machine from one hand to another, but to smash it, and this is essential for every real people's revolution on the Continent. And this is what our heroic Party comrades in Paris are attempting. . . . If they are defeated only their "good nature" will be to blame. They should have marched at once on Versailles, after first Vinoy and then the reactionary section of the Paris National Guard had themselves retreated. The right moment was missed because of conscientious scruples. They did not want to start the civil war with his attempt to disarm Paris. Second mistake: The Central Committee surrendered its power too soon, to make way for the Commune. Again from a too "honorable" scrupulosity![3]

Though not a clear prescription for the use of terror, Marx's analysis of the failures of the Commune leaves that possibility open. At least scruples were not to inhibit resolute action against the ruthless bourgeois enemy. And the underlying strategy of the proletariat in the final revolution must be to destroy the machinery by which the enemy has oppressed the workers, i.e., the bourgeois state. Repressive aspects of the old state had to be liquidated. Marx here reversed his former position, which held that the workers had only to seize the old state to begin the construction of socialism. The experience of the Commune revealed that the postrevolutionary government would be fundamentally different from all past states.

Marx outlined the characteristics of the Paris Com-

[3] Karl Marx, *The Civil War in France* (New York, 1962), p. 85.

mune, suggesting it as a model for a new, post-bourgeois organization of society. "The Commune was to be a working, not a parliamentary body, executive and legislative at the same time." All oppressive agencies of present governments, including the police and the army, were to be converted into agencies of the Communes, and all officials at all times could be recalled. Administration was to be in the hands of elected representatives, whose salaries would not exceed that of an average worker. On the provincial level, power would also be vested in local communes, and the standing army was to be replaced by a militia. But, though power would be fractionalized, decentralization would not lead to the disintegration of the nation. "The unity of the nation was not to be broken, but, on the contrary, to be organized by the Communal Constitution, and to become a reality by the destruction of the state power which claimed to be the embodiment of that unity independent of, and superior to, the nation itself, from which it was but a parasitic excrescence."[4]

While Marx did not refer to the Commune as a "state" or as "the dictatorship of the proletariat," his disciples were less restrained. Engels, in the introduction to the 1891 edition of *The Civil War in France*, simplified the argument of his dead collaborator on the postrevolutionary state:

> In reality, however, the state is nothing but a machine
> for the oppression of one class by another, and indeed
> in the democratic republic no less than in the monarchy;
> and at best an evil inherited by the proletariat after its
> victorious struggle for class supremacy, whose worst
> sides the proletariat, just like the Commune, cannot
> avoid having to lop off at the earliest possible moment,
> until such time as a new generation, reared in new and
> free social conditions will be able to throw the entire

[4] *Ibid.*, p. 58.

lumber of the state on the scrap-heap.

Of late, the Social-Democratic philistine has once more been filled with wholesome terror at the words: Dictatorship of the Proletariat. Well and good, gentlemen, do you want to know what this dictatorship looks like? Look at the Paris Commune. That was the Dictatorship of the Proletariat.[5]

In fact, in 1871 Marx was quite close to the anarchist Bakunin in his enthusiasm for the Commune as the spontaneous expression of the workers. Marx wrote that the Commune was not merely a new kind of class rule but had actually superseded class rule itself. On this point he writes:

While the merely repressive organs of the old governmental power were to be amputated, its legitimate functions were to be wrested from an authority usurping preeminence over society itself, and restored to the responsible agents of society. Instead of deciding once in three or six years which members of the ruling class were to misrepresent the people in Parliament, universal suffrage was to serve the people, constituted in Communes, as individual suffrage serves every other employer in the search for the workmen and managers in his business. And it is well-known that companies, like individuals, in matters of real business generally know how to put the right man in the right place, and, if they for once make a mistake, to redress it promptly. On the other hand, nothing could be more foreign to the spirit of the Commune than to supersede universal suffrage by hierarchic investiture.[6]

Universal suffrage and communal organization would prevent the recurrence of class rule and a repressive state order. All the people would elect the officials, and with the

5 *Ibid.*, p. 22.　　6 *Ibid.*, pp. 58–59.

power of immediate recall would maintain close and complete control over those elected.

In his *Civil War in France*, written before the fall of the Commune, Marx praises the libertarian aspects of the Parisian government. But in his letters to Dr. Kugelmann he criticizes the Communards for being overscrupulous and unwilling to use repressive measures against the bourgeoisie. One may justifiably point out that the democracy of the Commune and its tolerance of opposition did not permit the kind of repression that Marx demanded. In 1917 Lenin attempted to reconcile these two aspects of the Commune's dilemma, democracy and terror. His achievement represents a distortion of the Marx of 1871.

In his work *State and Revolution*, written while hiding from the Provisional Government's police in the late summer of 1917, Lenin launched a polemic on two fronts: against the anarchist-communists on the left and against the Mensheviks and Socialist Revolutionaries on the right. Lenin began by distinguishing the anarchists' plan to abolish the state totally from the Marxist contention that only the repressive aspects of the state should be destroyed at once. Lenin followed Engels in speaking of two stages: the first in which the bourgeois state after a violent revolution is seized by the proletariat, and the second in which the proletarian state withers away. The anarchists would have abolished the state as soon as the workers had gained control, and Lenin considered such action utopian.

Lenin attacked the Right socialists for supporting the Provisional Government and not heeding Marx's advice to destroy the bourgeois state when the opportunity arose. Marx had corrected his earlier position in the *Communist Manifesto* after the experience of the Commune and argued that the workers would not simply take over the bourgeois state intact but had to smash it up immediately. Lenin interpreted this as meaning "the old bureaucratic machine," not all of officialdom: "To destroy officialdom

(358)

immediately, everywhere, completely—this cannot be thought of. That is a Utopia. But to *break up* at once the old bureaucratic machine and to start immediately the construction of a new one which will enable us gradually to reduce all officialdom to naught—this is *no* Utopia, it is the experience of the Commune, it is the direct and urgent task of the revolutionary proletariat."[7] Lenin's position was between the anarchists' insistence on the total destruction of the state and the Right socialists' tolerance of the bourgeois state. But Lenin's position, I would argue, was not identical, as he would like to have had it, with Marx's. Marx saw the Commune as a non-statist road to socialism, a new form of society which had been freed from the evils of class rule; while Lenin, like Engels, saw the Commune as a kind of semistate through which socialism could be constructed. *State and Revolution* does not represent an aberration in Lenin's thinking on the state but rather an attempt to enlist the Marx of 1871 and the Paris Commune in the ranks of statist socialists.

Lenin's emphasis was squarely on destroying the bourgeoisie. There was to be no accommodation with this mortal class enemy. The mistakes of the Paris Commune were not to be repeated by its Marxist disciples. Lenin wrote:

> It is still necessary to suppress the bourgeoisie and crush its resistance. This was particularly necessary for the Commune; and one of the reasons of its defeat was that it did not do this with sufficient determination. But the organ of suppression is now the majority of the population, and not a minority as was always the case under slavery, serfdom, and wage labor. And, once the

[7] V. I. Lenin, *Polnoe sobranie sochineniia* (5th ed.), XXXIII, *passim*. This volume contains the text of *State and Revolution* with Lenin's notes and corrections. The translations here are taken from International Publishers' "Little Lenin Library" edition (New York, n.d.), p. 42.

majority of the people *itself* suppresses its oppressors,
a "special force" for suppression is *no longer necessary.*
In this sense the state *begins to wither away.*[8]

Lenin's postrevolutionary "commune" curiously enough
possessed the Marxist characteristics of a "state," i.e., the
rule by one class (now the majority) and the repression
of another (now a minority). The Paris Commune, with
its universal suffrage and tolerance for the middle classes,
had avoided in Marx's eyes these aspects of the traditional
state. In other words, Lenin was readapting the model of
the Commune to his personal vision of the postrevolutionary form of government. He was trying to resolve the very
dilemma which had defeated the original Communards—
how to reconcile democracy with repression. Lenin simply
subordinated minority rights to majority "needs."

Once the bourgeois state machinery had been shattered,
a new order, called by both Marx and Lenin the "commune," was to replace it. But Marx saw the commune as
democratic, with the workers ruling in conjunction with
other classes while the very concept of classes was being
eliminated. Lenin, on the other hand, saw the workers
ruling *over* the rest of society. In Lenin's scheme the
elimination of the bourgeoisie would permit the workers
to run all of society like a post office: "Overthrow the
capitalists, crush with the iron hand of armed workers
the resistance of these exploiters, break the bureaucratic
machine of the modern state—and you have before you a
mechanism of the highest technical equipment, freed of
'parasites,' capable of being set into motion by the united
workers themselves who hire their own technicians, managers, bookkeepers, and pay them *all*, as, indeed, every
'state' official with the usual workers' wage."[9]

Lenin agreed with Marx that parliamentarism was a
loquacious sickness of the modern democratic state. He

[8] *Ibid.*, p. 37.      [9] *Ibid.*, p. 43.

argued that a new system of representation was needed, and adopted the model of the Paris Commune: "Representative institutions remain, but parliamentarism as a special system, as a division of labor between the legislative and executive functions, as a privileged position for the deputies, *no longer exists*. Without representative institutions we cannot imagine democracy, not even proletarian democracy; but we can and *must* think of democracy without parliamentarism, if criticism of bourgeois society is not mere empty words for us."[10] In the context in which Lenin was writing *State and Revolution* it was clear that such representative institutions (joint executive-legislative bodies) existed in the soviets of workers', soldiers', and peasants' deputies. Thus for Lenin the transfer of power to these organs would once again give concrete form to the ideal of the Commune. The soviets would constitute the new proletarian "state."[11]

Lenin's enthusiasm for the Commune as the model for the postrevolutionary government did not extend to the adoption of its federalist program. Marx had favored federalism only in specific historical contexts and generally supported a centralized state. Engels had more explicitly advocated a strongly centralized state for economic reasons. Lenin too was a centralist and opposed the anarchist-federalist approach. That both centralist Marxists and federalist anarchists based their visions of the future state on the Paris Commune indicates that the primary attraction of the Commune was the heroism of its experience rather than its concrete achievements or its

[10] *Ibid.*, pp. 41–42.

[11] Nowhere in *State and Revolution* did Lenin speak about the party. The role of the party in the postrevolutionary state had not yet been worked out in Lenin's mind. Many of the seeming contradictions between the centralist and statist notions of the Bolsheviks and the decentralized and communal aspects of the Paris commune were eventually to be resolved in favor of a dictatorship by one party.

theoretical accomplishments. The experience of the Baku Commune suggests that tensions between local communal organizations and the center are inevitable. Even before the short-lived Commune fell in Baku, the relations between the center and the city on the Caspian had revealed that local autonomy could exist only when physical contact between the two had broken down. Party loyalty and subordination to the central authorities proved to be stronger than local pressure, and were contributing factors to the fall of the Bolsheviks.

For the actual experience of the Russian revolution, whether in central Russia or in a provincial city like Baku, the example of the Paris Commune could provide only a theoretical framework, for decisions finally had to be made in response to the situation at hand. And yet Paris was accepted as a guide to actions and, therefore, an inhibition on choices. History did teach lessons, thought the socialists, and those lessons could be applied.

# Bibliography

## I. ARCHIVAL MATERIALS

Public Record Office (London) contains documents pertinent to the British role in Transcaucasia. The records of Dunsterforce, of Vice-Consul MacDonell, and of British companies in Baku are available.

Russian Archive, Columbia University in the City of New York, contains memoirs of participants in the revolutionary movement and anti-Bolshevik resistance in Transcaucasia.

Tsentral'nyi Gosudarstvennyi Arkhiv Oktiabr'skoi Revoliutsii i Sotsialisticheskogo Stroitel'stva (Moscow) contains originals and copies of letters and information bulletins from Transcaucasia, 1917–1918. There are also documents from the Commissariat of Nationalities.

Tsentral'nyi Gosudarstvennyi Istoricheskii Arkhiv Armianskoi SSR (Erevan) contains documents on Shaumian, the Dashnaktsutiun, the Baku Armenian National Council, K. Vermishev (the Baku Kadet leader), and relations between the Armenian Republic and Baku.

## II. NEWSPAPERS AND JOURNALS, BAKU 1917–1918

*Arev* (1917–1918)—the most widely read Armenian newspaper in Baku; during the revolution it supported the Dashnaks.

*Ashkhatanki droshak* (1917–1918)—organ of the Armenian S.R.s.

*Azerbaidzhan* (1917–1920)—Russian organ of the Azerbaijani Republic.

*Bakinets*

*Bakinskie gubernskie vedomosti*

*Bakinskii rabochii* (April 22, 1917, to August 11, 1918)—organ of the Baku Organization of RSDRP until June 1917, when it became the organ of the Baku Bolsheviks. Shaumian was editor until October 1917 when he was succeeded by Arsen Amirian.

*Baku* (1917 to March 1918)—edited by K. A. Vermishev, this newspaper had a Kadet orientation, although it was ostensibly nonpartisan and geared to the whole population, particularly to the Armenians.

*Banvor* (1917–1918)—organ of the Armenian Social-Democratic Workers' Organization in Baku.

*Banvori khosk* (1918)—the theoretical journal of the Baku Bolsheviks.

*Biulleten' diktatury Tsentrokaspiia i prezidiuma vremennogo ispolnitel'nogo komiteta soveta* (August–September 1918)—official organ of the Dictatorship of Tsentrokaspii.

*Biulleten' komiteta revoliutsionnoi oborny* (April 1918)—the official organ of the Committee of Revolutionary Defense set up during the "March Days."

*Golos edinstva* (1917–1918)—organ of the Plekhanovites.

*Golos trudiaschegosia* (1918)—organ of the Left Dashnaks.

*Gorts* (January 1917)—an Armenian nonparty newspaper.

*Gudok* (June 1918)—organ of the Council of Oil Workers.

*Iskra* (August–September 1918)—organ of the Baku Mensheviks.

*Izvestiia bakinskogo ispolnitel'nogo komiteta obshchestvennykh organizatsii* (1917)—organ of the Baku IKOO.

*Izvestiia bakinskoi gorodskoi dumy* (1917–1918)

*Izvestiia revoliutsionnogo komiteta obshchestvennoi bezo-pastnosti* (1917)—organ of the Committee of Public Safety set up by the Right socialists after the October Revolution.

*Izvestiia sovetov rabochikh i soldatskikh deputatov bakins-kogo raiona* (1917–1918)—organ of the Baku Soviet of Workers' and Soldiers' Deputies, edited by Shaumian, Mandel'shtam, Karinian, Mikoyan, and others.

*Izvestiia voenno-revoliutsionnogo komiteta kavkazskoi armii* (1918)—organ of Korganov's Military-Revolutionary Committee of the Caucasian Army.

*Kaspii* (1917–1918)—a major newspaper in Baku, published by the wealthy Moslem, Z. A. Tagiev; this newspaper was aimed primarily at the Moslem community, although it was published in Russian. The *Izvestiia* of the Moslem National Council was published as the last page of *Kaspii* and is a primary source of information on the activities of the Moslem community.

*Kavkazskaia kooperatsiia* (1918)—organ of the cooperatives.

*Kavkazskaia krasnaia armiia* (1918)—organ of the Caucasian Red Army.

*Kavkazskii telegraf* (1917)

*Mer orer* (1918)—an Armenian newspaper.

*Molot* (1917)

*Narodnaia svoboda* (1917–1918)—organ of the Party of People's Freedom (Kadets), edited by P. M. Kara-Murza and later by D. Kireev.

*Nash golos* (1918)—organ of the Baku Mensheviks.

*Nashe znamiia* (1918)—organ of the Left S.R.s.

*Neftianoe delo* (1917–1918)—organ of the Council of the Congress of Oil Industrialists.

*Professional'nyi vestnik* (1917–1918)—organ of the trade unions.

*Rassvet* (1917)

*Samopomoshch'* (1917–1918)

*Sotsial-Demokrat* (1917)—the weekly Armenian organ of the Social Democrats, particularly the Bolsheviks, edited by Stepan Shaumian.

*Sotsial-Demokrat* (1917–1918)—organ of the Baku Mensheviks.

*Svobodnaia mysl'* (1917)

*Teghekatu* (1918)—the daily organ of the Baku soviet in the Armenian language, edited by A. I. Mikoyan.

*Tovarisch* (1917)

*Uchenicheskii kooperativ* (1917)

*Veratsnund* (1918)

*Vesti Baku* (1917–1918)—a weekly issued by the publishers of the newspaper *Baku*.

*Vestnik bakinskogo soveta narodnykh komissarov* (1918) —the organ of the Baku Council of People's Commissars; the official editorial board was in the commissariat of justice.

*Vestnik prikaspiiskoi kooperatsii* (1918)—organ of the cooperatives of the Caspian group.

*Vestnik soveta uchenicheskikh deputatov g. Baku* (1917)

*Volna* (1917)—organ of the sailors' union.

*Vpered* (1917–1918)—Russian organ of the Dashnaktsutiun.

*Znamiia truda* (1917–1918)—organ of the Right S.R.s.

III. COLLECTIONS OF DOCUMENTS, LETTERS, AND ARTICLES

A. *Works of the Principal Participants*

Amirian, Arsen. *Stat'i* (Baku, 1925).

Bukharin, N. I., V. I. Molotov, and I. I. Skvortsov-Stepanov, eds. *Leninskii sbornik* (Moscow, 1924–1940).

Dzhaparidze, Prokofiia A. *Izbrannye stat'i, rechi i pis'ma, 1905–1918 gg.* (Moscow, 1958).

Lenin, Vladimir Ilich. *Lenin ob interventsii*, ed. I. I. Mints and A. I. Gukovskii (Moscow, 1931).

————. *O natsional'nom i natsional'no-kolonial'nom voprose* (Moscow, 1956).

————. "Perepiska N. Lenina i N. K. Krupskoi s kavkazskoi organizatsiei," ed. A. M. Stopani and M. Leman, *Proletarskaia revoliutsiia*, no. 5 (40) (May 1925), pp. 6–56.

————. *Polnoe sobranie sochineniia*, 5th ed. (Moscow, 1958–1966).

————. *V. I. Lenin o Zakavkaz'e* (Erevan, 1963).

Narimanov, Nariman. *Stat'i i pis'ma s kratkim biograficheskim ocherkom* (Moscow, 1925).

Shaumian, Stepan Georgievich. *Azgayin-kulturakan avtonomiayi masin* (Erevan, 1953).

————. *Erker*, 3 vols. (Erevan, 1955–1958).

————. *Erkeri zhoghovatsu (1905–1918)*, 2 vols. (Moscow, 1925–1928).

————. *Grakanutyan masin* (Erevan, 1948).

————. *Hodvatsner ev jarer* (Erevan, 1953).

————. *Izbrannye proizvedeniia*, 2 vols. (Moscow, 1957–1958).

————. *Literaturno-kriticheskie stat'i*, ed. A. Voskerchian (Moscow, 1955).

————. *Namakner 1896–1918* (Erevan, 1959).

————. *Natsionalizmi dem (hodvatsneri zhoghovatsu)* (Erevan, 1928).

————. "Pis'ma iz tiurmy," *Molodaia gvardiia*, no. 10 (1958), pp. 218–220.

————. "Pis'ma S. G. Shaumiana (1904–1918 gg.)," *Istoricheskii arkhiv*, no. 2 (1957), pp. 41–64.

————. *Pis'ma, 1896–1918* (Erevan, 1959).

————. *S. Shahumyani ev S. Spandaryani namaknere irents erekhanerin* (Erevan, 1941).

————. *Stat'i i rechi, 1902–1918 gg.*, intro. A. Karinian (Baku, 1924).

Shaumian, Stepan Georgievich. *Stat'i i rechi, 1917–1918 gg.* (Baku, 1929).

———. *Untir erkeri zhoghovatsu* (Tiflis, 1931).

———. *Untir erker* (Erevan, 1948).

Shaumian, S. G., and Askanaz Mravian. *Maksim Gorki. Targmanutyunner ev hodvatsner* (Erevan, 1936).

Stalin, Iosif Vissarionovich. *Sochineniia* (Moscow, 1946–1953).

Stolypin, P. A., and I. I. Vorontsov-Dashkov. "Bor'ba s revoliutsionnym dvizheniem na Kavkaze v epokhu stolypinshchiny (Iz perepiski P. A. Stolypina s gr. I. I. Vorontsovym-Dashkovym)," *Krasnyi arkhiv,* no. 3 (34) (1929), pp. 184–221.

Vorontsov-Dashkov, I. I. *Vsepoddanneishii otchet za vosem' let upravleniia Kavkazom* (St. Petersburg, 1913).

Zhordaniia, Noi N. *Za dva goda* (Tiflis, 1919).

B. *Records of Party Congresses, meetings of the Central Committee, and Congresses of Soviets*

*Vtoroi s"ezd RSDRP, Iiul'–Avgust 1903 goda: Protokoly* (Moscow, 1959).

*Tretii s"ezd RSDRP, Aprel'–Mai 1905 goda: Protokoly* (Moscow, 1959).

*Tretii s"ezd RSDRP. Sbornik dokumentov i materialov* (Moscow, 1955).

*Chetvertyi (ob"edinitel'nyi) s"ezd RSDRP, Aprel' (Aprel'–Mai) 1906 goda: Protokoly* (Moscow, 1959).

*Piatii (londonskii) s"ezd RSDRP, Aprel'–Mai 1907 goda: Protokoly* (Moscow, 1963).

*Sed'maia (Aprel'skaia) vserossiiskaia konferentsiia RSDRP (bol'shevikov). Petrogradskaia obshchegorodskaia konferentsiia RSDRP (bol'shevikov). Aprel' 1917 goda: Protokoly* (Moscow, 1958).

*Pervyi vserossiiskii s"ezd sovetov rabochikh i soldatskikh deputatov 3–11 iiunia 1917 goda: Stenograficheskii otchet* (Moscow–Leningrad, 1930).

(368)

*Shestoi s"ezd RSDRP (bol'shevikov). Avgust 1917 goda:* Protokoly (Moscow, 1958).

*Protokoly tsentral'nogo komiteta RSDRP(b). Avgust 1917– Fevral' 1918* (Moscow, 1958).

*Sed'moi ekstrennyi s"ezd RKP(b). Mart 1918 goda: Steno- graficheskii otchet* (Moscow, 1962).

C. Published Documents

*Au congrès international socialiste de Londres. La Fédéra- tion révolutionnaire arménienne* (Geneva, 1896).

*Bor'ba za pobedu sovetskoi vlasti v Gruzii. Dokumenty i materialy (1917–1921 gg.)* (Tiflis, 1958).

(Britain. Parliamentary Papers) *Cmd. 1846 (Russia No. 1, [1923]), Correspondence between H. M. Govt. and the Soviet Govt. respecting the murder of Mr. C. F. Davison in Jan. 1920.*

Bunyan, James. *Intervention, Civil War, and Communism in Russia: Documents and Materials* (Baltimore, 1936).

Bunyan, James, and H. H. Fisher. *The Bolshevik Revolu- tion, 1917–1918: Documents and Materials* (Stanford, 1934).

Degras, Jane, ed. *Soviet Documents on Foreign Policy,* I: 1917–1924 (London, 1951).

Dimanshtein, S. M., ed. *Revoliutsiia i natsional'nyi vopros,* III (Moscow, 1930).

*Dokumenty i materialy po vneshnei politike Zakavkaz'ia i Gruzii* (Tiflis, 1919).

*Dokumenty vneshnei politiki SSSR,* I (Moscow, 1958).

*Germanskie okkupanty v Gruzii v 1918 godu. Sbornik dokumentov i materialov* (Tiflis, 1942).

Guliev, A. N., and I. V. Strigunov, eds. *Rabochee dvizhenie v Azerbaidzhane v gody novogo revoliutsionnogo pod"ema (1910–1914 gg.): Dokumenty i materialy,* I (Baku, 1967).

Guseinov, I. A., ed. *Velikii Oktiabr' i bor'ba za sovetskuiu vlast' v Azerbaidzhane. Sbornik dokumentov, materialov i statei* (Baku, 1958).

Ibragimov, Z. I., and M. S. Iskenderov, eds. *Bol'sheviki v bor'be za pobedu sotsialisticheskoi revoliutsii v Azerbaidzhane. Dokumenty i materialy, 1917–1918 gg.* (Baku, 1960).

*K protsessu F. Funtikova* (Baku, 1926). This volume contains Funtikov's diary and material on the shooting of the Twenty-six Commissars.

Kakurin, N. E., comp. *Razlozhenie armii v 1917 godu* (Moscow, 1925).

*L'action du Parti S. R. Arménien dit "Daschnaktzoutioun" 1914–1923 (Rapport présenté au Congrès Socialiste International de Hambourg, Mai 1923)* (Paris, 1923).

*Le 28 Mai, 1919: Le jour de premier anniversaire de l'indépendance de la République d'Azerbaidjan* (Baku, 1919).

Meller, V. L., and A. M. Pankratova. *Rabochee dvizhenie v 1917 godu* (Moscow–Leningrad, 1926).

Mints, I., and E. Gorodetskii, eds. *Dokumenty po istorii grazhdanskoi voiny v SSSR*, 1 (Moscow, 1940).

Piontkovskii, S. A. *Grazhdanskaia voina v Rossii: khrestomatiia* (Moscow, 1925).

*Politika sovetskoi vlasti po natsional'nym delam za tri goda. 1917.xi–1920* (Moscow, 1920).

*Programma armianskoi revoliutsionnoi i sotsialisticheskoi partii Dashnaktsutiun* (Geneva, 1908).

*Programme du parti arménien "Daschnaktzoutioun" (élaboré en 1907)* (Paris, 1919).

*Rapport présenté au Bureau Socialiste International par le parti socialiste et révolutionnaire arménien Daschnaktzoutioun* (Stuttgart, 1907).

RSDRP. *Otchet kavkazskoi delegatsii ob obshchepartiinoi konferentsii* (Paris, 1909).

Tashlieva, Sh., ed. *Turkmenistan v period inostrannoi voennoi interventsii i grazhdanskoi voiny 1918–1920 gg.: sbornik dokumentov* (Ashkhabad, 1957).

*The Treatment of Armenians in the Ottoman Empire: Documents Presented to Viscount Grey of Fallodon* (London, 1916).

Varandian, M. *Rapport présenté au congrès socialiste international de Copenhague par le parti arménien* "Daschnaktzoutioun": *Turquie—Caucase—Perse* (Geneva, 1910).

*Velikaia oktiabr'skaia sotsialisticheskaia revoliutsiia i pobeda sovetskoi vlasti v Armenii (Sbornik dokumentov)* (Erevan, 1957).

Zeman, Z. A. B., ed. *Germany and the Revolution in Russia, 1915–1918. Documents from the Archives of the German Foreign Ministry* (London, 1958).

IV. MEMOIRS AND TRAVELERS' ACCOUNTS

Andranik. *Zor Andranik ge khosi* (Paris, 1921).

Badayev (Badaev), A. *The Bolsheviks in the Tsarist Duma* (New York, n.d.).

Baikov, Boris. "Vospominaniia o revoliutsii v Zakavkaz'e (1917–1920 gg.)," *Arkhiv russkoi revoliutsii* (Berlin), IX (1923), pp. 91–194.

Barkhashov, Boris. *V bakinskom podpol'e* (Moscow, 1933).

———. *V podpol'e* (Moscow, 1931).

Bobrovskaia (Zelikson), Tsetsiliia Samoilovna. *Zapiski podpol'shchika 1894–1917* (Moscow, 1957).

Broido, Eva. *Memoirs of a Revolutionary*, trans. and ed. Vera Broido (New York and Toronto, 1967).

———. "Na balakhanskikh promyslakh. Vospominaniia o rabote sotsial-demokratov v Baku," *Sovremennyi mir*, no. 6 (June 1912), pp. 198–222, and no. 7 (July 1912), pp. 182–203.

Darbinian, Reuben. "A Mission to Moscow: Memoirs," *Armenian Review*, I, no. 2 (Spring 1948), pp. 23–37, and no. 3 (Summer 1948), pp. 27–41.

Donohoe, M. H. *With the Persian Expedition* (London, 1919).

Dunsterville, L. C. *The Adventures of Dunsterforce* (London, 1920).

*Dvadtsat' piat' let bakinskoi organizatsii bol'shevikov* (Baku, 1924). A collection of memoirs by Enukidze, Vasil'ev-Iuzhin, Nogin, Sarkisian, and Karinian.

Ellis, C. H. "A correspondent, The Revolt in Transcaspia 1918–1919," *Central Asian Review* (London), VIII (1959), pp. 117–130.

————. "Operations in Transcaspia, 1918–1919, and the 26 Commissars Case," *St. Antony's Papers*, No. 6: Soviet Affairs, no. 2, ed. David Footman (London, 1959), pp. 129–153.

————. *The British "Intervention" in Transcaspia, 1918–1919* (Berkeley, 1963).

Enukidze, Avel. *Nashi podpol'nye tipografii na Kavkaze* (Moscow, 1925).

Ernouf, Baron. *Le Caucase, la Perse et la Turquie d'Asie d'après la relation de M. le baron de Thielmann* (Paris, 1880).

Essad Bey. *Blood and Oil in the Orient* (New York, 1932).

Giulhandanian, A. "Bakvi herosamarte," *Hairenik Amsagir*, July 1941, pp. 89–102, and September/October 1941, pp. 101–115 and 81–92.

Golubev (Chetyrekhglazyi), Nik. "Podpol'naia rabota v Baku," *Proletarskaia revoliutsiia*, no. 6 (1922), pp. 124–135.

Gulbenkian, Calouste S. *La Transcaucasie et la Péninsule d'Apcheron. Souvenirs de voyage* (Paris, 1891).

*Hin Bolshevikneri Hishoghutiunner*, 2 vols. (Erevan, 1958–1961). A collection of memoirs by old Armenian Bolsheviks.

Jordania (Zhordaniia), I., and L. Zhgenti. "Rabochee dvizhenie v Baku i bol'sheviki" (Unpublished manuscript,

Russian Archive, Columbia University in the City of New York).

Kakhoian, A. S. *Hodvatsner ev husher* (Erevan, 1963). The author was a delegate to the London Congress of the RSDRP and knew Shaumian.

Karaev, Ali Geidar. *Iz nedavnego proshlogo; materialy k istorii azerbaidzhanskoi kommunisticheskoi partii* (Baku, 1926). Primarily on the period 1918–1920.

Karinian, A. B. "K kharakteristike bakinskoi periodicheskoi pechati v 1917–1918 gg. (Fakti. Vospominaniia)," *Trudy azerbaidzhanskogo filiala IMEL pri TsK KPSS, Voprosy istorii kompartii Azerbaidzhana*, XXVI (1962).

————. "Na fronte kultury v dni bakinskoi kommuny 1918 g. (Vospominaniia. Fakty)," *Izvestiia akademii nauk azerbaidzhanskoi SSR, Seriia istorii, filosofii, i prava*, no. 3 (1966), pp. 3–10.

Kerensky, Alexander. *Russia and History's Turning Point* (New York, 1963).

Knollys, Lt.-Col. D. E. "Military Operations in Transcaspia, 1918–1919," *Journal of the Central Asian Society* (London), XIII (1926), no. 2, pp. 89–110.

Kolesnikova, Nadezhda Nikolaevna. *Iz istorii bor'by za sovetskuiu vlast' v Baku (avgust 1917 g.—iiul' 1918 g.): Vospominaniia* (Baku, 1958).

————. *Massoviki-podpol'shchiki. Vospominaniia o bakinskikh rabochikh* (Moscow, 1935). Memoirs about worker activists in Baku, 1907–1912.

Krupskaia, Nadezhda Konstantinovna. *Vospominaniia o Lenine* (Moscow, 1957).

Liadov, M. N. *Iz zhizni partii v 1903–1907 godakh (Vospominaniia)* (Moscow, 1956).

Liadov, M. N., and S. M. Pozner, eds. *Leonid Borisovich Krasin ("Nikitich"): Gody podpol'ia. Sbornik vospominanii, stat'i i dokumentov* (Moscow–Leningrad, 1928).

BIBLIOGRAPHY

Lishin, N. N. *Na kaspiiskom more: Gody beloi bor'by* (Prague, 1938).

MacDonell, Ranald. *"And Nothing Long"* (London, 1938).

Marvin, Charles. *The Region of the Eternal Fire* (London, 1888).

Melik-Eolchian, S. "Bakvi herosamarte," *Hairenik Amsagir*, 1925 (May), pp. 105–128; (June), pp. 104–118; (July), pp. 68–74; (August), pp. 97–113; (September), pp. 68–78; (October), pp. 125–129.

Melikian, Ar. "Hisoghutyunner Stepan Shahumyani masin," *Nor Ashkharh*, no. 2 (September 1922), pp. 153–157.

Mikoyan, Anastas I. "As I look back," *Soviet Weekly* (London), October 28, 1967, p. 16.

————. "Bakinskaia organizatsiia v 17–18 gg.," *Pobeda velikoi oktiabr'skoi sotsialisticheskoi revoliutsii. Sbornik vospominanii* (Moscow, 1958), pp. 334–346. Essentially the same article as appeared in *Iz proshlogo* (Baku, 1923).

————. "Bakinskoe podpol'e pri angliiskoi okkupatsii (1919 god)," *Iunost'*, 1968, no. 9, pp. 88–99; no. 10, pp. 92–103; no. 11, pp. 84–93; no. 12, pp. 79–90, and 1969, no. 1, pp. 85–95; no. 2, pp. 90–100; no. 3, pp. 85–96; no. 4, pp. 76–91.

————. "O dniakh bakinskoi kommuny (Iz vospominanii)," *Iunost'*, 1967, no. 11, pp. 66–78; no. 12, pp. 51–62; and 1968, no. 1, 61–75; no. 2, pp. 81–95.

————. "Pamiati vozhdei bakinskoi kommuny," *Bakinskii rabochii*, September 2, 1928.

————. "Stepan Grigor'evich Shaumian," *Kommunist*, September 8, 1920.

————. "V tiur'makh Zakaspiia pri angliiskoi okkupatsii," *Iunost'*, 1968, no. 5, pp. 66–67; no. 6, pp. 81–94.

Mravian, V. *Vstrechi s Shaumianom* (Erevan, 1953).

Norris, Capt. David. "Caspian Naval Expedition, 1918–1919," *Journal of the Central Asian Society* (London), x (1923), no. 3, pp. 216–240.

(374)

Post, Wilber E. *A résumé of events in the Caucasus since the Russian Revolution* (unpublished manuscript, Hoover Institute, Stanford University).

Price, Morgan Phillips. *War and Revolution in Asiatic Russia* (London, 1918).

Rawlinson, Lt.-Col. A. *Adventures in the Near East, 1918–1922* (London, 1923).

Ruben (Ter Minasian, Ruben). *Hai Heghapoghakani me hishataknere*, 7 vols. (Los Angeles, 1951–1952).

Sarkisov, Grigori Khosrovovich. *Za rabochee delo* (*Vospominaniia*) (Baku, 1966).

Semenov, Iu. F. "Zakavkazskaia Respublika," *Vozrozhdenie* (Paris) I (1949), pp. 121–139. Semenov was the only Kadet member of the Transcaucasian Seim, editor of *Kavkazskoe slovo* from 1910 to 1918, and editor of the émigré journal, *Vozrozhdenie*, in Paris from 1927 to 1940.

Stasova, E. "Iz vospominanii o partiinoi rabote do revoliutsii 1917 g.," *Proletarskaia revoliutsiia*, no. 12 (71) (December 1927), pp. 186–202. Stasova worked in Tiflis from the fall of 1907 to the fall of 1910.

———. *Stranitsy zhizni i bor'by* (Moscow, 1957).

Tseretelli, I. G. *Vospominaniia o fevral'skoi revoliutsii*, 2 vols. (Paris and The Hague, 1963).

Uratadze, Grigorii. *Vospominaniia gruzinskogo sotsialdemokrata* (Stanford, Calif., 1968).

Zhordaniia, Noi. *Maia Zhizn'*, trans. from the Georgian by Ina Zhordaniia (Stanford, Calif., 1968).

V. SECONDARY ACCOUNTS

Abdurakhmanov, A. A. *Bakinskaia bol'shevistskaia organizatsiia v gody novogo revoliutsionnogo pod"ema* (Baku, 1963).

Agajanian, G. S. *Voprosy marksistsko-leninskoi teorii v trudakh St. Shaumiana* (Erevan, 1958).

BIBLIOGRAPHY

Akhtamzian, A. *Ot Bresta do Kilia: proval antisovetskoi politiki germanskogo imperializma v 1918 godu* (Moscow, 1963).

Akhundov, B. Iu. *Monopolisticheskii kapital v dorevoliutsionnoi bakinskoi neftianoi promyshlennosti* (Moscow, 1959).

————. "Razvitie bakinskoi neftianoi promyshlennosti posle otmeny otkupnoi sistemy," *Izvestiia akademii nauk Azerbaidzhanskogo SSR*, no. 10 (1949).

Akhundov, V. Iu. "Geroicheskie bortsy za kommunizm," *Bakinskii rabochii*, September 20, 1963. A speech given by the first secretary of the TsK of the Communist Party of Azerbaijan on the forty-fifth anniversary of the shooting of the Twenty-six Commissars.

Akindinova, T. "Iz istorii bakinskoi organizatsii bol'shevikov (1907–1909 gg.)," *Proletarskaia revoliutsiia*, no. 4 (1940), pp. 64–97.

*Aktivnye bortsy za sovetskuiu vlast' v Azerbaidzhane* (Baku, 1957).

Akubzhanova, Z. "Obrazovanie kavkazskogo soiuza RSDRP," *Teghekagir*, no. 9 (1962), pp. 3–14.

Aleksanian, T. P. *Stepan Shahumyane vorpes martnchogh materialist* (Erevan, 1957).

Aliev, Kh. "K voprosu istoriografii dvizhushchikh sil revoliutsii v Azerbaidzhane," *Uchenye zapiski azerbaidzhanskogo gosudarstvennogo universiteta imeni S. M. Kirova, Seriia istorii i filosofskikh nauk*, no. 1 (1967), pp. 3–13, and no. 2, pp. 10–19.

Aliev, P. M. *Deiatel'nost' bol'shevikov Karabakha v period bor'by za sovetskuiu vlast' v Azerbaidzhane (1917–1920 gg.)* (unpublished dissertation, Baku, 1961).

Aliiarov, S. S. "Chislennost', professional'nyi i natsional'nyi sostav bakinskogo proletariata v period pervoi mirovoi voiny," *Uchenye zapiski azerbaidzhanskogo gosudarstvennogo universiteta imeni S. M. Kirova, Seriia istorii i*

(376)

*filosofskikh nauk*, no. 1 (1967) pp. 72–79, and no. 2 (1967), pp. 31–37.

———. "Izmeneniia v sostave rabochikh Baku v gody pervoi mirovoi voiny," *Istoriia SSSR*, no. 2 (1969), pp. 49–61.

———. "K voprosu o sostave bakinskogo proletariata nakanune oktiabr'skoi revoliutsii," *Izvestiia akademii nauk azerbaidzhanskoi SSR*, no. 9 (1961), p. 15.

———. "Primenialsia li fakticheski kollektivnyi dogovor bakinskikh rabochikh 1917 g.," *Istoriia SSSR*, no. 1 (1966), pp. 110–123.

Alikhanian, S. T. *Haikakan gortseri komisariati gortsune-utyune (1917–1921)* (Erevan, 1958).

Allen, W. E. D., and Paul Muratoff. *Caucasian Battlefields. A History of the Wars on the Turco-Caucasian Border, 1828–1921* (Cambridge, 1953).

Ananoun, Davit. *Rusahaireri hasarakakan zargatsune*, III (1901–1918) (Venice, 1926).

Arazy, A. *Les tueries de Bakou (une page sur les exploits tzariens)* (Geneva, 1905). A Dashnak publication.

Arkomed, S. T. (G. Karjian). "Krasnyi terror na Kavkaze i okhrannoe otdelenie," *Katorga i ssylka*, no. 6 (13), pp. 71–83.

———. *Materialy po istorii otpadeniia Zakavkaz'ia ot Rossii* (Tiflis, 1923).

———. *Rabochee dvizhenie i sotsialdemokratiia na Kavkaze (s 80-kh gg. po 1903 g.)* (Moscow–Petrograd, 1923).

Arutiunov, G. A. *Rabochee dvizhenie v Zakavkaz'e v period novogo revoliutsionnogo pod"ema (1910–1914 gg.)* (Moscow–Baku, 1963).

Arzumanian, M. "Arsen Amiryane—akanavor zhurnalist-hraparakakhos," *Teghekagir*, no. 10 (1956), pp. 19–30.

———. "Stepan Shahumyane azgayin hartsi tesaban," *Patma-banasirakan handes*, nos. 2–3 (4–5) (1959), pp. 162–179.

Avagian, S. D. "Bagvi komunayi hayeren organe," *Patmabanasirakan handes*, no. 4 (7) (1959), pp. 123–131.

Avalishvili, Zourab. *The Independence of Georgia in International Politics, 1918–1921* (London, n.d.).

Avazian, V. L. *Ejer Andrkovkasum otarerkrya intrventsiya patmutyunits (1918)* (Erevan, 1957).

Avetisian, G. A. *Komsomol Zakavkaz'ia v bor'be za pobedu i uprochenie sovetskoi vlasti (1917–1921 gg.)* (Erevan, 1964).

Avetisian, V. *Stepan Shahumyan. Kensagrakan aknark* (Erevan, 1953).

*Azerbaidzhanskaia neftianaia promyshlennost' za desiat' let natsionalizatsii (1920–1930)* (Baku, 1930).

Azizbekova, P., A. Mnatsakanian, and M. Traskunov. *Sovetskaia Rossiia i bor'ba za ustanovlenie i uprochenie vlasti sovetov v Zakavkaz'e* (Baku, 1969).

Badalian, Kh. H. *Dashnakneri kontr-revolutsion gortsuneutyan mi kani pasteri masin, 1918–1920 Tvakannerin* (Erevan, 1955).

Baghdasarian, G. L. *Stepan Shahumyani paykare sotsialistakan revolyutsiayi haghtanaki ev sovetakan ishkhanutyan hamar* (Erevan, 1958).

Bagirov, M. D. *Iz istorii bol'shevistskoi organizatsii Baku i Azerbaidzhana* (Moscow, 1946). A reprint of a report made on December 19–20, 1939, at a meeting of the entire party *aktiv* celebrating the sixtieth birthday of I. V. Stalin, by the first secretary of the Communist Party of Azerbaijan.

Bairamov, G. M. "Vozniknovenie v Baku promyslovo-zavodskikh komissii v 1917 g.," *Izvestiia akademii nauk azerbaidzhanskoi SSR, Seriia obshchestvennykh nauk*, no. 4 (1964), pp. 25–26.

Barby, Henry. *Le débâcle russe. Les extravagances bolcheviques et l'épopée arménienne* (Paris, 1918).

Barseghian, Kh. H. *Bolshevikyan hay parberakan mamuli patmutyun, 1900-1920* (Erevan, 1956).

———. *Stepan Shaumian* (Moscow, 1960).

Begak, R. *Sud nad anglichanami, sdavshimi Baku turkam v 1918 g.* (Baku, 1927). A play of a trial of Dunsterville for use as agitational material. The audience is to decide on the guilt or innocence of the British.

Belen'kii, Semon Natanovich, and A. Manvelov. *Revoliutsiia 1917 g. v Azerbaidzhane (Khronika sobytii)* (Baku, 1927). A detailed chronicle of the events in Baku, 1917.

Bennigsen, Alexandre, and Chantal Lemercier-Quelquejay. *Islam in the Soviet Union* (London, 1967).

——— and ———. *La presse et le mouvement national chez les musulmans de Russie avant 1920* (Paris and The Hague, 1964).

——— and ———. *The Evolution of the Muslim Nationalities of the USSR and their Linguistic Problems* (London, 1961).

Beria, Lavrenti. *On the History of the Bolshevik Organizations in Transcaucasia. A lecture delivered at a meeting of active workers of the Tbilisi Party Organization, July 21–22, 1935* (Moscow, 1949).

Bibineishvili, Varfolomei Efimovich. *Akhcha-Kuimskaia tragediia. Vozhdi bakinskoi kommuny* (Tiflis, 1931).

Bilenko, Ia. *Muzhestvennye bortsy za kommunizm. (Geroicheskaia epopeia o 26 bakinskikh komissarov)* (Kiev, 1964).

*Bol'shevistskaia periodicheskaia pechat' Azerbaidzhana (1904—Aprel' 1920 gg.). Spravochnik* (Baku, 1964).

Bukshpan, A. S. "Anglo-eserovskii blok i bakinskaia kommuna. (Iz epokhi pervoi angliiskoi interventsii)," *Izvestiia vostochnogo fakul'teta azerbaidzhanskogo gosudarstvennogo universiteta imeni V. I. Lenina*, IV (1929), pp. 231–248.

———. "K desiatiletiiu gibeli '26' (1918–1928 gg.)," *Izvestiia vostochnogo fakulteta azerbaidzhanskogo gosudarstvennogo universiteta imeni V. I. Lenina, Vostokovedenie*, III (1928), pp. 124–135.

Bukshpan, A. S., comp. *Poslednie dni komissarov bakinskoi kommuny po materialam sudebnykh protsessov* (Baku, 1928).

Burdzhalov, E. *Dvadtsat' shest' bakinskikh komissarov* (Moscow, 1938).

———. "Iz istorii velikoi proletarskoi revoliutsii v Azerbaidzhane," *Proletarskaia revoliutsiia*, no. 3 (1939), and no. 1 (1940).

Chaikin, Vadim A. *K istorii rossiiskoi revoliutsii, 1: Kazn' 26 bakinskikh komissarov* (Moscow, 1922). This account by the S.R. Chaikin was the first source of information on the death of the Twenty-six Commissars. His earlier articles, contained in this book, were used by Stalin and the central Soviet government to blame the English for their murder.

Chesnais, P. G. la. *Les peuples de la Transcaucasie pendant la guerre et devant la paix* (Paris, 1921).

Chubinov, G. "K krest'ianskomu voprosu v Zakavkaz'e," *Delo naroda*, August 15, 1917.

Coates, W. P. and Zelda K. *Armed Intervention in Russia, 1918–1922* (London, 1935).

D. Z. T. "La première république musulmane: L'Azerbaidjan," *Revue du monde musulman* (Paris), xxxvi (1918–1919), pp. 229–270.

Dallakian, G. "Iz istorii klassovoi bor'by bakinskogo proletariata," *Teghekagir*, no. 6 (1956), pp. 3–16. On the Baku strike of 1914.

Devitt, V. *Dvadtsat' shest' bakinskikh komissarov v sovetskoi poezii (russkoi i azerbaidzhanskoi)* (Baku, 1965).

Drabkina, E. "Tiurkskii proletariat v revoliutsii i grazhdanskoi voine," *Istoriia proletariata SSSR*, no. 5 (1931), pp. 78–110, and no. 6, pp. 18–61.

Dubner, A. "Bakinskii proletariat v bor'be za vlast' 1918–1920 gg.," *Proletarskaia revoliutsiia*, no. 9 (104) (September 1930), pp. 75–93, and no. 10 (105) (October 1930), pp. 19–45.

BIBLIOGRAPHY

————. *Bakinskii proletariat v gody revoliutsii (1917–1920 gg.)* (Baku, 1931).

*Dvadtsat' piat' let bakinskoi organizatsii bol'shevikov (Osnovnye momenty razvitiia bakinskoi organizatsii)* (Baku, 1924).

*Dvadtsat' shest' komissarov, 1918–1948. Sbornik stikhov* (Moscow, 1948).

Dvinov, B. *Pervaia mirovaia voina i rossiiskaia sotsialdemokratiia* (Inter-university Project on the History of the Menshevik Movement, Paper no. 3) (New York, 1962).

Dzherzibashev, I. "Zemel'nye komitety na Kavkaze," *Delo naroda*, July 27, 1917.

Efendiev, Sultan Medzhid. *Borets za interesy azerbaidzhanskoi bednoty (materialy k biografii M. Azizbekova)* (Baku, 1930).

————. *Iz istorii revoliutsionnogo dvizheniia azerbaidzhanskogo proletariata* (Baku, 1957).

Eghikian, G. "Hnchakyannere ev nrants bolshevikneru het mianavu portsere," *Hayrenik Amsagir*, XVII, no. 3 (January 1939).

Emin, Ahmet. *Turkey in the World War* (New Haven, Conn., 1930).

Enukidze, D. *Krakh imperialisticheskoi interventsii v Zakavkaz'e* (Tiflis, 1954).

Fischer, Fritz. *Germany's Aims in the First World War* (New York, 1967).

Freund, Gerald. *Unholy Alliance: Russian–German Relations from the Treaty of Berlin* (London, 1957).

Frolov, V. I. *Zabastovki bakinskikh neftepromyshlennykh rabochikh v 1908 godu* (Baku, 1909).

Gadzhinskii, D. D. "Vozniknovenie v Baku promyslovo-zavodskikh komissii i ikh deiatel'nost' v 1905 g.," *Izvestiia akademii nauk azerbaidzhanskoi SSR, Seriia obshchestvennykh nauk*, no. 7 (1961), pp. 17–39.

BIBLIOGRAPHY

Galoian, G. A. *Rabochee dvizhenie i natsional'nyi vopros v Zakavkaz'e, 1900–1922* (Erevan, 1969).

———. *Sotsialisticheskaia revoliutsiia v Zakavkaz'e v osveshchenii burzhuaznoi istoriografii* (Moscow, 1960).

Galustian, Andranik Arutiunovich. *Iz istorii bor'by trudiashchikhsia gandzhinskoi (elizavetpol'skoi) gubernii Azerbaidzhana za sovetskuiu vlast' (1917–1920 gg.)* (Baku, 1963).

Garibdzanian, G. B. V. I. *Lenin i bol'shevistskie organizatsii Zakavkaz'ia* (Erevan, 1967).

Gasanov, G., and N. Sarkisov. "Sovetskaia vlast' v Baku v 1918 godu," *Istorik marksist*, no. 5/69 (1939), pp. 32–70.

Gasparian, N. M. *Stepan Shahumyane marksizmi akanavor tesaban u propagandiat* (Erevan, 1960).

Geghamiants, Eghishe A. Kan. *Tajiknere Kovkasum ev Bagvi ankume* (Baku, 1919).

Gharibjanian, G. B. V. I. *Lenin i osvobozhdenie narodov Zakavkaz'ia* (Erevan, 1960).

Gindin, A. M., and I. S. Muslimov. "Pervye sotsialisticheskie meropriiatiia sovetskoi vlasti v Azerbaidzhane," *Voprosy istorii*, no. 11 (1963), pp. 17–33.

Gleichen, Lord Edward, comp. *The Baltic and Caucasian States* (London, 1923).

Gukasian, A. R. "Bakinskii komitet RSDRP vo glave revoliutsionnykh vystuplenii bakinskogo proletariata (1901–1904 gg.)," *Trudy institut istorii akademii nauk azerbaidzhanskoi SSR*, XI (1957), pp. 157–204.

Guliev, A. N. *Bakinskii proletariat v gody novogo revoliutsionnogo pod"ema* (Baku, 1963).

———. "Dzhaparidze i soiuz neftepromyshlennykh rabochikh," *Izvestiia akademii nauk azerbaidzhanskoi SSR*, no. 1 (1957), pp. 155–169.

———. *I. P. Vatsek v revoliutsionnom dvizhenii v Baku* (Baku, 1965). A biography of Ivan Prokof'evich Vatsek (1870–1951), a Social Democrat and later a Bolshevik who worked in Baku from 1899.

———— and M. I. Naidel. *50 let profsoiuza rabochikh neftianoi promyshlennosti* (Baku, 1956).

Gurko-Kriazhin, V. A. "Angliiskaia interventsiia v 1918–19 gg. v Zakaspii i Zakavkaz'e," *Istorik marksist*, II (1926), pp. 115–139.

————. "Bakinskii protsess i istoriia 26 komissarov," *Novyi vostok*, nos. 13–14 (1926), pp. 179–184.

Guseinov, Geidar. "Geroicheskie bortsy za vlast' sovetov v Azerbaidzhane," *Trudy azerbaidzhanskogo filiala IMEL pri TsK VKP(b)*, XIII (1949), pp. 8–24.

————. "Pamiati 26 bakinskikh komissarov," *Trudy azerbaidzhanskogo filiala IMEL pri TsK VKP(b)*, XIII (1947), pp. 66–76.

Guseinov, I. A. *Bol'sheviki—organizatory pobedy sotsialisticheskoi revoliutsii v Azerbaidzhane* (unpublished dissertation, Moscow, 1946).

———— et al., eds. *Istoriia Azerbaidzhana*, 3 vols. (Baku, 1959–1963).

Guseinov, Mirza-Davud. *Tiurkskaia demokraticheskaia partiia federalistov "Musavat" v proshlom i v nastoiashchem*, 1: programma i taktika (Tiflis, 1927).

Guseinov, Sh. A. *Gazeta "Bakinskii rabochii" v bor'be za ustanovlenie sovetskoi vlasti v Azerbaidzhane (Aprel' 1917—Aprel' 1918 gg.)* (unpublished dissertation, Moscow, 1954).

————. "Rol' gazety 'Bakinskii rabochii' v ukreplenii druzhby trudiashchikhsia Azerbaidzhana s velikim russkim narodom v period podgotovki oktiabr'skoi revoliutsii," *Uchenye zapiski azerbaidzhanskogo gosudarstvennogo universiteta imeni S.M. Kirova, Seriia istorii i filosofskikh nauk*, no. 3 (1964), pp. 53–63.

Guseinov, T. *Oktiabr' v Azerbaidzhane (k semiletiiu aprel'skoi revoliutsii)* (Baku, 1927). Primarily on the revolution in 1920.

Haimson, Leopold. "The Problem of Social Stability in Urban Russia, 1905–1917," *Slavic Review*, XXIII, no. 4 (De-

BIBLIOGRAPHY

cember 1964), pp. 619–642, and XXIV, no. 1 (March 1965), pp. 1–22.
Hajibeyli, Jeyhoun Bei. "The Origins of the National Press in Azerbaijan," *Asiatic Review*, XXVI, no. 88 (October, 1930), pp. 757–765, and XXVII, nos. 90–91 (April and July, 1931), pp. 349–359 and 552–557.
Harutiunian, A. "Bakvi 26 komisarnere," *Teghekagir*, no. 9 (1958), pp. 7–16.
Hassmann, Heinrich. *Oil in the Soviet Union* (Princeton, 1953).
Hovannisian, Richard G. *Armenia on the Road to Independence, 1918* (Berkeley and Los Angeles, 1967).
Hovhannisian, Ashot. *Dashnaktsutyan aritov* (Moscow, 1929).
————. *Erku bnuytagir. Stepan Shahumyani ev Al. Rubeni* (Erevan, 1927).
Iakushkin, E., and S. Polunin. *Angliiskaia interventsiia v 1918–1920 gg.* (Moscow–Leningrad, 1928).
Ibragimov, M. D. "K voprosu o vliianii pervoi mirovoi voiny na neftianoe proizvodstvo bakinskogo raiona (1914–1917 gody)," *Uchenye zapiski azerbaidzhanskogo gosudarstvennogo universiteta imeni S. M. Kirova, Seriia istorii i filosofskikh nauk*, no. 1 (1968), pp. 62–69.
Ibragimov, Z. I. "Bratskaia pomoshch' Sovetskoi Rossii trudiashchimsia Azerbaidzhana v bor'be za pobedu sovetskoi vlasti (1917–1918 gg.)," *Izvestiia akademii nauk azerbaidzhanskoi SSR, Seriia obshchestvennykh nauk*, no. 3 (1964), pp. 9–22.
Ioffe, G. Z. "Anglo-Amerikanskaia burzhuaznaia istoriografiia o fevral'skoi revoliutsii v Rossii," *Istoricheskie zapiski*, no. 78 (1965), pp. 3–30.
Ishkhanian, B. *Bagvi mets sarsapnere anketayin usumnasirutyun septemberyan antskeri 1918 t.* (Tiflis, 1920).
————. *Velikie uzhasy v gorode Baku. Anketnoe issledovanie sentiabrskikh sobytii 1918 g.* (Tiflis, 1920). Russian translation of the preceding work.

————. *Dimaknere patravts (ovker en bolsheviknere?)* (Baku, 1918).

————. *Hakaheghapokhakan sharzhume Andrkovkasum (Bagvi aryunahegh antskeri aritov)* (Baku, 1918).

————. *Kontr-revoliutsiia v Zakavkaz'e*, 1: Tendentsii musul'manskogo dvizheniia (Sotsialno-istoricheskii kharakter martovskikh sobytii 1918 goda) (Baku, 1919). Russian translation of the preceding work.

Iskenderov, Mokhammed Salman ogly. *Iz istorii bor'by kommunisticheskoi partii Azerbaidzhana* (Baku, 1958).

———— *et al. Ocherki istorii kommunisticheskoi partii Azerbaidzhana* (Baku, 1963).

Israfilbekov (Kadirli), M. "Prichina padeniia sovetskoi vlasti v bakinskom raione," *Zhizn' natsional'nostei*, April 18, 1920.

*Istoriia grazhdanskoi voiny v SSSR* (Moscow, 1957).

*Istoriia kommunisticheskoi partii Azerbaidzhana*, part 1 (Baku, 1958).

*Iz proshlogo: sbornik materialov po istorii bakinskoi bol'shevistskoi organizatsii i oktiabr'skoi revoliutsii v Azerbaidzhane* (Baku, 1924).

*Iz proshlogo: stat'i i vospominaniia iz istorii bakinskoi organizatsii i rabochego dvizheniia v Baku* (Baku, 1923).

Kadishev, A. B. *Interventsiia i grazhdanskaia voina v Zakavkaz'e* (Moscow, 1960).

Kaltakhchian, S. T. *Bor'ba S. G. Shaumiana za teoriiu i taktiku leninizma* (Moscow, 1956).

Karapetian, S. *Stepan Shahumyani revolyutsion gortsuneutyune Kovkasum 1917–1918 tvakannerin* (Erevan, 1954).

Karinian, Artashes. *Dashnaktsutyune ev ir zinakitsnere* (Erevan, 1932).

————. *Shaumian i natsionalisticheskie techeniia na Kavkaze* (Baku, 1928).

Kazemzadeh, Firuz. *The Struggle for Transcaucasia (1917–1921)* (New York, 1951).

(385)

BIBLIOGRAPHY

Kaziev, M. A. *Iz istorii revoliutsionnoi bor'by bakinskogo proletariata* (Baku, 1956).

――――. *Zhizn' i revoliutsionnaia deiatel'nost' Meshadi Azizbekova* (Baku, 1956).

Keenan, E. L. "Remarques sur l'histoire du mouvement révolutionnaire à Bakou (1904–1905)," *Cahiers du monde russe et soviétique*, III, no. 2 (April/June, 1962), pp. 225–260.

Khachikian, Iakov Ivanovich. *Bor'ba S. G. Shaumiana za marksistsko-leninskoe ponimanie roli narodnykh mass v istorii* (Erevan, 1956).

Khaleian, E. "St. Shahumyani handipumnere V. I. Lenini het ev nrants namakagrutyune 1903–1918 tt.," *Teghekagir*, no. 11 (1953), pp. 3–22.

Khalikov, A. I. "Iz istorii potrebitel'skoi kooperatsii v Azerbaidzhane," *Izvestiia akademii nauk azerbaidzhanskoi SSR, Seriia obshchestvennikh nauk*, no. 3 (1962), pp. 27–40.

Kheifets, S. Ia. "Zakavkaz'e v pervuiu polovinu 1918 g. i Zakavkazskii Seim," *Byloe*, no. 21 (1923), pp. 298–310.

Khurshudian, L. A. "Bakvi proletariati 1917 tvakani herosakan paykari patmutyunits," *Teghekagir*, no. 5 (1957), pp. 3–15.

――――. *Stepan Shahumyan: petakan ev partiakan gortsuneutyun 1917–1918 tt.* (Erevan, 1959).

――――. "V. I. Lenine ev Bakvi komunan," *Teghekagir*, no. 10 (1956), pp. 3–18.

Kolesnikova, N. N. *Iakov Zevin* (Baku, 1948).

――――. *Ivan Fioletov. Kratkii biograficheskii ocherk* (Baku, 1948).

Korganoff, Gen. G. *La participation des arméniens à la guerre mondiale sur le front du Caucase (1914–1918)* (Paris, 1927).

Koshevoi, S. *26 komissarov* (Baku, 1933). On the first film made on the theme of the Twenty-six Commissars.

(386)

Kosian, Hair Rafael. *Liakatar tsutsak hayeren lragirneru, 1794–1921* (Vienna, 1924). A complete list of Armenian newspapers, 1794–1921.

Kuliev, Mustafa. *Vragi Oktiabr'ia v Azerbaidzhane (K 10-letiiu Oktiabr'ia)* (Baku, 1927).

Kuliev, N. M. "K sovetskoi istoriografii sotsialisticheskoi revoliutsii v Azerbaidzhane (20-seredina 30-kh gg.)," *Izvestiia akademii nauk azerbaidzhanskoi SSR, Seriia istorii, filosofii, i prava,* no. 3 (1966), pp. 11–19.

―――. "Sovetskaia istoriografiia sotsialisticheskoi revoliutsii v Azerbaidzhane," *Istoriia SSSR,* no. 3 (1967), pp. 38–50.

Kuligina, T. I. *Bakinskie komissary V. F. Polukhin i E. A. Berg* (Moscow, 1952).

Kuznetsova, S. I., and B. E. Shtein. "Angliiskaia i amerikanskaia istoriografiia oktiabr'skoi revolutsii, voennoi interventsii i grazhdanskoi voiny v Rossii," *Voprosy istorii,* no. 11 (1956), pp. 147–158.

*La Republique de l'Azerbaidjan du Caucase* (Paris, 1919).

Lang, David Marshall. *A Modern History of Soviet Georgia* (New York, 1962).

Larin, Iurii. *O soveshchanii s neftepromyshlennikami* (Baku, 1907).

―――. *Rabochie neftianogo dela (iz byta i dvizheniia 1903–1908 gg.)* (Moscow, 1909).

Lifshits, Lev Mikhailovich. *Geroicheskii podvig bakinskikh bol'shevikov (Iz istorii bor'by za pobedu sotsialisticheskoi revoliutsii v Azerbaidzhane)* (Baku, 1964).

Lifshits, Mikhail. *Kto vinovat v ubiistve 26-ti. S prilozheniem dnevnika Funtikova* (Tiflis, 1926).

―――― and P. Chagin, eds. *Pamiati 26. Materialy k istorii bakinskoi kommuny* (Baku, 1922).

Loris-Melikov, J. *La révolution russe et les républiques transcaucasiennes* (Paris, 1920).

Low, Alfred D. *Lenin on the Question of Nationality* (New York, 1958).

BIBLIOGRAPHY

Ludshuveit, Evgenii Fedorovich. *Turtsiia v gody pervoi mirovoi voiny, 1914–1918 gg.* (*Voenno-politicheskii ocherk*) (Moscow, 1966).

Lunkevich, Valentin-Valerian Viktorovich. *Podvigi tsarizma; krovavye dni v Baku* (Geneva, 1905).

L'vov, A. "1905 god v Baku (Kratkii obzor sobytii)," *Novyi Vostok*, nos. 13–14 (1926), pp. 132–157.

Makharadze, Filip. *K istorii kommunisticheskoi partii Zakavkaz'ia* (Tiflis, 1923).

————. *Ocherki revoliutsionnogo dvizheniia v Zakavkaz'e* (Tiflis, 1927).

————. *Sovety i bor'ba za sovetskuiu vlast' v Gruzii* (Tiflis, 1928).

Martov, L., P. Maslov, and A. Potresov, eds. *Obshchestvennoe dvizhenie v Rossii v nachale XX-go veka*, 4 vols. (St. Petersburg, 1909–1914).

Masurian, S. "Rusahayots Azgayin Hamagumare," *Mayis* 28 (Paris, 1926), pp. 4–22.

Matveev, A. M. "Angliiskii polkovnik zametaet sledy (po povodu knigi 'Zakaspiiskii episod 1918–1919')," *Istoriia SSSR*, no. 1 (1965), pp. 183–194. A review of C. H. Ellis's book on the intervention in Transcaspia.

Mekhti, Gussein Alievich. *Komissar* (Moscow, 1949). Stories about Meshadi Azizbekov.

Mil'man, Aron Shmul'evich. *Politicheskii stroi Azerbaidzhana v XIX—nachale XX vekov (administrativnyi apparat i sud, formy i metody kolonial'nogo upravleniia)* (Baku, 1966).

Miroshnikov, L. I. *Angliiskaia ekspansiia v Irane (1914–1920)* (Moscow, 1961).

Mirzoian, L. I. *Poslednie dni komissarov bakinskoi kommuny (po materialy sudebnykh protsessov)* (Baku, 1927).

Mneian, Georgii Manukovich. *Stepan Shahumyani partiakan ev petakan gortsuneutyune (1900–1918)* (Erevan, 1958).

————. "Stepan Shahumyani revolyutsion gortsuneutyunits (1911–1916)," *Teghekagir*, no. 10 (1958), pp. 29–34.

Moberly, Brig.-Gen. F. J., comp. *The Campaign in Mesopotamia, 1914–1918*, IV (London, 1927).

Movsisian, S. *Stepan Shahumyane ev Suren Spandaryane ajogh serndi dastiarakontyan masin* (Erevan, 1953).

Mravian, Iu. "K voprosu o vzgliadakh S. G. Shaumiana na gosudarstvennuiu federatsiiu," *Teghekagir*, no. 1 (1957), pp. 3–10.

Muslimov, I. S. "Bakinskaia kommuna i voprosy organizatsii revoliutsionnogo poriadka (1918 g.)," *Uchenye zapiski azerbaidzhanskogo gosudarsvennogo universiteta imeni S. M. Kirova, Seriia istorii i filosofskikh nauk,* no. 1 (1964), pp. 17–27.

————. "Bakinskaia kommuna v bor'be za povyshenie material'nogo urovnia trudiashchikhsia (1918 g.)," *Uchenye zapiski azerbaidzhanskogo politekhnicheskogo instituta imeni M. F. Akhundova*, XIV (1962).

Nalbandian, Louise. *The Armenian Revolutionary Movement: the Development of Armenian Political Parties through the Nineteenth Century* (Berkeley and Los Angeles, 1963).

Nasyrin, V. P. "O nekotorykh voprosakh sotsialisticheskogo preobrazovaniia promyshlennosti v SSSR," *Voprosy istorii*, no. 5 (1956), pp. 90–99.

Nersisian Mkrtich Gegamovich. *Plamennyi borets za kommunizm—S. G. Shaumian* (Moscow, 1954).

Nevskii, V. I., ed.; E. A. Korol'chuk and Sh. M. Levin, comps. *Deiateli revoliutsionnogo dvizheniia v Rossii: Biograficheskii-bibliograficheskii slovar'*, V: Sotsial-Demokraty, 1880–1904 (Moscow, 1931–1933).

Orakhelashvili, Mamia Dmitrievich. *Zakavkazskie bol'shevistskie organizatsii v 1917 godu* (Tiflis, 1927).

Ordzhonididze, G. K. "Svetloi pamiati 26 bakinskikh komissarov," *Bakinskii rabochii*, September 20, 1922.

"Pamiati 26 bakinskikh komissarov," *Krasnyi arkhiv*, nos. 4–5 (89–90) (1938), pp. 3–29. Contains documents and memorial articles by Stalin, Mikoyan, and Ordzhonikidze.

*Pamiati 26–ti kommunarov* (Erevan, 1928).

*Pamiati N. Narimanova. Sbornik statei* (Moscow, 1925).

Papazian, K. S. *Patriotism Perverted: A discussion of the deeds and misdeeds of the Armenian Revolutionary Federation, the so-called Dashnagtzoutune* (Boston, 1934).

Park, Alexander G. *Bolshevism in Turkestan, 1917–1927* (New York, 1957).

Pazhitnov, K. A. *Ocherki po istorii bakinskoi neftedobyvaiushchei promyshlennosti* (Moscow–Leningrad, 1940).

Pchelin, N. *Krest'ianskii vopros pri musavate (1918–1920). Ocherki* (Baku, 1931).

Petrosian, H. A. "Bakvi bolshevikneri paykare razmaardyunaperakan komiteneri dem," *Teghekagir*, no. 8 (1963), pp. 33–46.

Pipes, Richard. *The Formation of the Soviet Union: Communism and Nationalism, 1917–1923* (Cambridge, Mass., 1957).

Pokshishevskii, V. V. *Polozhenie bakinskogo proletariata nakanune revoliutsii (1914–1917 gg.)* (Baku, 1927).

Popov, A. L. "Iz epokhi angliiskoi interventsii v Zakavkaz'e," *Proletarskaia revoliutsiia*, nos. 6–7 (18–19) (1923), pp. 222–274, no. 8 (20), pp. 95–132, and no. 9 (21), pp. 185–217.

———. "Iz istorii revoliutsii v Vostochnom Zakavkaz'e (1917–1918 g.)," *Proletarskaia revoliutsiia*, no. 5 (28) (1924), pp. 13–35, no. 7 (30), pp. 110–143, no. 8–9 (31–32), pp. 99–116, and no. 11 (34), pp. 137–161.

———. *Iz istorii zabastovochnogo dvizheniia v Rossii nakanune imperialisticheskoi voiny: Bakinskaia zabastovka 1914 g.* (Leningrad, 1925).

———. "Revoliutsiia v Baku: Ocherk pervyi, Fevral'– Oktiabr' 1917 g.," *Byloe*, no. 22 (1923), pp. 278–312.

Rabinowitch, Alexander. *Prelude to Revolution: The Petro-grad Bolsheviks and the July 1917 Uprising* (Bloomington, Ind., 1968).

Radkey, Oliver H. *The Agrarian Foes of Bolshevism: Promise and Default of the Russian Socialist Revolutionaries, February to October, 1917* (New York, 1958).

———. *The Elections to the Russian Constituent Assembly of 1917* (Cambridge, Mass., 1950).

Raevskii, Aleksandr Mikhailovich. *Alesha Dzhaparidze (Politicheskii siluet)* (Baku, 1931).

———. *Angliiskaia interventsiia i musavatskoe pravitel'-stvo. Iz istorii interventsii i kontr-revoliutsii v Zakav-kaz'e* (Baku, 1927).

———. *Angliiskie "druz'ia" i musavatskie "patrioty"* (Baku, 1927).

———. *Bol'sheviki i Men'sheviki v Baku v 1904–05 godakh* (Baku, 1930).

———. *Musavatskoe pravitel'stvo na versal'skoi konfer-entsii. Doneseniia predsedatelia azerbaidzhanskoi musa-vatskoi delegatsii* (Baku, 1930).

———. *Partiia "Musavat" i ee kontrrevoliutsionnaia rabota* (Baku, 1928).

Ratgauzer, Ia. A. *Arest i gibel' komissarov bakinskoi kommuny* (Baku, 1928).

———. "Bakinskaia kommuna i narodnoe prosveshche-nie," *Izvestiia vostochnogo fakul'teta azerbaidzhanskogo gosudarstvennogo universiteta imeni V. I. Lenina, Vosto-kovedenie*, II (1928), pp. 109–121.

———. *Bor'ba bakinskogo proletariata za kollektivnyi dogovor 1917 g.* (Baku, 1927).

———. *Bor'ba za Sovetskii Azerbaidzhan. K istorii aprel'-skogo perevorota* (Baku, 1928).

Ratgauzer, Ia. A. *Revoliutsiia i grazhdanskaia voina v Baku*, I: 1917–1918 gg. (Baku, 1927).

Resul Zade, Mamed Emin. *Ideia svobody i molodezh'* (Istanbul, 1925).

———. *L'Azerbaidjan en lutte pour l'indépendance* (Paris, 1930).

———. *O panturanizme v sviazi s kavkazskoi problemoi*, with foreword by Noi Zhordaniia (Paris, 1930).

Riha, Thomas. "1917–A Year of Illusions," *Soviet Studies*, XIX, no. 1 (July 1967), pp. 115–121.

Rosenberg, William G. "Russian Liberals and the Bolshevik Coup," *The Journal of Modern History*, XL, no. 3 (September 1968), pp. 328–347.

Sarkis, *Bor'ba za vlast': Opyt istorii bakinskoi organizatsii AKP(b) za 1918–1920 gody* (Baku, 1930).

Sarkisian, E. K. *Ekspansionistskaia politika osmanskoi imperii v Zakavkaz'e* (Erevan, 1962).

Schafir, J. *Die Ermordung der 26 Kommunare in Baku und die Partei der Sozialrevolutionäre* (Hamburg, n.d.). A pamphlet published by the Communist International implicating the S.R.s in the execution of the Twenty-six Commissars.

Schwarz, Solomon M. *The Russian Revolution of 1905: The Workers' Movement and the Formation of Bolshevism and Menshevism* (Chicago, 1967).

Sef, Semen E. "Bakinskii Oktiabr'," *Proletarskaia revoliutsiia*, no. 11 (106) (1930), pp. 67–89.

———. *Bor'ba za Oktiabr' v Zakavkaz'i* (Tiflis, 1932).

———. "Iz istorii bakinskogo rabochego dvizheniia (otchet bakinskogo gradonachal'nika Martynova o vseobshchei stachke 1914 g.)," *Proletarskaia revoliutsiia*, no. 7 (54) (1926), pp. 227–259.

———. "Iz istorii bor'by za natsionalizatsiiu neftianoi promyshlennosti," *Istorik marksist*, nos. 18–19 (1930), pp. 29–62.

——. *Kak bol'sheviki prishli k vlasti v 1917–1918 gg. v bakinskom raione* (Baku, 1927).

——. *Rasstrel v aleksandrovskom sadu 10 fevralia 1918 g. v Tiflise* (Tiflis, 1927).

——. *Revoliutsiia 1917 g. v Zakavkaz'e (dokumenty, materialy)* (Tiflis, 1927).

——. *Revoliutsionnyi proletariat Baku v bor'be za vlast'* (Baku, 1939).

Semin, Orest. *Osnovnye voprosy mestnogo samoupravleniia: Zemskaia reforma na Kavkaze i v neftepromyshlennom raione g. Baku* (Baku, 1910).

Shatirian, M. "Drvagner motik antsyalits," *Hayrenik Amsagir*, May 1923, pp. 111–123.

——. "Ej me hay-trkakan krivneren," *Hayrenik Amsagir*, September 1923, pp. 96–100.

Shaumian, Lev Stepanovich. *Muzhestvennye bortsy za kommunizm k 35–letiiu rasstrela 26 bakinskikh komissarov* (Moscow, 1954).

——. *Rasstrel 26 bakinskikh komissarov angliiskimi interventami* (Moscow, 1954).

Shaumian, Suren Stepanovich. "Bakinskaia kommuna 1918 goda," *Proletarskaia revoliutsiia*, no. 12 (59) (1926).

——. *Bakinskaia kommuna* (Baku, 1927).

Shtein, G. *Bakinskaia kommuna, populiarnyi ocherk* (Baku, 1928).

*Sorok let so dnia zlodeiskogo rasstrela 26 bakinskikh komissarov (Materialy dlia dokladov i besed)* (Baku, 1958).

Staffi, Bagrat. *Stepan Shahumyan: Vep* (Erevan, 1960). A novel based on Shaumian's life.

Stavrovskii, Aleksandr Ivanovich. *Zakavkaz'e posle Oktiabria. Vzaimootnosheniia s Turtsei v pervoi polovine 1918 g.* (Moscow and Leningrad, 1925).

Steklov, A. *Krasnaia armiia Azerbaidzhana* (Baku, 1928). Primarily on the period after 1918.

Steklov, A. P. "Soldatskie massy tylovykh garizonov kavkaz-skogo fronta v bor'be za pobedu oktiabr'skoi revoliutsii," *Istoriia SSSR*, no. 5 (1962), pp. 120–135.

*Stepan Shahumyan 1879–1918: Bibliografia* (Erevan, 1957).

*Stepan Shaumian: Sbornik statei* (Baku, 1948).

Strigunov, I. V. "Zarabotnaia plata bakinskikh rabochikh v kontse XIX veka," *Trudy instituta istorii akademii nauk azerbaidzhanskoi SSR*, xv (1961), pp. 69–121.

Tevzaia, V. "Kavkazskaia sotsial-demokratiia i mirovaia voina," *International i voina*, no. 1 (1915), pp. 130–134.

Tokarzhevskii, Evgenii Alekseevich. *Bakinskie bol'sheviki—organizatory bor'by protiv turetsko-germanskikh i angliiskikh interventov v Azerbaidzhane v 1918 godu* (Baku, 1949).

————. *Iz istorii inostrannoi interventsii i grazhdanskoi voiny v Azerbaidzhane* (Baku, 1957).

———— and M. A. Kaziev. *Alesha Dzhaparidze. Kratkii biograficheskii ocherk* (Baku, 1949).

Trotsky, Leon. *Between Red and White: A Study of some Fundamental Questions of Revolution with Particular Reference to Georgia* (London, 1922). This work was dedicated to the memory of the Baku Commissars.

Trumpener, Ulrich. *Germany and the Ottoman Empire, 1914–1918* (Princeton, 1968).

Ullman, Richard H. *Anglo-Soviet Relations, 1917–1921: Intervention and the War* (Princeton, 1961).

Varandian, M. H. *H. Dashnaktsutyan batmutyun*, 2 vols. (Paris, 1932; Cairo, 1950).

Vateishvili, D. L. *Iz istorii legal'noi rabochei pechati Zakavkaz'ia* (Tiflis, 1963).

Zenkovsky, Serge A. *Pan-Turkism and Islam in Russia* (Cambridge, Mass., 1960).

Zhakov, M., S. E. Sef, and G. Khachapuridze, eds. *Istoriia klassovoi bor'by v Zakavkaz'i: Sbornik statei. Kniga pervaia* (Tiflis, 1930).

Zhordaniia, Noi N. *"Bol'shinstvo" ili "Men'shinstvo"?* (Geneva, 1905).

*Zoravar Andraniki kovkasyan kajati patmakan oragrutyune 1914–1917* (Boston, 1924).

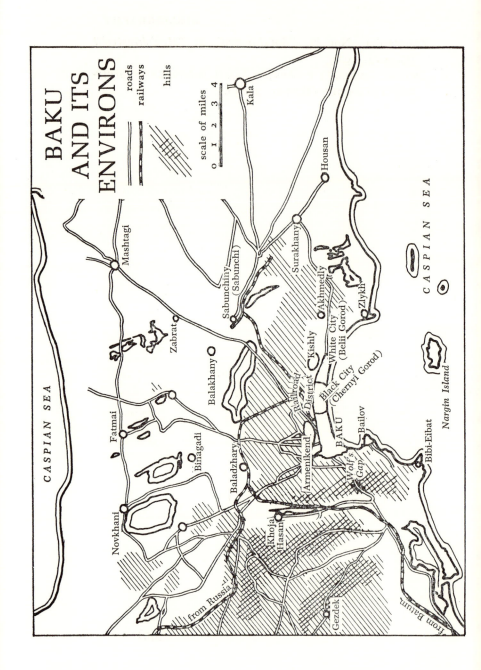

BAKU
AND ITS
ENVIRONS

roads
railways
hills

scale of miles
0   1   2   3   4

Kala

Housan

Mashtagi

Sabunchiny
(Sabunchi)

Surakhany

Akhmedly

Zlykh

Zabrat

White City
(Belii Gorod)

Balakhany

Kishly

Black City
(Chernyi Gorod)

Railroad
District

CASPIAN SEA

Fatmai

BAKU

Binagadi

Armenikend

Bailov

Bibi-Eibat

Nargin Island

Novkhani

Baladzhary

Wolf's
Gap

Khoja
Hasan

from Russia

Gezdek

from Batum

CASPIAN SEA

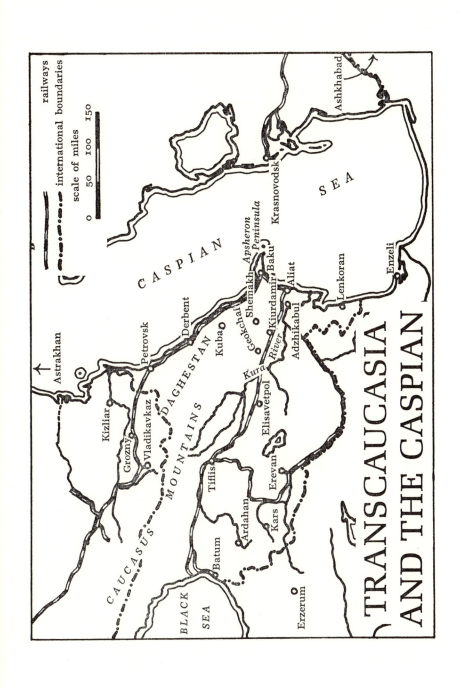

railways

international boundaries

scale of miles

0    50    100    150

SEA

Ashkhabad

Krasnovodsk

CASPIAN

Enzeli

Apsheron Peninsula

Shemakh

Baku

Kiurdamir

Aliat

Lenkoran

Astrakhan

Petrovsk

Derbent

Geokchai

Kuba

Kura River

Adzhikabul

DAGHESTAN

Kizliar

Grozny

Vladikavkaz

Elisavetpol

MOUNTAINS

CAUCASUS

Tiflis

Erevan

Batum

Ardahan

Kars

BLACK

SEA

Erzerum

TRANSCAUCASIA
AND THE CASPIAN

# INDEX

Abashidze, K.G. (member of
the Ozakom), 74n
Abramovich (soldier), 133n
*Achiz-soz*, 19-20, 139, 224
Adalet (leftist political
organization of the Persians
in Baku), 86n, 231
Adzhikabul, 219, 263, 269, 283n
Afanas'ev (SR), 137n
Agapov, 243
Agasiev, K.M. (Bolshevik), 264n
Agu-Dzhafat, 221
Aiollo, Grigorii Gustavovich
(Menshevik, member of the
Dictatorship of
Tsentrokaspii), 74, 89n,
96n, 105, 118n, 133, 211,
307, 313, 319, 325
Akhmedly, 7
Akhundov, G.-bek, 140n
Akhundzade, Mirza Feth-'Ali
(Azerbaijani playwright,
1812-1878), 16-17
Aleekseev-Meskhiev (Georgian
Social Federalist, member of
the Zavkom), 174n
Alexander II (1855-1881), 8
Alexander III (1881-1894), 8
Aliat, 283n, 291
Aliiarov, S.S. (historian), 99
Al'khavi, 279
Amazasp (Dashnak
commander), 204, 316
Amirago (opera singer), 255
Amirazhany, 7
Amirian, Arsen (Bolshevik, one
of the Twenty-Six
Commissars), 96n, 210,
267, 336, 342n
Amirian, Tatevos (Dashnak, one
of the Twenty-Six
Commissars), 336, 343n
Anabekov, 96n
Ansheles, I.S. (Menshevik),
89n, 95n, 96
Antranik (Ozanian), General,
198, 214
April Crisis, x
Arakelian, A. (Dashnak,
member of the Dictatorship of
Tsentrokaspii), 155n, 192,
313, 325

Ardahan, 260-61, 287
Armenian Church, 22
Armenian National Council
(Bureau): in Baku, 84, 171,
200, 204, 216, 218, 222,
225-26, 228, 252, 277, 317-20,
326, 350; in Tiflis, 335
Armenian National Democratic
Party, 202
Armenian People's Party,
176, 178
Armenian Republic, 266n
Armenian Social Democratic
Workers' Organization, 24-25
Armenians, 36, 94, 115, 138,
175, 178, 190, 197, 200,
203-4, 206-7, 215, 218, 220n,
226, 230, 257, 275, 284, 292,
294n, 323, 348, 350; attitude
toward the war, 59; in Baku,
4-5, 20, 160, 171, 177, 305,
326; bourgeoisie, 22-23, 37;
massacre of, 337; peasants,
15, 270; refugees from
massacres, 99; soldiers, 213,
218n, 223-24, 226, 261, 270,
316, 327, 334; Turkish
Armenians, 21, 25-26;
women, 20-21; workers, 10,
13-14, 18, 29, 56, 67,
77-78, 346
Armenikend, 7
Armeno-Azerbaijani conflicts,
22, 37-38, 110, 213-14, 218
Army of Islam, 262, 291, 326
Arutiunov, D., 222
Ashkhabad, 338-40, 342
*Ashkhatanki droshak*, 299n
Ashurbekov, B., 188
Ashurov, 222
Astrakhan, 52, 237, 263, 292,
297, 299, 315-16, 320,
330-31, 332n, 337-38, 342
Atabekian, Levon (SR), 222
Atebekov, N. (Menshevik), 161n
Avakian, Baghdasar
(Bolshevik, one of the
Twenty-Six Commissars),
342n-43n
Avakian, Osip (leader of Baku
soldiers), 137-38, 154-55,
157, 161

# STUDIES OF THE RUSSIAN INSTITUTE

## PUBLISHED BY COLUMBIA UNIVERSITY PRESS

THAD PAUL ALTON, *Polish Postwar Economy*

JOHN A. ARMSTRONG, *Ukrainian Nationalism*

ABRAM BERGSON, *Soviet National Income and Product in 1937*

EDWARD J. BROWN, *The Proletarian Episode in Russian Literature, 1928-1932*

HARVEY L. DYCK, *Weimar Germany and Soviet Russia, 1926-1933: A Study in Diplomatic Instability*

RALPH TALCOTT FISHER, JR., *Pattern for Soviet Youth: A Study of the Congresses of the Komsomol, 1918-1954*

MAURICE FRIEDBERG, *Russian Classics in Soviet Jackets*

ELLIOT R. GOODMAN, *The Soviet Design for a World State*

DAVID GRANICK, *Management of the Industrial Firm in the USSR: A Study in Soviet Economic Planning*

THOMAS TAYLOR HAMMOND, *Lenin on Trade Unions and Revolution, 1893-1917*

JOHN N. HAZARD, *Settling Disputes in Soviet Society: The Formative Years of Legal Institutions*

DAVID JORAVSKY, *Soviet Marxism and Natural Science, 1917-1932*

DAVID MARSHALL LANG, *The Last Years of the Georgian Monarchy, 1658-1832*

GEORGE S. N. LUCKYJ, *Literary Politics in the Soviet Ukraine, 1917-1934*

HERBERT MARCUSE, *Soviet Marxism: A Critical Analysis*

KERMIT E. MC KENZIE, *Comintern and World Revolution, 1928-1943: The Shaping of Doctrine*

CHARLES B. MC LANE, *Soviet Policy and the Chinese Communists, 1931-1946*

JAMES WILLIAM MORLEY, *The Japanese Thrust into Siberia, 1918*

ALEXANDER G. PARK, *Bolshevism in Turkestan, 1917-1927*

MICHAEL BORO PETROVICH, *The Emergence of Russian Panslavism, 1856-1870*

OLIVER H. RADKEY, *The Agrarian Foes of Bolshevism: Promise and Default of the Russian Socialist Revolutionaries, February to October, 1917*

OLIVER H. RADKEY, *The Sickle Under the Hammer: The Russian Socialist Revolutionaries in the Early Months of Soviet Rule*

ALFRED J. RIEBER, *Stalin and the French Communist Party, 1941-1947*

ALFRED ERICH SENN, *The Emergence of Modern Lithuania*

ERNEST J. SIMMONS, editor, *Through the Glass of Soviet Literature: Views of Russian Society*

THEODORE K. VON LAUE, *Sergei Witte and the Industrialization of Russia*

ALLEN S. WHITING, *Soviet Policies in China, 1917-1924*